PLOT SUMMARY INDEX

compiled by
Carol L. Koehmstedt

The Scarecrow Press, Inc.
Metuchen, N.J. 1973

Library of Congress Cataloging in Publication Data

Koehmstedt, Carol L
Plot summary index.

1. Literature--Stories, plots, etc.--Indexes.
I. Title.
Z6514.P66K63 809 72-13726
ISBN 0-8108-0584-7

Dedicated to my colleagues
in their time of need--
in particular, examination time.

PREFACE

This listing was the brain child of Kenton Forrest, at the time a student assistant in the reference department of the University of Northern Colorado Library. Its compilation during that period was the result of the endeavors of the student reference staff as a whole, initially being an index to the *Masterplots* series available at that time. Over the years it has been supplemented and added to as new compilations of summaries have been published and old ones discovered. In addition to other titles, the present listing indexes all the variant compilations of the *Masterplots* series.

The first half of the book is the "Title Index," arranged alphabetically, giving titles of literary works, their authors, symbols of the collections in which plot summaries of these works appear, and, in parentheses following each symbol, a reference to the page number of that collection on which the given plot summary falls. The second half of the book is, naturally, the "Author Index," giving the same information but arranged alphabetically by author. A key to the symbols used, with full citations to the various plot summary collections, follows this preface.

My appreciation is extended to Mrs. Beatrice Krogen, reference clerk, and Miss Susan Enquist, student assistant, of the reference department of the North Dakota State University Library, for their typing of the reference department copy which served as the basic listing that was expanded for publication. My gratitude is also due my mother for her assistance in various sorting phases of the project.

Carol L. Koehmstedt
Reference Librarian
North Dakota State
University Library

SYMBOLS FOR COLLECTIONS INDEXED

BM Masterplots Annual. Masterplots: Best Masterplots, 1954-1962: 175 Essay-Reviews from Masterplots Annuals Since 1954. Edited by Frank N. Magill; associate editor, Dayton Kohler. New York, Salem Press, 1963.

CAL Magill, Frank Northen. Masterpieces of Catholic Literature in Summary Form, edited by Frank N. Magill with associate editors A. Robert Caponigri and Thomas P. Neill. New York, Harper and Row, 1965.

CHL Magill, Frank Northen. Masterpieces of Christian Literature in Summary Form, edited by Frank N. Magill with Ian P. McGreal. New York, Harper and Row, 1963.

DGAP Lovell, John. Digests of Great American Plays; Complete Summaries of More Than 100 Plays from the Beginnings to the Present. New York, Crowell, 1961.

MAF Magill, Frank Northen. Masterplots: American Fiction Series. vol. 2. New York, Salem Press, 1964.

MCLE Magill, Frank Northen. Masterplots; Comprehensive Library Edition: Two Thousand and Ten Plot Stories and Essay Reviews from the World's Fine Literature. Edited by Frank N. Magill. Story editor: Dayton Kohler. Definitive ed. New York, Salem Press, 1968. 8 vols.

MD Magill, Frank Northen. Masterplots: Drama Series. vol. 1. New York, Salem Press, 1964.

MEF Magill, Frank Northen. Masterplots: English

Fiction Series. vol. 3. New York, Salem Press, 1964.

MEU — Magill, Frank Northen. Masterplots: European Fiction Series. vol. 4. New York, Salem Press, 1964.

MN — Magill, Frank Northen. Masterplots: Non-Fiction Series. vol. 6. New York, Salem Press, 1964.

MP — Magill, Frank Northen. Masterplots: Poetry Series. vol. 5. New York, Salem Press, 1964.

MP1-4 — Magill, Frank Northen. Masterpieces of World Literature in Digest Form. 1st-4th series. Edited by Frank N. Magill, with the assistance of Dayton Kohler and staff. New York, Harper, 1952-1969. 4 vols.

MPA1-5 — Magill, Frank Northen. Masterplots of American Literature. New York, Harper and Row, 1970? 5 vols.

PO — Goodman, Roland Arthur, ed. Plot Outlines of 100 Famous Novels: The First Hundred. Garden City, N. Y., Doubleday, 1962.

PO2 — Olfson, Lewy, ed. Plot Outlines of 100 Famous Novels: The Second Hundred. Garden City, N. Y., Doubleday, 1966.

PON — Grozier, Edwin Atkins, ed. Plot Outlines of 101 Best Novels: Condensations Based on Original Works. New York, Barnes & Noble, 1962.

POP — Cartmell, Van H., ed. Plot Outlines of 100 Famous Plays. Philadelphia, Blakiston Company, New Home Library. n. d. (Doubleday has a 1962 edition with different pagination; Dolphin Books.)

SCL — Magill, Frank Northen. Survey of Contemporary Literature; Updated Reprints of 1500 Essay-Reviews from Masterplots Annuals, 1954-1969. Edited by Frank N. Magill. Associate editor, Dayton Kohler. New York, Salem Press, 1971.

SCLs	_____. _____. Supplement, 1954-1968. New York, Salem Press, 1972.
SGAN	Lass, Abraham Harold. A Student's Guide to 50 American Novels, edited by Abraham H. Lass. New York, Washington Square Press, 1966.
SGAP	Lass, Abraham Harold. A Student's Guide to 50 American Plays, edited by Abraham H. Lass and Milton Levin. New York, Washington Square Press, 1969.
SGBN	Lass, Abraham Harold. A Student's Guide to 50 British Novels, edited by Abraham H. Lass. New York, Washington Square Press, 1966.
SGEN	Lass, Abraham Harold. A Student's Guide to 50 European Novels, edited by Abraham H. Lass and Brooks Wright. New York, Washington Square Press, 1967.
TCP	Sprinchorn, Evert, ed. 20th Century Plays in Synopsis. New York, Crowell, 1966.
WP	Magill, Frank Northen. Masterpieces of World Philosophy in Summary Form. Associate editor: Ian P. McGreal. 1st ed. New York, Harper, 1961.
[year]a	Masterplots Annual. 1954- . New York, Salem Press. Symbol: e.g., 1968a.

TITLE INDEX

A 1-12. Louis Zukofsky. SCL(1), 1968a(1).
Abbé Constantin, The. Ludovic Halévy. MCLE(1), MEU(1), MP1(1), PON(1).
Abe Lincoln in Illinois. Robert E. Sherwood. DGAP(304), MCLE(4), MD(1), MP1(3).
Abie's Irish Rose. Anne Nichols. DGAP(199), POP(35).
About the House. W. H. Auden. SCL(5), 1966a(1).
Abraham and Isaac. Unknown. MCLE(7), MD(4), MP3(1).
Abraham Lincoln. Carl Sandburg. BM(1), MCLE(9), MN(1), MP3(2), SCL(9), 1954a(1).
Absalom, Absalom! William Faulkner. MAF(1), MCLE(12), MP1(5).
Absalom and Achitophel. John Dryden. MCLE(15), MP(1), MP3(5).
Absentee, The. Maria Edgeworth. MCLE(17), MEF(1), MP2(1).
Abuse of Power. Theodore Draper. SCL(12), 1968a(4).
Acceptance World, The. Anthony Powell. BM(4), SCL(15), 1957a(1).
Acharnians, The. Aristophanes. MCLE(21), MD(6), MP3(7).
Act and Being. Michele Federico Sciacca. CAL(1031).
Act of Creation, The. Arthur Koestler. SCL(19), 1965a(1).
Act of God. Margaret Kennedy. SCL(22), 1955a(1).
Act of Love, An. Ira Wolfert. SCL(25), 1954a(4).
Act One. Moss Hart. SCL(28), 1960a(1).
Acte. Lawrence Durrell. SCL(31), 1967a(1).
Action, L'. Maurice Blondel. CAL(706).
Actress, The. Bessie Breuer. SCL(35), 1958a(1).
Ada or Ardor: A Family Chronicle. Vladimir Nabokov. 1970a(1).
Adam. David Bolt. SCL(38), 1962a(1).
Adam Bede. George Eliot. MCLE(23), MEF(5), MP1(8), PO(78), PON(6), SGBN(132).
Adam's Dream. Julia Randall. 1970a(4).
Adams Papers, The. John Adams. BM(8), SCL(42), 1962a(4).
Address of Tatian to the Greeks. Tatian. CHL(26).
Addresses. Abraham Lincoln. MCLE(25), MN(4), MP3(9).

Admirable Crichton, The. James M. Barrie. MCLE(28), MD(8), MP1(10), POP(121), TCP(42).
Adolphe. Benjamin Constant. MCLE(30), MEU(4), MP3(12).
Adornment of the Spiritual Marriage, The. John of Ruysbroeck. CHL(272).
Adrienne. André Maurois. SCL(45), 1962a(8).
Advancement of Learning, The. Sir Francis Bacon. WP(369).
Adventures in the Skin Trade. Dylan Thomas. SCL(50), 1955a(4).
Adventures of Augie March, The. Saul Bellow. MCLE(33), MP4(1), SGAN(337).
Adventures of Huckleberry Finn, The. Samuel L. Clemens. PO2(176), SGAN(45).
Adventures of Tom Sawyer, The. Samuel L. Clemens. PO2(171).
Advice to a Prophet. Richard Wilbur. SCL(53), 1962a(12).
Advise and Consent. Allen Drury. SCL(56), 1960a(3).
Aeneid, The. Virgil. MCLE(36), MP(3), MP1(11), PON(11).
Aesop's Fables. Aesop. MCLE(39), MEU(7), MP3(15).
Aesthetic. Benedetto Croce. MCLE(41), MP4(3), WP(745).
Aeterni patris. Pope Leo XIII. CAL(691).
Affair, The. C. P. Snow. BM(11), MCLE(44), MP4(6), SCL(59), 1961a(1).
Affinities. Vernon Watkins. SCL(62), 1964a(1).
Affluent Society, The. John Kenneth Galbraith. SCL(65), 1959a(1).
African Witch, The. Joyce Cary. SCL(68), 1963a(1).
After Experience. W. D. Snodgrass. SCL(71), 1968a(7).
After Strange Gods. T. S. Eliot. MCLE(48), MP4(9).
After the Fall. Arthur Miller. SCL(76), 1965a(3).
After the Trauma. Harvey Curtis Webster. 1971a(1).
Afternoon Men. Anthony Powell. SCL(78), 1964a(4).
Afternoon of an Author. F. Scott Fitzgerald. SCL(81), 1959a(3).
Against Celsus. Origen. CHL(66).
Against Eunomius. Saint Basil. CAL(98).
Against Heresies. Saint Irenaeus. CAL(37), CHL(35).
Against Interpretation. Susan Sontag. SCL(84), 1967a(5).
Against the American Grain. Dwight MacDonald. SCL(88), 1963a(3).
Against the Grain. Joris Karl Huysmans. MCLE(50), MEU(9), MP2(4).
Agape and Eros. Anders Nygren. CHL(946).
Age of Discontinuity, The. Peter F. Drucker. 1971a(7).
Age of Innocence, The. Edith Wharton. MAF(4), MCLE(53), MP1(14), PO2(194).
Age of Louis XIV, The. Will and Ariel Durant. SCL(92), 1964a(6).

Age of Reason, The. Thomas Paine. MCLE(56), MP4(11).
Age of Reason Begins, The. Will and Ariel Durant. BM(14), SCL(96), 1962a(15).
Age of Reform, The. Richard Hofstadter. SCLs(1).
Age of Revolution, The. Winston S. Churchill. BM(18), SCL(100), 1958a(4).
Age of Roosevelt, The, Vol. I. Arthur M. Schlesinger. SCL(104), 1958a(7).
Age of Roosevelt, The, Vol. II. Arthur M. Schlesinger. SCL(107), 1960a(7).
Age of Roosevelt, The, Vol. III. Arthur M. Schlesinger. SCL(111), 1961a(4).
Age of Voltaire, The. Will and Ariel Durant. SCL(115), 1966a(5).
Agnes Grey. Anne Brontë. MCLE(59), MEF(7), MP3(16).
Ah, Wilderness! Eugene O'Neill. DGAP(260), SGAP(20).
Aids to Reflection. Samuel Taylor Coleridge. CHL(663).
Aiglon, L'. Edmond Rostand. MCLE(2509), MD(438), MP2(551).
Ajax. Sophocles. MCLE(62), MD(10), MP2(6).
Akenfield. Ronald Blythe. 1970a(7).
Aku-Aku. Thor Heyerdahl. SCL(119), 1959a(6).
Al Filo del Agua. Agustín Yáñez. MCLE(64), MAF(7), MP3(19).
Albany Depot, The. William Dean Howells. DGAP(128).
Albert Gallatin. Raymond Walters, Jr. SCL(122), 1958a(10).
Alcestis. Euripides. MCLE(67), MD(12), MP1(16).
Alchemist, The. Ben Jonson. MCLE(69), MD(14), MP2(8).
Aleck Maury, Sportsman. Caroline Gordon. MAF(10), MCLE(72), MP1(17).
Aleph and Other Stories: 1933-1969, The. Jorge Luis Borges. 1971a(10).
Alexander Hamilton. Broadus Mitchell. SCL(125), 1958a(14).
Alexander Hamilton and the Constitution. Clinton Rossiter. SCL(128), 1965a(5).
Alexander Pope. Peter Quennell. 1970a(10).
Alexandria Quartet, The. Lawrence Durrell. MCLE(75), MP4(14).
Algiers Motel Incident, The. John Hersey. SCL(131), 1969a(1).
Alice Adams. Booth Tarkington. MAF(13), MCLE(83), MP1(20).
Alice in Wonderland. Lewis Carroll. MCLE(85), MEF(10), MP1(21), PO2(64), PON(14), SGBN(147).
All Fall Down. James Leo Herlihy. MCLE(88), MP4(21), SCL(135), 1961a(7).
All Fools. George Chapman. MCLE(90), MD(17), MP3(22).

All for Love. John Dryden. MCLE(92), MD(19), MP2(11).
All Green Shall Perish. Eduardo Mallea. SCL(138), 1967a(8).
All Hallows Eve. Charles Williams. MCLE(95), MP4(23).
All Men Are Brothers. Shih Nai-an. MCLE(98), MEU(12), MP3(24).
All Quiet on the Western Front. Erich Maria Remarque. MCLE(102), MEU(16), MP2(13), PO(384), SGEN(397).
All the King's Men. Robert Penn Warren. MAF(15), MCLE(104), MP2(15), PO2(281), SGAN(297).
All the Little Live Things. Wallace Stegner. SCL(143), 1968a(11).
Allegory of Love, The. C. S. Lewis. MCLE(107), MP4(26).
Alligator Bride, The. Donald Hall. SCLs(5).
All's Well That Ends Well. William Shakespeare. MCLE (112), MD(22), MP2(18).
Almanac for Moderns, An. Donald Culross Peattie. MCLE (115), MP4(30).
Almayer's Folly. Joseph Conrad. MCLE(118), MEF(13), MP2(20).
Alp. William Hjortsberg. 1970a(14).
Amadís de Gaul. Vasco de Lobeira. MCLE(121), MEU(18), MP3(27).
Ambassadors, The. Henry James. MAF(18), MCLE(124), MP2(22), MPA3(7).
Ambassador's Journal. John Kenneth Galbraith. 1970a(18).
Amédée or How to Get Rid of It. Eugene Ionesco. TCP (195).
Amelia. Henry Fielding. MCLE(127), MEF(16), MP1(24).
America as a Civilization. Max Lerner. SCL(147), 1958a (17).
American, The. Henry James. DGAP(121), MAF(21), MCLE(130), MP1(27), MPA3(12).
American Catholic Crossroads. Walter J. Ong, S.J. CAL (1076).
American Catholic Dilemma. Thomas O'Dea. CAL(1066).
American Challenge, The. Jean-Jacques Servan-Schreiber. SCL(150), 1969a(5).
American Commonwealth, The. James Bryce. MCLE(132), MP4(32).
American Elegies. Robert Hazel. 1970a(21).
American Grandfather, An. Marian Spencer Smith. DGAP (206).
American Notebooks, The. Nathaniel Hawthorne. MCLE (135), MP4(35), MPA2(31).
American Republic, The. Orestes Augustus Brownson. CAL(667).

American Tragedy, An. Theodore Dreiser. MAF(23), MCLE(138), MP1(29), PO(214), PON(19), SGAN(135).
American Visitor, An. Joyce Cary. SCL(154), 1962a(19).
Americans Roused, The. Jonathan Sewall. DGAP(9).
Americans: The National Experience, The. Daniel Joseph Boorstin. SCL(157), 1966a(8).
America's Coming-of-Age. Van Wyck Brooks. MCLE(140), MP4(38).
America's Western Frontiers. John A. Hawgood. SCLs(9).
Among the Dangs. George P. Elliott. SCL(161), 1962a(22).
Amores. Ovid. MCLE(144), MP4(41).
Amorosa Fiammetta, L'. Giovanni Boccaccio. MCLE(2525), MEU(424), MP3(550).
Amphitryon. Titus Maccius Plautus. MCLE(146), MD(25), MP2(24).
Amphitryon 38. Jean Giraudoux. MCLE(149), MD(28), MP3(30).
Amrita. R. Prawer Jhabvala. SCL(164), 1957a(4).
Amulet. Carl Rakosi. SCL(167), 1969a(8).
Anabasis. St.-John Perse. MCLE(152), MP(6), MP3(32).
Anabasis, The. Xenophon. MCLE(156), MN(7), MP3(36).
Analects of Confucius, The. (Lun Yü) Confucius. WP(5).
Analogy of Religion, The. Joseph Butler. CHL(573).
Analysis of Knowledge and Valuation, An. Clarence Irving Lewis. WP(1096).
Analysis of the Sensations, The. Ernst Mach. WP(691).
Anatol. Arthur Schnitzler. POP(297).
Anatomy of a Murder. Robert Traver. SCL(170), 1959a(9).
Anatomy of Melancholy, The. Robert Burton. MCLE(160), MN(11), MP3(39).
Anaxagoras: Fragments. Anaxagoras of Clazomenae. WP (22).
Anaximander: Fragments. Anaximander of Miletus. WP(1).
And Other Stories. John O'Hara. SCL(173), 1969a(10).
And Quiet Flows the Don. Mikhail Sholokhov. MCLE(162), MEU(21), MP1(30), SGEN(371).
Andersen's Fairy Tales (Selections). Hans Christian Andersen. MCLE(164), MEU(23), MP2(27).
Andersonville. MacKinlay Kantor. SCL(177), 1955a(7).
André. William Dunlap. DGAP(23).
Andria. Terence. MCLE(169), MD(31), MP2(31).
Andromache. Euripides. MCLE(171), MD(33), MP3(40).
Andromache. Jean Baptiste Racine. MCLE(173), MD(35), MP2(33).
Andromeda Strain, The. Michael Crichton. 1970a(24).
Anecdotes of Destiny. Isak Dinesen. SCL(181), 1959a(11).
Angel Guerra. Benito Pérez Galdós. MCLE(175), MEU(28),

MP3(42).
Anglo-Saxon Attitudes. Angus Wilson. SCL(184), 1957a(7).
Animal Kingdom, The. Philip Barry. SGAP(116).
Animals in That Country, The. Margaret Atwood. 1970a (28).
Anna Christie. Eugene O'Neill. DGAP(195), MCLE(177), MD(37), MP2(35).
Anna Karénina. Count Leo Tolstoy. MCLE(179), MEU(30), MP1(32), PO(363), PON(25), SGEN(164).
Anna of the Five Towns. Arnold Bennett. MCLE(181), MEF(19), MP2(37).
Annals of Tacitus, The. Cornelius Tacitus. MCLE(184), MN(13), MP3(44).
Annals of the Parish. John Galt. MCLE(188), MEF(22), MP2(39).
Annals of the Roman People. Livy. MCLE(191), MN(17), MP3(47).
Anonymous Sins and Other Poems. Joyce Carol Oates. 1970a(31).
Answer from Limbo, An. Brian Moore. SCL(188), 1963a(7).
Anthony Adverse. Hervey Allen. MAF(25), MCLE(194), MP1(34).
Antigone. Jean Anouilh. TCP(23).
Antigone. Sophocles. MCLE(197), MD(39), MP1(37).
Anti-Intellectualism in American Life. Richard Hofstadter. SCLs(11).
Anti-Memoirs. André Malraux. SCL(190), 1969a(14).
Antiquary, The. Sir Walter Scott. MCLE(199), MEF(25), MP2(41).
Antiworlds. Andrei Voznesensky. SCL(194), 1967a(12).
Antony and Cleopatra. William Shakespeare. MCLE(202), MD(41), MP2(43).
Anxiety and the Christian. Hans Urs von Balthasar. CAL (969).
Apes, Angels, and Victorians. William Irvine. BM(22), SCL(199), 1955a(11).
Apologia pro vita sua. John Henry Cardinal Newman. CAL (661), CHL(743), MCLE(205), MN(20), MP3(49).
Apology. Plato. WP(42).
Apology for Raimond Sebond. Michel Eyquem de Montaigne. WP(359).
Apology for the Life of Colley Cibber, Comedian, An. Colley Cibber. MCLE(208), MN(23), MP3(52).
Apology for the True Christian Divinity, An. Robert Barclay. CHL(526).
Apology of Aristides, The. Aristides. CAL(10), CHL(9).
Apology of Athenagoras, The. Athenagoras. CHL(29).

Apology of Tertullian, The. Tertullian. CAL(41), CHL(39).
Apostle, The. Sholem Asch. MAF(28), MCLE(211), MP1 (38).
Apostolic Tradition, The. Saint Hippolytus. CHL(54).
Appearance and Reality. Francis Herbert Bradley. WP(706).
Apple of the Eye, The. Glenway Wescott. MAF(31), MCLE (214), MP1(40).
Appointment in Samarra. John O'Hara. MAF(33), MCLE (216), MP2(46), SGAN(253).
Arabesque and Honeycomb. Sacheverell Sitwell. SCL(202), 1959a(14).
Arabian Nights, The. Princess Scheherazade. PON(29).
Arabian Nights' Entertainments, The (Selections). Unknown. MCLE(219), MEU(32), MP2(48).
Arabian Sands. Wilfred Thesiger. SCL(205), 1960a(10).
Arbitration, The. Menander. MCLE(224), MD(44), MP3(54).
Arcadia. Sir Philip Sidney. MCLE(227), MEF(28), MP3(56).
Areopagitica. John Milton. MCLE(230), MP4(42).
Argenis. John Barclay. MCLE(233), MEF(31), MP3(59).
Ariel. Sylvia Plath. SCL(208), 1967a(17).
Aristocrat, The. Conrad Richter. SCL(213), 1969a(18).
Armada, The. Garrett Mattingly. BM(25), SCL(217), 1960a(13).
Arme Heinrich, Der. Hartmann von Aue. MCLE(237), MP (10), MP3(63).
Armies of the Night, The. Norman Mailer. SCL(220), 1969a(21).
Arms and Men. Walter Millis. SCL(225), 1957a(10).
Arne. Björnstjerne Björnson. MCLE(239), MEU(37), MP1 (42).
Around the World in Eighty Days. Jules Verne. PO2(317).
Arrowsmith. Sinclair Lewis. MAF(36), MCLE(241), MP1 (44), PO(247), SGAN(147).
Ars amatoria. Ovid. MCLE(244), MP4(45).
Ars logica. John of St. Thomas. CAL(589).
Ars poetica. Horace. MCLE(246), MN(26), MP3(65).
Art and Scholasticism. Jacques Maritain. CAL(766).
Art as Experience. John Dewey. WP(986).
Artamène. Madeleine de Scudéry. MCLE(249), MEU(39), MP3(67).
Artamonov Business, The. Maksim Gorki. MCLE(252), MEU(42), MP3(69).
Arturo's Island. Elsa Morante. SCL(229), 1960a(16).
As I Lay Dying. William Faulkner. MAF(39), MCLE(255), MP2(52).
As I Walked Out One Midsummer Morning. Laurie Lee. 1970a(34).

As You Like It. William Shakespeare. MCLE(257), MD(47), MP1(46), POP(208).
Ascent of F6, The. W. H. Auden and Christopher Isherwood. TCP(37).
Ascent of Man, The. Henry Drummond. CHL(805).
Ascent of Mount Carmel and The Dark Night of the Soul, The. Saint John of the Cross. CAL(558).
Ascent to Truth. Thomas Merton. CAL(979).
Ascetic Life, The. Saint Maximus the Confessor. CAL(252).
Ash Wednesday. T. S. Eliot. MCLE(259), MP(12), MP3 (72).
Ashes. Stefan Zeromski. MCLE(261), MEU(45), MP2(54).
Ask at the Unicorn. Norman Thomas. SCL(232), 1964a(10).
Asquith. Roy Jenkins. SCL(235), 1966a(12).
Assistant, The. Bernard Malamud. SCL(238), SGAN(350), 1958a(19).
Assommoir, L'. Émile Zola. PO(347).
Astronomer and Other Stories, The. Doris Betts. SCL(240), 1967a(22).
At Lady Molly's. Anthony Powell. BM(28), SCL(246), 1959a(17).
At Play in the Fields of the Lord. Peter Matthiessen. SCL (249), 1966a(15).
At the Crossroads. Evan S. Connell, Jr. SCL(253), 1966a (19).
At the Sign of the Reine Pédauque. Anatole France. MCLE (264), MEU(48), MP2(57).
Atala. François René de Chateaubriand. MCLE(267), MEU (51), MP2(59).
Atalanta in Calydon. Algernon Charles Swinburne. MCLE (270), MP(14), MP2(61).
Ataturk. Patrick Balfour, Lord Kinross. SCL(255), 1966a (21).
Atheistic Communism. Pope Pius XI. CAL(858).
Atomic Quest. Arthur Holly Compton. SCL(258), 1957a(14).
Attack on Christendom. Søren Kierkegaard. CHL(728).
Aubrey's Brief Lives. Oliver Lawson Dick, Editor. SCL (262), 1958a(22).
Aucassin and Nicolette. Unknown. MCLE(273), MEU(54), MP1(48).
Audubon: A Vision. Robert Penn Warren. 1970a(39).
Auntie Mame. Patrick Dennis. SCL(266), 1955a(14).
Autobiography, An. Anthony Trollope. MCLE(275), MP4(46).
Autobiography of a Hunted Priest, The. John Gerard. CAL (571).
Autobiography of an Ex-Coloured Man, The. James Weldon Johnson. SCLs(14).

Autobiography of Benjamin Franklin, The. Benjamin Franklin. MCLE(278), MN(29), MP3(74).
Autobiography of Benjamin Robert Haydon, The. Benjamin Robert Haydon. MCLE(281), MP4(48).
Autobiography of Benvenuto Cellini, The. Benvenuto Cellini. MCLE(284), MN(32), MP2(64).
Autobiography of Bertrand Russell: 1872-1914, The. Bertrand Russell. SCL(269), 1968a(15).
Autobiography of Bertrand Russell: 1914-1944, The. Bertrand Russell. SCL(273), 1969a(26).
Autobiography of Bertrand Russell: 1944-1969, The. Bertrand Russell. 1970a(45).
Autobiography of Johannes Jörgensen, The. Johannes Jörgensen. CAL(801).
Autobiography of Leigh Hunt, The. Leigh Hunt. MCLE(287), MP4(51).
Autobiography of Malcolm X, The. Malcolm X. SCLs(17).
Autobiography of Mark Twain, The. Samuel L. Clemens. SCL(278), 1960a(19).
Autobiography of Saint Margaret Mary Alacoque, The. Saint Margaret Mary. CAL(615).
Autobiography of William Butler Yeats, The. William Butler Yeats. MCLE(290), MP4(54).
Autocrat of the Breakfast-Table, The. Oliver Wendell Holmes. MCLE(293), MN(35), MP3(76), MPA2(69).
Autumn Across America. Edwin Way Teale. SCL(282), 1957a(17).
Awake and Sing! Clifford Odets. SGAP(183), TCP(251).
Awakening Land, The. Conrad Richter. SCLs(21).
Awakening of Spring, The. Frank Wedekind. MCLE(297), MD(49), MP3(79).
Away All Boats. Kenneth Dodson. SCL(285), 1954a(7).
Awkward Age, The. Henry James. MCLE(300), MP4(56), MPA3(17).
Axe, The. Sigrid Undset. MCLE(304), MEU(56), MP2(66).
Axel's Castle. Edmund Wilson. MCLE(307), MP4(60).

Baal. Bertolt Brecht. MCLE(309), MP4(62), TCP(73).
Babbitt. Sinclair Lewis. MAF(41), MCLE(312), MP1(50), PO2(218), SGAN(142).
Babylonian Captivity of the Church, The. Martin Luther. CHL(334).
Bacchae, The. Euripides. MCLE(315), MD(52), MP2(68).
Bachelors, The. Henry de Montherlant. SCL(288), 1962a (24).
Bachelors, The. Muriel Spark. MCLE(318), MP4(64), SCL (291), 1962a(27).

Back Country, The. Gary Snyder. SCLs(25).
Back to Methuselah. George Bernard Shaw. MCLE(321), MD(55), MP3(82), TCP(337).
Background to Glory. John Bakeless. SCL(295), 1958a(26).
Bad Man, A. Stanley Elkin. SCL(299), 1968a(19).
Bad Seed, The. William March. SCL(302), 1954a(10).
Baldur's Gate. Eleanor Clark. 1971a(14).
Ballad of Peckham Rye, The. Muriel Spark. SCL(305), 1961a(10).
Ballad of the Sad Café, The. Edward Albee. SCL(309), 1964a(12).
Balthazar. Lawrence Durrell. BM(31), SCL(313), 1959a(20).
Bambi. Felix Salten. MCLE(324), MEU(59), MP1(52).
Bamboo Bed, The. William Eastlake. 1970a(49).
Band of Angels. Robert Penn Warren. SCL(317), 1955a(17).
Barabbas. Pär Lagerkvist. MCLE(327), MEU(62), MP3(85).
Barber of Seville, The. Pierre A. Caron de Beaumarchais. MCLE(330), MD(58), MP2(70), POP(255).
Barchester Towers. Anthony Trollope. MCLE(332), MEF (35), MP1(55), PO(174), SGBN(124).
Barnaby Rudge. Charles Dickens. MCLE(335), MEF(38), MP2(72).
Baron Münchausen's Narrative. Rudolph Erich Raspe. MCLE(339), MEU(65), MP2(76).
Barren Ground. Ellen Glasgow. MAF(44), MCLE(342), MP1(57).
Barretts of Wimpole Street, The. Rudolf Besier. POP(81).
Barry Lyndon. William Makepeace Thackeray. MCLE(345), MEF(42), MP2(78).
Bartholomew Fair. Ben Jonson. MCLE(348), MD(60), MP2 (80).
Baruch: The Public Years. Bernard M. Baruch. SCL(320), 1961a(13).
Basic Christian Ethics. Paul Ramsey. CHL(1117).
Basic Verities. Charles Péguy. CAL(879).
Batouala. René Maran. MCLE(351), MEU(68), MP3(87).
Battle. John Toland. SCL(323), 1960a(22).
Battle of Casino, The. Fred Majdalany. SCL(326), 1958a (30).
Battle of Dienbienphu, The. Jules Roy. SCL(330), 1966a(24).
Bay of Noon, The. Shirley Hazzard. 1971a(17).
Bay of Silence, The. Eduardo Mallea. MAF(47), MCLE (354), MP3(89).
Bazaar of Heraclides, The. Nestorius. CHL(162).
Beach of Falesá, The. Robert Louis Stevenson. MCLE(356), MEF(45), MP3(91).
Beardsley. Stanley Weintraub. SCL(333), 1968a(22).

Beastly Beatitudes of Balthazar B, The. J. P. Donleavy. SCL(340), 1969a(30).
Beasts and Men. Pierre Gascar. SCL(343), 1957a(20).
Beauchamp's Career. George Meredith. MCLE(343), MEF (48), MP2(83).
Beautyful Ones Are Not Yet Born, The. Ayi Kwei Armah. SCL(346), 1969a(33).
Beaux' Stratagem, The. George Farquhar. MCLE(362), MD(63), MP2(86), POP(184).
Beaver Coat, The. Gerhart Hauptmann. MCLE(365), MD (66), MP3(94).
Bech: A Book. John Updike. 1971a(21).
Becket, or The Honor of God. Jean Anouilh. TCP(26).
Bedford Forrest and His Critter Company. Andrew Lytle. SCL(349), 1961a(16).
Before My Time. Niccolò Tucci. SCL(352), 1963a(9).
Beggar, The. Rheinhard Johannes Sorge. TCP(372).
Beggar on Horseback. George S. Kaufman and Marc Connelly. DGAP(208).
Beggars' Bush, The. John Fletcher and Philip Massinger. MCLE(368), MD(69), MP3(96).
Beggar's Opera, The. John Gay. MCLE(371), MD(72), MP1(59), POP(177).
Beginners, The. Dan Jacobson. SCL(355), 1967a(28).
Beginning Again. Leonard Woolf. SCL(359), 1965a(8).
Being and Having. Gabriel Marcel. CHL(1003).
Being and Nothingness. Jean-Paul Sartre. WP(1079).
Being and Time. Martin Heidegger. WP(886).
Bel-Ami. Guy de Maupassant. MCLE(374), MEU(71), MP1 (62).
Belief and Faith. Josef Pieper. CAL(1121).
Bell, The. Iris Murdoch. BM(35), MCLE(377), MP4(67), SCL(362), 1959a(23).
Bell for Adano, A. John Hersey. MAF(49), MCLE(380), MP1(64).
Ben Hur: A Tale of the Christ. Lew Wallace. MAF(51), MCLE(382), MP1(66), PO(260), PON(34).
Benefactor, The. Susan Sontag. SCL(365), 1964a(16).
Benito Cereno. Herman Melville. MAF(54), MCLE(385), MP3(98), MPA4(38).
Benjamin Major. Richard of St. Victor. CAL(339).
Benjamin Minor. Richard of St. Victor. CHL(220).
Benjamin Minor and Benjamin Major. Richard of St. Victor. CAL(339).
Beowulf. Unknown. MCLE(388), MP(17), MP1(68).
Bérénice. Jean Baptiste Racine. MCLE(390), MD(75), MP3 (101).

Berlin. Theodor Plievier. SCL(371), 1958a(33).
Berlin Stories, The. Christopher Isherwood. SCL(374), 1954a(13).
Bernard Shaw. George Bernard Shaw. SCL(377), 1966a(27).
Berryman's Sonnets. John Berryman. SCL(383), 1968a(28).
Best Man, The. Gore Vidal. SCL(386), 1961a(19).
Betrothed, The. Alessandro Manzoni. MCLE(392), MEU (74), MP2(88).
Between the Acts. Virginia Woolf. MCLE(395), MEF(51), MP3(102).
Between Two Empires. Theodore Friend. SCLs(28).
Bevis of Hampton. Unknown. MCLE(398), MP(19), MP3 (105).
Beyond Good and Evil. Friedrich Wilhelm Nietzsche. MCLE(401), MN(39), MP3(108), WP(696).
Beyond Human Power, II. Björnstjerne Björnson. MCLE (404), MD(77), MP2(90).
Beyond the Aegean. Ilias Venezis. SCL(389), 1957a(23).
Beyond the Bridge. Jack Matthews. 1971a(24).
Bhowani Junction. John Masters. SCL(393), 1954a(16).
Bible in Spain, The. George Henry Borrow. MCLE(407), MP4(69).
Bid Me to Live. Hilda Doolittle. SCL(396), 1961a(21).
Big Sky, The. A. B. Guthrie, Jr. MAF(57), MCLE(410), MP1(70).
Big Woods. William Faulkner. SCL(399), 1955a(20).
Biglow Papers, The. James Russell Lowell. MCLE(413), MP(22), MP3(111), MPA4(19).
Billiards at Half Past Nine. Heinrich Böll. SCLs(31).
Billy Budd, Foretopman. Herman Melville. MAF(60), MCLE(416), MP2(92), MPA4(43), PO2(162), SGAN(10).
Billy Liar. Keith Waterhouse. SCL(402), 1961a(24).
Biographia Literaria. Samuel Taylor Coleridge. MCLE (419), MP4(72).
Biography. S. N. Behrman. DGAP(257), SGAP(92).
Birch Interval. Joanna Crawford. SCL(405), 1965a(11).
Birds, The. Aristophanes. MCLE(422), MD(80), MP2(94).
Birds, Beasts, and Relatives. Gerald Durrell. 1970a(53).
Birds Fall Down, The. Rebecca West. SCL(408), 1967a(31).
Birth of Britain, The. Winston S. Churchill. BM(38), SCL (412), 1957a(26).
Birthday King, The. Gabriel Fielding. SCL(415), 1964a(22).
Bishop's Bonfire, The. Sean O'Casey. SCL(418), 1955a(23).
Bismarck. Werner Richter. SCL(422), 1966a(32).
Bitter Honeymoon. Alberto Moravia. SCL(425), 1957a(29).
Bitter Lemons. Lawrence Durrell. SCL(428), 1959a(26).
Black Arrow, The. Robert Louis Stevenson. MCLE(425),

MEF(54), MP1(72).
Black Cloud, White Cloud. Ellen Douglas. SCL(430), 1964a (25).
Black Lamb and Grey Falcon. Rebecca West. MCLE(428), MN(42), MP1(75).
Black Like Me. John Howard Griffin. SCLs(34).
Black Obelisk, The. Erich Maria Remarque. SCL(433), 1958a(36).
Black Prince, The. Shirley Ann Grau. SCL(436), 1955a(26).
Black Swan, The. Thomas Mann. MCLE(431), MP4(74), SCL(439), 1954a(19).
Black Valley. Hugo Wast. MAF(63), MCLE(434), MP3(113).
Blacks, The. Jean Genêt. TCP(152).
Blast of War, The. Harold Macmillan. SCL(442), 1969a(36).
Bleak House. Charles Dickens. MCLE(437), MEF(57), MP1(77).
Bless the Beasts and Children. Glendon Swarthout. SCLs (37).
Bless This House. Norah Lofts. SCL(448), 1954a(22).
Blithe Spirit. Noel Coward. TCP(120).
Blithedale Romance, The. Nathaniel Hawthorne. MAF(66), MCLE(440), MP2(97), MPA2(38).
Blood Wedding. Federico García Lorca. MCLE(443), MD (83), MP2(99), TCP(143).
Bloodline. Ernest J. Gaines. SCL(452), 1969a(41).
Bloody Tenent of Persecution, The. Roger Williams. CHL (454).
Blot in the 'Scutcheon, A. Robert Browning. MCLE(446), MD(86), MP2(102).
Blue Denim. James Leo Herlihy and William Noble. SCLs (41).
Blue Estuaries, The. Louise Bogan. SCL(457), 1969a(45).
Blue Juniata. Malcolm Cowley. SCL(461), 1969a(48).
Blue Nile, The. Alan Moorehead. SCL(464), 1963a(12).
Blue Skies, Brown Studies. William Sansom. SCL(467), 1962a(30).
Body Rags. Galway Kinnell. SCL(470), 1968a(31).
Bohemians of the Latin Quarter, The. Henri Murger. MCLE(449), MEU(77), MP2(104).
Bondage of the Will, The. Martin Luther. CHL(347).
Bondman, The. Philip Massinger. MCLE(452), MD(89), MP3(116).
Bonds of Interest, The. Jacinto Benavente. MCLE(455), MD(92), MP2(107), POP(285).
Bonjour Tristesse. Françoise Sagan. SCL(473), 1955a(29).
Book of Proverbs. Otloh of St. Emmeram. CAL(276).
Book of Salvation, The. Avicenna. WP(278).

Book of Sentences, The. Peter Lombard. CAL(328).
Book of Songs. Heinrich Heine. MCLE(458), MP(25), MP3 (118).
Book of the Courtier, The. Baldassare Castiglione. MCLE (461), MP4(77).
Boon Island. Kenneth Roberts. SCL(476), 1957a(32).
Boris Godunov. Alexander Pushkin. MCLE(464), MD(95), MP2(109).
Born Free. Joy Adamson. SCL(480), 1961a(26).
Born Yesterday. Garson Kanin. SGAP(221).
Borough: A Poem in Twenty-Four Letters, The. George Crabbe. MCLE(467), MP4(79).
Borstal Boy. Brendan Behan. SCL(483), 1960a(25).
Bosnian Chronicle. Ivo Andrić. SCL(486), 1964a(27).
Boss, The. Edward Sheldon. DGAP(182).
Bostonians, The. Henry James. MCLE(470), MP4(82), MPA3(25).
Boswell. Stanley Elkin. SCL(490), 1965a(13).
Boswell for the Defence, 1769-1774. James Boswell. BM (41), SCL(493), 1960a(27).
Boswell in Search of a Wife, 1766-1769. James Boswell. BM(44), SCL(496), 1957a(36).
Boswell on the Grand Tour. James Boswell. BM(47), SCL (499), 1955a(32).
Boswell: The Ominous Years. James Boswell. SCL(503), 1964a(31).
Boswell's London Journal: 1762-1763. James Boswell. MCLE(473), MP4(85).
Bourgeois Gentleman, The. Molière. MCLE(476), MD(98), MP2(111).
Bouvard and Pécuchet. Gustave Flaubert. MCLE(478), MEU(80), MP3(121).
Boy Meets Girl. Samuel and Bella Spewack. SGAP(143).
Boys in the Band, The. Mart Crowley. SCL(509), 1969a(51).
Bracknels, The. Forrest Reid. MCLE(481), MEF(60), MP2 (113).
Braggart Soldier, The. Titus Maccius Plautus. MCLE(484), MD(100), MP3(123).
Braintree Mission, The. Nicholas E. Wyckoff. SCL(513), 1958a(39).
Brand. Henrik Ibsen. MCLE(487), MD(103), MP3(126).
Brautigan's. Richard Brautigan. 1970a(56).
Brave African Huntress, The. Amos Tutuola. SCLs(46).
Brave New World. Aldous Huxley. MCLE(490), MEF(63), MP1(79), PO2(135), SGBN(313).
Bread and Wine. Ignazio Silone. MCLE(492), MEU(83), MP1(81), SGEN(412).

Break of Noon. Paul Claudel. TCP(99).
Breakfast at Tiffany's. Truman Capote. SCLs(49).
Bride of Lammermoor, The. Sir Walter Scott. MCLE(495), MEF(65), MP3(128).
Bride of the Innisfallen, The. Eudora Welty. SCL(516), 1955a(35).
Brideshead Revisited. Evelyn Waugh. MCLE(498), MEF(68), MP1(83).
Bridge, The. Hart Crane. MCLE(501), MP(28), MP3(131).
Bridge at Andau, The. James A. Michener. SCL(519), 1958a(42).
Bridge of San Luis Rey, The. Thornton Wilder. MAF(69), MCLE(503), MP1(86), PO2(247), PON(38), SGAN(177).
Bridge on the Drina, The. Ivo Andrić. MCLE(506), MP4 (87), SCL(522), 1960a(30).
Bridge over the River Kwai, The. Pierre Boulle. SCL (525), 1954a(25).
Brief Lives. John Aubrey. MCLE(509), MP4(89).
Brigadier and the Golf Widow, The. John Cheever. SCL (528), 1965a(16).
Britannicus. Jean Baptiste Racine. MCLE(512), MD(106), MP3(133).
Broad and Alien Is the World. Ciro Alegría. MAF(72), MCLE(515), MP2(116).
Broken Ground, The. Wendell Berry. SCL(530), 1965a(18).
Broken Jug, The. Heinrich von Kleist. MCLE(518), MD (109), MP3(135).
Bronze Horseman: A Petersburg Tale, The. Alexander Pushkin. MCLE(521), MP4(91).
Brooklyn Bridge: Fact and Symbol. Alan Trachtenberg. SCL(534), 1966a(35).
Brother Ass. Eduardo Barrios. MCLE(524), MP4(94).
Brotherly Love. Gabriel Fielding. SCL(538), 1962a(33).
Brothers, The. Terence. MCLE(528), MD(112), MP3(138).
Brothers Ashkenazi, The. Israel Joshua Singer. MCLE(531), MEU(86), MP2(118).
Brothers Karamazov, The. Fyodor Mikhailovich Dostoevski. MCLE(534), MEU(89), MP1(88), PO(356), SGEN(152).
Brown Decades, The. Lewis Mumford. MCLE(537), MP4 (97).
Brushwood Boy, The. Rudyard Kipling. MCLE(540), MEF (71), MP2(120).
Brut, The. Layamon. MCLE(542), MP(30), MP3(140).
Brutal Friendship, The. F. W. Deakin. SCL(541), 1964a (37).
Buckdancer's Choice. James Dickey. SCL(544), 1966a(38).
Bucktails, The; or, Americans in England. James Kirke

Paulding. DGAP(64).
Buddenbrooks. Thomas Mann. MCLE(545), MEU(92), MP1 (91), SGEN(236).
Bull from the Sea, The. Mary Renault. SCL(549), 1963a (14).
Bullet Park. John Cheever. 1970a(63).
Bulwark, The. Theodore Dreiser. MAF(75), MCLE(548), MP3(142).
Buried Land, A. Madison Jones. SCL(554), 1964a(39).
Burning Glass, The. S. N. Behrman. SCL(558), 1969a(54).
Burning Glass, The. Charles Morgan. SCL(562), 1954a(28).
Burnt Ones, The. Patrick White. SCL(565), 1965a(22).
Burnt-Out Case, A. Graham Greene. MCLE(551), MP4(99), SCL(568), 1962a(36).
Bury the Dead. Irwin Shaw. SGAP(233).
Bus Stop. William Inge. SCLs(52).
Bussy D'Ambois. George Chapman. MCLE(554), MD(115), MP2(122).
But Not in Shame. John Toland. BM(51), SCL(572), 1962a (39).
Butterflies of the Province, The. Honor Tracy. 1971a(27).
By Daylight and in Dream. John Hall Wheelock. 1971a(29).
By Love Possessed. James Gould Cozzens. SCL(577), 1958a(44).
By the North Gate. Joyce Carol Oates. SCL(580), 1964a(43).
Byron. Leslie A. Marchand. BM(56), SCL(583), 1958a(47).

Cab at the Door, A. V. S. Pritchett. SCL(587), 1969a(57).
Cabala, The. Thornton Wilder. MAF(78), MCLE(557), MP1 (94).
Cabin, The. Vicente Blasco Ibáñez. MCLE(559), MEU(95), MP2(125).
Cabin Road, The. John Faulkner. 1970a(66).
Cabot Wright Begins. James Purdy. SCL(591), 1965a(25).
Cadmus. Folk tradition. MCLE(562), MEU(98), MP1(96).
Caesar and Cleopatra. George Bernard Shaw. MCLE(564), MD(118), MP3(145).
Caesar or Nothing. Pío Baroja. MCLE(567), MEU(100), MP1(97).
Caged Panther, The. Harry Meacham. SCL(595), 1968a(34).
Cain. George Gordon, Lord Byron. MCLE(570), MD(121), MP2(127).
Cakes and Ale. W. Somerset Maugham. MCLE(573), MEF (73), MP1(99).
Cale. Sylvia Wilkinson. 1971a(32).
Caleb Williams. William Godwin. MCLE(575), MEF(75), MP1(101).

Call It Sleep. Henry Roth. MCLE(577), MP4(102), SCL (599), 1965a(28).
Call of All Nations, The. Saint Prosper of Aquitaine. CAL (204).
Call of the Wild, The. Jack London. MAF(80), MCLE(581), MP1(103), PO2(208), SGAN(96).
Call to Honour, The. Charles de Gaulle. SCL(604), 1955a (38).
Camille. Alexandre Dumas (son). MCLE(584), MD(124), MP1(105), PO(289), PON(43), POP(247).
Camino Real. Tennessee Williams. TCP(443).
Campaspe. John Lyly. MCLE(586), MD(126), MP3(148).
Cancer Ward, The. Aleksandr I. Solzhenitsyn. SCL(608), 1969a(61).
Candida. George Bernard Shaw. MCLE(588), MD(128), MP3(150), TCP(342).
Candide. Voltaire. MCLE(590), MEU(103), MP1(107), PO (339), PON(48), SGEN(29).
Cane. Jean Toomer. SCLs(55).
Cannibal, The. John Hawkes. MCLE(592), MP4(105).
Canterbury Tales, The (Selections). Geoffrey Chaucer. MCLE(598), MP(33), MP2(129).
Cántice. Jorge Guillén. SCL(612), 1966a(43).
Cantos. Ezra Pound. MCLE(603), MP(38), MP3(151).
Capable of Honor. Allen Drury. SCL(615), 1967a(35).
Cape Cod Lighter, The. John O'Hara. SCL(619), 1963a(18).
Captain Cook and the South Pacific. John Gwyther. SCL (621), 1955a(41).
Captain from Köpenick. Carl Zuckmayer. TCP(462).
Captain Horatio Hornblower. C. S. Forester. MCLE(606), MEF(77), MP1(109).
Captain Singleton. Daniel Defoe. MCLE(609), MEF(80), MP3(154).
Captain Steele. Calhoun Winton. SCL(624), 1965a(32).
Captains Courageous. Rudyard Kipling. MCLE(612), MEF (83), MP1(111), PON(52).
Captain's Daughter, The. Alexander Pushkin. MCLE(615), MEU(105), MP1(113).
Captive and the Free, The. Joyce Cary. SCL(626), 1960a (33).
Captives, The. Titus Maccius Plautus. MCLE(618), MD (130), MP2(134).
Cards of Identity. Nigel Dennis. SCL(629), 1955a(44).
Caretaker, The. Harold Pinter. MCLE(620), MP4(110).
Carmen. Prosper Mérimée. MCLE(623), MEU(108), MP1 (116).
Carmen Deo nostro. Richard Crashaw. CAL(600).

Carmina. Gaius Valerius Catullus. MCLE(625), MP(41), MP3(156).
Casanova's Chinese Restaurant. Anthony Powell. BM(60), SCL(632), 1961a(30).
Case of Sergeant Grischa, The. Arnold Zweig. MCLE(628), MEU(110), MP1(118).
Cass Timberlane. Sinclair Lewis. MAF(83), MCLE(631), MP1(120).
Cassandra Singing. David Madden. 1970a(69).
Caste. Thomas William Robertson. MCLE(633), MD(132), MP2(135), POP(158).
Casti connubii. Pope Pius XI. CAL(808).
Castle, The. Franz Kafka. MCLE(636), MEU(113), MP1 (122), SGEN(345).
Castle Keep. William Eastlake. SCL(635), 1966a(46).
Castle of Fratta, The. Ippolito Nievo. MCLE(638), MEU (115), MP3(158), SCL(638), 1959a(28).
Castle of Otranto, The. Horace Walpole. MCLE(641), MEF (86), MP1(124).
Castle Rackrent. Maria Edgeworth. MCLE(643), MEF(88), MP1(126).
Casuals of the Sea. William McFee. MCLE(645), MEF(90), MP1(128).
Cat and Mouse. Günter Grass. MCLE(647), MP4(113), SCL(641), 1964a(46).
Cat on a Hot Tin Roof. Tennessee Williams. BM(63), MCLE(650), MP4(115), SCL(644), TCP(447), 1955a(47).
Catch-22. Joseph Heller. MCLE(653), MP4(117), PO2(285), SCL(647), 1962a(44).
Catcher in the Rye, The. J. D. Salinger. SCLs(58), SGAN (316).
Catechetical Lectures, The. Saint Cyril, Bishop of Jerusalem. CAL(90), CHL(92).
Catherine Carmier. Ernest J. Gaines. SCLs(61).
Catholicism. Henri de Lubac, S. J. CAL(856).
Catiline. Ben Jonson. MCLE(657), MD(135), MP3(161).
Cat's Cradle. Kurt Vonnegut, Jr. SCLs(65).
Caucasian Chalk Circle, The. Bertolt Brecht. TCP(76).
Caught in That Music. Seymour Epstein. SCL(651), 1968a (37).
Cause for Wonder. Wright Morris. SCL(655), 1964a(49).
Cavalleria Rusticana. Giovanni Verga. MCLE(660), MEU (118), MP2(137).
Cave, The. Robert Penn Warren. SCL(658), 1960a(35).
Cawdor. Robinson Jeffers. MCLE(662), MP(44), MP1(130).
Cecilia. Fanny Burney. MCLE(664), MEF(92), MP3(163).
Celestina. Fernando de Rojas. MCLE(667), MEU(120),

MP2(139).
Cenci, The. Percy Bysshe Shelley. MCLE(670), MD(138), MP1(131).
Centaur, The. John Updike. SCL(662), 1964a(52).
Centuries of Santa Fe, The. Paul Horgan. SCL(666), 1957a(39).
Ceremonies in Dark Old Men. Lonne Elder, III. 1970a(72).
Ceremony in Lone Tree. Wright Morris. BM(66), MCLE (672), MP4(121), SCL(670), 1961a(33).
Certain Smile, A. Françoise Sagan. SCL(673), 1957a(42).
César Birotteau. Honoré de Balzac. MCLE(676), MEU(123), MP2(142).
Chainbearer, The. James Fenimore Cooper. MAF(85), MCLE(679), MP3(166).
Chairs, The. Eugene Ionesco. TCP(197).
Chance. Joseph Conrad. PO2(86).
Change of Skin, A. Carlos Fuentes. SCL(676), 1969a(65).
Change of Weather. Winfield Townley Scott. SCL(680), 1965a(34).
Changeling, The. Thomas Middleton and William Rowley. MCLE(683), MD(140), MP3(169).
Character of Man, The. Emmanuel Mounier. CAL(902).
Characteristics. Anthony Ashley Cooper, Earl of Shaftesbury. WP(459).
Charles Demailly. Edmond and Jules de Goncourt. MCLE (686), MEU(124), MP3(171).
Charles Francis Adams. Martin Duberman. SCL(683), 1962a(48).
Charles O'Malley. Charles Lever. MCLE(689), MEF(95), MP1(133).
Charles Summer and the Coming of the Civil War. David Donald. BM(69), SCL(687), 1961a(36).
Charles XII. August Strindberg. TCP(376).
Charley Is My Darling. Joyce Cary. SCL(690), 1961a(38).
Charley's Aunt. Brandon Thomas. POP(147).
Charmed Life, A. Mary McCarthy. SCL(693), 1955a(50).
Charterhouse of Parma, The. Stendhal. MCLE(692), MEU (129), MP1(135), PO2(303), SGEN(48).
Chaste Maid in Cheapside, A. Thomas Middleton. MCLE (694), MD(143), MP3(174).
Château, The. William Maxwell. SCL(696), 1962a(51).
Chekhov. Ernest J. Simmons. SCL(700), 1963a(20).
Chéri. Sidonie Gabrielle Claudine Colette. MCLE(697), MEU(131), MP3(176).
Cherry Orchard, The. Anton Chekhov. MCLE(700), MD (146), MP2(144), POP(353).

Chevalier of the Maison Rouge, The. Alexandre Dumas (father). MCLE(702), MEU(134), MP3(179).
Chicago Poems. Carl Sandburg. MCLE(706), MP4(124).
Chickamauga. Glenn Tucker. SCLs(68).
Child Buyer, The. John Hersey. SCL(703), 1961a(41).
Child of Montmartre, The. Paul Léautaud. SCL(706), 1960a(39).
Child of Our Time. Michel del Castillo. SCL(709), 1959a (31).
Childe Harold's Pilgrimage. George Gordon, Lord Byron. MCLE(709), MP4(127).
Childhood, Boyhood, Youth. Count Leo Tolstoy. MCLE (712), MP4(129).
Children at the Gate, The. Edward Lewis Wallant. SCL (712), 1965a(37).
Children Is All. James Purdy. SCL(715), 1963a(23).
Children of God. Vardis Fisher. MAF(89), MCLE(715), MP1(137).
Children of Herakles, The. Euripides. MCLE(718), MD (148), MP3(182).
Children of Sánchez, The. Oscar Lewis. BM(72), SCL(718), 1962a(55).
Children of the Ghetto. Israel Zangwill. MCLE(720), MEF (98), MP2(146).
Children of Violence: Vols. I and II. Doris Lessing. SCL (723), 1965a(40).
Children of Violence: Vols. III and IV. Doris Lessing. SCL(728), 1967a(38).
Children's Hour, The. Lillian Hellman. TCP(189).
Chips with Everything. Arnold Wesker. MCLE(723), MP4 (132).
Chita. Lafcadio Hearn. MAF(92), MCLE(727), MP2(149), MPA2(64).
Chosen, The. Chaim Potok. SCL(731), 1968a(41).
Chouans, The. Honoré de Balzac. MCLE(730), MEU(138), MP2(151).
Christ and Culture. H. Richard Niebuhr. CHL(1121).
Christ and Society. Charles Gore. CHL(942).
Christ and Time. Oscar Cullmann. CHL(1072).
Christ of Faith, The. Karl Adam. CAL(1000).
Christian Directory, A. Richard Baxter. CHL(501).
Christian Discourses. Søren Kierkegaard. CHL(709).
Christian Doctrine. J. S. Whale. CHL(1051).
Christian Doctrine of Justification and Reconciliation, The. Albrecht Ritschl. CHL(758).
Christian Dogmatics. Hans Lassen Martensen. CHL(712).
Christian Education of Youth, The. Pope Pius XI. CAL(801).

Christian Faith, The. Friedrich Schleiermacher. CHL(657).
Christian Humanism. Louis Bouyer. CAL(1058).
Christian Message in a Non-Christian World, The. Hendrik Kraemer. CHL(1038).
Christian Mysticism. William Ralph Inge. CHL(816).
Christian Nurture. Horace Bushnell. CHL(736).
Christian Pastor, The. Washington Gladden. CHL(812).
Christian System, The. Alexander Campbell. CHL(672).
Christian Theology: An Ecumenical Approach. Walter Marshall Horton. CHL(1148).
Christian Theology in Outline. William Adams Brown. CHL (840).
Christian Understanding of God, The. Nels Ferré. CHL (1124).
Christianity among the Religions of the World. Arnold Toynbee. SCL(735), 1958a(50).
Christianity and Liberalism. John Gresham Machen. CHL (908).
Christianity and Paradox. Ronald W. Hepburn. CHL(1171).
Christianity as Old as the Creation. Matthew Tindal. CHL (569).
Christianity Not Mysterious. John Toland. CHL(554).
Christians and the State. John Coleman Bennett. CHL(1175).
Christmas Carol, A. Charles Dickens. MCLE(733), MEF (101), MP1(139), PO2(32).
Christopher Columbus, Mariner. Samuel Eliot Morison. BM(76), SCL(738), 1955a(53).
Christus Victor. Gustaf Aulén. CHL(950).
Chronica majora. Matthew Paris. CAL(376).
Chronicle of the Conquest of Granada, A. Washington Irving. MCLE(736), MN(45), MP3(183).
Chronicles of Froissart. Jean Froissart. MCLE(739), MN (48), MP3(185).
Chronicles of Hell. Michel de Ghelderode. TCP(155).
Chronique. St.-John Perse. BM(80), MCLE(742), MP4(134), SCL(742), 1962a(58).
Chuang Tzu. Chuan Chou. WP(185).
Church, The. Giovanni Battista Cardinal Montini (Pope Paul VI). CAL(1118).
Church and State. Luigi Sturzo. CAL(864).
Church Dogmatics. Karl Barth. CHL(981).
Church of the Word Incarnate, The. Charles Journet. CAL (875).
Churchills, The. A. L. Rowse. SCL(745), 1959a(34).
Cicero's Orations. Marcus Tullius Cicero. MCLE(745), MN(51), MP3(188).
Cid, The. Pierre Corneille. MCLE(747), MD(150), MP1

(142), POP(269).
Cinna. Pierre Corneille. MCLE(749), MD(152), MP3(190).
Cinq-Mars. Alfred de Vigny. MCLE(752), MEU(141), MP2 (153).
Circle, The. W. Somerset Maugham. TCP(215).
Circle of Chalk, The. Unknown. MCLE(755), MD(155), MP3(193).
Citadel of Learning, The. James Bryant Conant. SCL(748), 1957a(45).
Citizen Hearst. W. A. Swanberg. SCL(752), 1962a(61).
City, The. Clyde Fitch. POP(57).
City in History, The. Lewis Mumford. SCL(756), 1962a(64).
City Life. Donald Barthelme. 1971a(36).
City of God. Saint Augustine. CAL(188), CHL(140), WP (258).
City Without Walls and Other Poems. W. H. Auden. 1971a (38).
Civil War: A Narrative, The, Vol. I. Shelby Foote. SCL (759), 1959a(37).
Civil War: A Narrative, The, Vol. II. Shelby Foote. SCL(763), 1964a(55).
Clarissa Harlowe. Samuel Richardson. MCLE(758), MEF (104), MP1(143).
Claudius the God. Robert Graves. MCLE(761), MEF(107), MP1(146).
Clayhanger Trilogy, The. Arnold Bennett. MCLE(763), MEF(109), MP1(148).
Clea. Lawrence Durrell. BM(83), SCL(765), 1961a(44).
Cligés. Chrétien de Troyes. MCLE(766), MP(46), MP3(195).
Climbers, The. Clyde Fitch. DGAP(143).
Clock Without Hands. Carson McCullers. SCL(771), 1962a (67).
Cloister and the Hearth, The. Charles Reade. MCLE(770), MEF(112), MP1(150), PO(136).
Closed Garden, The. Julian Green. MCLE(773), MEU(144), MP2(155).
Cloud Forest, The. Peter Matthiessen. BM(89), MCLE (776), MP4(136), SCL(775), 1962a(71).
Cloud of Unknowing, The. Unknown. CAL(466), CHL(288).
Clouds, The. Aristophanes. MCLE(779), MD(158), MP1 (152).
Clown, The. Heinrich Böll. SCL(779), 1966a(49).
Clown on Fire. Aaron Judah. SCL(782), 1968a(45).
Cock-a-Doodle Dandy. Sean O'Casey. TCP(239).
Cocktail Party, The. T. S. Eliot. MCLE(781), MD(160), MP2(158).
Cocteau: A Biography. Francis Steegmuller. 1971a(42).

Coffin for King Charles, A. C. V. Wedgwood. SCL(785), 1965a(45).
Cold Comfort Farm. Stella Gibbons. MCLE(784), MP4(139).
Cold Ground Was My Bed Last Night. George Garrett. SCL(788), 1965a(47).
Collapse of the Third Republic, The. William L. Shirer. 1970a(75).
Collected Essays. Thomas Henry Huxley. WP(712).
Collected Letters of D. H. Lawrence, The. D. H. Lawrence. MCLE(787), MP4(141), SCL(791), 1963a(26).
Collected Papers. Charles Sanders Peirce. WP(952).
Collected Poems. John Betjeman. BM(93), SCL(794), 1960a (41).
Collected Poems. Lawrence Durrell. SCL(798), 1961a(49).
Collected Poems. Horace Gregory. SCL(801), 1965a(50).
Collected Poems. Walter De la Mare. MCLE(790), MP(50), MP3(198).
Collected Poems. Kathleen Raine. SCL(803), 1958a(53).
Collected Poems. Edith Sitwell. BM(97), SCL(806), 1955a (59).
Collected Poems, 1955. Robert Graves. SCL(809), 1955a (56).
Collected Poems, 1961. Robert Graves. SCL(813), 1962a (74).
Collected Poems, 1934-1952. Dylan Thomas. MCLE(793), MP(53), MP3(201).
Collected Poems of James Agee, The. James Agee. SCL (817), 1969a(72).
Collected Poems of Wallace Stevens, The. Wallace Stevens. BM(100), SCL(820), 1954a(31).
Collected Poems: I. Muriel Spark. SCL(823), 1969a(69).
Collected Short Prose of James Agee, The. James Agee. SCL(827), 1969a(74).
Collected Stories, The. Isaac Emmanuelovich Babel. SCL (830), 1955a(62).
Collected Stories of Ellen Glasgow, The. Ellen Glasgow. SCL(833), 1964a(57).
Collected Stories of Jean Stafford, The. Jean Stafford. SCLs(72).
Collected Stories of Katherine Anne Porter, The. Katherine Ann Porter. SCL(835), 1966a(51).
Collected Stories of Peter Taylor, The. Peter Taylor. 1971a(46).
Collected Works of Jane Bowles, The. Jane Bowles. SCL (841), 1967a(41).
Collector, The. John Fowles. SCL(846), 1964a(59).
Collegians, The. Gerald Griffin. MCLE(796), MEF(115),

MP2(160).
Colloquia peripatetica. John Duncan. CHL(762).
Colomba. Prosper Mérimée. MCLE(799), MEU(147), MP2 (162).
Color of Darkness. James Purdy. MCLE(802), MP4(144), SCLs(74).
Colossus and Other Poems, The. Sylvia Plath. SCLs(77).
Come Back, Little Sheba. William Inge. SGAP(227).
Come Gentle Spring. Jesse Stuart. 1970a(78).
Come, Let Us Worship. Godfrey Diekmann, O. S. B. CAL (1103).
Come Out into the Sun. Robert Francis. SCL(849), 1967a (45).
Comedians, The. Graham Greene. SCL(853), 1967a(49).
Comedy of Errors, The. William Shakespeare. MCLE(805), MD(163), MP2(164).
Coming Fury, The. Bruce Catton. SCL(858), 1962a(78).
Coming of Rain, The. Richard Marius. 1970a(82).
Command Decision. William Wister Haines. DGAP(370).
Commentaries. Gaius Julius Caesar. MCLE(808), MN(53), MP3(204).
Commentary on Aristotle's De anima. Saint Albert the Great. CAL(360).
Commentary on Galatians. Ragnar Bring. CHL(1180).
Commentary on the Apostles' Creed, A. Rufinus of Aquileia. CAL(169).
Commentary on the Summa theologica of Saint Thomas. Saint Cajetan. CAL(516).
Commonitory, A. Saint Vincent of Lérins. CAL(198), CHL (153).
Communism and the Conscience of the West. Fulton J. Sheen. CAL(944).
Communist World and Ours, The. Walter Lippmann. SCL (863), 1960a(45).
Complaint: Or, Night Thoughts, The. Edward Young. MCLE(810), MP4(146).
Complaisant Lover, The. Graham Greene. SCL(866), 1962a (82).
Compleat Angler, The. Izaak Walton. MCLE(812), MN(55), MP3(206).
Complete Poems. Elizabeth Bishop. 1970a(86).
Complete Poems. Marianne Moore. SCL(869), 1968a(47).
Complete Poems of Cavafy, The. Constantine P. Cavafy. SCL(874), 1962a(84).
Complete Ronald Firbank, The. Arthur Annesley Ronald Firbank. SCL(877), 1962a(87).

Complete Works of Nathanael West, The. Nathanael West. BM(103), SCL(881), 1958a(55).
Comrades. August Strindberg. MCLE(815), MD(166), MP3 (208).
Comus. John Milton. MCLE(817), MD(168), MP3(210).
Concept of Mind, The. Gilbert Ryle. WP(1109).
Concerning Illustrious Men. Gaius Suetonius Tranquillus. MCLE(820), MP4(148).
Concerning Rhetoric and Virtue. Alcuin. CAL(261).
Concluding Unscientific Postscript. Søren Kierkegaard. CHL(704), WP(626).
Confessions. Jean Jacques Rousseau. MCLE(826), MN(61), MP3(215).
Confessions of a Disloyal European. Jan Myrdal. SCL(885), 1969a(76).
Confessions of an English Opium Eater. Thomas De Quincey. MCLE(829), MN(64), MP2(167).
Confessions of Felix Krull, Confidence Man, The. Thomas Mann. BM(107), MCLE(832), MEU(150), MP3(218), SCL(889), 1955a(65).
Confessions of Nat Turner, The. William Styron. SCL(893), 1968a(53).
Confessions of Saint Augustine, The. Saint Augustine. CAL (165), CHL(128), MCLE(823), MN(58), MP3(213), WP (252).
Confessions of Zeno. Italo Svevo. PO2(472).
Confidence Man, The. Herman Melville. MAF(94), MCLE (835), MP3(221), MPA4(48), PO2(472).
Confidential Clerk, The. T. S. Eliot. BM(111), MCLE(838), MP4(150), SCL(897), 1954a(34).
Coningsby. Benjamin Disraeli. MCLE(841), MEF(118), MP2(170).
Conjure Woman, The. Charles Waddell Chesnutt. MAF(97), MCLE(844), MP2(172), MPA1(39).
Connecticut Yankee in King Arthur's Court, A. Samuel L. Clemens. MAF(100), MCLE(847), MP1(154), MPA5 (64), PO(203).
Connection, The. Jack Gelber. SGAP(295).
Conquest of Everest, The. John Hunt. SCL(900), 1954a(37).
Conquistador. Archibald MacLeish. MCLE(850), MP(56), MP3(223).
Conscience of the Rich, The. C. P. Snow. MCLE(853), MP4(152), SCL(903), 1959a(40).
Conscious Lovers, The. Sir Richard Steele. MCLE(856), MD(171), MP2(174).
Consciousness in Concord. Henry David Thoreau. SCL(906), 1959a(43).

Considerations on the Principal Events of the French Revolution. Madame de Staël. MCLE(859), MP4(155).
Consolation of Philosophy, The. Saint Anicius Manlius Severinus Boethius. CAL(229), MCLE(863), MN(67), MP3(225), WP(264).
Constant Circle, The. Sara Mayfield. SCL(909), 1968a(57).
Consuelo. George Sand. MCLE(865), MEU(153), MP1(156).
Contemplative Life, The. Julianus Pomerius. CAL(220).
Contemporary European Thought and Christian Faith. Albert Dondeyne. CAL(1061).
Contemporary Writers. Virginia Woolf. SCL(913), 1967a(53).
Contenders, The. John Wain. SCL(916), 1959a(45).
Contra celsum. Origen. CAL(71).
Contrast, The. Royall Tyler. DGAP(15).
Conversations of Goethe with Eckermann and Soret. Johann Peter Eckermann. MCLE(868), MP4(158).
Cooper's Creek. Alan Moorehead. SCL(919), 1965a(52).
Coorinna. Erle Wilson. SCL(923), 1954a(40).
Copperhead, The. Harold Frederic. MAF(103), MCLE(872), MP3(227).
Coriolanus. William Shakespeare. MCLE(875), MD(174), MP2(176).
Cornerstone, The. Zoé Oldenbourg. MCLE(878), MP4(162), SCL(926), 1955a(68).
Corrida at San Feliu, The. Paul Scott. SCL(929), 1965a(56).
Corridors of Power. C. P. Snow. SCL(933), 1965a(59).
Corsican Brothers, The. Alexandre Dumas (father). MCLE (881), MEU(156), MP2(179).
Cossacks, The. Count Leo Tolstoy. MCLE(884), MEU(159), MP2(181).
Cost of Discipleship, The. Dietrich Bonhoeffer. CHL(1028).
Council, Reform and Reunion, The. Hans Küng. CAL(1110).
Count Frontenac and New France Under Louis XIV. Francis Parkman. MCLE(886), MP4(164).
Count of Monte Cristo, The. Alexandre Dumas (father). MCLE(889), MEU(161), MP1(158), PO(282), PON(57), SGEN(101).
Counterfeiters, The. André Gide. MCLE(892), MEU(164), MP1(160), PO2(336), SGEN(273).
Countess de Charny, The. Alexandre Dumas (father). MCLE(895), MEU(167), MP3(230).
Country Doctor, A. Sarah Orne Jewett. MAF(106), MCLE (898), MP2(183), MPA3(97).
Country Doctor, The. Honoré de Balzac. MCLE(900), MEU (170), MP2(185).
Country House, The. John Galsworthy. MCLE(903), MEF (121), MP3(232).

Country of Old Men. Paul Olsen. SCL(937), 1967a(56).
Country of the Minotaur. Brewster Ghiselin. 1971a(51).
Country of the Pointed Firs, The. Sarah Orne Jewett. MAF (108), MCLE(905), MP1(163), MPA3(101).
Country Wife, The. William Wycherley. MCLE(907), MD (177), MP2(187).
Couples. John Updike. SCL(941), 1969a(80).
Courage to Be, The. Paul Tillich. WP(1146).
Course on the Positive Philosophy. Auguste Comte. WP (588).
Courtesan, The. Pietro Aretino. MCLE(909), MD(179), MP3(234).
Courtship of Miles Standish, The. Henry Wadsworth Longfellow. MCLE(911), MP(59), MP1(165), MPA4(7).
Cousin Bette. Honoré de Balzac. MCLE(913), MEU(173), MP1(166).
Cousin Pons. Honoré de Balzac. MCLE(916), MEU(176), MP2(189), PON(62).
Coxcomb, The. Francis Beaumont and John Fletcher. MCLE(919), MD(181), MP3(236).
Cradle Song, The. Gregorio Martínez Sierra. MCLE(922), MD(184), MP2(192).
Craig's Wife. George Kelly. SGAP(1).
Cranford. Mrs. Elizabeth Gaskell. MCLE(925), MEF(123), MP2(194).
Crazy in Berlin. Thomas Berger. SCLs(81).
Cream of the Jest, The. James Branch Cabell. MAF(110), MCLE(927), MP1(168).
Creative Evolution. Henri Bergson. WP(767).
Creed of a Savoyard Priest, The. Jean Jacques Rousseau. CHL(605).
Cress Delehanty. Jessamyn West. SCL(944), 1954a(43).
Crest Jewel of Wisdom. S'añkara. WP(268).
Crime and Punishment. Fyodor Mikhailovich Dostoevski. MCLE(929), MEU(179), MP1(170), PO(352), PON(70), SGEN(145).
Crime of Galileo, The. Giorgio De Santillana. SCL(947), 1955a(71).
Crime of Sylvestre Bonnard, The. Anatole France. MCLE (932), MEU(182), MP2(196), SGEN(215).
Crisis, The. Winston S. Churchill. MAF(112), MCLE(935), MP1(172), PON(77).
Crisis, The. Thomas Paine. MCLE(938), MN(69), MP3 (238).
Critic, The. Richard Brinsley Sheridan. MCLE(941), MD (187), MP2(199).

Critical Essays of William Hazlitt, The. William Hazlitt. MCLE(943), MP4(166).
Critique of Judgment. Immanuel Kant. WP(556).
Critique of Practical Reason. Immanuel Kant. WP(545).
Critique of Pure Reason. Immanuel Kant. MCLE(946), MN (72), MP3(240), WP(531).
Crito. Plato. WP(54).
Crock of Gold, The. James Stephens. MCLE(949), MEF (125), MP1(175), PO2(115), SGBN(257).
Crocodile Fever. Lawrence Earl. SCL(951), 1954a(46).
Crome Yellow. Aldous Huxley. MCLE(951), MEF(127), MP1 (177).
Cross of Iron, The. Willi Heinrich. SCL(954), 1957a(48).
Crossbowman's Story, A. George Millar. SCL(958), 1955a (74).
Crossroads. James McConkey. SCL(962), 1968a(60).
Crotchet Castle. Thomas Love Peacock. MCLE(953), MEF (129), MP2(201).
Crucial Decade, The. Eric G. Goldman. SCL(965), 1957a (51).
Crucible, The. Arthur Miller. SGAP(251), TCP(223).
Cruise of the Cachalot, The. Frank T. Bullen. MCLE(955), MEF(131), MP1(178).
Crusades, The. Zoé Oldenbourg. SCL(969), 1967a(59).
Cry, The Beloved Country. Alan Paton. MCLE(957), MEU (185), MP2(202), PO2(490).
Crying of Lot 49, The. Thomas Pynchon. SCL(973), 1967a (63).
Cuba: Island of Paradox. R. Hart Phillips. SCL(976), 1960a(48).
Cudjo's Cave. John Townsend Trowbridge. MAF(115), MCLE(959), MP2(205).
Culture and Anarchy. Matthew Arnold. MCLE(962), MP4 (169).
Cunning of the Dove, The. Alfred Duggan. SCL(979), 1961a (51).
Cupid and Psyche. Folk tradition. MCLE(965), MEU(187), MP1(180).
Cur Deus homo. Saint Anselm of Canterbury. CAL(286), CHL(202).
Cursus theologicus. John of St. Thomas. CAL(605).
Custom of the Country, The. Edith Wharton. MAF(118), MCLE(967), MP3(243).
Cyclops, The. Euripides. MCLE(969), MD(189), MP3(245).
Cymbeline. William Shakespeare. MCLE(971), MD(191), MP2(207).
Cypresses Believe in God, The. José María Gironella.

MCLE(974), MP4(172), SCL(983), 1955a(78).
Cyrano de Bergerac. Edmond Rostand. MCLE(976), MD (194), MP2(210), POP(243).
Cyropaedia. Xenophon. MCLE(979), MP4(174).

D. H. Lawrence: A Composite Biography. Edward Nehls, Editor. BM(129), SCL(1159), 1960a(60).
Dagon. Fred Chappell. SCL(986), 1969a(82).
Daisy Miller. Henry James. MAF(120), MCLE(982), MP1 (182), MPA3(31).
Damaged Souls. Gamaliel Bradford. MCLE(984), MP4(176).
Dame Care. Hermann Sudermann. MCLE(986), MEU(189), MP2(212).
Damnation of Theron Ware, The. Harold Frederic. MAF (122), MCLE(989), MP2(214), MPA2(7).
Dance in the Sun, A. Dan Jacobson. SCL(990), 1957a(55).
Dance of Death, The. August Strindberg. MCLE(992), MD (196), MP2(217), TCP(379).
Dance the Eagle to Sleep. Marge Piercy. 1971a(55).
Dance to the Music of Time, A. Anthony Powell. MCLE (995), MP4(178), SCL(993), 1963a(28).
Dance to the Music of Time: Second Movement, A. Anthony Powell. MCLE(1000), MP4(183).
Dancer in Darkness, A. David Stacton. SCL(997), 1963a(32).
Dangerous Acquaintances. Pierre Choderlos de Laclos. MCLE(1006), MEU(192), MP3(246).
Daniel Deronda. George Eliot. MCLE(1009), MEF(133), MP3(249).
Dante. Thomas Bergin. SCL(1001), 1966a(56).
Dante. T. S. Eliot. MCLE(1012), MP4(188).
Daphnis and Chloë. Attributed to Longus. MCLE(1014), MEU(195), MP1(183).
Dark and the Light, The. Elio Vittorini. SCL(1005), 1962a (90).
Dark as the Grave Wherein My Friend Is Laid. Malcolm Lowry. SCL(1008), 1969a(86).
Dark at the Top of the Stairs, The. William Inge. SCL (1011), 1959a(48).
Dark is Light Enough, The. Christopher Fry. SCL(1014), 1954a(150).
Dark Journey, The. Julian Green. MCLE(1016), MEU(197), MP2(219).
Dark Labyrinth, The. Lawrence Durrell. SCL(1017), 1963a (35).
Dark Laughter. Sherwood Anderson. MAF(125), MCLE (1019), MP1(185).

Dark Night of the Soul, The. Saint John of the Cross. CAL(558), CHL(406).
Dark of the Moon. Howard Richardson and William Berney. DGAP(362).
Darkness at Noon. Arthur Koestler. MCLE(1021), MEU(200), MP1(187), PO2(484), SGEN(432).
Darwin and the Darwinian Revolution. Gertrude Himmelfarb. SCL(1020), 1960a(51).
Das Kapital. Karl Marx. MN(166).
Daughter of France. V. Sackville-West. SCL(1023), 1960a (54).
Daughter of Silence. Morris L. West. SCL(1027), 1962a(93).
Daughter of the Legend. Jesse Stuart. SCL(1031), 1966a(60).
Daughter to Napoleon. Constance Wright. SCL(1034), 1962a (96).
Daumier: Man of His Time. Oliver W. Larkin. SCL(1038), 1967a(66).
David Copperfield. Charles Dickens. MCLE(1023), MEF (136), MP1(189), PO(55), PON(81), SGBN(83).
David Harum. Edward Noyes Westcott. MAF(127), MCLE (1027), MP1(192).
Davy Crockett. Frank Hitchcock Murdoch. DGAP(99).
Day After Sunday, The. Hollis Summers. SCL(1042), 1969a (89).
Day I Stopped Dreaming About Barbara Steele and Other Poems, The. R. H. W. Dillard. SCL(1047), 1967a (69).
Day in Late September, A. Merle Miller. SCL(1050), 1964a(61).
Day Is Dark, The and Three Travelers. Marie-Claire Blais. SCL(1054), 1968a(63).
Day Lincoln Was Shot, The. Jim Bishop. SCL(1058), 1955a (81).
Day of Infamy. Walter Lord. BM(114), SCL(1061), 1958a (60).
Day of the Lion, The. Giose Rimanelli. SCL(1064), 1954a (49).
Day Sailing. David Slavitt. 1970a(90).
Day the Money Stopped, The. Brendan Gill. SCL(1067), 1958a(63).
Day the Perfect Speakers Left, The. Leonard Nathan. 1970a(94).
Days in the Yellow Leaf. William Hoffman. SCL(1070), 1959a(50).
Days of Henry Thoreau, The. Walter Harding. SCL(1073), 1966a(63).
Days of the Phoenix. Van Wyck Brooks. SCL(1076), 1958a(66).

De contemptu mundi. Pope Innocent III. CAL(342).
De corpore. Thomas Hobbes. WP(399).
De corpore Christi. William of Ockham. CHL(267).
De magistro. Saint Augustine. CAL(140).
De monarchia. Dante Alighieri. CAL(438), CHL(255).
De potestate regia et papali. John of Paris. CAL(432).
De primo principio. John Duns Scotus. CAL(423).
De principiis. Origen. WP(240).
De profundis. Oscar Wilde. MCLE(1030), MP4(190).
De regno Christi. Martin Bucer. CHL(396).
De religione laici. Edward Herbert, First Lord of Cherbury. CHL(467).
De rerum natura. Lucretius. MCLE(1033), MN(75), MP3 (252), WP(218).
De sacro altaris mysterio. Pope Innocent III. CAL(345).
De trinitate. Saint Augustine. CAL(173).
De trinitate. Saint Anicius Manlius Severinus Boethius. CAL(223).
De veritate. Saint Thomas Aquinas. CAL(379).
De viris illustribus. Saint Jerome. CAL(148).
Dead End. Sidney Kingsley. DGAP(273), SGAP(190).
Dead Fires. José Lins do Rêgo. MAF(130), MCLE(1035), MP3(254).
Dead Souls. Nikolai V. Gogol. MCLE(1038), MEU(202), MP1(194), PO2(384), SGEN(94).
Dear Brutus. James M. Barrie. MCLE(1041), MD(199), MP1(196), TCP(44).
Death and Immortality. Michele Federico Sciacca. CAL (1078).
Death at an Early Age. Jonathan Kozol. SCL(1079), 1968a (67).
Death Comes for the Archbishop. Willa Cather. MAF(133), MCLE(1043), MP1(199), PO2(204).
Death Dance. Angus Wilson. 1970a(98).
Death in Life: Survivors of Hiroshima. Robert Jay Lifton. SCLs(84).
Death in Midsummer and Other Stories. Yukio Mishima. SCL(1084), 1967a(71).
Death in the Family, A. James Agee. BM(117), MCLE (1046), MP4(192), SCL(1088), 1958a(69).
Death in the Sanchez Family, A. Oscar Lewis. 1970a(101).
Death in Venice. Thomas Mann. MCLE(1049), MEU(205), MP2(221).
Death Kit. Susan Sontag. SCL(1092), 1968a(72).
Death of a Hero. Richard Aldington. MCLE(1052), MEF (140), MP2(223).
Death of a Nobody, The. Jules Romains. PO2(371).

Death of a Salesman. Arthur Miller. DGAP(378), MCLE (1054), MD(201), MP2(225), SGAP(244), TCP(226).
Death of Artemio Cruz, The. Carlos Fuentes. MCLE(1057), MP4(195), SCL(1096), 1965a(63).
Death of Ivan Ilyich, The. Count Leo Tolstoy. MCLE(1061), MEU(208), MP3(256).
Death of the Gods, The. Dmitri Merejkowski. MCLE(1063), MEU(210), MP1(201).
Death of the Heart, The. Elizabeth Bowen. MCLE(1066), MEF(142), MP2(228).
Death of Virgil, The. Hermann Broch. MCLE(1069), MEU (213), MP3(258).
Death Ship, The. B. Traven. MCLE(1072), MP4(199).
Death's Duell. John Donne. MCLE(1075), MP4(202).
Debit and Credit. Gustav Freytag. MCLE(1077), MEU(216), MP3(261).
Decades, The. Johann Heinrich Bullinger. CHL(381).
Decameron, The (Selections). Giovanni Boccaccio. MCLE (1080), MEU(219), MP2(230).
Decision at Trafalgar. Dudley Pope. BM(121), SCL(1102), 1961a(55).
Decision to Intervene, The. George F. Kennan. BM(125), SCL(1106), 1959a(54).
Declaration of Faith (and Other Writings), A. Gregory Thaumaturges. CHL(64).
Declaration of Sentiments, The. Jacobus Arminius. CHL (424).
Decline and Fall. Evelyn Waugh. MCLE(1085), MEF(145), MP2(235), SGBN(321).
Decline of the West, The. Oswald Spengler. SCL(1110), 1963a(38).
Decretum gratiani. Johannes Gratian. CAL(324).
Deephaven. Sarah Orne Jewett. MAF(136), MCLE(1088), MP2(238).
Deerslayer, The. James Fenimore Cooper. MAF(139), MCLE(1091), MP1(203), MPA1(44), PO2(158), PON(86).
Defeat, The. Nordahl Grieg. TCP(178).
Defence of Guenevere and Other Poems, The. William Morris. MCLE(1094), MP4(204).
Defence of Poesie. Sir Philip Sidney. MCLE(1097), MP4 (206).
Defence of Poetry, A. Percy Bysshe Shelley. MCLE(1100), MP4(208).
Defense, The. Vladimir Nabokov. SCL(1114), 1965a(69).
Defense of the Constitutions of Government of the United States of America, A. John Adams. MCLE(1103), MN(77), MP3(263).

Defense of the True and Catholic Doctrine of the Sacrament, A. Thomas Cranmer. CHL(385).
Degrees of Knowledge. Jacques Maritain. CAL(828), WP (963).
Deirdre. James Stephens. MCLE(1105), MEF(148), MP2 (240).
Deirdre of the Sorrows. John Millington Synge. MCLE(1108), MD(204), MP3(265).
Delicate Balance, A. Edward Albee. SCL(1117), 1967a(75).
Deliverance. James Dickey. 1971a(58).
Delphine. Madame de Staël. MCLE(1110), MEU(224), MP2 (243).
Delta Wedding. Eudora Welty. MAF(142), MCLE(1113), MP2(245).
Demian. Hermann Hesse. SCL(1121), 1966a(66).
Democracy in America. Alexis de Tocqueville. MCLE(1116), MP4(211).
Democratic Vistas. Walt Whitman. MCLE(1119), MP4(213), MPA5(99).
Democritus: Fragments. Democritus of Abdera. WP(37).
Demon: An Eastern Tale, The. Mikhail Yurievich Lermontov. MCLE(1122), MP4(216).
Demons, The. Heimito von Doderer. SCL(1124), 1962a(100).
Demonstration of Apostolic Teaching, The. Saint Irenaeus. CAL(47).
Deputy, The. Rolf Hochhuth. SCL(1127), 1965a(71).
Descent into Hell. Charles Williams. MCLE(1125), MP4 (218).
Descent of Man, and Selection in Relation to Sex, The. Charles Darwin. MCLE(1128), MP4(221).
Desert Music and Other Poems, The. William Carlos Williams. SCL(1131), 1954a(52).
Desert Solitaire. Edward Abbey. SCL(1134), 1969a(93).
Deserted House, The. Lydia Chukovskaya. SCL(1137), 1968a(75).
Design for Living. Noel Coward. POP(77).
Desire Under the Elms. Eugene O'Neill. DGAP(221), MCLE(1131), MD(206), MP2(247), SGAP(7), TCP(259).
Despair. Vladimir Nabokov. SCL(1141), 1967a(78).
Destiny Bay. Donn Byrne. MCLE(1133), MEF(151), MP2 (249).
Destiny of Man, The. Nikolai Berdyaev. CHL(960), WP (940).
Devil and the Good Lord, The. Jean-Paul Sartre. TCP(319).
Devil Drives, The. Fawn M. Brodie. SCL(1145), 1968a(79).
Devil Rides Outside, The. John Howard Griffin. SCLs(88).

Devil to Pay in the Backlands, The. João Guimarães Rosa. SCL(1150), 1964a(65).
Devil's Advocate, The. Morris L. West. SCL(1153), 1960a (57).
Devil's Elixir, The. Ernst Theodor Amadeus Hoffmann. MCLE(1136), MEU(227), MP3(267).
Devil's Yard. Ivo Andrić. SCL(1156), 1963a(42).
Devotion of the Cross, The. Pedro Calderón de la Barca. MCLE(1139), MD(208), MP3(270).
Devotions upon Emergent Occasions. John Donne. CHL(441).
Diable Boiteux, Le. Alain René Le Sage. MCLE(1141), MEU(230), MP3(271).
Dialogue Between the Soul and the Body, The. Saint Catherine of Genoa. CAL(530).
Dialogue Concerning the Two Chief World Systems. Galileo Galilei. CAL(593).
Dialogue des Héros de Roman. Nicolas Boileau-Despréaux. MCLE(1145), MN(79), MP3(275).
Dialogue of Comfort Against Tribulation, A. Sir Thomas More. CHL(354).
Dialogue of Saint Catherine of Siena, The. Saint Catherine of Siena. CAL(473), CHL(280).
Dialogues, The. Saint Gregory the Great. CAL(241).
Dialogues, The. Theodoret of Cyrus. CHL(156).
Dialogues Concerning Cause, Principle, and One. Giordano Bruno. WP(365).
Dialogues Concerning Natural Religion. David Hume. CHL (615), WP(525).
Dialogues of Plato, The. Plato. MCLE(1148), MN(82), MP3(277).
Dialogues of Sulpicius Severus, The. Sulpicius Severus. CAL(157).
Dialogues on Metaphysics and on Religion. Nicolas de Malebranche. WP(422).
Diana of the Crossways. George Meredith. MCLE(1152), MEF(154), MP1(206), PO(133).
Diaries of Kafka: 1910-1923, The. Franz Kafka. MCLE (1155), MP4(224).
Diary. John Evelyn. MCLE(1158), MN(86), MP3(281).
Diary. Samuel Pepys. MCLE(1161), MN(89), MP3(283).
Diary and Letters of Mme. d'Arblay, The. Fanny Burney. MCLE(1163), MP4(226).
Diary of a Country Priest, The. Georges Bernanos. MCLE (1167), MEU(234), MP2(251).
Diary of a Rapist, The. Evan S. Connell, Jr. SCL(1163), 1967a(82).

Diary of a Writer. Fyodor Mikhailovich Dostoevski. MCLE (1170), MP4(230).

Diary of Anaïs Nin: 1931-1934, The. Anaïs Nin. SCL (1166), 1967a(84).

Diary of Anaïs Nin: 1934-1939, The. Anaïs Nin. SCL (1170), 1968a(83).

Diary of Anne Frank, The. Frances Goodrich and Albert Hackett. DGAP(395).

Diary of David Brainerd, The. David Brainerd. CHL(594).

Diary of Henry Crabb Robinson, The. Henry Crabb Robinson. MCLE(1173), MP4(232).

(Diblos) Notebook, The. James Merrill. SCL(1173), 1966a (69).

Dick, The. Bruce Jay Friedman. 1971a(61).

Didache or The Teaching of the Twelve Apostles, The. Unknown. CAL(1), CHL(23).

Didactica magna. Johannes Amos Comenius. CHL(489).

Digby Grand. George J. Whyte-Melville. MCLE(1176), MEF (157), MP2(253).

Dignity of Man, The. Russell W. Davenport. SCL(1176), 1955a(83).

Dinner Party, The. Claude Mauriac. MCLE(1179), MP4 (235), SCL(1179), 1961a(58).

Dirty Hands. Jean-Paul Sartre. MEU(237), TCP(326).

Disciple, The. Paul Bourget. MCLE(1182), MP1(209).

Discourse Against the Greeks, The. Tatian. CAL(23).

Discourse Concerning the Holy Spirit. John Owen. CHL (518).

Discourse on Method. René Descartes. WP(380).

Discourse on the Origin of Inequality. Jean Jacques Rousseau. MCLE(1185), MP4(237).

Discourse on the Priesthood. Saint John Chrysostom. CAL (123).

Discourse on Universita History. Jacques Bénigne Bossuet. CAL(608).

Discourses. Pietro Aretino. MCLE(1187), MP4(239).

Discourses Against the Arians. Saint Athanasius. CAL(94).

Discourses and Manual. Epictetus. WP(224).

Discourses upon the Existence and Attributes of God. Stephen Charnock. CHL(539).

Discovery of God, The. Henri de Lubac, S. J. CAL(1025).

Discrepancies and Apparitions. Diane Wakoski. SCL(1183), 1966a(72).

Disputation of the Sacrament of the Eucharist, A. Peter Martyr Vermigli. CHL(376).

Disraeli. Louis Napoleon Parker. POP(109).

Distant Music, The. H. L. Davis. SCL(1186), 1958a(73).

Divan, The. Haifiz Hāfiz. MCLE(1190), MP(61), MP3(285).
Divine Comedy, The. Dante Alighieri. CAL(443), CHL(259), MCLE(1192), MP(63), MP1(211).
Divine Fire, The. May Sinclair. MCLE(1195), MEF(160), MP2(256).
Divine Imperative, The. Emil Brunner. CHL(986).
Divine Institutes, The. Lucius Caecilius Firmianus Lactantius. CAL(81), CHL(79).
Divine Love and Wisdom. Emanuel Swedenborg. MCLE(1197), MN(91), MP3(287).
Divine Milieu, The. Pierre Teilhard de Chardin, S.J. CAL (1054), CHL(1152).
Divine Names, The. Dionysius, the Pseudo-Areopagite. CHL(165).
Divine Relativity, The. Charles Hartshorne. CHL(1088).
Divinity School Address, The. Ralph Waldo Emerson. CHL (684).
Divino afflante Spiritu. Pope Pius XII. CAL(883).
Do, Lord, Remember Me. George Garrett. SCL(1190), 1966a(74).
Doctor Faustus. Thomas Mann. MCLE(1199), MEU(240), MP2(258).
Doctor Faustus. Christopher Marlowe. MCLE(1202), MD (210), MP2(261).
Doctor in Spite of Himself, The. Molière. MCLE(1205), MD(213), MP3(289).
Dr. Jekyll and Mr. Hyde. Robert Louis Stevenson. MCLE (1208), MEF(162), MP1(214), PO(159), PON(90), POP (151).
Doctor Pascal. Émile Zola. MCLE(1210), MEU(243), MP3 (291).
Doctor Thorne. Anthony Trollope. MCLE(1213), MEF(164), MP2(263).
Doctor Zhivago. Boris Pasternak. BM(133), MCLE(1216), MP4(241), PON(96), SCL(1194), SGEN(467), 1959a(57).
Dodsworth. Sinclair Lewis. MAF(145), MCLE(1220), MP2 (265).
Dog Who Wouldn't Be, The. Farley Mowat. SCL(1199), 1958a(76).
Dog Years. Günter Grass. SCL(1202), 1966a(78).
Dogmatics. Emil Brunner. CHL(1076).
Dollmaker, The. Harriette Simpson Arnow. SCL(1206), 1954a(55).
Doll's House, A. Henrik Ibsen. MCLE(1223), MD(216), MP1(216), POP(321).
Domains. James Whitehead. SCL(1210), 1969a(96).
Dombey and Son. Charles Dickens. MCLE(1225), MEF(167),

MP2(267).
Domestic Relations. Frank O'Connor. SCL(1213), 1958a(78).
Dominique. Eugène Fromentin. MCLE(1228), MEU(246), MP3(294).
Don Carlos. Johann Christoph Friedrich von Schiller. MCLE(1231), MD(218), MP2(270).
Don Flows Home to the Sea, The. Mikhail Sholokhov. MCLE(1234), MEU(249), MP2(272).
Don Juan. George Gordon, Lord Byron. MCLE(1237), MP (66), MP1(217).
Don Juan. Molière. MCLE(1240), MD(221), MP3(296).
Don Juan Tenorio. José Zorrilla y Moral. MCLE(1243), MD(224), MP2(274).
Don Quixote de la Mancha. Miguel de Cervantes Saavedra. MCLE(1246), MEU(252), MP1(220), PO(372), PON(102), SGEN(15).
Don Segundo Sombra. Ricardo Güiraldes. MAF(148), MCLE (1250), MP2(277).
Doña Barbara. Rómulo Gallegos. MAF(151), MCLE(1253), MP2(277).
Dona Flor and Her Two Husbands. Jorge Amado. 1971a(63).
Doña Perfecta. Benito Pérez Galdós. MCLE(1256), MEU (256), MP3(298).
Don't Go Near the Water. William Brinkley. SCL(1215), 1957a(58).
Dostoevsky. Nikolai Berdyaev. MCLE(1258), MP4(245).
Dostoevsky. David Magarshack. SCL(1219), 1964a(67).
Double-Dealer, The. William Congreve. MCLE(1261), MD (227), MP2(281).
Double Helix, The. James D. Watson. SCL(1222), 1969a(98).
Down There. Joris Karl Huysmans. MCLE(1263), MEU(258), MP3(300).
Downfall, The. Émile Zola. MCLE(1265), MEU(260), MP1 (223).
Dracula. Bram Stoker. MCLE(1269), MEF(170), MP2(283).
Dragon: Fifteen Stories, The. Yevgeny Zamyatin. SCL (1226), 1967a(87).
Dragon Seed. Pearl S. Buck. MAF(154), MCLE(1271), MP1 (226).
Dragon's Wine. Borden Deal. SCL(1230), 1961a(61).
Dramatic Monologues and Lyrics of Browning. Robert Browning. MCLE(1274), MP4(247).
Dramatis Personae. Robert Browning. MCLE(1277), MP4 (250).
Dream of Arcadia, The. Van Wyck Brooks. SCL(1233), 1959a(62).

Dream of Kings, A. Davis Grubb. SCL(1237), 1955a(86).
Dream of Kings, A. Harry Mark Petrakis. SCL(1240), 1968a(86).
Dream of the Red Chamber. Tsao Hsueh-chin. BM(138), MCLE(1281), MEU(263), MP3(302), PO2(429), SCL (1243), 1959a(65).
Dream Play, A. August Strindberg. TCP(383).
Dreiser. W. A. Swanberg. SCL(1247), 1966a(81).
Drink. Émile Zola. MCLE(1285), MEU(267), MP3(305).
Drowning with Others. James Dickey. SCL(1251), 1963a(44).
Drums. James Boyd. MAF(157), MCLE(1288), MP1(228).
Drums Along the Mohawk. Walter D. Edmonds. MAF(160), MCLE(1291), MP1(230).
Drums of Father Ned, The. Sean O'Casey. SCL(1255), 1961a(64).
Drunkard, The; or, The Fallen Saved. William H. Smith. DGAP(55).
Duchess of Malfi, The. John Webster. MCLE(1294), MD (229), MP1(232).
Ductor dubitantium. Jeremy Taylor. CHL(497).
Duino Elegies. Rainer Maria Rilke. MCLE(1296), MP(69), MP3(307).
Dunciad, The. Alexander Pope. MCLE(1299), MP(72), MP3 (310).
Dybbuk, The. S. Ansky. POP(364).
Dyer's Hand and Other Essays, The. W. H. Auden. SCL (1258), 1963a(47).
Dylan. Sidney Michaels. SCL(1262), 1965a(74).
Dynasts, The. Thomas Hardy. MCLE(1302), MD(231), MP1 (234).

Eagle and the Serpent, The. Martín Luis Guzmán. MCLE (1305), MP4(253).
Ear in Bartram's Tree, An. Jonathan Williams. 1970a(105).
Early Theological Writings. Georg Wilhelm Friedrich Hegel. CHL(633).
Earth. Émile Zola. MCLE(1308), MEU(270), MP3(312).
Earth-Spirit. Frank Wedekind. TCP(425).
Earth Walk. William Meredith. 1971a(66).
Earthly Paradise, The. William Morris. MCLE(1311), MP4 (255).
Easiest Way, The. Eugene Walter. DGAP(170), POP(46).
East Lynne. Mrs. Henry Wood. POP(155).
East of Eden. John Steinbeck. MAF(163), MCLE(1313), MP3(315).
East to West. Arnold Toynbee. BM(142), SCL(1265), 1959a (68).

Eastward Ho! George Chapman with Ben Jonson and John Marston. MCLE(1316), MD(234), MP3(317).
Ebony and Ivory. Llewelyn Powys. MCLE(1319), MEF(173), MP3(320).
Ecce homo. Sir John Robert Seeley. CHL(747).
Ecclesiastical History. Eusebius of Caesarea. CHL(87).
Ecclesiastical History. Eusebius Pamphili. CAL(88).
Ecclesiastical History of the English People. Saint Bede. CAL(258), CHL(181).
Ecclesiazusae, The. Aristophanes. MCLE(1321), MD(237), MP3(322).
Eclogues. Publius Vergilius Maro. MCLE(1323), MP4(257).
Edge of Darkness, The. Mary Ellen Chase. SCL(1268), 1958a(80).
Edge of Day, The. Laurie Lee. SCL(1271), 1961a(67).
Edge of Sadness, The. Edwin O'Connor. SCL(1275), 1962a (103).
Edge of the Sea, The. Rachel Carson. BM(145), SCL(1279), 1955a(89).
Edge of the Storm, The. Agustín Yáñez. SCL(1282), 1964a (70).
Edge of the Woods, The. Heather Ross Miller. SCL(1285), 1965a(77).
Edison: A Biography. Matthew Josephson. BM(148), SCL (1288), 1960a(63).
Edmund Campion. Evelyn Waugh. CAL(838), MCLE(1326), MN(93), MP1(237).
Education of Henry Adams, The. Henry Adams. MCLE (1328), MN(95), MP1(238).
Edward the Second. Christopher Marlowe. MCLE(1331), MD(239), MP2(286).
Effi Briest. Theodore Fontane. MCLE(1334), MEU(273), MP3(323).
Egmont. Johann Wolfgang von Goethe. MCLE(1337), MD (242), MP2(288).
Egoist, The. George Meredith. MCLE(1340), MEF(175), MP1(241), PO2(55), PON(106).
Ehrengard. Isak Dinesen. PO2(497).
Eighth Day, The. Thornton Wilder. SCL(1291), 1968a(89).
Eirenicon, An. Edward B. Pusey. CHL(751).
Either/Or. Søren Kierkegaard. WP(612).
Elder Statesman, The. T. S. Eliot. BM(152), MCLE(1344), MP4(262), SCL(1297), 1960a(67).
Elective Affinities. Johann Wolfgang von Goethe. MCLE (1347), MEU(276), MP3(326).
Electra. Euripides. MCLE(1350), MD(245), MP1(243), POP (372).

Electra. Jean Giraudoux. TCP(158).
Electric Kool-Aid Acid Test, The. Tom Wolfe. SCL(1301), 1969a(102).
Elegies of Propertius, The. Sextus Propertius. MCLE (1352), MP4(265).
Elizabeth the Great. Elizabeth Jenkins. BM(156), SCL(1305), 1960a(70).
Ellen Terry. Roger Manvell. SCL(1309), 1969a(106).
Elmer Gantry. Sinclair Lewis. MCLE(1355), MP4(268).
Èlogie and Other Poems. St.-John Perse. BM(160), MCLE (1359), MP4(271), SCL(1314), 1957a(61).
Embezzler, The. Louis Auchincloss. SCL(1317), 1967a(91).
Emergence of the New South, 1913-1945, The. George Brown Tindall. SCL(1320), 1968a(94).
Emerging South, The. Thomas D. Clark. BM(163), SCL (1323), 1962a(106).
Emigrants, The. Johan Bojer. MCLE(1362), MEU(279), MP1(244).
Emigrants, The. José Maria Ferreira de Castro. SCL(1327), 1963a(51).
Emigrants of Ahadarra, The. William Carleton. MCLE (1364), MEF(177), MP3(328).
Émile. Jean Jacques Rousseau. MCLE(1366), MEU(281), MP3(330).
Emilia Galotti. Gotthold Ephraim Lessing. MCLE(1369), MD(247), MP3(333).
Emily Dickinson. Thomas H. Johnson. SCL(1330), 1955a(92).
Eminent Victorians. Lytton Strachey. MCLE(1371), MN(98), MP3(335).
Emma. Jane Austen. MCLE(1374), MEF(179), MP1(246), PO2(24).
Empedocles: Fragments. Empedocles of Acragas. WP(26).
Emperor Jones, The. Eugene O'Neill. MCLE(1377), MD (249), MP2(291), POP(27).
Emperor of Ice-Cream, The. Brian Moore. SCL(1334), 1966a(85).
Empress Josephine. Ernest John Knapton. SCL(1337), 1965a(80).
Empty Canvas, The. Alberto Moravia. SCL(1340), 1962a (110).
En Route. Joris-Karl Huysmans. CAL(716).
Enarrations on the Psalms. Saint Augustine. CAL(196).
Enchanted, The. Jean Giraudoux. TCP(160).
Enchiridion militis Christiani. Desiderius Erasmus. CAL (498), CHL(321).
Enchiridion on Faith, Hope, and Love, The. Saint Augustine. CHL(149).

Enchiridion symbolorum et definitionum. Heinrich Joseph Dominicus Denzinger. CAL(658).
End of It, The. Mitchell Goodman. SCL(1343), 1962a(112).
End of Obscenity, The. Charles Rembar. SCL(1346), 1969a(110).
End of Summer. S. N. Behrman. TCP(67).
End of the Affair, The. Graham Greene. PO2(154).
End of the Battle, The. Evelyn Waugh. BM(167), SCL(1351), 1962a(115).
End of the Road, The. John Barth. MCLE(1379), MP4(273).
End of Time, The. Josef Pieper. CAL(964).
Enderby. Anthony Burgess. SCL(1356), 1969a(115).
Endymion. John Lyly. MCLE(1381), MD(251), MP3(337).
Enemy Camp, The. Jerome Weidman. SCL(1361), 1959a(71).
Enemy of the People, An. Henrik Ibsen. MCLE(1383), MD (253), MP2(292).
England Under the Stuarts. George Macaulay Trevelyan. MCLE(1386), MP4(275).
English Notebooks, The. Nathaniel Hawthorne. MCLE(1389), MP4(277), MPA2(43).
Enlightenment: An Interpretation, The. Peter Gay. SCL (1363), 1967a(94).
Enlightenment: An Interpretation, The, Vol. II. Peter Gay. 1970a(109).
Enneads. Plotinus. WP(245).
Enoch Arden. Alfred, Lord Tennyson. MCLE(1392), MP(75), MP1(249).
Enormous Room, The. E. E. Cummings. MAF(166), MCLE (1394), MP1(250).
Enquiry Concerning Human Understanding, An. David Hume. MCLE(1397), MN(101), MP3(339).
Enquiry Concerning the Principles of Morals, An. David Hume. WP(488).
Enthusiasm. Ronald Knox. CAL(961).
Epic of Gilgamesh, The. Unknown. MCLE(1400), MP(77), MP3(342).
Epigrams of Martial. Martial. MCLE(1403), MP(80), MP3(344).
Epigrams of Meleager, The. Meleager. MCLE(1405), MP4 (280).
Epinicia, The. Pindar. MCLE(1408), MP(82), MP3(346).
Episode of Sparrows, An. Rumer Godden. SCL(1367), 1955a(95).
Epistle of Barnabas, The. Unknown, but attributed to the Apostle Barnabas. CHL(3).
Epistle to Diognetus, The. Unknown. CAL(62), CHL(48).
Epistle to the Philippians. Saint Polycarp of Smyrna. CHL(17).
Epistle to the Romans, The. Karl Barth. CHL(894).

Epistle XXI: To the Most Clement Emperor and Most Blessed Augustus. Saint Ambrose. CAL(127).
Epistles and The Martyrdom of Saint Polycarp, The. Saint Polycarp of Smyrna. CAL(16).
Epistles of Horace, The. Horace. MCLE(1411), MP4(282).
Epistles of Saint Ignatius of Antioch, The. Saint Ignatius, Bishop of Antioch. CAL(7).
Epitaph for Dixie, An. Harry S. Ashmore. SCL(1370), 1959a(73).
Epitaph of a Small Winner. Joaquim Maria Machado de Assis. MAF(169), MCLE(1414), MP2(294).
Era of Reconstruction, 1865-1877, The. Kenneth M. Stampp. SCL(1373), 1966a(87).
Erasers, The. Alain Robbe-Grillet. SCL(1379), 1965a(83).
Erec and Enide. Chrétien de Troyes. MCLE(1417), MP(85), MP3(348).
Erewhon. Samuel Butler. MCLE(1421), MEF(182), MP1 (252), SGBN(154).
Ernest Hemingway. Carlos Baker. 1970a(112).
Esau and Jacob. Joaquim Maria Machado de Assis. SCL (1382), 1966a(93).
Escape of Socrates, The. Robert Pick. SCL(1386), 1954a (58).
Essais. Michel Eyquem de Montaigne. MCLE(1423), MN (104), MP3(352).
Essay Concerning Human Understanding, An. John Locke. MCLE(1426), MN(107), MP3(354), WP(428).
Essay of Dramatic Poesy, An. John Dryden. MCLE(1429), MP4(285).
Essay on Catholicism, Liberalism, and Socialism. Juan Francisco Maria de la Saludad Donoso Cortés. CAL (650).
Essay on Criticism. Alexander Pope. MCLE(1432), MP4 (287).
Essay on Human Love. Jean Guitton. CAL(923).
Essay on Indifference in Matters of Religion. Félicité Robert de Lamennais. CAL(632).
Essay on Liberty. John Stuart Mill. WP(644).
Essay on Man. Alexander Pope. MCLE(1435), MP4(290).
Essay on Metaphysics, An. Robin George Collingwood. WP (1046).
Essay on the Development of Christian Doctrine, An. John Henry Cardinal Newman. CAL(644).
Essay Towards a New Theory of Vision, An. George Berkeley. MCLE(1438), MP4(292).
Essays. Sir Francis Bacon. MCLE(1440), MN(110), MP3 (357).

Essays: First and Second Series. Ralph Waldo Emerson. MCLE(1443), MN(113), MP3(359), MPA1(110).
Essays of a Biologist. Julian Huxley. MCLE(1446), MP4 (294).
Essay of Aldous Huxley, The. Aldous Huxley. MCLE(1449), MP4(297).
Essays of Edgar Allan Poe, The. Edgar Allan Poe. MCLE (1452), MP4(299), MPA5(7).
Essays of Elia and Last Essays of Elia. Charles Lamb. MCLE(1455), MN(116), MP3(362).
Essays of G. K. Chesterton, The. Gilbert Keith Chesterton. MCLE(1457), MP4(302).
Essays of Henry David Thoreau, The. Henry David Thoreau. MCLE(1461), MP4(305), MPA5(37).
Essays of Max Beerbohm, The. Max Beerbohm. MCLE (1464), MP4(307).
Essays on the Intellectual Powers of Man and Essays on the Active Powers of the Human Mind. Thomas Reid. WP(538).
Essence of Christianity, The. Ludwig Feuerbach. CHL(697).
Estate of Memory, An. Ilona Karmel. 1970a(117).
Esther Waters. George Moore. MCLE(1468), MEF(184), MP1(254), PO2(83).
Eternal Now, The. Paul Tillich. SCL(1389), 1964a(72).
Ethan Frome. Edith Wharton. MAF(172), MCLE(1471), MP1 (256), PO(263), SGAN(102).
Ethica Nicomachea. Aristotle. WP(157).
Ethical Studies. Francis Herbert Bradley. WP(676).
Ethics. Dietrich Bonhoeffer. CHL(1101).
Ethics. Nicolai Hartmann. WP(868).
Ethics. Frank Chapman Sharp. WP(901).
Ethics. Benedictus de Spinoza. MCLE(1473), MN(118), MP3 (364), WP(416).
Ethics and Language. Charles Leslie Stevenson. WP(1089).
Etymologies, The. Saint Isidore of Seville. CAL(248).
Eugene Aram. Edward George Earle Bulwer-Lytton. MCLE (1476), MEF(187), MP2(297).
Eugene Onegin. Alexander Pushkin. MCLE(1479), MP(89), MP2(299).
Eugénie Grandet. Honoré de Balzac. MCLE(1482), MEU (284), MP1(258), PO(272), SGEN(75).
Eunuch, The. Terence. MCLE(1485), MD(256), MP2(302).
Euphues and His England. John Lyly. MCLE(1487), MEF (190), MP3(366).
Euphues, the Anatomy of Wit. John Lyly. MCLE(1489), MEF(192), MP3(368).
Euthyphro. Plato. WP(49).

Eva Trout. Elizabeth Bowen. SCL(1392), 1969a(119).
Evan Harrington. George Meredith. MCLE(1492), MEF(195), MP2(304).
Evangeline. Henry Wadsworth Longfellow. MCLE(1495), MP (92), MP1(261), MPA4(10).
Eve of St. Agnes, The. John Keats. MCLE(1498), MP(95), MP1(263).
Evelina. Fanny Burney. MCLE(1500), MEF(198), MP2(306).
Evening of the Holiday, The. Shirley Hazzard. SCL(1395), 1967a(98).
Everlasting Man, The. Gilbert Keith Chesterton. CAL(785).
Every Man in His Humour. Ben Jonson. MCLE(1503), MD (258), MP2(309).
Every Man Out of His Humour. Ben Jonson. MCLE(1506), MD(261), MP2(312).
Everyman. Unknown. MCLE(1509), MD(264), MP2(314), POP(221).
Everything That Rises Must Converge. Flannery O'Connor. SCL(1398), 1966a(97).
Evolution and Religion. Henry Ward Beecher. CHL(793).
Evolution of Political Thought, The. C. Northcote Parkinson. SCL(1401), 1959a(75).
Exemplary Novels. Miguel de Cervantes Saavedra. MCLE (1512), MEU(287), MP3(370).
Exile and the Kingdom. Albert Camus. BM(172), MCLE (1515), MP4(311), SCL(1404), 1959a(78).
Exiles. James Joyce. MCLE(1518), MD(267), MP3(373).
Expedition of Humphry Clinker. Tobias Smollett. PO2(16).
Expensive People. Joyce Carol Oates. SCL(1408), 1969a (122).
Experience and Substance. De Witt Henry Parker. WP(1070).
Exploding Metropolis, The. The Editors of Fortune. SCL (1413), 1959a(81).
Exploration and Empire. William H. Goetzmann. SCL(1416), 1967a(101).
Extant Fragments of the Works of Dionysius. Saint Dionysius of Alexandria. CHL(77).
Extant Writings of Julius Africanus, The. Sextus Julius Africanus. CHL(61).
Extant Writings of Saint Francis of Assisi, The. Saint Francis of Assisi. CAL(349).
Extreme Occident, The. Petru Dumitriu. SCL(1419), 1967a (104).
Eye-Beaters, Blood, Victory, Madness, Buckhead and Mercy, The. James Dickey. 1971a(69).
Eye for an I, An. Harriet Zinnes. SCL(1423), 1966a(100).

FBI Story, The. Don Whitehead. SCL(1498), 1957a(67).
Fable, A. William Faulkner. BM(176), MAF(174), MCLE (1521), MP3(375), SCL(1427), 1954a(61).
Fable for Critics, A. James Russell Lowell. MCLE(1524), MP4(313), MPA4(25).
Fables. Jean de La Fontaine. MCLE(1527), MP(97), MP3 (378).
Fables of La Fontaine, The. Marianne Moore, Translator. SCL(1431), 1954a(65).
Faerie Queene, The. Edmund Spenser. MCLE(1529), MP (99), MP1(264).
Fair Maid of Perth, The. Sir Walter Scott. MCLE(1532), MEF(201), MP3(380).
Fair Sister, The. William Goyen. SCL(1434), 1964a(75).
Fairly Good Time, A. Mavis Gallant. SCLs(91).
Faith and History. Reinhold Niebuhr. CHL(1104).
Faith and Knowledge. John Hick. CHL(1156).
Faith, Hope, and Charity. Saint Augustine. CAL(184).
Faith of a Moralist, The. Alfred Edward Taylor. CHL(954).
Faith of the Christian Church, The. Gustaf Aulén. CHL (912).
Faithful Shepherdess, The. John Fletcher. MCLE(1535), MD(270), MP3(383).
Falkners of Mississippi: A Memoir, The. Murry C. Falkner. SCL(1437), 1968a(97).
Fall, The. Albert Camus. BM(180), MCLE(1537), MP4 (316), SCL(1440), 1958a(83).
Fall of a Sparrow, The. Nigel Balchin. SCL(1443), 1957a (64).
Fall of a Titan, The. Igor Gouzenko. SCL(1446), 1954a(68).
Fall of Paris, The. Alistair Horne. SCL(1449), 1967a(107).
Fall of the House of Hapsburg, The. Edward Crankshaw. SCL(1453), 1964a(77).
Fall of the House of Usher, The. Edgar Allan Poe. MCLE (1540), MAF(177), MP2(316), MPA5(14).
Familiar Essays of William Hazlitt, The. William Hazlitt. MCLE(1542), MP4(319).
Family at Gilje, The. Jonas Lie. MCLE(1545), MEU(290), MP2(318).
Family Moskat, The. Isaac Bashevis Singer. SCL(1456), 1966a(103).
Family of Pascual Duarte, The. Camilio José Cela. MCLE (1548), MP4(321), SCL(1459), 1965a(86).
Family Reunion, The. T. S. Eliot. MCLE(1551), MD(272), MP2(321).
Fantasticks, The. Tom Jones and Harvey Schmidt. SCLs (94).

Far Away and Long Ago. W. H. Hudson. MCLE(1554), MN(121), MP2(323).
Far Cry, A. Earl Rovit. SCL(1463), 1968a(100).
Far Field, The. Theodore Roethke. SCL(1469), 1965a(89).
Far from the Madding Crowd. Thomas Hardy. MCLE(1557), MEF(204), MP1(266), PO(101), PON(111).
Faraway Country, The. Louis D. Robin, Jr. SCL(1471), 1964a(80).
Farewell to Arms, A. Ernest Hemingway. MAF(179), MCLE(1560), MP1(269), PO(229), SGAN(166).
Farmers' Daughters, The. William Carlos Williams. SCL (1474), 1962a(119).
Fashion. Anna Cora Mowatt Ritchie. DGAP(59).
Fat City. Leonard Gardner. 1970a(120).
Fatal Impact, The. Alan Moorehead. SCL(1477), 1967a(111).
Father, The. R. V. Cassill. SCL(1481), 1966a(106).
Father, The. August Strindberg. MCLE(1562), MD(275), MP2(325), POP(329), TCP(388).
Father and His Fate, A. Ivy Compton-Burnett. SCL(1485), 1959a(84).
Father Goriot. Honoré de Balzac. MCLE(1565), MEU(293), MP1(271).
Fathers. Herbert Gold. SCL(1488), 1968a(105).
Fathers, The. Allen Tate. BM(183), MCLE(1568), MP4 (324), SCL(1491), 1961a(71).
Fathers and Sons. Ivan Turgenev. MCLE(1571), MEU(296), MP1(273), PO(366), PON(116), SGEN(128).
Faust. Johann Wolfgang von Goethe. MCLE(1574), MD(278), MP1(276), POP(305).
Fausto and Anna. Carlo Cassola. SCL(1495), 1961a(75).
Feast of July, The. H. E. Bates. SCL(1502), 1954a(71).
Feast of Lupercal, The. Brian Moore. SCL(1505), 1958a(86).
Feast of St. Barnabas, The. Jesse Hill Ford. 1970a(123).
Federalist, The. Alexander Hamilton, James Madison, and John Jay. MCLE(1577), MN(124), MP3(384).
Felix Holt, Radical. George Eliot. MCLE(1581), MEF(207), MP3(388).
Fellowship of the Ring, The. J. R. R. Tolkien. MCLE (1584), MP4(326).
Fête. Roger Vailland. SCL(1508), 1962a(123).
Fêtes galantes and Other Poems. Paul Verlaine. MCLE (1587), MP(102), MP3(390).
Ficciones. Jorge Luis Borges. MCLE(1589), MP4(329), SCL(1511), 1963a(53).
Field of Vision, The. Wright Morris. MCLE(1591), MP4 (331), SCLs(98).
Fields, The. Conrad Richter. MAF(181), MCLE(1595),

MP2(327).
Fiesta in November. Eduardo Mallea. MCLE(1598), MP4 (335).
Fiestas. Juan Goytisolo. SCL(1514), 1961a(77).
Fifteen Sermons Preached at the Rolls Chapel. Joseph Butler. WP(465).
Fifth Column, The. Ernest Hemingway. 1970a(125).
Fifth Queen, The. Ford Madox Ford. MCLE(1601), MP4 (337), SCL(1518), 1964a(83).
Fig Tree, The. Aubrey Menen. SCL(1522), 1960a(74).
Fight Night on a Sweet Saturday. Mary Lee Settle. SCL (1525), 1965a(92).
Figures in a Landscape. Barry England. SCL(1528), 1968a (108).
File No. 113. Émile Gaboriau. MCLE(1604), MEU(299), MP1(278), PON(121).
File on Stanley Patton Buchta, The. Irvin Faust. SCLs(102).
Filostrato, Il. Giovanni Boccaccio. MCLE(1607), MP4(340).
Final Solutions. Frederick Seidel. SCL(1531), 1964a(86).
Financial Expert, The. R. K. Narayan. SCLs(105).
Financier, The. Theodore Dreiser. MAF(184), MCLE(1610), MP1(280).
Findings. Wendell Berry. 1970a(129).
Fine Madness, A. Elliot Baker. SCL(1533), 1965a(95).
Finest Stories of Seán O'Faoláin, The. Seán O'Faoláin. SCL(1538), 1958a(88).
Finn Cycle, The. Unknown. MCLE(1612), MEF(210), MP3 (392).
Finnegans Wake. James Joyce. MCLE(1615), MEF(213), MP3(395).
Fire from Heaven. Mary Renault. 1970a(132).
Fire Next Time, The. James Baldwin. SCL(1541), 1964a (88).
Fire-Raisers, The. Marris Murray. SCL(1544), 1954a(74).
Fire Screen, The. James Merrill. 1971a(73).
Fires on the Plain. Shohei Ooka. SCL(1547), 1958a(91).
Firmament of Time, The. Loren Eiseley. SCL(1550), 1961a (80).
First Apology and The Second Apology, The. Saint Justin Martyr. CAL(19), CHL(19).
First Blood: The Story of Fort Sumter. W. A. Swanberg. SCL(1553), 1959a(87).
First Catechetical Instruction, The. Saint Augustine. CAL (161).
First Circle, The. Aleksandr I. Solzhenitsyn. SCL(1556), 1969a(126).
First Day of Friday, The. Honor Tracy. SCL(1560), 1964a(91).

First Epistle of Clement to the Corinthians, The. Saint Clement of Rome. CHL(1).
First Lady of the South. Ishbel Ross. SCL(1562), 1959a(89).
First Principles. Herbert Spencer. WP(649).
Fisher Maiden, The. Björnstjerne Björnson. MCLE(1618), MEU(302), MP2(330).
Fishes, Birds and Sons of Men. Jesse Hill Ford. SCL (1565), 1968a(111).
Five Smooth Stones. Ann Fairbairn. SCL(1568), 1967a(115).
Five Theological Orations. Saint Gregory of Nazianzus. CAL(116), CHL(113).
Five Women Who Loved Love. Ibara Saikaku. MCLE(1620), MEU(304), MP3(398).
Fixer, The. Bernard Malamud. SCL(1571), 1967a(118).
Flame Trees of Thika, The. Elspeth Huxley. SCL(1575), 1960a(77).
Flaubert. Enid Starkie. SCL(1579), 1968a(114).
Flies, The. Mariano Azuela. MCLE(1622), MP4(342).
Flies, The. Jean-Paul Sartre. MCLE(1626), MP4(346).
Flight from the Enchanter, The. Iris Murdoch. SCL(1584), 1957a(70).
Flint Anchor, The. Sylvia Townsend Warner. SCL(1587), 1954a(77).
Floating Opera, The. John Barth. SCLs(108).
Flood. Robert Penn Warren. SCL(1590), 1965a(99).
Flower Girls, The. Clemence Dane. SCL(1593), 1955a(98).
Flower Herding on Mount Monadnock. Galway Kinnell. SCL (1596), 1965a(101).
Flowering of the Cumberland. Harriette Simpson Arnow. SCL(1600), 1964a(93).
Flowering Peach, The. Clifford Odets. TCP(253).
Flowers of Evil. Charles Baudelaire. MCLE(1629), MP (104), MP3(399).
Flying Swans, The. Padraic Colum. SCL(1603), 1958a(94).
Folks, The. Ruth Suckow. MCLE(1631), MP4(349).
Folkways, The. William Graham Sumner. MCLE(1634), MP4(351).
Following of Christ, The. Gerhard (Geert de) Groote. CHL (291).
Foma Gordyeeff. Maksim Gorki. MCLE(1637), MEU(306), MP2(331).
Fontamara. Ignazio Silone. BM(187), MCLE(1640), MP4 (353), SCL(1606), 1966a(83).
Fool Killer, The. Helen Eustis. SCL(1610), 1954a(80).
Fool of Quality, The. Henry Brooke. MCLE(1643), MEF (216), MP2(333).

Fool's Errand, A. Albion W. Tourgée. MCLE(1646), MP4 (356), MPA5(57).
For a Bitter Season. George Garrett. SCL(1613), 1968a(118).
For the Union Dead. Robert Lowell. SCL(1617), 1965a(105).
For Whom the Bell Tolls. Ernest Hemingway. MAF(186), MCLE(1649), MP1(282), PO2(251).
Force and Matter. Friedrich Karl Christian Ludwig Büchner. WP(633).
Ford: Decline and Rebirth, 1933-1962. Allan Nevins and Frank Ernest Hill. SCL(1619), 1964a(96).
Ford: Expansion and Challenge, 1915-1933. Allan Nevins and Frank Ernest Hill. SCL(1622), 1958a(96).
Ford: The Times, The Man, The Company. Allan Nevins. SCL(1625), 1954a(83).
Forest of the Night. Madison Jones. SCL(1628), 1961a(87).
Forest Rose, The. Samuel Woodworth. DGAP(41).
Form of the Personal, The. John Macmurray. CHL(1162).
Forsyte Saga, The. John Galsworthy. MCLE(1652), MEF (219), MP1(284).
Fortitude. Hugh Walpole. MCLE(1655), MEF(222), MP1(286).
Fortress, The. Hugh Walpole. MCLE(1657), MEF(224), MP1(288).
Fortunata and Jacinta. Benito Pérez Galdós. MCLE(1660), MEU(309), MP2(336).
Fortunes of Nigel, The. Sir Walter Scott. MCLE(1663), MEF(227), MP2(338).
Fortunes of Richard Mahony, The. Henry Handel Richardson. MCLE(1666), MEF(230), MP2(341).
Forty Days of Musa Dagh, The. Franz Werfel. MCLE (1669), MEU(312), MP1(291).
42nd Parallel, The. John Dos Passos. SGAN(217).
Foundation of Christian Doctrine. Menno Simons. CHL(367).
Foundations of Freedom, The. John Lilburne. CHL(470).
Fountain of Wisdom, The. Saint John of Damascus. CHL (186).
Fountain Overflows, The. Rebecca West. SCL(1632), 1957a (73).
Four-Gated City, The. Doris Lessing. 1970a(135).
Four Horsemen of the Apocalypse, The. Vicente Blasco Ibáñez. PO(375), PON(125).
Four Loves, The. C. S. Lewis. BM(191), SCL(1635), 1961a(91).
Four Plays for Dancers. William Butler Yeats. TCP(457).
Four Quartets. T. S. Eliot. MCLE(1672), MP(106), MP3 (401).
Fourth of June, The. David Benedictus. SCL(1639), 1963a (56).

Fox and the Camellias, The. Ignazio Silone. SCL(1642), 1962a(125).
Fox in the Attic, The. Richard Hughes. SCL(1645), 1963a (59).
Fragments. Ayi Kwei Armah. 1971a(77).
Framley Parsonage. Anthony Trollope. MCLE(1675), MEF (233), MP1(293).
Francesca da Rimini. George Henry Boker. DGAP(80).
Francis Bacon. Catherine Drinker Bowen. SCL(1648), 1964a (99).
Frankenstein. Mary Godwin Shelley. MCLE(1677), MEF(235), MP1(295), PO(155).
Franny and Zooey. J. D. Salinger. BM(195), MCLE(1679), MP4(359), SCL(1651), 1962a(127).
Fraternity. John Galsworthy. MCLE(1681), MEF(237), MP2 (343).
Free Fall. William Golding. BM(198), MCLE(1684), MP4 (361), SCL(1654), 1961a(94).
Freedom and the Spirit. Nikolai Berdyaev. CHL(929).
Freedom of the Will. Jonathan Edwards. CHL(598), WP(501).
Freedom or Death. Nikos Kazantzakis. MCLE(1687), MP4 (364), SCL(1658), 1957a(76).
Freedom Road. Howard Fast. SCLs(111).
French Lieutenant's Woman, The. John Fowles. 1970a(139).
French Revolution, The. Thomas Carlyle. MCLE(1690), MN(128), MP3(404).
Friar Bacon and Friar Bungay. Robert Greene. MCLE (1693), MD(281), MP2(345).
Friend in Power, A. Carlos Baker. SCL(1661), 1959a(92).
Friend of Kafka, A. Isaac Bashevis Singer. 1971a(80).
Frithiof's Saga. Esaias Tegnér. MCLE(1696), MP(109), MP2(348).
Frogs, The. Aristophanes. MCLE(1698), MD(284), MP1(297).
From Morn to Midnight. Georg Kaiser. TCP(209).
From the Danube to the Yalu. General Mark W. Clark. BM (202), SCL(1664), 1954a(86).
From the Hand of the Hunter. John Braine. SCL(1667), 1961a(98).
From the Terrace. John O'Hara. SCL(1670), 1959a(94).
Front Page, The. Ben Hecht and Charles MacArthur. DGAP (234), SGAP(104).
Frontenacs, The. François Mauriac. SCL(1673), 1962a(130).
Frontier in American History, The. Frederick Jackson Turner. MCLE(1700), MP4(366).
Fruit of the Tree, The. Edith Wharton. MAF(189), MCLE (1703), MP3(406).
Full Fathom Five. John Stewart Carter. SCL(1676), 1966a(109).

Funeral, The. Sir Richard Steele. MCLE(1706), MD(286), MP2(350).
Further Fables for Our Time. James Thurber. SCL(1681), 1957a(79).
Future of Mankind, The. Karl Jaspers. SCL(1684), 1962a (132).
Future Shock. Alvin Toffler. 1971a(82).

Gabriela, Clove and Cinnamon. Jorge Amado. MCLE(1709), MP4(369), SCL(1687), 1963a(62).
Galileo. Bertolt Brecht. TCP(79).
Gallipoli. Alan Moorehead. BM(205), SCL(1690), 1957a(81).
Gambler, The. Fyodor Mikhailovich Dostoevski. MCLE (1712), MEU(315), MP2(352).
Game of Hearts, The. Harriette Wilson. SCL(1693), 1955a (101).
Gandhi's Truth. Erik H. Erikson. 1971a(91).
Garden, The. Yves Berger. SCL(1696), 1964a(102).
Garden, The. L. A. G. Strong. MCLE(1715), MEF(240), MP2(354).
Garden of Earthly Delights, A. Joyce Carol Oates. SCL (1702), 1968a(122).
Garden of the Finzi-Continis, The. Giorgio Bassani. SCL (1706), 1966a(114).
Gardener's Dog, The. Lope de Vega. MCLE(1718), MD (289), MP2(356).
Gardner and Other Poems, The. John Hall Wheelock. SCL (1710), 1962a(135).
Gargantua and Pantagruel. François Rabelais. MCLE(1721), MEU(318), MP1(298), SGEN(3).
Gate to the Sea. Bryher. SCL(1713), 1959a(96).
Gaucho: Martín Fierro, The. José Hernández. MCLE(1724), MP(111), MP2(358).
General Introduction to Psychoanalysis, A. Sigmund Freud. MCLE(1726), MP4(371).
General Theory of Value. Ralph Barton Perry. WP(874).
"Genius," The. Theodore Dreiser. MAF(192), MCLE(1729), MP3(409).
Generous Man, A. Reynolds Price. SCLs(115).
Gentleman Dancing Master, The. William Wycherley. MCLE (1732), MD(292), MP3(411).
Gentleman Usher, The. George Chapman. MCLE(1735), MD (295), MP3(413).
George. Emlyn Williams. SCL(1715), 1963a(65).
George Bernard Shaw. Archibald Henderson. SCL(1718), 1957a(84).

George C. Marshall: Education of a General. Forrest C. Pogue. SCL(1722), 1964a(107).
George C. Marshall: Ordeal and Hope, 1939-1942. Forrest C. Pogue. SCL(1725), 1967a(122).
George Eliot: A Biography. Gordon S. Haight. SCL(1729), 1969a(130).
George Meredith and English Comedy. V. S. Pritchett. 1971a(96).
Georgia Scenes. Augustus Baldwin Longstreet. MAF(195), MCLE(1738), MP3(416).
Georgics. Publius Vergilius Maro. MCLE(1741), MP4(373).
Germinal. Émile Zola. MCLE(1743), MEU(321), MP2(360), SGEN(202).
Germinie Lacerteux. Edmond and Jules de Goncourt. MCLE (1746), MEU(324), MP2(363), SGEN(137).
Gettysburg. Elsie Singmaster. MAF(198), MCLE(1749), MP2 (365).
Ghost at Noon, A. Alberto Moravia. SCL(1734), 1955a(104).
Ghost Sonata. August Strindberg. TCP(391).
Ghost Voyage, The. Gontran de Poncins. SCL(1737), 1954a (89).
Ghosts. Henrik Ibsen. MCLE(1752), MD(298), MP1(301).
Giant Dwarfs, The. Gisela Elsner. SCL(1740), 1966a(118).
Giants in the Earth. Thomas Job. DGAP(238).
Giants in the Earth. O. E. Rölvaag. MAF(201), MCLE (1754), MP1(303), SGAN(184).
Gideon's Trumpet. Anthony Lewis. SCL(1743), 1965a(107).
Gift, The. Vladimir Nabokov. SCL(1746), 1964a(110).
Gift from the Sea. Anne Morrow Lindbergh. SCL(1749), 1955a(107).
Gil Blas de Santillane. Alain René Le Sage. MCLE(1757), MEU(327), MP1(305), PO(311), PON(129).
Gilded Age, The. Samuel L. Clemens and Charles Dudley Warner. MAF(204), MCLE(1759), MP2(368), MPA5(69).
Giles Goat-Boy. John Barth. SCL(1752), 1967a(126).
Ginger Man, The. J. P. Donleavy. SCL(1757), 1959a(98).
Girl in Winter, A. Philip Larkin. SCL(1760), 1963a(67).
Girl of the Golden West, The. David Belasco. DGAP(148).
Girl Who Sang with the Beatles and Other Stories. Robert Hemenway. 1971a(99).
Girls of Slender Means, The. Muriel Spark. SCL(1763), 1964a(112).
Give Us This Day. Sidney Stewart. SCL(1767), 1958a(99).
Gladiator, The. Robert Montgomery Bird. DGAP(50).
Glance at New York, A. Benjamin A. Baker. DGAP(68).
Glass Key, The. Dashiell Hammett. MAF(207), MCLE (1762), MP1(307).

Glass Menagerie, The. Tennessee Williams. DGAP(358), MCLE(1764), MD(300), MP3(418), SGAP(208), TCP (449).
Glories of Mary. Saint Alphonsus Mary de' Liguori. CAL (624).
Glosses on Porphyry, The. Peter Abelard. WP(290).
Go-Between, The. L. P. Hartley. SCL(1770), 1954a(92).
Go Down, Moses. William Faulkner. MCLE(1766), MP4 (375).
Go Tell It on the Mountain. James Baldwin. MCLE(1770), MP4(379).
Goat Song. Franz Werfel. MCLE(1773), MD(302), MP2(370).
God and His Gifts, A. Ivy Compton-Burnett. SCL(1773), 1965a(110).
God and Intelligence in Modern Philosophy. Fulton J. Sheen. CAL(788).
God in Christ. Horace Bushnell. CHL(716).
God in Modern Philosophy. James D. Collins. CAL(1071).
God Was in Christ. Donald M. Baillie. CHL(1093).
Gods Are Athirst, The. Anatole France. MCLE(1776), MEU (329), MP3(420).
God's Grace and Man's Hope. Daniel Day Williams. CHL (1108).
God's Little Acre. Erskine Caldwell. SGAN(247).
God's Oddling. Jesse Stuart. SCL(1776), 1961a(101).
Goethe. Richard Friedenthal. SCL(1780), 1966a(120).
Gog. Andrew Sinclair. SCL(1783), 1968a(126).
Going Away. Clancy Sigal. SCL(1787), 1963a(70).
Gold Bug, The. Edgar Allan Poe. MAF(209), MCLE(1779), MP2(373), MPA5(18).
Golden Apples, The. Eudora Welty. MCLE(1781), MP4(382).
Golden Ass of Lucius Apuleius, The. Lucius Apuleius. MCLE(178), MEU(332), MP1(309), PO2(418).
Golden Bough, The. Sir James George Frazer. MCLE(1787), MP4(384).
Golden Bowl, The. Henry James. MAF(211), MCLE(1790), MP2(374), MPA3(34), PO2(189).
Golden Boy. Clifford Odets. MCLE(1793), MD(305), MP3 (422), TCP(255).
Golden Echo, The. David Garnett. SCL(1790), 1954a(95).
Golden Fruits, The. Nathalie Sarraute. SCL(1793), 1965a (112).
Golden Notebook, The. Doris Lessing. SCL(1796), 1963a(72).
Golden Sovereign, The. Richard Church. SCL(1800), 1958a (101).
Golden Spur, The. Dawn Powell. SCL(1803), 1963a(76).
Golden Weather, The. Louis Rubin. SCL(1805), 1962a(138).

Goncourt Journals, The. Edmond and Jules de Goncourt. MCLE(1795), MP4(387).
Gondoliers, The. W. S. Gilbert and Arthur Sullivan. MCLE (1798), MD(307), MP2(377).
Gone a Hundred Miles. Heather Ross Miller. SCL(1809), 1969a(135).
Gone with the Wind. Margaret Mitchell. MAF(214), MCLE (1800), MP3(424), PO2(260).
Good Companions, The. J. B. Priestley. MCLE(1803), MEF(243), MP1(311).
Good Earth, The. Pearl S. Buck. MAF(217), MCLE(1806), MP1(313), PO(195), SGAN(226).
Good Light, The. Karl Bjarnhof. SCL(1812), 1961a(104).
Good Man Is Hard to Find, A. Flannery O'Connor. SCL (1815), 1955a(109).
Good Morning, Midnight. Jean Rhys. 1971a(102).
Good News Yesterday and Today, The. Josef Andreas Jungmann, S. J. CAL(843).
Good Shepherd, The. C. S. Forester. SCL(1818), 1955a (112).
Good Soldier: Schweik, The. Jaroslav Hašek. MCLE(1809), MP4(390).
Good Times/Bad Times. James Kirkwood. SCL(1821), 1969a(138).
Good Woman of Setzuan. Bertolt Brecht. TCP(82).
Goodbye. William Sansom. SCL(1824), 1967a(131).
Goodbye, Columbus. Philip Roth. SCLs(117).
Goodbye, Mr. Chips. James Hilton. MCLE(1812), MEF(246), MP1(316).
Goodbye to a River. John Graves. SCL(1827), 1961a(107).
Goodbye to Uncle Tom. J. C. Furnas. SCL(1830), 1957a (87).
Gorboduc. Thomas Norton and Thomas Sackville. MCLE (1814), MD(309), MP2(379).
Gorgias. Plato. WP(70).
Gospel and the Church, The. Alfred Loisy. CHL(832).
Gösta Berling's Saga. Selma Lagerlöf. SGEN(228).
Grace Abounding to the Chief of Sinners. John Bunyan. CHL(506).
Grammar of Assent, A. John Henry Cardinal Newman. CAL(678), WP(666).
Grand Hotel. Vicki Baum. MCLE(1816), MEU(335), MP1 (318), POP(293).
Grand Inquisitor, The. Fyodor Mikhailovich Dostoevski. CHL(786).
Grand Mademoiselle, The. Francis Steegmuller. SCL(1833), 1957a(90).

Grandfather Stories. Samuel Hopkins Adams. SCL(1836), 1955a(115).
Grandfathers, The. Conrad Richter. SCL(1840), 1965a(115).
Grandissimes, The. George W. Cable. MAF(220), MCLE (1819), MP1(320), MPA1(34).
Grandmothers, The. Glenway Wescott. MAF(222), MCLE (1821), MP1(322).
Granite and Rainbow. Virginia Woolf. SCL(1846), 1959a(101).
Grant Moves South. Bruce Catton. BM(208), SCL(1849), 1961a(109).
Grapes of Wrath, The. John Steinbeck. MAF(225), MCLE (1824), MP1(324), PO2(276), SGAN(267).
Gray Fox. Burke Davis. SCL(1853), 1957a(93).
Great American Jackpot, The. Herbert Gold. 1970a(143).
Great Captains, The. Henry Treece. SCL(1856), 1957a(96).
Great Catechism, The. Saint Gregory of Nyssa. CAL(120), CHL(125).
Great Christian Doctrine of Original Sin Defended, The. Jonathan Edwards. CHL(602).
Great Conspiracy Trial, The. Jason Epstein. 1971a(105).
Great Democracies, The. Winston S. Churchill. BM(212), SCL(1859), 1959a(103).
Great Diamond Robbery, The. Edward M. Alfriend and A. C. Wheeler. DGAP(131).
Great Divide, The. William Vaughn Moody. DGAP(157).
Great Expectations. Charles Dickens. MCLE(1827), MEF (248), MP1(326), PO2(36), SGBN(94).
Great Galeoto, The. José Echegaray. MCLE(1830), MD (311), MP2(381).
Great Gatsby, The. F. Scott Fitzgerald. MAF(228), MCLE (1832), MP1(329), PO2(229), SGAN(155).
Great God Brown, The. Eugene O'Neill. TCP(261).
Great Highway, The. August Strindberg. TCP(394).
Great Hunger, The. Cecil Woodham-Smith. SCL(1862), 1964a(115).
Great Learning, The. Attributed to Tseng Tzu or Tzu Sau. WP(212).
Great Meadow, The. Elizabeth Madox Roberts. MAF(231), MCLE(1835), MP2(383).
Great Plains, The. Walter Prescott Webb. MCLE(1838), MP4(393).
Great River. Paul Horgan. BM(216), SCL(1866), 1954a(98).
Great Terror, The. Robert Conquest. SCL(1870), 1969a (140).
Great Testament, The. François Villon. MCLE(1841), MP (113), MP3(426).

Great Valley, The. Mary Johnston. MAF(234), MCLE(1843), MP3(428).
Great White Hope, The. Howard Sackler. 1970a(146).
Greek Passion, The. Nikos Kazantzakis. MCLE(1846), MP4(395), SCL(1874), 1954a(102).
Green Bay Tree, The. Louis Bromfield. MAF(237), MCLE (1849), MP1(331).
Green Goddess, The. William Archer. POP(98).
Green Grow the Lilacs. Lynn Riggs. MCLE(1852), MD(313), MP3(430).
Green House, The. Mario Vargas Llosa. 1970a(150).
Green Man, The. Kingsley Amis. SCLs(121).
Green Mansions. W. H. Hudson. MCLE(1855), MEF(251), MP1(333), PO(113), SGBN(235).
Green Mare, The. Marcel Aymé. SCL(1877), 1957a(99).
Green Mountain Boys, The. Daniel Pierce Thompson. MAF (240), MCLE(1858), MP2(385).
Green Pastures, The. Marc Connelly. DGAP(249), POP(20), SGAP(69).
Greenback Era, The. Irwin Unger. SCLs(125).
Greene's Groatsworth of Wit Bought with a Million of Repentance. Robert Greene. MCLE(1862), MP4(397).
Greengage Summer, The. Rumer Godden. SCL(1880), 1959a (106).
Greening of America, The. Charles Reich. 1971a(108).
Greenwillow. B. J. Chute. SCL(1883), 1957a(102).
Grettir the Strong. Unknown. MCLE(1864), MEU(338), MP1 (335).
Gringa, La. Florencio Sánchez. MCLE(1867), MD(316), MP2(389).
Group, The. Mary McCarthy. SCL(1887), 1964a(119).
Group, The. Mercy Warren. DGAP(12).
Growing into Love. X. J. Kennedy. 1970a(154).
Growth of the Idea of God, The. Shailer Mathews. CHL (965).
Growth of the Soil. Knut Hamsun. MCLE(1870), MEU(341), MP1(338), SGEN(329).
Growth or Decline?: The Church Today. Emmanuel Cardinal Suhard. CAL(920).
Grüne Heinrich, Der. Gottfried Keller. MCLE(1873), MEU (344), MP3(432).
Guard of Honor. James Gould Cozzens. MAF(244), MCLE (1876), MP3(435).
Guardsman, The. Ferenc Molnár. POP(333).
Guest and His Going, A. P. H. Newby. SCL(1890), 1961a (113).

Guest the One-Eyed. Gunnar Gunnarsson. MCLE(1878), MEU(347), MP3(437).
Guide, The. R. K. Narayan. MCLE(1880), MP4(399), SCL (1893), 1959a(109).
Guide for the Perplexed. Maimonides. WP(300).
Gulliver's Travels. Jonathan Swift. MCLE(1883), MEF(254), MP1(341), PO(163), PON(134), SGBN(16).
Gull's Hornbook, The. Thomas Dekker. MCLE(1886), MP4 (401).
Guns of August, The. Barbara W. Tuchman. SCL(1896), 1963a(78).
Guy Mannering. Sir Walter Scott. MCLE(1889), MEF(257), MP2(391).
Guy of Warwick. Unknown. MCLE(1892), MP(115), MP3(439).
Guzmán de Alfarache. Mateo Alemán. MCLE(1895), MEU (349), MP2(393).
Guzman, Go Home. Alan Sillitoe. 1970a(157).

H. G. Wells. Lovat Dickson. 1970a(164).
H. M. S. Pinafore. W. S. Gilbert and Arthur Sullivan. MCLE(2082), MD(353), MP1(370).
Hadrian VII. Peter Luke. 1970a(161).
Hadrian's Memoirs. Marguerite Yourcenar. MCLE(1900), MP4(404), SCL(1900), 1954a(105).
Hairy Ape, The. Eugene O'Neill. DGAP(202).
Hajji Baba of Ispahan. James Morier. MCLE(1903), MEF (260), MP1(343).
Hakluyt's Voyages. Richard Hakluyt. MCLE(1906), MN(346), MP1(346).
Half Sun Half Sleep. May Swenson. SCL(1903), 1968a(130).
Hall of Mirrors, A. Robert Stone. SCL(1907), 1968a(134).
Hamlet, The. William Faulkner. MCLE(1909), MP2(398).
Hamlet, Prince of Denmark. William Shakespeare. MAF (246), MCLE(1912), MD(319), MP1(348), POP(201).
Hampshire Days. W. H. Hudson. MCLE(1914), MP4(406).
Han Fei Tzu. Han Fei. WP(201).
Handful of Dust, A. Evelyn Waugh. MCLE(1916), MEF(263), MP1(350).
Handley Cross. Robert Smith Surtees. MCLE(1919), MEF (266), MP1(352).
Handy Andy. Samuel Lover. MCLE(1922), MEF(269), MP2 (400).
Hanger Stout, Awake! Jack Mathews. SCL(1911), 1968a(137).
Hangman's House. Donn Byrne. MCLE(1925), MEF(272), MP2(403).
Happy Exiles, The. Felicity Shaw. SCL(1915), 1957a(105).

Happy Families Are All Alike. Peter Taylor. SCL(1918), 1960a(80).
Happy Marriage, The. R. V. Cassill. SCL(1921), 1967a (133).
Hard Blue Sky, The. Shirley Ann Grau. SCL(1925), 1959a (111).
Hard Hours, The. Anthony Hecht. SCL(1928), 1968a(140).
Hard Times. Charles Dickens. MCLE(1928), MEF(275), MP2(405).
Hard Times. Studs Terkel. 1971a(112).
Harmless People, The. Elizabeth Marshall Thomas. SCL (1933), 1960a(82).
Harmonium. Wallace Stevens. MCLE(1931), MP(118), MP3 (442).
Harold Nicolson: Diaries and Letters, 1930-1939. Sir Harold Nicolson. SCL(1936), 1967a(138).
Harold Nicolson: Diaries and Letters, 1939-1945. Sir Harold Nicolson. SCL(1941), 1968a(145).
Harold Nicolson: Diaries and Letters, 1945-1962. Sir Harold Nicolson. SCL(1945), 1969a(144).
Harp of a Thousand Strings. H. L. Davis. MAF(249), MCLE(1935), MP2(407).
Harp-Weaver and Other Poems, The. Edna St. Vincent Millay. MCLE(1938), MP(122), MP3(445).
Harvest on the Don. Mikhail Sholokhov. SCL(1950), 1962a (142).
Hat on the Bed, The. John O'Hara. SCL(1953), 1964a(121).
Hatful of Rain, A. Michael Vincente Gazzo. DGAP(399).
Havelok the Dane. Unknown. MCLE(1941), MP(125), MP2 (410).
"Having Wonderful Time." Arthur Kober. SGAP(149).
Hawaii. James A. Michener. SCL(1956), 1960a(85).
Hazard of New Fortunes, A. William Dean Howells. MAF (252), MCLE(1944), MP2(412), MPA2(76).
He Who Flees the Lion. J. Klein-Haparash. SCL(1960), 1964a(124).
He Who Gets Slapped. Leonid Andreyev. POP(345).
He Who Rides a Tiger. Bhabani Bhattacharya. SCL(1963), 1954a(108).
Headlong Hall. Thomas Love Peacock. MCLE(1947), MEF (278), MP2(414).
Hear Us O Lord from Heaven Thy Dwelling Place. Malcolm Lowry. BM(220), SCL(1966), 1962a(145).
Heart Is a Lonely Hunter, The. Carson McCullers. MAF (255), MCLE(1949), MP2(416), SGAN(282).
Heart of Darkness. Joseph Conrad. MCLE(1952), MEF(280), MP3(447), PO2(91), SGBN(214).

Heart of Man, The. Gerald Vann, O. P. CAL(889).
Heart of Midlothian, The. Sir Walter Scott. MCLE(1955), MEF(283), MP1(355), PO(152), PON(138).
Heart of the Matter, The. Graham Greene. MCLE(1958), MEF(286), MP2(418), PO2(150).
Heartbreak House. George Bernard Shaw. MCLE(1961), MD(321), MP3(449), TCP(345).
Heart's Needle. W. D. Snodgrass. BM(224), SCL(1970), 1960a(88).
Heat of the Day, The. Elizabeth Bowen. MCLE(1964), MEF (289), MP2(420).
Heaven's My Destination. Thornton Wilder. MAF(258), MCLE(1967), MP1(357).
Hedda Gabler. Henrik Ibsen. MCLE(1970), MD(324), MP1 (359), POP(317).
Heights of Macchu Picchu, The. Pablo Neruda. SCL(1974), 1968a(149).
Heiké Story, The. Eiji Yoshikawa. SCL(1978), 1957a(107).
Heimskringla, The. Snorri Sturluson. MCLE(1972), MEU (354), MP2(423).
Helen. Euripides. MCLE(1977), MD(326), MP3(452).
Hell-Bent for Heaven. Hatcher Hughes. DGAP(211).
Hellenism. Arnold Toynbee. SCL(1981), 1960a(91).
Helmets. James Dickey. SCL(1984), 1965a(121).
Henderson the Rain King. Saul Bellow. MCLE(1979), MP4 (408), SCL(1987), 1960a(94).
Henrietta, The. Bronson Howard. DGAP(190).
Henry Adams: 1877-1890. Ernest Samuels. BM(228), SCL(1990), 1959a(114).
Henry Adams: 1890-1918. Ernest Samuels. SCL(1993), 1965a(124).
Henry Esmond. William Makepeace Thackeray. MCLE(1982), MEF(292), MP1(361), PO(171), PON(143).
Henry James. Leon Edel. SCL(2002), 1963a(81).
Henry James: Autobiography. Henry James. 1957a(110).
Henry Knox. North Callahan. SCLs(128).
Henry IV. Luigi Pirandello. TCP(293).
Henry the Fourth, Part One. William Shakespeare. MCLE (1990), MD(333), MP2(430).
Henry the Fourth, Part Two. William Shakespeare. MCLE (1993), MD(336), MP2(432).
Henry the Fifth. William Shakespeare. MCLE(1988), MD (331), MP1(364).
Henry the Sixth, Part One. William Shakespeare. MCLE (1996), MD(339), MP2(434).
Henry the Sixth, Part Two. William Shakespeare. MCLE (1999), MD(342), MP2(437).

Henry the Sixth, Part Three. William Shakespeare. MCLE (2002), MD(345), MP2(439).
Henry VIII. J. J. Scarisbrick. SCL(1997), 1969a(148).
Henry the Eighth. William Shakespeare. MCLE(1985), MD (328), MP2(427).
Heraclitus: Fragments. Heraclitus of Ephesus. WP(11).
Herakles. Archibald MacLeish. SCL(2005), 1968a(152).
Herakles Mad. Euripides. MCLE(2005), MD(348), MP3(454).
Hercules and His Twelve Labors. Folk tradition. MCLE (2007), MEU(359), MP1(366).
Herdsmen, The. Elizabeth Marshall Thomas. SCL(2010), 1966a(123).
Hereward the Wake. Charles Kingsley. MCLE(2009), MEF (295), MP1(367).
Heritage. Anthony West. SCL(2014), 1955a(118).
Heritage and Its History, A. Ivy Compton-Burnett. MCLE (2012), MP4(411), SCL(2017), 1961a(116).
Hernani. Victor Hugo. POP(251).
Hero of Our Time, A. Mikhail Yurievich Lermontov. MCLE(2015), MEU(361), MP3(456).
Herod's Children. Ilse Aichinger. SCL(2021), 1964a(126).
Heroides. Ovid. MCLE(2019), MP4(413).
Heron, The. Giorgio Bassani. 1971a(115).
Herself Surprised. Joyce Cary. MCLE(2021), MEF(298), MP3(459), PO2(127).
Herzog. Saul Bellow. SCL(2025), 1965a(127).
Hesperides. Robert Herrick. MCLE(2024), MP(128), MP3 (461).
Hidden Persuaders, The. Vance Packard. BM(231), SCL (2028), 1958a(104).
High and Low. John Betjeman. SCL(2031), 1968a(157).
High New House, A. Thomas Williams. SCL(2035), 1964a (130).
High Tide at Gettysburg. Glenn Tucker. SCL(2040), 1959a (117).
High Valley, The. Kenneth E. Read. SCL(2043), 1966a(127).
High Water. Richard Bissell. SCL(2046), 1954a(111).
High, Wide and Lonesome. Hal Borland. SCL(2049), 1957a (113).
High Wind Rising, A. Elsie Singmaster. MAF(261), MCLE (2027), MP2(442).
Hill of Dreams, The. Arthur Machen. MCLE(2030), MEF (301), MP2(445).
Hillingdon Hall. Robert Smith Surtees. MCLE(2033), MEF (304), MP2(447).
him. E. E. Cummings. TCP(125).
Hind and the Panther, The. John Dryden. CAL(611).

Hippolytus. Euripides. MCLE(2036), MD(350), MP2(449).
Hiroshima Diary. Michihiko Hachiya. BM(234), SCL(2052), 1955a(121).
His Toy, His Dream, His Rest. John Berryman. SCL (2056), 1969a(152).
Historia calamitatum. Pierre Abelard. CAL(307), MCLE (2039), MN(134), MP3(464).
Historian's Approach to Religion, An. Arnold Toynbee. BM(238), SCL(2060), 1957a(116).
Historical and Critical Dictionary, The. Pierre Bayle. WP (441).
History of Colonel Jacque, The. Daniel Defoe. MCLE(2042), MEF(307), MP2(451).
History of England, The. John Lingard. CAL(638).
History of England, The. Thomas Babington Macaulay. MCLE(2045), MN(137), MP3(466).
History of Frederick II of Prussia. Thomas Carlyle. MCLE (2048), MP4(415).
History of Freedom and Other Essays, The. John Emerich Edward Dalberg Acton. CAL(739).
History of King Richard III. Sir Thomas More. MCLE (2051), MP4(417).
History of Mr. Polly, The. H. G. Wells. MCLE(2054), MEF(310), MP2(454).
History of New York by Diedrich Knickerbocker, A. Washington Irving. MCLE(2056), MN(140), MP3(469).
History of the Catholic Church in the United States, A. John Dawson Gilmary Shea. CAL(702).
History of the Conquest of Mexico. William Hickling Prescott. MCLE(2059), MN(143), MP3(471).
History of the Councils. Karl Joseph von Hefele. CAL(686).
History of the Decline and Fall of the Roman Empire, The. Edward Gibbon. MCLE(2062), MN(146), MP3(474).
History of the Development of the Doctrine of the Person of Christ. Isaac August Dorner. CHL(692).
History of the Franks. Saint Gregory of Tours. CAL(244).
History of the Peloponnesian War. Thucydides. MCLE(2065), MN(149), MP3(476).
History of the Persian Wars, The. Herodotus. MCLE(2068), MN(152), MP3(479).
History of the Popes from the Close of the Middle Ages, The. Ludwig von Pastor. CAL(796).
History of the Rebellion and Civil Wars in England. Edward Hyde, Earl of Clarendon. MCLE(2071), MP4(420).
History of the Reformation in Scotland. John Knox. CHL (409).

History of the Reign of King Henry VII. Sir Francis Bacon. MCLE(2073), MP4(421).
Hitler. Alan L. C. Bullock. SCL(2064), 1965a(130).
Hive, The. Camilio José Cela. MCLE(2076), MP4(424).
Hiza-Kurige. Jippensha Ikku. MCLE(2080), MEU(365), MP3 (481).
Hogan's Goat. William Alfred. SCL(2068), 1967a(143).
Hogarth's Progress. Peter Quennell. SCL(2072), 1955a(124).
Hold April. Jesse Stuart. SCL(2076), 1963a(84).
Holiday. Philip Barry. DGAP(242).
Hollow Universe, The. George De Koninck. CAL(1084).
Holy State and the Profane State, The. Thomas Fuller. MCLE(2084), MP4(428).
Holy Terrors, The. Jean Cocteau. MCLE(2087), MEU(367), MP3(483).
Holy Week. Louis Aragon. SCL(2079), 1962a(149).
Homage to Clio. W. H. Auden. SCL(2082), 1961a(119).
Homage to Mistress Bradstreet. John Berryman. MCLE (2090), MP4(430), SCL(2084), 1957a(119).
Home from the Hill. William Humphrey. SCL(2087), 1959a (119).
Home Is the Sailor. Jorge Amado. SCL(2090), 1965a(133).
Home of the Brave. Arthur Laurents. SGAP(271).
Homecoming. C. P. Snow. SCL(2093), 1957a(123).
Homilies. Aelfric. CAL(272).
Homilies of Saint John Chrysostom. Saint John Chrysostom. CAL(154).
Homilies on the Statues. Saint John Chrysostom. CHL(117).
Homo viator. Gabriel Marcel. CAL(893).
Honest Whore, Part One, The. Thomas Dekker. MCLE (2092), MD(355), MP3(485).
Honest Whore, Part Two, The. Thomas Dekker. MCLE (2095), MD(358), MP3(487).
Honey in the Horn. H. L. Davis. MAF(264), MCLE(2098), MP1(371).
Hoosier Schoolmaster, The. Edward Eggleston. MAF(267), MCLE(2101), MP1(373), MPA1(105).
Hopscotch. Julio Cortázar. SCL(2097), 1967a(146).
Horace. Pierre Corneille. MCLE(2104), MD(361), MP3(490).
Horatio. Hyam Plutzik. SCL(2102), 1962a(152).
Horizon. Augustin Daly. DGAP(95).
Horse Knows the Way, The. John O'Hara. SCL(2105), 1965a(136).
Horse Show at Midnight, The. Henry Taylor. SCL(2108), 1967a(150).
Horseman on the Roof, The. Jean Giono. SCL(2112), 1954a (114).

Horse's Mouth, The. Joyce Cary. MCLE(2106), MEF(312), MP2(456), PON(148).
Horseshoe Robinson. John P. Kennedy. MAF(270), MCLE (2109), MP1(376).
Hostage, The. Brendan Behan. TCP(64).
Hotel Universe. Philip Barry. TCP(55).
Hound of Heaven, The. Francis Thompson. CAL(709).
Hound of the Baskervilles, The. Arthur Conan Doyle. PO2 (75).
House at Adampur, The. Anand Lall. SCL(2115), 1957a(126).
House by the Churchyard, The. Joseph Sheridan Le Fanu. MCLE(2112), MEF(315), MP2(458).
House by the Medlar Tree, The. Giovanni Verga. MCLE (2115), MEU(370), MP2(460).
House in Paris, The. Elizabeth Bowen. MCLE(2118), MEF (318), MP2(463).
House Made of Dawn. N. Scott Momaday. SCL(2119), 1969a(156).
House of Atreus, The. Aeschylus. MCLE(2121), MD(363), MP1(378).
House of Bernarda Alba. Federico García Lorca. TCP(146).
House of Five Talents, The. Louis Auchincloss. SCL(2124), 1961a(121).
House of Gentlefolk, A. Ivan Turgenev. MCLE(2124), MEU (373), MP2(465).
House of Intellect, The. Jacques Barzun. BM(242), SCL (2128), 1960a(96).
House of Lies. Françoise Mallet-Joris. SCL(2131), 1958a (107).
House of Mirth, The. Edith Wharton. MAF(273), MCLE (2127), MP1(380).
House of the Seven Gables, The. Nathaniel Hawthorne. MAF (276), MCLE(2130), MP1(383), MPA2(49), PO(222), PON(153), SGAN(26).
House with the Green Shutters, The. George Douglas. MCLE(2133), MEF(321), MP2(467).
Housebreaker of Shady Hill, The. John Cheever. SCL(2134), 1959a(122).
How Green Was My Valley. Richard Llewellyn. MCLE (2136), MEF(324), MP1(385).
Howards End. E. M. Forster. MCLE(2139), MEF(327), MP2(469).
Huasipungo. Jorge Icaza. MAF(279), MCLE(2142), MP2 (472).
Huckleberry Finn. Samuel L. Clemens. MAF(282), MCLE (2145), MP1(387), MPA5(74), PON(158).
Hudibras. Samuel Butler. MCLE(2148), MP(131), MP3(492).

Huey Long. T. Harry Williams. 1970a(169).
Hugh Wynne, Free Quaker. Silas Weir Mitchell. MAF(285), MCLE(2151), MP1(390).
Human Comedy, The. William Saroyan. MAF(288), MCLE (2154), MP1(392), SGAN(289).
Human Destiny. Pierre Lecomte du Noüy. CAL(913).
Human Nature and Conduct. John Dewey. WP(835).
Humanity of Christ, The. Romano Guardini. CAL(1064).
Humboldt. Helmut De Terra. SCL(2137), 1955a(128).
Humphry Clinker. Tobias Smollett. MCLE(2156), MEF(330), MP1(394), SGBN(47).
Hunchback of Notre Dame, The. Victor Hugo. MCLE(2159), MEU(376), MP1(397), PO(304), SGEN(65).
Hunger. Knut Hamsun. MCLE(2163), MEU(380), MP1(400), SCL(2141), 1968a(160).
Hungerfield and Other Poems. Robinson Jeffers. SCLs(130).
Huon de Bordeaux. Unknown. MCLE(2165), MEU(382), MP3 (494).
Hyde Park. James Shirley. MCLE(2168), MD(366), MP3 (497).
Hydriotaphia: Urn-Burial. Sir Thomas Browne. MCLE (2171), MP4(432).
Hymns of Ephraem the Syrian, The. Ephraem the Syrian. CHL(103).
Hymns of Saint Ambrose, The. Saint Ambrose. CAL(152).
Hymns of Saint Thomas Aquinas, The. Saint Thomas Aquinas. CAL(421).
Hypatia. Charles Kingsley. MCLE(2174), MEF(333), MP1 (402).
Hypochondriac, The. Molière. MCLE(2178), MD(369), MP2 (474).

I Am Mary Dunne. Brian Moore. SCL(2145), 1969a(160).
I and Thou. Martin Buber. CHL(917), WP(856).
I, Claudius. Robert Graves. MCLE(2181), MEF(337), MP1 (406).
I Don't Need You Any More. Arthur Miller. SCL(2149), 1968a(164).
I Know Why the Caged Bird Sings. Maya Angelou. SCLs (133).
I Remember! I Remember! Seán O'Faoláin. SCL(2152), 1963a(86).
I Remember Mama. John Van Druten. SGAP(154).
I Speak for Thaddeus Stevens. Elsie Singmaster. MCLE (2184), MN(155), MP1(408).
Iceland Fisherman, An. Pierre Loti. MCLE(2187), MEU (385), MP1(410).

Iceman Cometh, The. Eugene O'Neill. SGAP(24), TCP(265).
Icon and the Axe, The. James H. Billington. SCL(2155), 1967a(154).
Iconographs. May Swenson. 1971a(119).
Idea of a Christian Society, The. T. S. Eliot. CHL(1043).
Idea of a University, The. John Henry Cardinal Newman. CAL(653).
Idea of Christ in the Gospels, The. George Santayana. CHL (1080).
Idea of the Holy, The. Rudolf Otto. CHL(882), WP(810).
Idealist View of Life, An. Sarvepalli Radhakrishnan. WP (974).
Ideas: General Introduction to Pure Phenomenology. Edmund Husserl. WP(795).
Ideological Origins of the American Revolution, The. Bernard Bailyn. SCLs(135).
Ides of March, The. Thornton Wilder. MAF(290), MCLE (2190), MP1(413).
Idiot, The. Fyodor Mikhailovich Dostoevski. MCLE(2193), MEU(388), MP1(415), PO2(396).
Idiot's Delight. Robert E. Sherwood. SGAP(123).
Idiots First. Bernard Malamud. SCL(2159), 1964a(135).
Idler, The. Samuel Johnson. MCLE(2196), MP4(434).
Idylls of the King, The. Alfred, Lord Tennyson. MCLE (2199), MP(134), MP1(417).
If I Were King. Justin Huntly McCarthy. POP(117).
If Winter Comes. A. S. M. Hutchinson. MCLE(2203), MEF (340), MP1(421).
Ignatius His Conclave. John Donne. MCLE(2206), MP4(437).
Illiad, The. Homer. MCLE(2209), MP(138), MP1(423), PON(163).
I'm Expecting to Live Quite Soon. Paul West. 1971a(122).
Image of America. R. L. Bruckberger. SCL(2162), 1960a (99).
Images of Truth. Glenway Wescott. SCL(2165), 1963a(89).
Imaginary Conversations. Walter Savage Landor. MCLE (2212), MN(158), MP3(499).
Imaginations. William Carlos Williams. 1971a(124).
Imitation of Christ, The. Thomas à Kempis. CAL(491), CHL(308), MCLE(2215), MN(161), MP3(501).
Imitations. Robert Lowell. SCLs(137).
Immoralist, The. André Gide. PO2(330), SGEN(267).
Immortale Dei. Pope Leo XIII. CAL(695).
Imperial Woman. Pearl S. Buck. SCL(2169), 1957a(130).
Importance of Being Earnest, The. Oscar Wilde. MCLE (2217), MD(372), MP2(476), POP(141).
In a Summer Season. Elizabeth Taylor. SCL(2172), 1962a

(155).
In a Wild Sanctuary. William Harrison. 1970a(174).
In Cold Blood. Truman Capote. SCL(2175), 1967a(158).
In Dubious Battle. John Steinbeck. MAF(293), MCLE(2219), MP2(478).
In His Steps. Charles M. Sheldon. CHL(808).
In Memoriam. Alfred, Lord Tennyson. MCLE(2221), MP4 (439).
In My Father's Court. Isaac Bashevis Singer. SCL(2179), 1967a(162).
In Parenthesis. David Jones. SCL(2182), 1963a(93).
In the American Grain. William Carlos Williams. MCLE (2224), MP4(442).
In the Clearing. Robert Frost. BM(245), SCL(2185), 1963a (95).
In the Days of McKinley. Margaret Leech. SCL(2192), 1960a(102).
In the Heart of the Country. William H. Gass. SCL(2196), 1969a(164).
In the Rose of Time. Robert Fitzgerald SCL(2200), 1958a (109).
In the Time of Greenbloom. Gabriel Fielding. SCL(2202), 1958a(111).
In the Wilderness. Sigrid Undset. MCLE(2229), MEU(391), MP2(480).
Inadmissible Evidence. John Osborne. SCL(2205), 1966a (129).
Inazuma-Byôshi. Santô Kyôden. MCLE(2232), MEU(394), MP3(503).
Incarnation of the Word of God, The. Saint Athanasius. CAL(84), CHL(83).
Incarnations. Robert Penn Warren. SCL(2208), 1969a(167).
Incense to Idols. Sylvia Ashton-Warner. SCL(2211), 1961a (124).
Incognito. Petru Dumitriu. MCLE(2235), MP4(446), SCL (2215), 1965a(139).
Incoherence of the Incoherence, The. Averroës. WP(294).
Independent People. Halldór Laxness. MCLE(2239), MEU (397), MP1(425).
India Today. Frank Moraes. SCL(2219), 1961a(127).
Indian Princess, The. James Nelson Barker. DGAP(26).
Indian Summer. William Dean Howells. MAF(295), MCLE (2242), MP2(482), MPA2(81).
Indiana. George Sand. MCLE(2245), MEU(400), MP2(485).
Indians. Arthur Kopit. 1970a(177).
Inês de Castro. António Ferreira. MCLE(2247), MD(374), MP3(506).

Infernal Machine, The. Jean Cocteau. TCP(113).
Infernal Machine and Other Plays, The. Jean Cocteau. SCL (2222), 1965a(143).
Infinity of Mirrors, An. Richard Condon. SCL(2226), 1965a (146).
Informer, The. Liam O'Flaherty. MCLE(2249), MEF(343), MP2(486).
Ingoldsby Legends, The. Thomas Ingoldsby. MCLE(2252), MP4(449).
Inherit the Wind. Jerome Lawrence and Robert E. Lee. DGAP(403), SGAP(238).
Inheritors, The. William Golding. MCLE(2255), MP4(452), SCL(2229), 1963a(101).
Inkling, The. Fred Chappell. SCL(2233), 1966a(132).
Innocent, The. Madison Jones. SCL(2237), 1958a(114).
Innocent Party, The. John Hawkes. SCL(2240), 1967a(165).
Innocent Voyage, The. Richard Hughes. MCLE(2258), MEF (346), MP2(488).
Inquiry Concerning Political Justice, An. William Godwin. MCLE(2261), MP4(454).
Inquiry into Meaning and Truth, An. Bertrand Russell. WP(1052).
Inquisitor's House, The. Robert Somerlott. 1970a(181).
Insect Comedy. Karel and Joseph Čapek. TCP(95).
Inside Africa. John Gunther. SCL(2243), 1955a(131).
Inside Russia Today. John Gunther. SCL(2246), 1959a(125).
Inside the Blood Factory. Diane Wakoski. SCL(2250), 1969a(169).
Inside the Third Reich. Albert Speer. 1971a(128).
Insight. Bernard J. F. Lonergan, S. J. CAL(1043).
Insolent Chariots, The. John Keats. BM(252), SCL(2253), 1959a(128).
Inspector, The. Jan de Hartog. SCL(2256), 1961a(130).
Inspector General, The. Nikolai V. Gogol. MCLE(2264), MD(376), MP2(491).
Institutes of the Christian Religion, The. John Calvin. CHL (358).
Institutes of the Monastic Life, The. John Cassian. CAL (193).
Instructions in Favor of Christian Discipline. Commodianus. CHL(71).
Instrument, The. John O'Hara. SCL(2258), 1968a(166).
Intellectual Life, The. Antonin Gilbert Sertillanges. CAL (771).
Interior Castle, The. Saint Teresa of Ávila. CAL(561).
Interpretation of Dreams, The. Sigmund Freud. MCLE (2267), MN(163), MP3(508).

Introduction to Mathematical Philosophy. Bertrand Russell. WP(816).
Introduction to Metaphysics, An. Henri Bergson. WP(749).
Introduction to Semantics. Rudolf Carnap. WP(1075).
Introduction to the Devout Life. Saint Francis de Sales. CAL(568), CHL(428).
Introduction to the Philosophy of Religion. Peter Anthony Bertocci. CHL(1130).
Introduction to the Principles of Morals and Legislation, An. Jeremy Bentham. WP(551).
Intruder in the Dust. William Faulkner. MAF(298), MCLE (2270), MP3(511).
Invisible Man. Ralph Ellison. MCLE(2272), MP4(457), SGAN(330).
Invisible Man, The. H. G. Wells. MCLE(2275), MEF(349), MP1(428).
Invisible Writing, The. Arthur Koestler. SCL(2261), 1954a (117).
Iolanthe. W. S. Gilbert and Arthur Sullivan. MCLE(2278), MD(379), MP2(493).
Ion. Euripides. MCLE(2280), MD(381), MP3(513).
Iphigenia in Aulis. Euripides. MCLE(2283), MD(384), MP2 (495).
Iphigenia in Tauris. Euripides. MCLE(2285), MD(386), MP2(497).
Ippolita. Alberto Denti di Pirajno. SCL(2264), 1962a(157).
Irish Melodies. Thomas Moore. MCLE(2288), MP4(460).
Islam Inflamed. James Morris. SCL(2266), 1958a(117).
Island. Aldous Huxley. SCL(2269), 1963a(105).
Island, The. Robert Creeley. SCL(2272), 1964a(138).
Islanders, The. Philip Booth. SCL(2275), 1962a(159).
Islands in the Stream. Ernest Hemingway. 1971a(135).
Israel Potter. Herman Melville. MAF(300), MCLE(2291), MP3(515), MPA4(53).
It Is Better than It Was. Pedro Calderón de la Barca. MCLE(2294), MD(389), MP3(517).
It Is Worse than It Was. Pedro Calderón de la Barca. MCLE(2296), MD(391), MP3(519).
Italian, The. Mrs. Ann Radcliffe. MCLE(2298), MEF(352), MP3(521).
Itching Parrot, The. José Joaquín Fernández de Lizardi. MAF(303), MCLE(2304), MP2(499).
Ivanhoe. Sir Walter Scott. MCLE(2307), MEF(358), MP1 (430), PO(145), PON(167), SGBN(63).

J. B. Archibald MacLeish. BM(255), DGAP(410), SCL (2307), SGAP(85), 1959a(131).

Jack of Newberry. Thomas Deloney. MCLE(2311), MEF (361), MP2(501).
Jack Sheppard. William Harrison Ainsworth. MCLE(2313), MEF(364), MP2(504).
Jacob's Ladder, The. Denise Levertov. SCL(2278), 1964a (140).
Jalna. Mazo de la Roche. MAF(306), MCLE(2316), MP2 (506).
James Boswell: The Earlier Years, 1740-1769. Frederick A. Pottle. SCL(2281), 1967a(168).
James Forrestal. Arnold A. Rogow. SCL(2285), 1965a(148).
James Joyce. Richard Ellmann. SCL(2289), 1960a(105).
James Madison: 1809-1812. Irving Brant. SCL(2292), 1957a(132).
James Madison: 1812-1836. Irving Brant. SCL(2296), 1962a(162).
James Russell Lowell. Martin Duberman. SCL(2300), 1967a (171).
Jane Eyre. Charlotte Brontë. MCLE(2319), MEF(367), MP1 (432), PO(24), PON(171), SGBN(102).
Japanese Inn. Oliver Statler. SCL(2304), 1962a(165).
Jason and the Golden Fleece. Folk tradition. MCLE(2322), MEU(402), MP1(435).
Java Head. Joseph Hergesheimer. MAF(309), MCLE(2324), MP1(437).
Jean-Christophe. Romain Rolland. MCLE(2327), MEU(404), MP1(439), PO(323), SGEN(285).
Jean Santeuil. Marcel Proust. SCL(2310), 1957a(135).
Jeb Stuart, The Last Cavalier. Burke Davis. SCL(2313), 1958a(120).
Jefferson and Hamilton: The Struggle for Democracy in America. Claude G. Bowers. MCLE(2330), MP4 (462).
Jefferson and the Ordeal of Liberty. Dumas Malone. SCL (2316), 1963a(108).
Jefferson Davis: American Patriot. Hudson Strode. BM (258), SCL(2320), 1955a(134).
Jefferson Davis: Confederate President. Hudson Strode. BM(261), SCL(2323), 1960a(108).
Jefferson Davis: Private Letters, 1823-1889. Hudson Strode. SCL(2326), 1967a(175).
Jefferson Davis: Tragic Hero. Hudson Strode. SCL(2330), 1965a(152).
Jefferson the President. Dumas Malone. 1971a(140).
Jennie Gerhardt. Theodore Dreiser. MAF(312), MCLE (2333), MP1(526).
Jeremy's Version. James Purdy. 1971a(144).

Jerome: A Poor Man. Mary E. Wilkins-Freeman. PON (176).
Jerusalem Delivered. Torquato Tasso. CAL(548), MCLE (2337), MP(141), MP1(441).
Jesse Stuart. Ruel E. Foster. SCL(2334), 1969a(172).
Jesus and His Times. Henri Daniel-Rops. CAL(1006).
Jesus the Lord. Karl Heim. CHL(1008).
Jew of Malta, The. Christopher Marlowe. MCLE(2339), MD(393), MP1(444).
Jewess of Toledo, The. Franz Grillparzer. MCLE(2341), MD(395), MP3(528).
Joanna Godden. Sheila Kaye-Smith. MCLE(2344), MEF(370), MP2(509).
Joel Chandler Harris. Paul M. Cousins. SCL(2340), 1969a (177).
John Adams. Page Smith. SCL(2344), 1963a(112).
John Brown's Body. Stephen Vincent Benét. MCLE(2347), MP(144), MP1(445).
John Donne: A Life. R. C. Bald. 1971a(148).
John Dryden: The Poet, the Dramatist, the Critic. T. S. Eliot. MCLE(2350), MP4(465).
John Halifax, Gentleman. Dinah Maria Mulock. MCLE (2353), MEF(373), MP2(511).
John Inglesant. Joseph Henry Shorthouse. MCLE(2356), MEF(376), MP2(513).
John Keats. Walter Jackson Bate. SCLs(141).
John Keats. Aileen Ward. SCL(2348), 1964a(143).
John Keats: The Living Year. Robert Gittings. SCL(2352), 1954a(120).
John Paul Jones: A Sailor's Biography. Samuel Eliot Morison. BM(264), SCL(2355), 1960a(111).
John Ploughman's Talks. Charles Haddon Spurgeon. CHL (755).
John Quincy Adams and the Union. Samuel Flagg Bemis. BM(268), SCL(2359), 1957a(138).
Jonathan Wild. Henry Fielding. MCLE(2359), MEF(379), MP2(516).
Jorrocks' Jaunts and Jollities. Robert Smith Surtees. MCLE (2362), MEF(382), MP2(518).
Joseph and His Brothers. Thomas Mann. SGEN(252).
Joseph Andrews. Henry Fielding. MCLE(2365), MEF(385), MP1(448), PO2(12).
Joseph Conrad. Jocelyn Baines. BM(272), SCL(2362), 1961a (132).
Joseph: The Man Closest to Jesus. Francis L. Filas, S.J. CAL(1115).
Joseph Vance. William De Morgan. MCLE(2368), MEF(388),

MP1(450).
Journal of a Tour to the Hebrides. James Boswell. MCLE (2371), MP4(467).
Journal of Edwin Carp, The. Richard Haydn. SCL(2368), 1954a(123).
Journal of Francis Asbury, The. Francis Asbury. CHL (654).
Journal of George Fox, The. George Fox. CHL(546).
Journal of John Wesley, The. John Wesley. CHL(581).
Journal of John Woolman, The. John Woolman. CHL(612).
Journal of the Plague Year, A. Daniel Defoe. MCLE(2374), MP4(469).
Journal of Thoreau, The. Henry David Thoreau. MCLE (2377), MP4(471), MPA5(43).
Journal to Eliza. Laurence Sterne. MCLE(2380), MP4(474).
Journal to Stella. Jonathan Swift. MCLE(2383), MP4(476).
Journals of André Gide, The. André Gide. MCLE(2386), MP4(478).
Journals of Dorothy Wordsworth. Dorothy Wordsworth. MCLE(2389), MP4(481).
Journals of George Whitefield. George Whitefield. CHL(577).
Journals of Henry Melchior Mühlenberg, The. Henry Melchior Mühlenberg. CHL(620).
Journals of Lewis and Clark, The. Meriwether Lewis and William Clark. MCLE(2392), MP4(484).
Journey, The. Jiro Osaragi. SCL(2371), 1961a(137).
Journey, The. Lillian Smith. SCL(2374), 1954a(126).
Journey for Joedel. Guy Owen. 1971a(152).
Journey into Summer. Edwin Way Teale. SCL(2377), 1961a (140).
Journey Not the Arrival Matters, The. Leonard Woolf. 1971a(156).
Journey of the Mind to God. Saint Bonaventure. CHL(237), WP(308).
Journey to Matecumbe, A. Robert Lewis Taylor. SCL (2380), 1962a(168).
Journey to the End of the Night. Louis-Ferdinand Céline. MCLE(2395), MEU(407), MP1(453).
Journey Without End. Manes Sperber. SCL(2384), 1954a (129).
Journey's End. Robert Cedric Sherriff. MCLE(2398), MD (398), MP2(520), POP(86), TCP(366).
Jovial Crew, A. Richard Brome. MCLE(2400), MD(400), MP3(531).
Judaism: Profile of a Faith. Ben Zion Bokser. SCLs(145).
Jude the Obscure. Thomas Hardy. MCLE(2402), MEF(391), MP1(455), PO2(60), SGBN(177).

Judith Paris. Hugh Walpole. MCLE(2405), MEF(394), MP1 (457).
Julian. Gore Vidal. SCL(2387), 1965a(155).
Julius Caesar. William Shakespeare. MCLE(2408), MD(402), MP2(522), POP(204).
Jungle, The. Upton Sinclair. MAF(315), MCLE(2411), MP1 (459).
Jungle Books, The. Rudyard Kipling. MCLE(2413), MEF (397), MP1(461).
Juno and the Paycock. Sean O'Casey. MCLE(2416), MD (405), MP3(533), POP(227), TCP(241).
Jurgen. James Branch Cabell. MAF(317), MCLE(2418), MP1(464), SGAN(123).
Justice. John Galsworthy. MCLE(2421), MD(407), MP1 (466), POP(102), TCP(139).
Justice Oliver Wendell Holmes. Mark DeWolfe Howe. BM (278), SCL(2391), 1958a(122).
Justine. Lawrence Durrell. BM(282), SCL(2395), 1958a(125).

Kalevala, The. Elias Lönnrot. MCLE(2423), MP(147), MP3(535).
Kamongo. Homer W. Smith. MCLE(2427), MP4(486).
Kandy-Kolored Tangerine-Flake Streamline Baby, The. Tom Wolfe. SCL(2397), 1966a(135).
Kapital, Das. Karl Marx. MCLE(2429), MP3(538).
Kate Fennigate. Booth Tarkington. MAF(320), MCLE(2432), MP1(467).
Katherine. Anya Seton. SCL(2400), 1954a(132).
Keepers of the House, The. Shirley Ann Grau. SCL(2403), 1965a(159).
Kenilworth. Sir Walter Scott. MCLE(2434), MEF(400), MP1 (469), PO(148), PON(181).
Kenneth Grahame: A Biography. Peter Green. SCL(2406), 1960a(114).
Kettle of Fire. H. L. Davis. SCL(2409), 1960a(117).
Key to the Doctrine of the Eucharist, A. Dom Anscar Vonier, O. S. B. CAL(793).
Keys of the Kingdom of Heaven, The. John Cotton. CHL (458).
Kidnap. George Waller. SCL(2413), 1962a(172).
Kidnapped. Robert Louis Stevenson. MCLE(2436), MEF (402), MP1(471), PON(186).
Killing Frost, A. Sylvia Wilkinson. SCLs(148).
Killing Time. Thomas Berger. SCL(2417), 1968a(169).
Kim. Rudyard Kipling. MCLE(2438), MD(409), MEF(404), MP1(473), PO2(79), SGBN(227).
Kindly Ones, The. Anthony Powell. SCL(2421), 1963a(115).
King and No King, A. Francis Beaumont and John Fletcher.

MCLE(2441), MP3(541).
King Edward the Seventh. Philip Magnus. SCL(2424), 1965a(161).
King Horn. Unknown. MCLE(2444), MP4(487).
King John. John Bale. MCLE(2447), MD(412), MP3(543).
King John. William Shakespeare. MCLE(2450), MD(415), MP2(524).
King Lear. William Shakespeare. MCLE(2453), MD(418), MP2(526).
King Must Die, The. Mary Renault. BM(284), SCL(2427), 1959a(133).
King of Pontus. Alfred Duggan. SCL(2431), 1960a(121).
King of Rome, The. André Castelot. BM(287), SCL(2434), 1961a(143).
King of the Golden River, The. John Ruskin. MCLE(2456), MEF(407), MP2(529).
King of the Mountains, The. Edmond François About. MCLE(2459), MEU(410), MP2(531).
King Paradox. Pío Baroja. MCLE(2462), MEU(413), MP2 (533).
King, Queen, Knave. Vladimir Nabokov. SCL(2438), 1969a (181).
King Ranch, The. Tom Lea. SCL(2442), 1958a(127).
King Solomon's Mines. H. Rider Haggard. MCLE(2465), MEF(410), MP1(475).
King, the Greatest Alcalde, The. Lope de Vega. MCLE (2469), MD(421), MP2(536).
Kingdom of Christ, The. Frederick Denison Maurice. CHL (688).
Kingdom of God, The. Gregorio Martínez Sierra. MCLE (2471), MD(423), MP3(545).
Kingdom of This World, The. Alejo Carpentier. SCL(2445), 1958a(130).
Kings in Exile. Alphonse Daudet. MCLE(2474), MEU(416), MP2(538).
King's Row. Henry Bellamann. MAF(322), MCLE(2476), MP1(478).
King's War: 1641-1647, The. C. V. Wedgwood. BM(291), SCL(2448), 1960a(124).
Kipps. H. G. Wells. MCLE(2478), MEF(414), MP2(540).
Kiss, Kiss. Roald Dahl. SCL(2451), 1961a(147).
Kiss Me, Kate. Samuel and Bella Spewack and Cole Porter. DGAP(374).
Knight of the Burning Pestle, The. Francis Beaumont. MCLE(2480), MD(426), MP2(542).
Knightly Quest, The. Tennessee Williams. SCL(2454), 1967a(179).

Knights, The. Aristophanes. MCLE(2483), MD(429), MP1 (480).
Knock on Any Door. Willard Motley. SCLs(151).
Know Thyself. Peter Abelard. CHL(212).
Knowledge of God and the Service of God, The. Karl Barth. WP(1027).
Kreutzer Sonata, The. Count Leo Tolstoy. MCLE(2485), MEU(418), MP1(481), PO2(412).
Krishna Fluting. John Berry. SCL(2457), 1960a(126).
Kristin Lavransdatter. Sigrid Undset. MCLE(2488), MEU (421), MP1(483), PO2(464), SGEN(381).
Kung-sun Lung Tzu. Kung-sun Lung. WP(195).

Labyrinth of Solitude, The. Octavio Paz. MCLE(2491), MP4(489), SCL(2462), 1963a(117).
L'Action, see Action, L'.
Ladder of Divine Ascent, The. Saint John Climacus. CAL (254), CHL(179).
Ladder of Perfection, The. Walter Hilton. CAL(494).
Lady, The. Conrad Richter. SCL(2465), 1958a(133).
Lady Chatterley's Lover. D. H. Lawrence. PO2(123), SCL(2468), 1960a(129).
Lady for Ransom, The. Alfred Duggan. MCLE(2494), MP4 (492), SCL(2473), 1954a(135).
Lady from the Sea, The. Henrik Ibsen. MCLE(2497), MD (431), MP2(544).
Lady in the Dark. Moss Hart, Ira Gershwin and Kurt Weill. DGAP(334).
Lady into Fox. David Garnett. MCLE(2500), MEF(416), MP1(486).
Lady of the Lake, The. Sir Walter Scott. MCLE(2502), MP(151), MP2(547).
Lady Windermere's Fan. Oscar Wilde. MCLE(2505), MD (434), MP1(488), POP(144).
Lady's Not for Burning, The. Christopher Fry. MCLE (2507), MD(436), MP2(549), TCP(136).
Lafcadio Hearn. Elizabeth Stevenson. SCL(2476), 1962a (175).
L'Aiglon, see Aiglon, L'.
Lais, Le. François Villon. MCLE(2512), MP4(494).
Lais of Marie de France, The. Marie de France. MCLE (2516), MP4(497).
Lalla Rookh. Thomas Moore. MCLE(2522), MP(154), MP3 (548).
Lamb, The. François Mauriac. SCL(2479), 1957a(141).
Lament for the Molly Maguires. Arthur H. Lewis. SCL (2482), 1965a(164).

L'Amorosa Fiammetta, see Amorosa Fiammetta, L'.
Lamp Post, The. Martin Gregor-Dellin. SCL(2485), 1965a (167).
Land They Fought For, The. Clifford Dowdey. SCL(2488), 1955a(137).
Land Without Justice. Milovan Djilas. SCL(2492), 1959a (137).
Language, Truth and Logic. Alfred Jules Ayer. WP(1010).
Lanterns and Lances. James Thurber. SCL(2496), 1962a (178).
L'Assommoir, see Assommoir, L'.
Last Analysis, The. Saul Bellow. SCL(2498), 1966a(138).
Last Angry Man, The. Gerald Green. SCL(2501), 1958a (136).
Last Athenian, The. Viktor Rydberg. MCLE(2528), MEU (427), MP2(553).
Last Chronicle of Barset, The. Anthony Trollope. MCLE (2531), MEF(418), MP2(556).
Last Day the Dogbushes Bloomed, The. Lee Smith. SCL (2504), 1969a(185).
Last Days of Pompeii, The. Edward George Earle Bulwer-Lytton. MCLE(2533), MEF(420), MP1(490), PO(31), PON(190), SGBN(71).
Last Gentleman, The. Walker Percy. SCL(2508), 1967a (184).
Last Hunt, The. Milton Lott. SCL(2511), 1954a(138).
Last Hurrah, The. Edwin O'Connor. BM(294), SCL(2514), 1957a(144).
Last Innocence, The. Célia Bertin. SCL(2518), 1955a(141).
Last of Summer, The. Kate O'Brien. MCLE(2535), MEF (422), MP2(558).
Last of the Barons, The. Edward George Earle Bulwer-Lytton. MCLE(2538), MEF(425), MP1(492).
Last of the Crazy People, The. Timothy Findley. SCL (2521), 1968a(173).
Last of the Just, The. André Schwarz-Bart. SCL(2524), 1961a(149).
Last of the Mohicans, The. James Fenimore Cooper. MAF (324), MCLE(2541), MP1(494), MPA1(50), PO(207), PON(195), SGAN(3).
Last of the Vikings, The. Johan Bojer. MCLE(2544), MEU (430), MP2(560).
Last of the Wine, The. Mary Renault. BN(298), MCLE (2547), MP4(503), SCL(2527), 1957a(147).
Last Picture Show, The. Larry McMurtry. SCLs(154).
Last Puritan, The. George Santayana. MAF(327), MCLE (2550), MP1(497).

Last Tales. Isak Dinesen. SCL(2530), 1958a(138).
Last Temptation of Christ, The. Nikos Kazantzakis. SCL (2533), SGEN(458), 1961a(153).
Last Things. C. P. Snow. 1971a(161).
Last Tycoon, The. F. Scott Fitzgerald. MAF(330), MCLE (2553), MP3(552).
Last Unicorn, The. Peter S. Beagel. SCL(2537), 1969a (188).
Late George Apley, The. John P. Marquand. MAF(332), MCLE(2555), MP1(499), PO2(223), SGAN(260).
Late Lord Byron, The. Doris Langley Moore. BM(301), SCL(2542), 1962a(180).
Late Mattia Pascal, The. Luigi Pirandello. MCLE(2558), MEU(433), MP2(562).
Laughter. Henri Bergson. MCLE(2561), MP4(505).
Laurette. Marguerite Courtney. BM(305), SCL(2546), 1955a (144).
Laval. Hubert Cole. SCL(2550), 1964a(146).
Lavengro. George Henry Borrow. MCLE(2564), MEF(428), MP1(501).
Law, The. Roger Vailland. SCL(2553), 1959a(141).
Laws. Plato. WP(131).
Lay of Igor's Campaign, The. Unknown. MCLE(2567), MP4 (507).
Lay of the Last Minstrel, The. Sir Walter Scott. MCLE (2570), MP(157), MP2(564).
Lazarillo de Tormes. Unknown. MCLE(2573), MEU(436), MP2(567).
Leatherstocking Saga, The. James Fenimore Cooper. SCL (2556), 1954a(141).
Leaves of Grass. Walt Whitman. MCLE(2576), MP(160), MP3(554), MPA5(106).
Lectures on Calvinism. Abraham Kuyper. CHL(969).
Lectures on Godmanhood. Vladimir Solovyev. CHL(782).
Lectures on Preaching. Phillips Brooks. CHL(778).
Lectures on Revivals of Religion. Charles Grandison Finney. CHL(675).
Lectures on the Philosophy of Life. Friedrich von Schlegel. CAL(635).
Legend of Good Women, The. Geoffrey Chaucer. MCLE (2580), MP(164), MP3(557).
Legend of Sleepy Hollow, The. Washington Irving. MAF (335), MCLE(2583), MP2(569), MPA2(92), PO(236), PON(199).
Legend of the Moor's Legacy. Washington Irving. MAF (337), MCLE(2585), MP2(571).
Legend of Tyl Ulenspiegel, The. Charles de Coster. MCLE

(2588), MEU(439), MP2(573).
Leisure the Basis of Culture. Josef Pieper. CAL(940).
Leopard, The. Giuseppe di Lampedusa. BM(309), MCLE
 (2591), MP4(510), SCL(2559), 1961a(156).
Leopards and Lilies. Alfred Duggan. MCLE(2594), MP4
 (512), SCL(2563), 1954a(144).
Lesson, The. Eugene Ionesco. TCP(200).
Let Me Count the Ways. Peter De Vries. SCL(2566),
 1966a(141).
Let No Man Write My Epitaph. Willard Motley. SCLs(157).
Let Not Your Hart. James Seay. 1971a(164).
Let Us Now Praise Famous Men. James Agee. BM(313),
 MCLE(2597), MP4(515), SCL(2570), 1961a(160).
Letter of the Church of Rome to the Church of Corinth, The.
 Saint Clement I. CAL(4).
Letter to the Grand Duchess Christina. Galileo Galilei.
 CAL(579).
Letters and Sermons of Saint Leo the Great, The. Saint
 Leo the Great. CAL(211).
Letters from an American Farmer. Michet-Guillaume Jean
 de Crèvecoeur. MCLE(2600), MN(169), MP3(560).
Letters from Madame La Marquise de Sévigné. Madame
 Marie de Sévigné. SCL(2573), 1957a(150).
Letters from the Earth. Samuel L. Clemens. SCL(2576),
 1963a(120).
Letters from the Underworld. Fyodor Mikhailovich Dosto-
 evski. MCLE(2603), MEU(442), MP2(576).
Letters of C. S. Lewis. C. S. Lewis. SCL(2582), 1967a
 (187).
Letters of Carl Sandburg, The. Carl Sandburg. SCL(2578),
 1969a(193).
Letters of Charles Lamb, The. Charles Lamb. MCLE
 (2606), MP4(517).
Letters of Emily Dickinson, The. Emily Dickinson. BM
 (319), MCLE(2609), MP4(520), SCL(2586), 1959a(144).
Letters of F. Scott Fitzgerald, The. F. Scott Fitzgerald.
 MCLE(2612), MP4(523), SCL(2589), 1964a(149).
Letters of James Agee to Father Flye. James Agee. SCL
 (2593), 1963a(122).
Letters of James Joyce. James Joyce. SCL(2597), 1958a
 (141).
Letters of John Keats, The. John Keats. MCLE(2615),
 MP4(525).
Letters of Madame de Sévigné, The. Madame Marie de
 Sévigné. MCLE(2618), MP4(528).
Letters of Oscar Wilde, The. Oscar Wilde. BM(316), SCL
 (2600), 1963a(126).

Letters of Pliny the Younger, The. Gaius Plinius Caecilius Secundus (Pliny). MCLE(2620), MP4(530).
Letters of Robert Frost, The. Robert Frost. MCLE(2623), MP4(532).
Letters of Robert Frost to Louis Untermeyer, The. Robert Frost. SCL(2603), 1964a(152).
Letters of Rupert Brooke, The. Rupert Brooke. SCL(2608), 1969a(196).
Letters of Saint Basil, The. Saint Basil. CAL(110).
Letters of Saint Bernard of Clairvaux, The. Saint Bernard. CAL(332).
Letters of Saint Jerome, The. Saint Jerome. CAL(180), CHL(108).
Letters of Thomas Gray, The. Thomas Gray. MCLE(2626), MP4(535).
Letters of Thomas Wolfe, The. Thomas Wolfe. BM(322), MCLE(2629), MP4(538), SCL(2612), 1957a(152).
Letters of Wallace Stevens. Wallace Stevens. SCL(2616), 1967a(190).
Letters of Walpole, The. Horace Walpole. MCLE(2633), MN(172), MP3(563).
Letters of William Cowper, The. William Cowper. MCLE (2636), MP4(541).
Letters to His Son. Philip Dormer Stanhope, Lord Chesterfield. MCLE(2639), MN(175), MP3(565).
Letting Go. Philip Roth. SCL(2620), 1963a(129).
Leviathan. Thomas Hobbes. MCLE(2641), MN(177), MP3 (567), WP(392).
Lex rex. Samuel Rutherford. CHL(462).
Leyte: June 1944-January 1945. Samuel Eliot Morison. BM(326), SCL(2624), 1959a(147).
Liars, The. Henry Arthur Jones. POP(130).
Liber amoris. William Hazlitt. MCLE(2644), MN(180), MP3(570).
Liber de corpore et sanguine domini. Lanfranc. CAL(283).
Liberation of Lord Byron Jones, The. Jesse Hill Ford. SCL(2627), 1966a(144).
Liberator, The. John L. Thomas. SCL(2631), 1964a(157).
Lie, The. Alberto Moravia. SCL(2634), 1967a(194).
Lie Down in Darkness. William Styron. MCLE(2647), MP4 (544), SGAN(322).
Lieh Kuo Chih. Feng Meng-lung. MCLE(2650), MEU(445), MP3(572).
Lies. C. K. Williams. 1970a(184).
Life and Death of Cardinal Wolsey, The. George Cavendish. MCLE(2653), MP4(546).
Life and Death of Mr. Badman, The. John Bunyan. MCLE

(2656), MEF(431), MP3(575).
Life and Times of Lucrezia Borgia, The. Maria Bellonici. SCL(2638), 1954a(147).
Life and Work of Sigmund Freud, The. Ernest Jones, M. D. SCL(2641), 1958a(144).
Life at the Top. John Braine. SCL(2644), 1963a(132).
Life in London. Pierce Egan. MCLE(2658), MEF(433), MP2(578).
Life Is a Dream. Pedro Calderón de la Barca. MCLE (2661), MD(441), MP2(580), POP(289).
Life of Alfred. John Asser. CAL(268).
Life of Antony, The. Saint Athanasius. CHL(95).
Life of Charlemagne, The. Einhard. CAL(265).
Life of Dylan Thomas, The. Constantine FitzGibbon. SCL (2647), 1966a(148).
Life of Ezra Pound, The. Noel Stock. 1971a(167).
Life of Jesus, The. Ernest Renan. CHL(739).
Life of Jesus Critically Examined, The. David Friedrich Strauss. CHL(679).
Life of Lady Mary Wortley Montagu, The. Robert Halsband. SCL(2651), 1958a(147).
Life of Lenin, The. Louis Fischer. SCL(2654), 1965a(170).
Life of Nelson. Robert Southey. MCLE(2664), MN(183), MP3(576).
Life of Our Lord Jesus Christ, The. Louis Veuillot. CAL (665).
Life of Reason, The. George Santayana. WP(761).
Life of Richard Savage. Samuel Johnson. MCLE(2667), MP4(549).
Life of Saint Louis, The. Jean de Joinville. CAL(435).
Life of St. Martin, The. Sulpicius Severus. CHL(137).
Life of St. Teresa of Ávila, The. Saint Teresa of Ávila. CHL(392).
Life of Samuel Johnson, LL. D. , The. James Boswell. MCLE(2670), MN(186), MP3(579).
Life of Samuel Johnson, LL. D. , The. Sir John Hawkins, Knt. SCL(2659), 1962a(184).
Life of the Mind in America, The. Perry Miller. SCLs (160).
Life on the Mississippi. Samuel L. Clemens. MCLE(2673), MN(189), MP1(504), MPA5(80).
Life Studies. Robert Lowell. BM(329), SCL(2662), 1960a (133).
Life with Father. Clarence Day, Jr. MAF(340), MCLE (2676), MP1(506).
Life with Father. Howard Lindsay and Russel Crouse. DGAP(317), POP(1), SGAP(58).

Ligeia. Edgar Allan Poe. MAF(343), MCLE(2679), MP2 (583), MPA5(22).
Light Around the Body, The. Robert Bly. SCL(2665), 1968a(176).
Light in August. William Faulkner. MAF(345), MCLE (2681), MP1(509), PO2(242), SGAN(206).
Light in the Piazza, The. Elizabeth Spencer. SCL(2668), 1961a(163).
Light Infantry Ball, The. Hamilton Basso. SCL(2671), 1960a(136).
Light Is Dark Enough, The. Christopher Fry. 1954a (150).
Light That Failed, The. Rudyard Kipling. PO(120).
Lightnin'. Winchell Smith and Frank Bacon. POP(38).
Like a Bulwark. Marianne Moore. BM(332), SCL(2675), 1957a(156).
Liliom. Ferenc Molnár. MCLE(2684), MD(444), MP1(511), POP(337), TCP(232).
Lime Twig, The. John Hawkes. MCLE(2686), MP4(551), SCL(2678), 1962a(186).
Lincoln Finds a General. Kenneth P. Williams. BM(335), SCL(2681), 1960a(140).
Lincoln the President. James G. Randall and Richard N. Current. BM(340), SCL(2686), 1955a(147).
Lindmann. Frederic Raphael. SCL(2690), 1965a(174).
Link, The. August Strindberg. MCLE(2689), MD(446), MP3 (581).
Lion and the Throne, The. Catherine Drinker Bowen. BM (344), SCL(2692), 1958a(150).
Lion in the Garden. James B. Meriwether and Michael Millgate, Eds. SCL(2695), 1968a(179).
Lion of Flanders, The. Hendrik Conscience. MCLE(2691), MEU(448), MP3(583).
Literary Essays of Virginia Woolf, The. Virginia Woolf. MCLE(2694), MP4(553).
Literature and Dogma. Matthew Arnold. CHL(770).
Little Big Man. Thomas Berger. SCL(2698), 1965a(176).
Little Book of Eternal Wisdom, The. Blessed Henry Suso, O. P. CAL(458).
Little Clay Cart, The. Shudraka. MCLE(2696), MD(448), MP3(586).
Little Dorrit. Charles Dickens. MCLE(2699), MEF(436), MP2(585).
Little Flowers of Saint Francis, The. Unknown. CAL(448), CHL(264).
Little Foxes, The. Lillian Hellman. DGAP(321), MCLE (2702), MD(451), MP3(588), SGAP(196), TCP(191).

Little Girls, The. Elizabeth Bowen. SCL(2705), 1964a(160).
Little Hut, The. André Roussin. SCL(2708), 1954a(153).
Little Karoo, The. Pauline Smith. SCL(2711), 1960a(144).
Little Learning, A. Evelyn Waugh. SCL(2714), 1965a(183).
Little Minister, The. James M. Barrie. MCLE(2704), MEF(439), MP1(513), PO(17), PON(204).
Little Prince, The. Antoine de Saint-Exupéry. PO2(351).
Little Women. Louisa May Alcott. MAF(348), MCLE(2707), MP1(515), MPA1(7), PO(188), PON(208).
Liturgical Piety. Louis Bouyer. CAL(1014).
Liturgy and Personality. Dietrich von Hildebrand. CAL(835).
Live or Die. Anne Sexton. SCL(2719), 1967a(197).
Lives. Izaak Walton. MCLE(2709), MP4(555).
Lives of the Caesars. Gaius Suetonius Tranquillus. MCLE (2712), MN(192), MP3(590).
Lives of the Poets. Samuel Johnson. MCLE(2716), MP4 (558).
Living God, The. Nathan Söderblom. CHL(994).
Living Room, The. Graham Greene. SCL(2724), 1954a(156).
Living Sea, The. Jacques-Yves Cousteau. SCL(2727), 1964a (163).
Living Word, The. Gustaf Wingren. CHL(1112).
Liza of Lambeth. W. Somerset Maugham. MCLE(2719), MEF(442), MP2(587).
Lizzie Borden. Edward D. Radin. SCL(2730), 1962a(189).
Local Anaesthetic. Günter Grass. 1971a(170).
Loci communes rerum theologicarum. Philipp Melanchthon. CHL(343).
Logic. Georg Wilhelm Friedrich Hegel. WP(577).
Logic of Modern Physics, The. Percy Williams Bridgman. WP(880).
Logic, the Theory of Inquiry. John Dewey. WP(1033).
Lolita. Vladimir Nabokov. SCL(2733), 1959a(150).
Loneliness of the Long-Distance Runner, The. Alan Sillitoe. SCL(2736), 1961a(165).
Lonely Passion of Judith Hearne, The. Brian Moore. SCL (2739), 1957a(159).
Lonesome Traveler and Other Stories, The. John William Corrington. SCL(2742), 1969a(200).
Long and Happy Life, A. Reynolds Price. MCLE(2721), MP4(561), SCL(2748), 1963a(135).
Long Day's Journey into Night. Eugene O'Neill. BM(347), DGAP(339), MCLE(2731), SCL(2753), SGAP(30), 1957a (162).
Long Journey, The. Johannes V. Jensen. MCLE(2724), MEU(451), MP2(589).
Long-Legged House, The. Wendell Berry. SCLs(163).

Long March, The. William Styron. SCLs(168).
Long Night, The. Andrew Lytle. MAF(350), MCLE(2728), MP2(593).
Long Ships, The. Frans G. Bengtsson. SCL(2756), 1954a (159).
Long Street, The. Donald Davidson. BM(350), SCL(2759), 1962a(192).
Long Voyage, The. Jorge Semprun. SCL(2763), 1965a(188).
Longer Rules and The Shorter Rules, The. Saint Basil. CHL(99).
Longest Day: June 6, 1944, The. Cornelius Ryan. SCL (2768), 1960a(146).
Longest Journey, The. E. M. Forster. MCLE(2731), MEF (444), MP3(593).
Look Back in Anger. John Osborne. BM(354), MCLE(2734), MP4(563), SCL(2771), TCP(288), 1958a(153).
Look Homeward, Angel. Thomas Wolfe. MAF(353), MCLE (2738), MP1(517), PO2(267), SGAN(189).
Looking Backward. Edward Bellamy. MAF(356), MCLE (2741), MP1(520), MPA1(17), PO(191), SGAN(77).
Looking Up at Leaves. Barbara Howes. SCL(2773), 1967a (201).
Lord, The. Romano Guardini. CAL(849).
Lord Byron's Wife. Malcolm Elwin. SCL(2777), 1964a(165).
Lord Grizzly. Frederick F. Manfred. SCL(2781), 1954a (162).
Lord Jim. Joseph Conrad. MCLE(2744), MEF(447), MP1 (522), PO(48), PON(212), SGBN(219).
Lord of History, The. Jean Daniélou, S.J. CAL(997).
Lord of the Flies. William Golding. MCLE(2747), MP4 (566), SGBN(350).
Lord's Prayer, The. Saint Gregory of Nyssa. CAL(136).
Lorna Doone. Richard D. Blackmore. MCLE(2750), MEF (450), MP1(524), PO(21), PON(216).
Losing Battles. Eudora Welty. 1971a(175).
Loss of El Dorado, The. V. S. Naipaul. 1971a(178).
Lost Horizon. James Hilton. MCLE(2753), MEF(453), MP1 (527), PO2(138), SGBN(329).
Lost Illusions. Honoré de Balzac. MCLE(2756), MEU(455), MP2(595).
Lost in the Funhouse. John Barth. SCL(2784), 1969a(205).
Lost Lady, A. Willa Cather. MAF(359), MCLE(2759), MP1 (529).
Lost Revolution, The. Robert Shaplen. SCL(2787), 1966a (151).
Lost Weekend, The. Charles Jackson. MAF(362), MCLE (2762), MP1(531).

Lost World, The. Randall Jarrell. SCL(2790), 1966a(154).
Love and Its Derangements. Joyce Carol Oates. 1971a(181).
Love and Will. Rollo May. 1970a(187).
Love and Work. Reynolds Price. SCL(2793), 1969a(208).
Love for Love. William Congreve. MCLE(2764), MD(453), MP2(597).
Love-Girl and the Innocent, The. Aleksandr I. Solzhenitsyn. 1971a(186).
Love in a Wood. William Wycherley. MCLE(2767), MD (456), MP3(595).
Love of God, The. Saint Francis de Sales. CAL(584).
Love Poems. Anne Sexton. SCL(2797), 1969a(212).
Love Story. Erich Segal. 1971a(189).
Love, the Law of Life. Toyohiko Kagawa. CHL(921).
Lovely Ambition, The. Mary Ellen Chase. SCL(2800), 1961a(168).
Love's Body. Norman O. Brown. SCL(2803), 1967a(205).
Love's Labour's Lost. William Shakespeare. MCLE(2770), MD(459), MP2(599).
Loving. Henry Green. MCLE(2773), MEF(456), MP2(602).
Lower Depths, The. Maksim Gorki. MCLE(2776), MD(462), MP2(604), POP(349), TCP(174).
Low's Autobiography. David Low. SCL(2807), 1958a(155).
Loyalties. John Galsworthy. MCLE(2779), MD(465), MP1 (533).
Lucien Leuwen. Stendhal. MCLE(2781), MEU(458), MP2 (606).
Luck of Ginger Coffey, The. Brian Moore. SCL(2810), 1961a(171).
Luck of Roaring Camp and Other Sketches, The. Bret Harte. MAF(364), MCLE(2784), MP3(597), MPA2(25).
Lucky Jim. Kingsley Amis. MCLE(2787), MP4(569).
Lunar Landscapes. John Hawkes. 1970a(190).
Lusiad, The. Luis Vaz de Camoëns. MCLE(2790), MP(167), MP2(608).
Luther. John Osborne. TCP(290).
Lyfe of Sir Thomas More, Knighte. William Roper. CAL (543).
Lyric Poetry of Byron, The. George Gordon, Lord Byron. MCLE(2793), MP4(571).
Lyric Poetry of Lowell, The. James Russell Lowell. MCLE(2796), MP4(574), MPA4(31).
Lyric Poetry of Milton, The. John Milton. MCLE(2800), MP4(577).
Lyric Poetry of Spenser, The. Edmund Spenser. MCLE (2804), MP4(581).
Lyrical and Critical Essays. Albert Camus. SCL(2813),

1969a(215).
Lysistrata. Aristophanes. MCLE(2809), MD(467), MP2(610), POP(369).
Lytton Strachey. Michael Holroyd. SCL(2817), 1969a(218).

Mabinogion, The. Unknown. MCLE(2811), MEF(459), MP3 (600).
Macbeth. William Shakespeare. MCLE(2815), MD(469), MP1 (534), POP(197).
Mackerel Plaza, The. Peter De Vries. SCL(2821), 1959a (152).
McTeague. Frank Norris. MAF(367), MCLE(2818), MP1 (537), MPA4(102).
Madame Bovary. Gustave Flaubert. MCLE(2821), MEU(461), MP1(539), PO(293), PON(220), SGEN(113).
Madame Butterfly. David Belasco and John Luther Long. DGAP(140).
Mademoiselle de Maupin. Théophile Gautier. MCLE(2824), MEU(464), MP1(542), PO(296), SGEN(86).
Madras House, The. Harley Granville-Barker. MCLE(2826), MD(472), MP3(604).
Madwoman of Chaillot, The. Jean Giraudoux. MCLE(2828), MD(474), MP3(606), TCP(163).
Magdeburg Centuries, The. Matthias Flacius (and others). CHL(388).
Maggie: A Girl of the Streets. Stephen Crane. MAF(370), MCLE(2831), MP1(543), MPA1(86).
Magic Barrel, The. Bernard Malamud. SCLs(171).
Magic Mountain, The. Thomas Mann. MCLE(2833), MEU (466), MP1(545), PO2(451), SGEN(245).
Magnalia Christi Americana. Cotton Mather. CHL(557), MCLE(2836), MN(196), MP3(608).
Magnificent Obsession, The. Lloyd C. Douglas. MAF(372), MCLE(2839), MP1(547).
Magus, The. John Fowles. SCLs(174).
Mahabharata, The. Unknown. MCLE(2842), MP(170), MP3 (611).
Maias, The. José Maria Eça de Queiroz. SCL(2824), 1966a(157).
Maid of Honour, The. Philip Massinger. MCLE(2845), MD (477), MP3(613).
Maid's Tragedy, The. Francis Beaumont and John Fletcher. MCLE(2848), MD(480), MP2(612).
Mail Boat, The. Alexander Randolph. SCL(2828), 1954a(165).
Main Currents in American Thought. Vernon Louis Parrington. MCLE(2851), MP4(586).
Main Street. Sinclair Lewis. MAF(375), MCLE(2854), MP1

(549), PO2(212).
Main-Travelled Roads. Hamlin Garland. MAF(378), MCLE (2857), MP3(615), MPA2(12).
Major Barbara. George Bernard Shaw. MCLE(2859), MD (483), MP3(617), TCP(349).
Makepeace Experiment, The. Abram Tertz. SCL(2831), 1966a(161).
Making of Charles Dickens, The. Christopher Hibbert. SCL(2834), 1968a(182).
Making of Europe, The. Christopher Dawson. CAL(824).
Making of the President, 1960, The. Theodore H. White. BM(356), SCL(2838), 1962a(195).
Making of the President, 1964, The. Theodore H. White. SCL(2842), 1966a(164).
Making of the President, 1968, The. Theodore H. White. 1970a(193).
Malcolm. James Purdy. MCLE(2862), MP4(588), SCL(2847), 1960a(149).
Malcontent, The. John Marston. MCLE(2865), MD(486), MP3(619).
Male Animal, The. James Thurber and Elliott Nugent. DGAP(330), SGAP(110).
Malefactors, The. Caroline Gordon. SCLs(176).
Maltaverne. François Mauriac. 1971a(192).
Maltese Falcon, The. Dashiell Hammett. MAF(380), MCLE (2868), MP1(551).
Man a Machine. Julien Offray de La Mettrie. WP(482).
Man Against the Sky, The. Edwin Arlington Robinson. MCLE(2871), MP(173), MP3(622).
Man and Superman. George Bernard Shaw. MCLE(2874), MD(489), MP3(624), TCP(352).
Man and the Masses. Ernst Toller. TCP(417).
Man and the State. Jacques Maritain. CAL(973).
Man and Two Women, A. Doris Lessing. SCL(2851), 1964a (169).
Man-Eater of Malgudi, The. R. K. Narayan. SCL(2888), 1962a(199).
Man in Motion. Michael Mewshaw. 1971a(195).
Man in the Gray Flannel Suit, The. Sloan Wilson. SCL (2854), 1955a(150).
Man Just Ahead of You, The. Robert M. Coates. SCL (2857), 1965a(193).
Man of Feeling, The. Henry Mackenzie. MCLE(2876), MEF(463), MP2(615).
Man of La Mancha. Dale Wasserman. SCL(2860), 1967a (209).
Man of Mode, The. Sir George Etherege. MCLE(2879), MD

(491), MP2(617).
Man of Property, The. John Galsworthy. PO(92), SGBN (242).
Man Who Cried I Am, The. John A. Williams. SCLs(179).
Man Who Laughs, The. Victor Hugo. PO(308).
Man Who Loved Children, The. Christina Stead. SCL(2865), 1966a(168).
Man Who Never Was, The. Ewen Montagu. SCL(2868), 1954a(168).
Man Who Was Thursday, The. Gilbert Keith Chesterton. MCLE(2882), MEF(466), MP2(619).
Man with a Bull-Tongue Plow. Jesse Stuart. MCLE(2885), MP(176), MP3(626).
Man Without a Country, The. Edward Everett Hale. MAF (383), MCLE(2888), MP1(553), MPA2(16), PO2(167).
Man Without Qualities: Volume II, The. Robert Musil. SCL(2871), 1954a(171).
Manchild in the Promised Land. Claude Brown. SCL(2874), 1966a(171).
Mandarins, The. Simone de Beauvoir. SCL(2878), 1957a (165).
Mandate for Change, 1953-1956. Dwight D. Eisenhower. SCL(2881), 1964a(172).
Mandelbaum Gate, The. Muriel Spark. SCL(2885), 1966a (175).
Manette Salomon. Edmond and Jules de Goncourt. MCLE (2890), MEU(469), MP3(628).
Manfred. George Gordon, Lord Byron. MCLE(2893), MP (179), MP2(621).
Manhattan Transfer. John Dos Passos. MAF(385), MCLE (2895), MP1(555).
Mani. Patrick Leigh Fermor. SCL(2891), 1961a(173).
Manjiro. Hisakazu Kaneko. SCL(2894), 1957a(168).
Manner Is Ordinary, The. John LaFarge, S. J. CAL(1010).
Manon Lescaut. Abbé Prévost. MCLE(2898), MEU(472), MP1(557), PO2(297).
Manor, The. Isaac Bashevis Singer. SCL(2897), 1968a(186).
Man's Fate. André Malraux. MCLE(2901), MEU(475), MP1 (559), PO2(375), SGEN(403).
Mansfield Park. Jane Austen. MCLE(2904), MEF(469), MP1(562).
Mansion, The. William Faulkner. BM(360), MCLE(2907), MP4(591), SCL(2900), 1960a(152).
Marat. Peter Weiss. TCP(432).
Marble Faun, The. Nathaniel Hawthorne. MAF(388), MCLE (2910), MP1(564), MPA2(54), PO(225), PON(227).
Marching On. James Boyd. MAF(390), MCLE(2912), MP1

(566).
Mardi. Herman Melville. MAF(393), MCLE(2915), MP2 (623), MPA4(58).
Margaret Fleming. James A. Herne. DGAP(117).
Maria Chapdelaine. Louis Hémon. MAF(396), MCLE(2919), MP2(626).
Maria Magdalena. Friedrich Hebbel. MCLE(2922), MD(494), MP2(628).
Marianne. Pierre Carlet de Chamblain de Marivaux. MCLE (2925), MEU(478), MP3(631).
Marianne Thornton. E. M. Forster. SCL(2904), 1957a(170).
Marius the Epicurean. Walter Pater. MCLE(2928), MEF (472), MP2(630).
Marjorie Morningstar. Herman Wouk. SCL(2907), 1955a (153).
Mark Twain: An American Prophet. Maxwell Geismar. 1971a(200).
Market Harborough. George J. Whyte-Melville. MCLE (2931), MEF(475), MP2(632).
Markings. Dag Hammarskjold. SCL(2910), 1965a(195).
Marlborough's Duchess. Louis Kronenberger. SCL(2914), 1959a(155).
Marmion. Sir Walter Scott. MCLE(2934), MP(181), MP2 (635).
Marquise Went Out at Five, The. Claude Mauriac. SCL (2918), 1963a(139).
Marriage à la Mode. John Dryden. MCLE(2937), MD(497), MP3(634).
Marriage of Figaro, The. Pierre A. Caron de Beaumarchais. MCLE(2939), MD(499), MP2(637).
Marse Chan. Thomas Nelson Page. MAF(399), MCLE(2941), MP2(638).
Martereau. Nathalie Sarraute. SCL(2921), 1960a(156).
Martin Chuzzlewit. Charles Dickens. MCLE(2943), MEF (478), MP2(640).
Martyrdom of Saint Polycarp, The. Saint Polycarp of Smyrna. CAL(16).
Martyred, The. Richard E. Kim. SCL(2924), 1965a(199).
Mary. Vladimir Nabokov. 1971a(202).
Mary Barton. Mrs. Elizabeth Gaskell. MCLE(2947), MP4 (594).
Mary Queen of Scots. Lady Antonia Fraser. 1970a(198).
Mass for the Dead, A. William Gibson. SCL(2927), 1969a (222).
Mass of the Roman Rite, The. Josef Andreas Jungmann, S.J. CAL(949).
Massacre at Montségur. Zoé Oldenbourg. SCL(2934),

1963a(142).
Master Builder, The. Henrik Ibsen. MCLE(2950), MD(501), MP2(643).
Master of Ballantrae, The. Robert Louis Stevenson. MCLE (2952), MEF(482), MP1(568), PON(231).
Masters, The. C. P. Snow. MCLE(2955), MP4(596).
Masters of Deceit. J. Edgar Hoover. SCL(2937), 1959a (158).
Mastro-don Gesualdo. Giovanni Verga. MCLE(2958), MEU (481), MP3(636).
Mater et magistra. Pope John XXIII. CAL(1106).
Matter and Memory. Henri Bergson. MCLE(2962), MP4 (599).
Max. Lord David Cecil. SCL(2941), 1966a(178).
Max Havelaar. Multatuli. MCLE(2964), MEU(485), MP3 (639).
Max Jamison. Wilfrid Sheed. 1971a(206).
Maxims, The. François, Duc de La Rochefoucauld. MCLE (2967), MN(199), MP3(642).
May We Borrow Your Husband? Graham Greene. SCL (2945), 1968a(188).
Mayor of Casterbridge, The. Thomas Hardy. MCLE(2969), MEF(485), MP1(571), SGBN(172).
Mayor of Zalamea, The. Pedro Calderón de la Barca. MCLE(2972), MD(503), MP2(645).
Maze Maker, The. Michael Aytron. SCL(2949), 1968a(192).
Meaning of God in Human Experience, The. William Ernest Hocking. CHL(869).
Meaning of Man, The. Jean Mouroux. CAL(933).
Meaning of Revelation, The. H. Richard Niebuhr. CHL (1054).
Meaning of Truth, The. William James. WP(784).
Measure for Measure. William Shakespeare. MCLE(2975), MD(506), MP2(648).
Measure My Love. Helga Sandburg. SCL(2954), 1960a(158).
Measure of Man, The. Joseph Wood Krutch. SCLs(182).
Medea. Euripides. MCLE(2978), MD(509), MP1(573).
Mediator Dei. Pope Pius XII. CAL(915).
Medieval Foundation of England, The. Sir Arthur Bryant. SCL(2958), 1968a(196).
Meditations. Marcus Aurelius. MCLE(2980), MN(201), MP3 (644), WP(229).
Meditations on First Philosophy. René Descartes. WP(386).
Meditations on the Life of Christ. Unknown Franciscan Monk and Saint Bonaventure. CAL(455).
Medium, The. Gian-Carlo Menotti. DGAP(366).
Meek Heritage. Frans Eemil Sillanpää. MCLE(2982), MEU

(488), MP2(650).
Meeting of Love and Knowledge, The. Martin Cyril D'Arcy, S. J. CAL(1040).
Melbourne. Lord David Cecil. BM(364), SCL(2961), 1954a (174).
Melmoth the Wanderer. Charles Robert Maturin. MCLE (2985), MEF(488), MP2(653).
Member of the Wedding, The. Carson McCullers. MAF (401), MCLE(2988), MP2(655), SGAP(259).
Memed, My Hawk. Yashar Kemal. SCL(2964), 1962a(202).
Memento Mori. Muriel Spark. MCLE(2991), MP4(601).
Memoirs. Giovanni Jacopo Casanova de Seingalt. MCLE (2994), MN(203), MP3(646).
Memoirs, Volume I. Harry S. Truman. SCL(2967), 1955a (156).
Memoirs, Volume II. Harry S. Truman. SCL(2971), 1957a (173).
Memoirs: 1925-1950. George F. Kennan. SCL(2975), 1968a(198).
Memoirs of a Cavalier, The. Daniel Defoe. MCLE(2997), MEF(491), MP3(649).
Memoirs of a Fox-Hunting Man. Siegfried Sassoon. MCLE (3000), MEF(494), MP1(575).
Memoirs of a Midget. Walter De la Mare. MCLE(3003), MEF(497), MP1(577).
Memoirs of a Physician. Alexandre Dumas (father). MCLE (3005), MEU(491), MP3(651).
Memoirs of an Infantry Officer. Siegfried Sassoon. MCLE (3009), MEF(499), MP1(579).
Memoirs of Field-Marshal Montgomery, The. Viscount Montgomery. SCL(2983), 1959a(162).
Memoirs of Hecate County. Edmund Wilson. SCL(2987), 1960a(162).
Memories of a Catholic Girlhood. Mary McCarthy. SCL (2991), 1958a(158).
Men and Women. Robert Browning. MCLE(3012), MP4(603).
Men Die. H. L. Humes. SCL(2994), 1960a(165).
Men to Match My Mountains. Irving Stone. SCL(2997), 1957a(177).
Menaechmi, The. Titus Maccius Plautus. MCLE(3015), MD(511), MP3(654), POP(387).
Meng Tzu. Mencius. WP(180).
Meno. Plato. WP(64).
Menteur, Le. Pierre Corneille. MCLE(3017), MD(513), MP3(656).
Merchant of Venice, The. William Shakespeare. MCLE (3020), MD(516), MP1(581), POP(211).

Mercy of God, The. Jean Cau. SCL(3000), 1964a(175).
Meriwether Lewis: A Biography. Richard Dillon. SCL (3003), 1966a(182).
Mermaid Madonna, The. Stratis Myrivilis. SCL(3008), 1960a(168).
Mermaids, The. Eva Boros. SCL(3011), 1957a(180).
Merry Christmas of the Old Woman Who Lived in a Shoe, The. George Melville Baker. DGAP(102).
Merry Monarch. Hesketh Pearson. BM(367), SCL(3014), 1961a(177).
Merry Wives of Windsor, The. William Shakespeare. MCLE(3023), MD(519), MP2(657).
Messer Marco Polo. Donn Byrne. MCLE(3026), MEF(502), MP1(584).
Metalogicon. John of Salisbury. CAL(335).
Metamora: or, The Last of the Wampanoags. John Augustus Stone. DGAP(45).
Metamorphoses, The. Ovid. MCLE(3028), MP(184), MP3 (658).
Metaphysics. Aristotle. WP(152).
Methods of Ethics, The. Henry Sidwick. WP(671).
Micah Clarke. Arthur Conan Doyle. MCLE(3031), MEF (504), MP1(585).
Michael and His Lost Angel. Henry Arthur Jones. MCLE (3034), MD(522), MP2(660).
Microcosmus. Rudolf Hermann Lotze. WP(638).
Midcentury. John Dos Passos. SCL(3018), 1962a(205).
Mid-Channel. Arthur Wing Pinero. MCLE(3037), MD(525), MP3(661).
Middle Age of Mrs. Eliot, The. Angus Wilson. SCL(3023), 1960a(171).
Middlemarch. George Eliot. MCLE(3039), MEF(507), MP1 (588), PO2(47).
Midnight Cowboy. James Leo Herlihy. SCL(3026), 1966a (186).
Midpoint and Other Poems. John Updike. 1970a(203).
Midsummer Night's Dream, A. William Shakespeare. MCLE(3042), MD(527), MP2(662).
Midway. Mitsuo Fuchida and Masatake Okumiya. SCL(3029), 1955a(160).
Mighty and Their Fall, The. Ivy Compton-Burnett. BM (371), MCLE(3045), MP4(606), SCL(3033), 1963a(145).
Mighty Stonewall. Frank E. Vandiver. SCL(3036), 1958a (161).
Mikado, The. W. S. Gilbert and Arthur Sullivan. MCLE (3048), MD(530), MP1(591).
Military Philosophers. Anthony Powell. 1970a(207).

Mill on the Floss, The. George Eliot. MCLE(3050), MEF (510), MP1(593), PO(82).
Mill on the Po, The. Riccardo Bacchelli. MCLE(3053), MEU(495), MP2(664).
Millennium of Europe, The. Oscar Halecki. CAL(1128).
Mind and Heart of Love, The. Martin Cyril D'Arcy, S.J. CAL(909).
Mind and Its Place in Nature, The. Charlie Dunbar Broad. WP(862).
Mind and the World Order. Clarence Irving Lewis. WP (914).
Mind of Primitive Man, The. Franz Boas. MCLE(3056), MP4(608).
Mind Parasites, The. Colin Wilson. SCL(3039), 1968a(205).
Mind, Self, and Society. George Herbert Mead. WP(992).
Mind's Road to God, The. Saint Bonaventure. CAL(371).
Ministry of Fear, The. Graham Greene. MCLE(3059), MEF(513), MP2(666).
Minna von Barnhelm. Gotthold Ephraim Lessing. MCLE (3062), MD(532), MP2(668).
Mirror for Witches, A. Esther Forbes. MAF(404), MCLE (3065), MP2(671).
Mirrors & Windows: Poems. Howard Nemerov. SCL(3043), 1959a(165).
Misanthrope, The. Molière. MCLE(3068), MD(535), MP1 (595), POP(259).
Miscellanies. Saint Clement of Alexandria. CHL(43).
Miscellanies. Abraham Cowley. MCLE(3070), MP(187), MP3(663).
Miser, The. Molière. MCLE(3072), MD(537), MP2(673).
Misérables, Les. Victor Hugo. MCLE(3074), MEU(498), MP1(597), PO(300), PON(235), SGEN(58).
Miss Julie. August Strindberg. MCLE(3077), MD(539), MP2(675), TCP(397).
Miss Leonora When Last Seen. Peter Taylor. SCL(3045), 1965a(202).
Miss Lonelyhearts. Nathanael West. MAF(407), MCLE (3080), MP3(664).
Miss Ravenel's Conversion. John William De Forest. MAF (410), MCLE(3083), MP2(677).
Missolonghi Manuscript, The. Frederic Prokosch. SCL (3048), 1969a(228).
Mr. Baruch. Margaret L. Coit. SCL(3051), 1958a(163).
Mr. Bridge. Evan S. Connell, Jr. 1970a(212).
Mr. Britling Sees It Through. H. G. Wells. MCLE(3086), MEF(516), MP1(600).
Mr. Bullivant and His Lambs. Ivy Compton-Burnett. MCLE

(3089), MP4(611).
Mr. Clemens and Mark Twain. Justin Kaplan. SCL(3054), 1967a(221).
Mr. Facey Romford's Hounds. Robert Smith Surtees. MCLE (3091), MEF(519), MP2(679).
Mr. Gallion's School. Jesse Stuart. SCL(3058), 1968a(209).
Mr. Midshipman Easy. Frederick Marryat. MCLE(3096), MEF(524), MP1(602), PON(239).
Mister Roberts. Thomas Heggen. MAF(413), MCLE(3099), MP1(605).
Mr. Sammler's Planet. Saul Bellow. 1971a(208).
Mr. Sponge's Sporting Tour. Robert Smith Surtees. MCLE (3102), MEF(527), MP2(684).
Mr. Weston's Good Wine. T. F. Powys. MCLE(3105), MEF(530), MP2(686).
Mistress of the Inn, The. Carlo Goldoni. MCLE(3114), MD(545), MP2(691), POP(280).
Mistress to an Age. J. Christopher Herold. BM(374), SCL (3061), 1959a(167).
Mit brennender Sorge. Pope Pius XI. CAL(860).
Mithridate. Jean Baptiste Racine. MCLE(3117), MD(548), MP3(667).
Mo Tzu. Mo Ti. WP(31).
Moby Dick. Herman Melville. MAF(416), MCLE(3120), MP1 (609), MPA4(63), PO(251), PON(244), SGAN(13).
Mock Astrologer, The. Pedro Calderón de la Barca. MCLE (3123), MD(551), MP3(669).
Modern Chivalry. Hugh Henry Brackenridge. MAF(419), MCLE(3125), MP2(693).
Modern Comedy, A. John Galsworthy. MCLE(3128), MEF (536), MP1(612).
Modern Instance, A. William Dean Howells. MAF(422), MCLE(3130), MP2(695).
Modern Midas, A. Maurus Jókai. MCLE(3133), MEU(501), MP2(697).
Moll Flanders. Daniel Defoe. MCLE(3137), MEF(538), MP1 (614), PO(52).
Mon Cher Papa. Calude-Anne Lopez. SCL(3065), 1967a(214).
Monadology. Gottfried Wilhelm von Leibniz. WP(601).
Monastic Order in England, The. Dom David Knowles, O. S. B. CAL(870).
Monday Conversations. Charles Augustin Sainte-Beuve. MCLE(3139), MP4(612).
Monk, The. Matthew Gregory Lewis. MCLE(3141), MEF (540), MP2(701).
Monkey. Wu Ch'eng-en. MCLE(3144), MEU(505), MP3(671).
Monologion. Saint Anselm of Canterbury. CHL(194).

Monologion and Proslogion. Saint Anselm of Canterbury. WP(284).
Monroe Doctrine and American Expansionism, 1843-1849, The. Frederick Merk. SCL(3068), 1967a(217).
Monsieur Beaucaire. Booth Tarkington. MAF(425), MCLE (3147), MP1(616), POP(61).
Monsieur d'Olive. George Chapman. MCLE(3149), MD(553), MP3(674).
Monsieur Lecoq. Émile Gaboriau. MCLE(3152), MEU(508), MP2(703).
Monsignor Ronald Knox. Evelyn Waugh. SCL(3073), 1961a (181).
Mont-Oriol. Guy de Maupassant. MCLE(3155), MEU(511), MP1(618).
Mont-Saint-Michel and Chartres. Henry Adams. MCLE (3158), MP4(614).
Month in the Country, A. Ivan Turgenev. MCLE(3161), MD(556), MP2(705).
Moon and Sixpence, The. W. Somerset Maugham. MCLE (3164), MEF(543), MP1(621).
Moonstone, The. Wilkie Collins. MCLE(3167), MEF(546), MP1(623), PO(41), PON(251).
Moral Philosophy. Jacques Maritain. CAL(1094).
Morning and the Evening, The. Joan Williams. SCL(3077), 1962a(209).
Morning in Antibes. John Knowles. SCL(3080), 1963a(148).
Morning Noon and Night. James Gould Cozzens. SCL(3083), 1969a(231).
Morte d'Arthur, Le. Sir Thomas Malory. MCLE(3170), MEF(549), MP1(625).
Morte d'Urban. J. F. Powers. SCL(3087), 1963a(151).
Mosby's Memoirs and Other Stories. Saul Bellow. SCL (3091), 1969a(234).
Moscow. Theodor Plievier. SCL(3096), 1954a(177).
Moss on the North Side. Sylvia Wilkinson. SCL(3099), 1967a(225).
Most Likely to Succeed. John Dos Passos. SCL(3103), 1954a(180).
Mother, The. Grazia Deledda. MCLE(3173), MEU(514), MP2(708).
Mother, The. Maksim Gorki. MCLE(3176), MEU(517), MP3 (676), PO(359).
Mother and Son. Ivy Compton-Burnett. BM(378), MCLE (3179), MP4(617), SCL(3106), 1955a(163).
Mother Courage and Her Children. Bertolt Brecht. TCP (86).
Mother Hubberd's Tale. Edmund Spenser. MCLE(3181),

MP4(619).
Mother Night. Kurt Vonnegut, Jr. SCLs(185).
Mother's Kisses, A. Bruce Jay Friedman. SCL(3109), 1965a(205).
Mountolive. Lawrence Durrell. BM(381), SCL(3112), 1960a (174).
Mourning Becomes Electra. Eugene O'Neill. MCLE(3184), MD(559), MP2(710), SGAP(12), TCP(273).
Moveable Feast, A. Ernest Hemingway. MCLE(3187), MP4 (621), SCL(3116), 1965a(208).
Moviegoer, The. Walker Percy. SCL(3119), 1962a(212).
Moving On. Larry McMurtry. SCLs(188).
Moving Target, The. W. S. Merwin. SCL(3123), 1964a(177).
Mrs. Dalloway. Virginia Woolf. MCLE(3108), MEF(533), MP1(607), PO2(118), SGBN(300).
Mrs. Dane's Defence. Henry Arthur Jones. MCLE(3111), MD(542), MP2(688).
Mrs. Wallop. Peter De Vries. 1971a(213).
Much Abused Letter, A. George Tyrrell. CHL(844).
Much Ado about Nothing. William Shakespeare. MCLE(3190), MD(562), MP2(712).
Mulata, The. Miguel Ángel Asturias. SCL(3128), 1968a(212).
Mulligan Guard Ball, The. Edward Harrigan. DGAP(105).
Murder in the Cathedral. T. S. Eliot. MCLE(3192), MD (564), MP2(714), TCP(133).
Museum Pieces. William Plomer. SCL(3133), 1954a(183).
Music School, The. John Updike. SCL(3136), 1967a(228).
Mutiny on the Bounty. Charles Nordhoff and James Norman Hall. MAF(427), MCLE(3195), MP1(628), SGAN(233).
My Antonia. Willa Cather. MAF(430), MCLE(3198), MP1 (630), SGAN(108).
My Autobiography. Charles Chaplin. SCL(3140), 1965a(211).
My Bones Being Wiser. Vassar Miller. SCLs(191).
My Brother's Keeper. Stanislaus Joyce. SCL(3144), 1959a (171).
My Fair Lady. Alan Jay Lerner. BM(385), SCL(3148), 1957a(182).
My Father's House. Philip B. Kunhardt, Jr. SCLs(194).
My Father's Son. Frank O'Connor. 1970a(215).
My Heart's in the Highlands. William Saroyan. TCP(316).
My Lady Suffolk. Evelyn Read. SCL(3151), 1964a(183).
My Lai 4. Seymour M. Hersh. 1971a(216).
My Land Has a Voice. Jesse Stuart. SCL(3154), 1967a(231).
My Life and Hard Times. James Thurber. MCLE(3201), MN(206), MP3(678).
My Life for My Sheep. Alfred Duggan. SCL(3157), 1955a (166).

My Several Worlds. Pearl S. Buck. SCL(3160), 1954a(186).
Mysteries of Christianity, The. Matthias Joseph Scheeben. CAL(672).
Mysteries of Paris, The. Eugène Sue. MCLE(3204), MEU (520), MP1(632), PON(255).
Mysteries of Udolpho, The. Mrs. Ann Radcliffe. MCLE (3207), MEF(552), MP1(635).
Mysterious Island, The. Jules Verne. MCLE(3210), MEU (523), MP3(681).
Mystery and Manners. Flannery O'Connor. SCLs(196).
Mystery-Bouffe. W. Somerset Maugham. TCP(219).
Mystery of Being, The. Gabriel Marcel. CAL(966), WP (1120).
Mystery of Edwin Drood, The. Charles Dickens. MCLE (3213), MEF(555), MP2(717).
Mystical Body of Christ, The. Pope Pius XII. CAL(886).
Mystical Element of Religion, The. Baron Friedrich John von Hügel. CAL(749).
Mystical Theology, The. Dionysius the Pseudo-Areopagite. CAL(218).
Myth of Sisyphus, The. Albert Camus. MCLE(3216), MP4 (624).

Naked. Luigi Pirandello. TCP(296).
Naked and the Dead, The. Norman Mailer. SCLs(199), SGAN(305).
Naked Ape, The. Desmond Morris. SCL(3163), 1969a(239).
Naked to Mine Enemies. Charles W. Ferguson. SCL(3168), 1959a(174).
Naked Year, The. Boris Pilnyak. MCLE(3219), MEU(526), MP2(719).
Names and Faces of Heroes, The. Reynolds Price. SCL (3172), 1964a(185).
Nana. Émile Zola. MCLE(3222), MEU(529), MP1(638), PO (343), SGEN(197).
Nanga Parbat. Karl M. Herrligkoffer. SCL(3175), 1954a (189).
Napoleon of Notting Hill, The. Gilbert Keith Chesterton. MCLE(3225), MEF(558), MP2(721).
Narrative of Arthur Gordon Pym, The. Edgar Allan Poe. MAF(433), MCLE(3228), MP1(640), MPA5(26).
Narrative of the Life of David Crockett, A. David Crockett. MCLE(3231), MN(209), MP2(724).
Narratives of Exploration and Adventure. John Charles Frémont. SCL(3178), 1957a(185).
Nathan the Wise. Gotthold Ephraim Lessing. MCLE(3234), MD(567), MP3(683), POP(312).

Nationalism: A Religion. Carlton J. H. Hayes. CAL(1091).
Native Son. Richard Wright. MAF(436), MCLE(3236), MP1 (643).
Native Son. Richard Wright and Paul Green. DGAP(344).
Natural and the Supernatural, The. John Wood Oman. CHL (973).
Natural Religion and Christian Theology. Charles E. Raven. CHL(1143).
Natural Theology. William Paley. CHL(641).
Nature and Destiny of Man, The. Reinhold Niebuhr. CHL (1059), WP(1064).
Nature and Mind. Frederick James E. Woodbridge. WP (1021).
Nature, Man and God. William Temple. CHL(999).
Nature, Mind, and Death. Curt John Ducasse. WP(1132).
Nature of Faith, The. Gerhard Ebeling. CHL(1184).
Nature of Passion, The. R. Prawer Jhabvala. SCL(3181), 1958a(166).
Nature of the Atonement, The. John McLeod Campbell. CHL(731).
Nature of Thought, The. Brand Blanshard. WP(1040).
Nature of Truth, The. Harold Henry Joachim. WP(773).
Naughty Marietta. Victor Herbert and Rida Johnson Young. DGAP(173).
Nausea. Jean-Paul Sartre. MCLE(3239), MEU(532), MP2 (726), SGEN(423).
Nazarene, The. Sholem Asch. MAF(439), MCLE(3242), MP1(645).
Near the Ocean. Robert Lowell. SCL(3184), 1967a(234).
Necessities of Life: Poems, 1962-1965. Adrienne Rich. SCL(3187), 1967a(237).
Necessity of Reforming the Church, The. John Calvin. CHL(371).
Nectar in a Sieve. Kamala Markandaya. SCL(3190), 1955a (169).
Nephew, The. James Purdy. SCL(3194), 1961a(185).
Nest of Simple Folk, A. Seán O'Faoláin. MCLE(3245), MEF(561), MP2(728).
Never Call Retreat. Bruce Catton. SCL(3197), 1966a(189).
New and Selected Poems. David Wagoner. 1970a(217).
New Atlantis. Sir Francis Bacon. MCLE(3248), MN(212), MP3(685).
New Class, The. Milovan Djilas. SCL(3202), 1958a(169).
New Criticism, The. John Crowe Ransom. MCLE(3250), MP4(626).
New Critique of Theoretical Thought, A. Herman Dooyeweerd. CHL(1016).

New English Bible, The. Oxford/Cambridge University Presses. SCL(3205), 1962a(215).
New Essays on the Human Understanding. Gottfried Wilhelm von Leibniz. WP(518).
New Faces of 1952. John Murray Anderson and Others. DGAP(382).
New Grub Street, The. George Gissing. MCLE(3253), MEF (564), MP1(647).
New Héloïse, The. Jean Jacques Rousseau. MCLE(3256), MEU(535), MP2(730).
New Life, A. Bernard Malamud. SCL(3207), 1962a(217).
New Men, The. C. P. Snow. BM(388), SCL(3210), 1955a (172).
New Poems: 1965-1969. A. D. Hope. 1971a(220).
New Reformation. Paul Goodman. 1971a(223).
New Science, The. Giovanni Battista Vico. CAL(618), WP (477).
New South Creed, The. Paul M. Gaston. 1971a(225).
New Way to Pay Old Debts, A. Philip Massinger. MCLE (3259), MD(569), MP2(732).
New World, The. Winston S. Churchill. BM(391), SCL (3213), 1957a(188).
New York Idea, The. Langdon Mitchell. DGAP(161).
Newcomes, The. William Makepeace Thackeray. MCLE (3261), MEF(567), MP1(650).
Nez Perce Indians and the Opening of the Northwest, The. Alvin M. Josephy, Jr. SCL(3217), 1966a(193).
Nibelungenlied, The. Unknown. MCLE(3264), MEU(538), MP1(652).
Nicholas and Alexandra. Robert K. Massie. SCL(3220), 1968a(217).
Nicholas Nickleby. Charles Dickens. MCLE(3267), MEF (570), MP2(734).
Nick of the Woods. Robert Montgomery Bird. MAF(442), MCLE(3270), MP2(737).
Nickel Miseries. Ivan Gold. SCLs(202).
Niels Lyhne. Jens Peter Jacobsen. MCLE(3275), MEU(541), MP2(741).
Nigger of the Narcissus, The. Joseph Conrad. MCLE(3278), MEF(573), MP2(743).
Night at Sea, A. Margaret Lane. SCL(3225), 1966a(196).
Night Comes to the Cumberlands. Harry M. Caudill. SCL (3229), 1964a(188).
Night Flight. Antoine de Saint-Exupéry. MCLE(3281), MEU (544), MP3(687).
Night in the Luxembourg, A. Remy de Gourmont. MCLE (3284), MEU(547), MP1(655).

Night Light. Donald Justice. SCL(3233), 1968a(221).
Night of the Hunter, The. Davis Grubb. SCL(3236), 1954a (192).
Night of the Iguana, The. Tennessee Williams. SCL(3239), 1963a(154).
Night of Time, The. René Fülöp-Miller. SCL(3242), 1955a (175).
Night Rider. Robert Penn Warren. MCLE(3286), MP4(628).
Night to Remember, A. Walter Lord. SCL(3245), 1955a (178).
Night Visitor and Other Stories, The. B. Traven. SCL (3249), 1967a(239).
Nightmare Abbey. Thomas Love Peacock. MCLE(3289), MEF(576), MP1(657), PO2(28).
Nightmares of Eminent Persons. Bertrand Russell. SCL (3253), 1955a(181).
Nights and Days. James Merrill. SCL(3257), 1967a(243).
Nightwalker and Other Poems. Thomas Kinsella. SCL(3261), 1969a(243).
Nine Hours to Rama. Stanley Wolpert. SCL(3267), 1963a (157).
900 Days, The. Harrison E. Salisbury. 1970a(221).
Nine Rivers from Jordan. Denis Johnston. SCL(3270), 1955a(184).
1918: The Last Act. Barrie Pitt. SCL(3273), 1964a(191).
Nineteen Eighty-Four. George Orwell. MCLE(3291), MEF (578), MP2(746), PO2(143), SGBN(343).
Ninth Wave, The. Eugene Burdick. SCL(3279), 1957a(191).
95 Poems. E. E. Cummings. BM(395), SCL(3276), 1959a (177).
No Exit. Jean-Paul Sartre. TCP(329).
No Laughing Matter. Angus Wilson. SCL(3283), 1968a(224).
No Mother to Guide Her. Lillian Mortimer. DGAP(152).
No Name. Wilkie Collins. MCLE(3294), MEF(581), MP1 (659).
No Time for Sergeants. Mac Hyman. SCL(3287), 1954a(195).
No Trifling with Love. Alfred de Musset. MCLE(3297), MD(571), MP2(748).
Noah's Ark. Hugh of St. Victor. CAL(304).
Nobody Knows My Name. James Baldwin. BM(398), SCL (3290), 1962a(219).
Nocturne. Frank Swinnerton. MCLE(3300), MEF(584), MP1 (661).
North Toward Home. Willie Morris. SCL(3292), 1968a(227).
Northanger Abbey. Jane Austen. MCLE(3302), MEF(586), MP2(750).
Northern Lass, The. Richard Brome. MCLE(3305), MD

(574), MP3(689).
Northwest Passage. Kenneth Roberts. MCLE(3308), MP4 (631).
Nostromo. Joseph Conrad. MCLE(3311), MEF(589), MP2 (752).
Not by Bread Alone. Vladimir Dudintsev. SCL(3297), 1958a (172).
Not for Publication. Nadine Gordimer. SCL(3301), 1966a (200).
Not Honour More. Joyce Cary. SCL(3305), 1955a(187).
Not This Pig. Philip Levine. SCL(3308), 1969a(248).
Notebook 1967-68. Robert Lowell. 1970a(225).
Notebooks: 1935-1942. Albert Camus. SCL(3312), 1964a (194).
Notebooks: 1942-1951. Albert Camus. SCL(3314), 1966a (203).
Notebooks of Leonardo da Vinci, The. Leonardo da Vinci. MCLE(3314), MP4(633).
Notes from a Bottle Found on the Beach at Carmel. Evan S. Connell, Jr. MCLE(3317), MP4(636), SCL(3317), 1964a(196).
Notes on the State of Virginia. Thomas Jefferson. MCLE (3319), MN(214), MP3(692).
Nothing Ever Breaks Except the Heart. Kay Boyle. SCL (3320), 1967a(246).
Nothing Like the Sun. Anthony Burgess. SCL(3323), 1965a (215).
Nothing New Under the Sun. Riccardo Bacchelli. SCL(3326), 1955a(190).
Novel, a Novella and Four Stories, A. Andrew Lytle. SCL (3330), 1959a(179).
Novice, The. Mikhail Yuievich Lermontov. MCLE(3322), MP4(637).
Novum organum. Sir Francis Bacon. WP(373).
Nowhere but Light: Poems 1964-1969. Ben Belitt. 1971a (228).
Nunquam. Lawrence Durrell. 1971a(232).
Nun's Story, The. Kathryn Hulme. SCL(3334), 1957a(195).

O Lovely England. Walter De la Mare. SCL(3337), 1957a (197).
O Pioneers! Willa Cather. MAF(447), MCLE(3324), MP1 (663).
O Taste and See. Denise Levertov. SCL(3340), 1965a(217).
O the Chimneys. Nelly Sachs. SCL(3342), 1968a(231).
O to Be a Dragon. Marianne Moore. BM(401), SCL(3345), 1960a(177).

Oblomov. Ivan Alexandrovich Goncharov. MCLE(3326), MEU(549), MP2(755), SGEN(121).
Occurrences of the Times; or, The Transactions of Four Days. Unknown. DGAP(20).
Octavius. Minucius Felix. CAL(50), CHL(51).
Octopus, The. Frank Norris. SGAN(85).
Octoroon, The. Boucicault. DGAP(85).
Ode to Aphrodite. Sappho. MCLE(3329), MP(189), MP3 (694).
Odyssey, The. Homer. MCLE(3331), MP(191), MP1(665), PON(264).
Odyssey: A Modern Sequel, The. Nikos Kazantzakis. SCLs(205).
Odyssey of a Friend. Whittaker Chambers. 1971a(235).
Oedipus at Colonus. Sophocles. MCLE(3334), MD(577), MP2(757).
Oedipus Rex, see Oedipus Tyrannus.
Oedipus the King, see Oedipus Tyrannus.
Oedipus Tyrannus. Sophocles. MCLE(3336), MD(579), MP1 (668), POP(379).
Of Being Numerous. George Oppen. SCL(3349), 1969a(252).
Of Civil Government: The Second Treatise. John Locke. WP(436).
Of Conscience, Its Power and Cases. William Ames. CHL (445).
Of Human Bondage. W. Somerset Maugham. MCLE(3338), MEF(592), MP1(670), PO2(105), PON(267), SGBN(270).
Of Learned Ignorance. Nicholas of Cusa (Nicholas Cusanus). CAL(482), CHL(312), WP(343).
Of Mice and Men. John Steinbeck. DGAP(300), MAF(449), MCLE(3341), MP1(672), PO2(272), SGAP(160).
Of Plimouth Plantation. William Bradford. MCLE(3343), MP4(639).
Of the Farm. John Updike. SCL(3353), 1966a(206).
Of Thee I Sing. George S. Kaufman, Morrie Ryskind, Ira and George Gershwin. DGAP(253), SGAP(53).
Of Time and the River. Thomas Wolfe. MAF(451), MCLE (3346), MP1(674).
Of Whales and Men. Robert B. Robertson. SCL(3356), 1954a(198).
Office Politics. Wilfrid Sheed. SCL(3359), 1967a(248).
Officers and Gentlemen. Evelyn Waugh. BM(405), SCL (3363), 1955a(193).
Oklahoma. Richard Rodgers and Oscar Hammerstein. DGAP (353).
Old and the Young, The. Luigi Pirandello. MCLE(3349), MEU(552), MP1(676).

Old Bachelor, The. William Congreve. MCLE(3352), MD (581), MP2(759).
"Old Bruin." Samuel Eliot Morison. SCL(3366), 1968a(234).
Old Calabria. Norman Douglas. MCLE(3355), MP4(641).
Old Curiosity Shop, The. Charles Dickens. MCLE(3358), MEF(595), MP2(761).
Old Fortunatus. Thomas Dekker. MCLE(3361), MD(584), MP3(696).
Old Glory, The. Robert Lowell. SCL(3369), 1966a(209).
Old Homestead, The. Denman Thompson and George W. Ryer. DGAP(112), POP(68).
Old Maid, The. Edith Wharton. MAF(454), MCLE(3364), MP1(679).
Old Man and the Sea, The. Ernest Hemingway. MAF(457), MCLE(3367), MP2(764), PO2(257), SGAN(171).
Old Men at the Zoo, The. Angus Wilson. SCL(3373), 1962a (222).
Old Mortality. Katherine Anne Porter. MAF(460), MCLE (3370), MEF(598), MP2(766).
Old Mortality. Sir Walter Scott. MCLE(3373), MP1(681).
Old Red and Other Stories. Caroline Gordon. SCL(3376), 1964a(198).
Old Regime in Canada, The. Francis Parkman. MCLE (3376), MP4(643).
Old St. Paul's. William Harrison Ainsworth. MCLE(3379), MEF(601), MP2(768).
Old Soldiers Never Die. Wolf Mankowitz. SCL(3378), 1957a (200).
Old Wives' Tale, The. Arnold Bennett. MCLE(3382), MD (587), MEF(604), MP1(684), PO2(102), PON(274), SGBN(250).
Old Wives' Tale, The. George Peele. MCLE(3385), MP2 (771).
Old Woman, the Wife, and the Archer, The. Donald Keene, Ed. SCL(3381), 1962a(224).
Oldtown Folks. Harriet Beecher Stowe. MAF(463), MCLE (3388), MP2(773).
Oliver Cromwell's Letters and Speeches. Oliver Cromwell. CHL(493).
Oliver Twist. Charles Dickens. MCLE(3392), MEF(607), MP1(686), PO(63), PON(279).
Olympio. André Maurois. SCL(3384), 1957a(203).
Omensetter's Luck. William H. Gass. SCLs(209).
Omoo. Herman Melville. MAF(467), MCLE(3396), MP1 (689), MPA4(69).
On a Lonesome Porch. Ovid Williams Pierce. SCL(3387), 1961a(188).

On Being and Essence. Saint Thomas Aquinas. CAL(364).
On Borrowed Time. Leonard Mosley. 1970a(228).
On Ecclesiastical Unity. John Gerson. CHL(299).
On Education. Juan Luis Vives. CAL(519).
On First Principles. Origen. CAL(65), CHL(57).
On Free Choice. Saint Thomas Aquinas. CAL(406).
On Heroes, Hero-Worship and the Heroic in History. Thomas Carlyle. MCLE(3399), MP4(646).
On His Own Ignorance. Francisco Petrarch. CAL(469).
On Kingship. Saint Thomas Aquinas. CAL(391).
On Liberty. John Stuart Mill. MCLE(3401), MN(217), MP3 (698).
On Poetry and Poets. T. S. Eliot. BM(408), SCL(3391), 1958a(175).
On Religion: Speeches to Its Cultured Despisers. Friedrich Schleiermacher. CHL(637).
On Revolution. Hannah Arendt. SCL(3393), 1964a(200).
On Spiritual Creatures. Saint Thomas Aquinas. CAL(402).
On the Adaptation of External Nature to the Moral and Intellectual Constitution of Man. Thomas Chalmers. CHL(668).
On the Beach. Nevil Shute. SCL(3396), 1958a(177).
On the Christian Faith. Saint Ambrose. CAL(112).
On the Divine Names. Dionysius the Pseudo-Areopagite. CAL(215).
On the Division of Nature. Johannes Scotus Erigena. WP (273).
On the Duties of the Clergy. Saint Ambrose. CAL(145), CHL(121).
On the Education of a Gentleman. Pier Paolo Vergerio. CAL(479).
On the Errors of the Trinity. Michael Servetus. CHL(351).
On the Eternal in Man. Max Scheler. CHL(904).
On the Genesis of the Species. St. George Jackson Mivart. CAL(682).
On the Holy Trinity. Saint Anicius Manlius Severinus Boethius. CHL(169).
On the Law of War and Peace. Hugo Grotius. MCLE(3404), MP4(648).
On the Necessity of Loving God. Saint Bernard. CAL(311).
On the Origin of Species. Charles Darwin. MCLE(3407), MN(220), MP3(700).
On the Power of God. Saint Thomas Aquinas. CAL(394).
On the Reduction of the Arts to Theology. Saint Bonaventure. WP(305).
On the Resurrection of the Dead. Athenagoras. CAL(30).
On the Road. Jack Kerouac. SCL(3398), 1958a(179).

On the Sublime. Unknown, long attributed to Longinus. MCLE(3409), MP4(650).
On the Soul. Saint Thomas Aquinas. CAL(409).
On the Soul. Aristotle. WP(147).
On the Steps of Humility and Pride. Saint Bernard. CAL (296).
On the Theology of Death. Karl Rahner. CAL(1047).
On the Trinity. Saint Augustine. CHL(134).
On the Trinity. Saint Hilary of Poitiers. CHL(106).
On the Unity of the Catholic Church. Saint Cyprian of Carthage. CAL(75), CHL(73).
On the Virtues in General. Saint Thomas Aquinas. CAL (413).
Once and Future King, The. T. H. White. BM(410), MCLE (3412), MP4(653), SCL(3401), 1959a(183).
Once to Sinai. H. F. M. Prescott. SCL(3406), 1959a(187).
Ondine. Jean Giraudoux. SCL(3409), TCP(167), 1954a(201).
One Day. Wright Morris. SCL(3412), 1966a(213).
One Day in the Life of Ivan Denisovich. Alexander I. Solzhenitsyn. SCL(3418), 1964a(203).
One Fat Englishman. Kingsley Amis. SCL(3421), 1965a (219).
One Flew over the Cuckoo's Nest. Ken Kesey. SCL(3423), 1963a(160).
One Hundred Years of Solitude. Gabriel Garcia Marquez. 1971a(240).
One in Twenty. Bryan Magee. SCL(3426), 1967a(252).
"...one-third of a nation..." Arthur Arent. DGAP(309), SGAP(178).
One to Count Cadence. James Crumley. 1970a(231).
O'Neill. Arthur and Barbara Gelb. BM(415), SCL(3429), 1963a(162).
Only Child, An. Frank O'Connor. SCL(3432), 1962a(227).
Only in America. Harry Golden. SCL(3435), 1959a(190).
Open Letter to the Christian Nobility of the German Nation, An. Martin Luther. CHL(330).
Openings. Wendell Berry. SCL(3438), 1969a(255).
Operators, The. Frank Gibney. SCL(3441), 1961a(191).
Optimistic Tragedy, The. Vsevolod Vishnevski. TCP(421).
Opus majus. Roger Bacon. CAL(398).
Opus oxoniense. John Duns Scotus. CAL(427).
Opus posthumous. Wallace Stevens. SCL(3444), 1958a(182).
Oration and Panegyric Addressed to Origen, The. Saint Gregory Thaumaturgus. CAL(69).
Oration on the Dignity of Man. Giovanni Pico della Mirandola. CAL(487), MCLE(3416), MP4(655).
Orchard Keeper, The. Cormac McCarthy. SCL(3448), 1966a

(218).
Orde Wingate. Christopher Sykes. SCL(3452), 1960a(181).
Ordeal of Gilbert Pinfold, The. Evelyn Waugh. MCLE (3418), MP4(657).
Ordeal of Richard Feverel, The. George Meredith. MCLE (3421), MEF(611), MP1(692), PO(129), SGBN(139).
Ordinatio: Oxford Commentary on the Sentences of Peter Lombard. John Duns Scotus. CHL(251).
Ordways, The. William Humphrey. SCL(3456), 1966a(221).
Oregon Trail, The. Francis Parkman. MCLE(3425), MN (222), MP1(695).
Orfeo. Politian. MCLE(3428), MD(590), MP3(702).
Organization Man, The. William H. Whyte, Jr. SCL(3459), 1958a(185).
Organon. Aristotle. WP(137).
Origin of the Brunists, The. Robert Coover. SCL(3462), 1967a(255).
Origin of the Jesuits, The. James Brodrick, S.J. CAL (868).
Orlando. Virginia Woolf. MCLE(3430), MEF(615), MP1(698).
Orlando Furioso. Ludovico Ariosto. MCLE(3433), MP(194), MP2(776).
Orlando Innamorato. Matteo Maria Boiardo. MCLE(3437), MP(198), MP3(703).
Orley Farm. Anthony Trollope. MCLE(3441), MEF(618), MP2(780).
Ornifle. Jean Anouilh. TCP(29).
Oroonoko. Mrs. Aphra Behn. MCLE(3445), MEF(622), MP2 (783).
Orphan, The. Thomas Otway. MCLE(3448), MD(592), MP3 (707).
Orpheus. Jean Cocteau. TCP(116).
Orpheus and Eurydice. Folk tradition. MCLE(3450), MEU (555), MP1(700).
Orpheus Descending with Battle of Angels. Tennessee Williams. SCL(3466), 1959a(193).
Orthodoxy. Gilbert Keith Chesterton. CAL(744).
Othello. William Shakespeare. MCLE(3452), MD(594), MP1 (701).
Other One, The. Sidonie Gabrielle Claudine Colette. MCLE (3455), MEU(557), MP3(709).
Our Calling. Einar Billing. CHL(857).
Our Experience of God. H. D. Lewis. CHL(1189).
Our Knowledge of the External World. Bertrand Russell. WP(799).
Our Man in Havana. Graham Greene. SCL(3469), 1959a(196).
Our Mutual Friend. Charles Dickens. MCLE(3458), MEF

(625), MP2(785), PON(282).
Our Nuclear Future. Edward Teller and Albert L. Latter. SCL(3472), 1959a(198).
Our Samoan Adventure. Fanny and Robert Louis Stevenson. SCL(3475), 1955a(196).
Our Town. Thornton Wilder. DGAP(313), MCLE(3461), MD (597), MP1(704), SGAP(130), TCP(436).
Our Village. Mary Russell Mitford. MCLE(3464), MEF (628), MP2(788).
Ourselves to Know. John O'Hara. SCL(3478), 1961a(195).
Out of My Life and Thought. Albert Schweitzer. MCLE (3467), MP4(660).
Outcasts, The. Stephen Becker. SCL(3481), 1968a(237).
Outer Dark. Cormac McCarthy. SCL(3484), 1969a(258).
Outlines of Pyrrhonism. Sextus Empiricus. WP(234).
Outsider, The. Colin Wilson. SCL(3487), 1957a(206).
Outward Bound. Sutton Vane. POP(94).
Overcoat, The. Nikolai V. Gogol. MCLE(3470), MEU(560), MP2(790).
Ox-Bow Incident, The. Walter Van Tilburg Clark. MAF (470), MCLE(3473), MP1(706), SGAN(275).
Oysters of Locmariaquer, The. Eleanor Clark. SCLs(213).

P. G. T. Beauregard. T. Harry Williams. BM(428), SCL (3553), 1955a(199).
P. S. Wilkinson. C. D. B. Bryan. SCLs(231).
Pacem in terris. Pope John XXIII. CAL(1131).
Painted Bird, The. Jerzy Kosinski. SCL(3491), 1966a(224).
Palace, The. Claude Simon. SCL(3494), 1964a(206).
Pale Fire. Vladimir Nabokov. BM(418), MCLE(3476), MP4 (662), SCL(3497), 1963a(165).
Pale Horse, Pale Rider. Katherine Anne Porter. MCLE (3479), MP4(665).
Palm-Wine Drinkard, The. Amos Tutuola. MCLE(3483), MP4(668).
Pamela. Samuel Richardson. MCLE(3486), MEF(631), MP1 (708), PO2(5).
Panarion. Saint Epiphanius of Salamis. CHL(111).
Pandora's Box. Frank Wedekind. TCP(428).
Papa Hemingway. A. E. Hotchner. SCL(3501), 1967a(259).
Paper Horse, A. Robert Watson. SCL(3504), 1963a(168).
Papers of Benjamin Franklin, The. Benjamin Franklin. SCL(3507), 1960a(184).
Papillon. Henri Charrière. 1971a(245).
Parables of the Kingdom, The. Charles Harold Dodd. CHL (1012).
Paraclesis, The. Desiderius Erasmus. CAL(505).

Parade's End. Ford Madox Ford. MCLE(3489), MEF(634), MP2(792).
Paradise Lost. John Milton. CHL(511), MCLE(3493), MP (202), MP1(711).
Paradise Reclaimed. Halldór Laxness. SCL(3509), 1963a (171).
Paradise Regained. John Milton. MCLE(3495), MP(204), MP3(711).
Parallel Lives. Plutarch. MCLE(3498), MN(225), MP3(713).
Parish Life in Mediaeval England. Francis Neil Aidan Cardinal Gasquet. CAL(736).
Parliament of Fowls, The. Geoffrey Chaucer. MCLE(3501), MP(207), MP3(716).
Parmenides. Plato. WP(106).
Parnassus Corner. W. S. Tryon. SCL(3513), 1964a(208).
Part of the Truth: An Autobiography. Granville Hicks. SCL(3516), 1966a(227).
Particular Place, A. Dabney Stuart. 1970a(234).
Partisans. Peter Matthiessen. SCLs(216).
Parzival. Wolfram von Eschenbach. MCLE(3503), MP(209), MP2(795).
Passage to India, A. E. M. Forster. MCLE(3506), MEF (638), MP1(713), PO2(147), SGBN(292).
Passing of the Third Floor Back, The. Jerome K. Jerome. POP(113).
Passion Flower, The. Jacinto Benavente. MCLE(3509), MD(600), MP3(718).
Passions of the Soul, The. René Descartes. MCLE(3512), MP4(670).
Paston Letters, The. Paston Family. MCLE(3515), MP4 (673).
Pastoral Care. Saint Gregory the Great. CAL(237), CHL (176).
Pastors and Masters. Ivy Compton-Burnett. MCLE(3518), MP4(675).
Paterson. William Carlos Williams. MCLE(3521), MP(212), MP3(720).
Paterson Five. William Carlos Williams. SCL(3520), 1959a (201).
Path to Rome, The. Hilaire Belloc. CAL(734), MCLE (3523), MN(228), MP3(722).
Pathfinder, The. James Fenimore Cooper. MAF(473), MCLE(3526), MP1(715), MPA1(56).
Patience. W. S. Gilbert and Arthur Sullivan. MCLE(3528), MD(603), MP2(798).
Patrician, The. John Galsworthy. MCLE(3530), MEF(641), MP3(724).

Patriot, The. Antonio Fogazzaro. MCLE(3532), MEU(563), MP2(800).
Patriotic Gore. Edmund Wilson. BM(422), SCL(3523), 1963a(174).
Patterns. Rod Serling. DGAP(407).
Paul and Virginia. Bernardin de Saint-Pierre. PO(326), PON(286).
Paul Bunyan. James Stevens. MAF(475), MCLE(3535), MP1 (717).
Pax Britannica. James Morris. SCL(3526), 1969a(260).
Peace, The. Aristophanes. MCLE(3538), MD(605), MP3 (726).
Peace of Soul. Fulton J. Sheen. CAL(958).
Peacemakers, The. Richard B. Morris. SCL(3530), 1966a (230).
Peasants, The. Ladislas Reymont. MCLE(3540), MEU(566), MP1(720).
Peder Victorious. O. E. Rölvaag. MAF(478), MCLE(3543), MP2(802).
Pedro Martínez. Oscar Lewis. SCL(3534), 1965a(221).
Pedro Páramo. Juan Rulfo. BM(425), MCLE(3546), MP4 (678), SCL(3537), 1960a(186).
Pedro Sánchez. José María de Pereda. MCLE(3549), MEU (569), MP3(728).
Peer Gynt. Henrik Ibsen. MCLE(3551), MD(607), MP1(722), POP(325).
Peg O' My Heart. J. Hartley Manners. DGAP(186).
Peg Woffington. Charles Reade. MCLE(3553), MEF(643), MP1(724), PON(291).
Peking and Moscow. Klaus Mehnert. SCL(3540), 1964a(211).
Pelle the Conqueror. Martin Andersen Nexö. MCLE(3555), MEU(571), MP3(730), SGEN(304).
Pélléas and Mélisande. Maurice Maeterlinck. MCLE(3558), MD(609), MP2(806), POP(273).
Peñas arriba. José María de Pereda. MCLE(3561), MEU (574), MP3(730).
Pendennis. William Makepeace Thackeray. MCLE(3563), MEF(645), MP1(726), PO2(39), PON(297).
Penguin Island. Anatole France. MCLE(3566), MEU(576), MP1(729), SGEN(219).
Pensées. Blaise Pascal. CHL(515), MCLE(3569), MN(231), MP3(732), WP(410).
People of Juvik, The. Olav Duun. MCLE(3572), MEU(579), MP2(809).
People of the Book. David Stacton. SCL(3544), 1966a(233).
People, Yes, The. Carl Sandburg. MCLE(3577), MP(214), MP3(734).

Pepita Jimenez. Juan Valera. MCLE(3579), MEU(584), MP2(813).
Perception. Henry Habberley Price. WP(968).
Père Goriot. Honoré de Balzac. PO(268), SGEN(78).
Peregrine Pickle. Tobias Smollett. MCLE(3582), MEF(648), MP1(731).
Pericles on 31st Street. Harry Mark Petrakis. SCLs(219).
Pericles, Prince of Tyre. William Shakespeare. MCLE (3586), MD(612), MP2(816).
Permanent Errors. Reynolds Price. 1971a(250).
Persecution and Assassination of Jean-Paul Marat, The. Peter Weiss. SCLs(222).
Persian Letters. Charles de Montesquieu. MCLE(3589), MN(234), MP3(736).
Persians, The. Aeschylus. MCLE(3591), MD(615), MP2 (818).
Person and Place of Jesus Christ, The. Peter Taylor Forsyth. CHL(861).
Personae. Ezra Pound. MCLE(3593), MP4(681).
Personal Anthology, A. Jorge Luis Borges. SCL(3547), 1967a(262).
Personal Realism. James Bissett Pratt. WP(1016).
Personalism. Borden Parker Bowne. CHL(851).
Persuasion. Jane Austen. MCLE(3596), MEF(652), MP1 (734).
Peter Ibbetson. George Du Maurier. MCLE(3599), MEF (655), MP1(736), PO(75).
Peter Pan. James M. Barrie. MCLE(3602), MD(617), MP2 (820), POP(126), TCP(47).
Peter Simple. Frederick Marryat. MCLE(3605), MEF(658), MP2(822).
Peter Whiffle. Carl Van Vechten. MAF(481), MCLE(3608), MP1(739).
Petrified Forest, The. Robert E. Sherwood. DGAP(269), POP(15), TCP(369).
Petty Demon, The. Fyodor Sologub. SCL(3550), 1963a(177).
Phaedo. Plato. WP(81).
Phaèdra (Phedre). Jean Baptiste Racine. MCLE(3611), MD (620), MP1(741), POP(265).
Phaedrus. Plato. WP(95).
Phèdre, see Phaèdra.
Phenomenology of Spirit, The. Georg Wilhelm Friedrich Hegel. CHL(645).
Phenomenon of Man, The. Pierre Teilhard de Chardin, S.J. CAL(1017), MCLE(3613), MP4(683), SCL(3557), 1960a (189).
Philaster. Francis Beaumont and John Fletcher. MCLE

(3616), MD(622), MP2(825).
Philebus. Plato. WP(120).
Philippics, The. Demosthenes. MCLE(3619), MN(236), MP3(738).
Philoctetes. Sophocles. MCLE(3622), MD(625), MP3(741).
Philosopher and Theology, The. Étienne Gilson. CAL(1088).
Philosopher or Dog? Joaquim Maria Machado de Assis. MCLE(3625), MP4(686), SCL(3561), 1954a(204).
Philosophiae naturalis principia mathematica. Sir Isaac Newton. MCLE(3628), MN(239), MP3(743).
Philosophical Bases of Theism, The. George Dawes Hicks. CHL(1031).
Philosophical Fragments. Søren Kierkegaard. WP(619).
Philosophical Investigations. Ludwig Wittgenstein. WP(1160).
Philosophical Studies. George Edward Moore. WP(842).
Philosophical Theology. Frederick Robert Tennant. CHL (933).
Philosophical Treatises and Moral Reflections of Seneca. Lucius Annaeus Seneca. MCLE(3631), MP4(688).
Philosophy and Logical Syntax. Rudolf Carnap. WP(997).
Philosophy and Psycho-Analysis. John Wisdom. WP(1153).
Philosophy of Art. Hippolyte Taine. MCLE(3635), MN(242), MP3(745).
Philosophy of Democratic Government. Yves René Marie Simon. CAL(982).
Philosophy of History, The. Georg Wilhelm Friedrich Hegel. WP(593).
Philosophy of Physical Realism, The. Roy Wood Sellars. WP(980).
Philosophy of Religion, A. Edgar Sheffield Brightman. CHL(1047).
Philosophy of Religion, The. Harald Höffding. CHL(828).
Philosophy of Symbolic Forms, The. Ernst Cassirer. WP (850).
Philosophy of the Unconscious, The. Eduard von Hartmann. WP(660).
Phineas Finn. Anthony Trollope. MCLE(3637), MEF(661), MP3(748).
Phineas Redux. Anthony Trollope. MCLE(3640), MEF(664), MP3(750).
Phoenician Women, The. Euripides. MCLE(3643), MD(628), MP3(753).
Phormio. Terence. MCLE(3645), MD(630), MP2(827).
Physical Basis of Life, The. Thomas Henry Huxley. MCLE (3649), MN(245), MP3(754).
Physicists. Friedrich Dürrenmatt. TCP(128).
Physics. Aristotle. WP(143).

Pickett's Charge. George R. Stewart. SCL(3564), 1960a (192).
Pickwick Papers. Charles Dickens. MCLE(3652), MEF(667), MP1(743), PO(66), PON(301), SGBN(78).
Picnic. William Inge. DGAP(386).
Picnic at Sakkara, The. P. H. Newby. SCL(3567), 1955a (202).
Picture of Dorian Gray, The. Oscar Wilde. MCLE(3656), MEF(671), MP1(746), PO(181), SGBN(193).
Pictures from an Institution. Randall Jarrell. SCL(3570), 1954a(207).
Pictures from Brueghel. William Carlos Williams. BM(432), SCL(3573), 1963a(179).
Pictures of Fidelman. Bernard Malamud. 1970a(238).
Pierre. Herman Melville. MAF(484), MCLE(3659), MP2 (829), MPA4(74).
Pigeon Feathers. John Updike. SCL(3577), 1963a(182).
Pilgrim Hawk, The. Glenway Westcott. MCLE(3662), MP4 (691), SCL(3581), 1968a(240).
Pilgrimage. Dorothy M. Richardson. MCLE(3665), MEF (674), MP3(757).
Pilgrimage of Charlemagne, The. Unknown. MCLE(3669), MP(216), MP3(760).
Pilgrim's Progress, The. John Bunyan. CHL(530), MCLE (3672), MEF(678), MP1(748), PO(35), PON(304), SGBN(1).
Pillars of Society, The. Henrik Ibsen. MCLE(3675), MD (633), MP2(831).
Pilot, The. James Fenimore Cooper. MAF(487), MCLE (3678), MP1(750), MPA1(60), PON(310).
Ping-Pong. Arthur Adamov. MCLE(3681), MP4(694).
Pioneers, The. James Fenimore Cooper. MAF(490), MCLE (3684), MP1(753), MPA1(66).
Pirates of Penzance, The. W. S. Gilbert and Arthur Sullivan. MCLE(3687), MD(636), MP2(834).
Pit, The. Frank Norris. MAF(493), MCLE(3689), MP1(756), MPA4(107).
Place on Earth, A. Wendell Berry. SCL(3586), 1968a(244).
Plague, The. Albert Camus. MCLE(3692), MEU(587), MP2 (836), PO2(365).
Plaideurs, Les. Jean Baptiste Racine. MCLE(3695), MD (638), MP3(763).
Plain Account of Christian Perfection, A. John Wesley. CHL(608).
Plain Dealer, The. William Wycherley. MCLE(3697), MD (640), MP2(838).
Plan of Salvation, The. Benjamin Warfield. CHL(890).

Plantation Boy. José Lins do Rêgo. MCLE(3700), MP4(696), SCL(3590), 1967a(264).
Platero and I. Juan Ramón Jiménez. BM(436), MCLE(3704), MEU(590), MP3(764), SCL(3595), 1958a(188).
Play It as It Lays. Joan Didion. 1971a(253).
Playboy of the Western World, The. John Millington Synge. MCLE(3707), MD(643), MP1(758), POP(231), TCP(412).
Player King, The. Earl Rovit. SCL(3598), 1966a(236).
Plays of Cocteau, The. Jean Cocteau. MCLE(3709), MP4 (699).
Plea for the Christians, The. Athenagoras. CAL(27).
Pledge, The. Friedrich Düerrenmatt. SCL(3600), 1960a(195).
Ploesti. James Dugan and Carroll Stewart. SCL(3604), 1963a(186).
Plough and the Stars, The. Sean O'Casey. MCLE(3712), MD(645), MP2(840), TCP(244).
Plowshare in Heaven. Jesse Stuart. SCL(3607), 1959a(204).
Plumed Serpent, The. D. H. Lawrence. MCLE(3715), MEF (681), MP2(843).
Plutus. Aristophanes. MCLE(3718), MD(648), MP2(845).
Pnin. Vladimir Nabokov. SCL(3611), 1958a(191).
Poem of the Cid. Unknown. MCLE(3720), MP(219), MP3 (766).
Poems. Barbara Guest. SCL(3614), 1963a(189).
Poems. A. D. Hope. SCL(3617), 1963a(191).
Poems. C. S. Lewis. SCL(3620), 1966a(238).
Poems. Boris Pasternak. SCL(3624), 1960a(199).
Poems. Alfred, Lord Tennyson. MCLE(3723), MP4(702).
Poems and Ballads. Algernon Charles Swinburne. MCLE (3726), MP4(704).
Poems, Chiefly in the Scottish Dialect. Robert Burns. MCLE(3729), MP(222), MP3(769).
Poems: 1951-1961. Robert Hazel. BM(442), SCL(3628), 1962a(229).
Poems: 1957-1967. James Dickey. SCL(3631), 1968a(247).
Poems: 1923-1954. E. E. Cummings. BM(439), SCL (3635), 1954a(210).
Poems of Alice Meynell, The. Alice Meynell. CAL(775).
Poems of Emily Dickinson, The. Emily Dickinson. BM (445), SCL(3638), 1955a(205).
Poems of Ernest Dowson, The. Ernest Christopher Dowson. CAL(720).
Poems of Gerard Manley Hopkins, The. Gerard Manley Hopkins. CAL(760).
Poems 2. Alan Dugan. SCLs(225).
Poems Written in Early Youth. T. S. Eliot. SCL(3641), 1967a(268).

Poetical Works of Edward Taylor, The. Edward Taylor. MCLE(3732), MP(225), MP3(771).
Poetics. Aristotle. MCLE(3735), MN(248), MP3(774), WP (174).
Poetry and Truth from My Own Life. Johann Wolfgang von Goethe. MCLE(3738), MP4(706).
Poetry of "A. E.," The. George William Russell. MCLE (3741), MP4(709).
Poetry of Aiken, The. Conrad Aiken. MCLE(3744), MP4 (711).
Poetry of Anacreon, The. Anacreon. MCLE(3747), MP4 (714).
Poetry of André Breton, The. André Breton. MCLE(3748), MP4(715).
Poetry of Apollinaire, The. Guillaume Apollinaire. MCLE (3751), MP4(718).
Poetry of Arnold, The. Matthew Arnold. MCLE(3754), MP4 (720).
Poetry of Auden, The. W. H. Auden. MCLE(3757), MP(228), MP3(777).
Poetry of Barker, The. George Barker. MCLE(3760), MP4 (723).
Poetry of Bashô, The. Matsuo Bashô. MCLE(3762), MP (231), MP3(779).
Poetry of Beddoes, The. Thomas Lovell Beddoes. MCLE (3765), MP4(725).
Poetry of Betjeman, The. John Betjeman. MCLE(3768), MP4(727).
Poetry of Bion, The. Bion. MCLE(3771), MP4(729).
Poetry of Blake, The. William Blake. MCLE(3773), MP (234), MP3(781).
Poetry of Blok, The. Aleksandr Blok. MCLE(3776), MP4 (731).
Poetry of Blunden, The. Edmund Charles Blunden. MCLE (3779), MP4(733).
Poetry of Booth, The. Philip Booth. MCLE(3781), MP4 (735).
Poetry of Brooke, The. Rupert Brooke. MCLE(3784), MP4 (737).
Poetry of Bryant, The. William Cullen Bryant. MCLE(3787), MP(237), MP3(784), MPA1(28).
Poetry of Campion, The. Thomas Campion. MCLE(3790), MP4(740).
Poetry of Carducci, The. Giosuè Carducci. MCLE(3793), MP(240), MP3(787).
Poetry of Carew, The. Thomas Carew. MCLE(3796), MP4 (743).

Poetry of Cavafy, The. Constantine P. Cavafy. MCLE (3800), MP4(746).
Poetry of Chatterton, The. Thomas Chatterton. MCLE (3803), MP4(748).
Poetry of Christina Rossetti, The. Christina Rossetti. MCLE(3806), MP(243), MP3(789).
Poetry of Clare, The. John Clare. MCLE(3809), MP4(751).
Poetry of Claudel, The. Paul Claudel. MCLE(3812), MP4 (754).
Poetry of Coleridge, The. Samuel Taylor Coleridge. MCLE (3815), MP4(756).
Poetry of Collins, The. William Collins. MCLE(3819), MP4(760).
Poetry of Corbière, The. Tristan Corbière. MCLE(3822), MP4(763).
Poetry of Cowper, The. William Cowper. MCLE(3826), MP4(766).
Poetry of Crashaw, The. Richard Crashaw. MCLE(3829), MP4(768).
Poetry of Cummings, The. E. E. Cummings. MCLE(3833), MP4(772).
Poetry of Daniel, The. Samuel Daniel. MCLE(3835), MP4 (774).
Poetry of Dante Gabriel Rossetti, The. Dante Gabriel Rossetti. MCLE(3839), MP(246), MP3(791).
Poetry of Dickey, The. James Dickey. MCLE(3842), MP4 (778).
Poetry of Donne, The. John Donne. MCLE(3846), MP(249), MP3(793).
Poetry of Dowson, The. Ernest Christopher Dowson. MCLE (3849), MP4(781).
Poetry of Drayton, The. Michael Drayton. MCLE(3852), MP(252), MP3(796).
Poetry of Dryden, The. John Dryden. MCLE(3855), MP4 (784).
Poetry of Du Bellay, The. Joachim Du Bellay. MCLE (3860), MP4(788).
Poetry of Eberhart, The. Richard Eberhart. MCLE(3864), MP4(792).
Poetry of Edith Sitwell, The. Edith Sitwell. MCLE(3866), MP4(793).
Poetry of Eichendorff, The. Josef von Eichendorff. MCLE (3869), MP4(795).
Poetry of Elinor Wylie, The. Elinor Wylie. MCLE(3871), MP4(798).
Poetry of Emerson, The. Ralph Waldo Emerson. MCLE (3874), MP4(800), MPA1(116).

Poetry of Emily Brontë, The. Emily Brontë. MCLE(3878), MP4(803).
Poetry of Emily Dickinson, The. Emily Dickinson. MCLE (3881), MP(255), MP3(798), MPA1(99).
Poetry of Esenin, The. Sergei Esenin. MCLE(3884), MP4 (806).
Poetry of Flecker, The. James Elroy Flecker. MCLE (3887), MP4(808).
Poetry of Freneau, The. Philip Freneau. MCLE(3889), MP(258), MP3(801).
Poetry of Frost, The. Robert Frost. MCLE(3892), MP (261), MP3(803).
Poetry of Gabriela Mistral, The. Gabriela Mistral. MCLE (3895), MP4(810).
Poetry of Garrett, The. George Garrett. MCLE(3898), MP4(812).
Poetry of Gascoigne, The. George Gascoigne. MCLE(3901), MP4(814).
Poetry of Gautier, The. Théophile Gautier. MCLE(3907), MP4(820).
Poetry of Goldsmith, The. Oliver Goldsmith. MCLE(3910), MP4(823).
Poetry of Graves, The. Robert Graves. MCLE(3914), MP4 (826).
Poetry of Gray, The. Thomas Gray. MCLE(3917), MP(264), MP3(805).
Poetry of H. D., The. Hilda Doolittle. MCLE(3925), MP4 (834).
Poetry of Hall, The. Donald Hall. MCLE(3919), MP4(829).
Poetry of Hardy, The. Thomas Hardy. MCLE(3922), MP4 (831).
Poetry of Henley, The. William Ernest Henley. MCLE(3928), MP4(836).
Poetry of Hérédia, The. José María de Hérédia. MCLE (3930), MP4(838).
Poetry of Hodgson, The. Ralph Hodgson. MCLE(3932), MP4(840).
Poetry of Hofmannsthal, The. Hugo von Hofmannsthal. MCLE(3934), MP4(842).
Poetry of Hölderlin, The. Johann Christian Friedrich Hölderlin. MCLE(3937), MP4(845).
Poetry of Hopkins, The. Gerard Manley Hopkins. MCLE (3940), MP(266), MP3(807).
Poetry of Horace, The. Horace. MCLE(3943), MP(269), MP3(810).
Poetry of Hugo, The. Victor Hugo. MCLE(3946), MP4(848).
Poetry of Jarrell, The. Randall Jarrell. MCLE(3949),

MP4(851).
Poetry of Jeffers, The. Robinson Jeffers. MCLE(3952), MP4(853).
Poetry of Jiménez, The. Juan Ramón Jiménez. MCLE (3955), MP4(856).
Poetry of Johnson, The. Samuel Johnson. MCLE(3957), MP4(857).
Poetry of Jonson, The. Ben Jonson. MCLE(3960), MP4(860).
Poetry of Kipling, The. Rudyard Kipling. MCLE(3965), MP4(865).
Poetry of Laforgue, The. Jules Laforgue. MCLE(3968), MP4(868).
Poetry of Lamartine, The. Alphonse de Lamartine. MCLE (3971), MP4(870).
Poetry of Landor, The. Walter Savage Landor. MCLE (3974), MP4(873).
Poetry of Lanier, The. Sidney Lanier. MCLE(3978), MP (272), MP3(812).
Poetry of Larkin, The. Philip Larkin. MCLE(3981), MP4 (876).
Poetry of Lawrence, The. D. H. Lawrence. MCLE(3983), MP4(877).
Poetry of Leopardi, The. Giacomo Leopardi. MCLE(3986), MP4(880).
Poetry of Lewis, The. Cecil Day Lewis. MCLE(3989), MP (275), MP3(815).
Poetry of Lindsay, The. Vachel Lindsay. MCLE(3992), MP (278), MP3(817).
Poetry of Lovelace, The. Richard Lovelace. MCLE(3994), MP(280), MP3(819).
Poetry of Machado, The. Antonio Machado. MCLE(3997), MP4(883).
Poetry of MacLeish, The. Archibald MacLeish. MCLE (4000), MP4(885).
Poetry of MacNeice, The. Louis MacNeice. MCLE(4003), MP4(887).
Poetry of Mallarmé, The. Stéphane Mallarmé. MCLE(4005), MP(283), MP3(821).
Poetry of Marianne Moore, The. Marianne Moore. MCLE (4008), MP4(889).
Poetry of Marot, The. Clément Marot. MCLE(4010), MP4 (890).
Poetry of Marvell, The. Andrew Marvell. MCLE(4013), MP(286), MP3(823).
Poetry of Mayakovsky, The. Vladimir Mayakovsky. MCLE (4016), MP4(893).
Poetry of Melville, The. Herman Melville. MCLE(4019),

MP4(896), MPA4(79).
Poetry of Meredith, The. George Meredith. MCLE(4023), MP4(899).
Poetry of Michelangelo, The. Michelangelo Buonarroti. MCLE(4026), MP4(902).
Poetry of Mörike, The. Eduard Mörike. MCLE(4030), MP4 (904).
Poetry of Moschus, The. Moschus. MCLE(4033), MP4(907).
Poetry of Musset, The. Alfred de Musset. MCLE(4035), MP4(908).
Poetry of Nekrasov, The. Nikolai Nekrasov. MCLE(4038), MP4(911).
Poetry of Neruda, The. Pablo Neruda. MCLE(4041), MP4 (913).
Poetry of Nerval, The. Gérard de Nerval. MCLE(4044), MP4(916).
Poetry of Nicholas Breton, The. Nicholas Breton. MCLE (4049), MP4(920).
Poetry of Owen, The. Wilfred Owen. MCLE(4051), MP4 (922).
Poetry of Pasternak, The. Boris Pasternak. MCLE(4053), MP4(924).
Poetry of Paz, The. Octavio Paz. MCLE(4055), MP4(926).
Poetry of Péguy, The. Charles Péguy. MCLE(4058), MP4 (928).
Poetry of Prior, The. Matthew Prior. MCLE(4061), MP4 (930).
Poetry of Raleigh, The. Sir Walter Raleigh. MCLE(4064), MP4(933).
Poetry of Robert Lowell, The. Robert Lowell, Jr. MCLE (4067), MP4(936).
Poetry of Roethke, The. Theodore Roethke. MCLE(4072), MP4(940).
Poetry of Ronsard, The. Pierre de Ronsard. MCLE(4077), MP(289), MP3(826).
Poetry of Shapiro, The. Karl Shapiro. MCLE(4079), MP4 (944).
Poetry of Sidney, The. Sir Philip Sidney. MCLE(4082), MP4(947).
Poetry of Skelton, The. John Skelton. MCLE(4087), MP4 (951).
Poetry of Smart, The. Christopher Smart. MCLE(4092), MP4(955).
Poetry of Sor Juana Inés de la Cruz, The. Sor Juana Inés de la Cruz. MCLE(4095), MP4(958).
Poetry of Spender, The. Stephen Spender. MCLE(4098), MP (291), MP3(828).

Poetry of Stefan George, The. Stefan George. MCLE(4101), MP(294), MP3(831).
Poetry of Stephen Vincent Benét, The. Stephen Vincent Benét. MCLE(4105), MP4(960).
Poetry of Stevens, The. Wallace Stevens. MCLE(4107), MP4(962).
Poetry of Suckling, The. Sir John Suckling. MCLE(4110), MP4(965).
Poetry of Swift, The. Jonathan Swift. MCLE(4113), MP4 (968).
Poetry of Tate, The. Allen Tate. MCLE(4118), MP4(972).
Poetry of Theocritus, The. Theocritus. MCLE(4121), MP (298), MP3(834).
Poetry of Thompson, The. Francis Thompson. MCLE(4123), MP4(974).
Poetry of Thoreau, The. Henry David Thoreau. MCLE(4125), MP4(976).
Poetry of Traherne, The. Thomas Traherne. MCLE(4127), MP4(978).
Poetry of Valéry, The. Paul Valéry. MCLE(4130), MP4 (981).
Poetry of Vaughan, The. Henry Vaughan. MCLE(4133), MP4(984).
Poetry of Vigny, The. Alfred de Vigny. MCLE(4137), MP4 (987).
Poetry of Waller, The. Edmund Waller. MCLE(4140), MP4 (989).
Poetry of Warren, The. Robert Penn Warren. MCLE(4143), MP4(992).
Poetry of Whittier, The. John Greenleaf Whittier. MCLE (4146), MP4(995), MPA5(119).
Poetry of Wilbur, The. Richard Wilbur. MCLE(4149), MP4 (997).
Poetry of Wilde, The. Oscar Wilde. MCLE(4152), MP4 (1000).
Poetry of Williams, The. William Carlos Williams. MCLE (4155), MP4(1002).
Poetry of Wither, The. George Wither. MCLE(4158), MP4 (1004).
Poetry of Wordsworth, The. William Wordsworth. MCLE (4161), MP4(1007).
Poetry of Wyatt and Surrey, The. Sir Thomas Wyatt and Henry Howard, Earl of Surrey. MCLE(4165), MP4 (1010).
Poetry of Yeats, The. William Butler Yeats. MCLE(4170), MP(300), MP3(836).
Poets in a Landscape. Gilbert Highet. SCL(3644), 1958a(193).

Point Counter Point. Aldous Huxley. MCLE(4173), MEF (684), MP1(760), PO2(130), SGBN(308).
Point of No Return. John P. Marquand. PON(314).
Points of My Compass, The. E. B. White. SCL(3647), 1963a(194).
Policraticus. John of Salisbury. CHL(216).
Policraticus and Metalogicon. John of Salisbury. CAL(335).
Political Theory: The Foundations of Twentieth-Century Political Thought. Arnold Brecht. SCLs(228).
Political Writings. Saint Robert Cardinal Bellarmine. CAL (564).
Politics. Aristotle. WP(163).
Polyeucte. Pierre Corneille. MCLE(4176), MD(650), MP3 (839).
Ponder Heart, The. Eudora Welty. MCLE(4179), MP4(1014), SCL(3650), 1954a(213).
Ponteach; or The Savages of America. Major Robert Rogers. DGAP(1).
Poor People. Fyodor Mikhailovich Dostoevski. MCLE(4182), MEU(593), MP2(847).
Poor White. Sherwood Anderson. MAF(496), MCLE(4185), MP1(762).
Poorhouse Fair, The. John Updike. BM(448), MCLE(4187), MP4(1016), SCL(3653), 1960a(202).
Porgy. Dorothy Heyward and DuBose Heyward. MAF(498), MCLE(4190), MP1(764), SGAP(64).
Porgy and Bess. George Gershwin, Ira Gershwin and DuBose Heyward. DGAP(277).
Portnoy's Complaint. Philip Roth. 1970a(242).
Portrait in Brownstone. Louis Auchincloss. SCL(3657), 1963a(196).
Portrait of a Lady, The. Henry James. MAF(500), MCLE (4192), MP1(766), MPA3(39), PO(243), PON(318), SGAN(61).
Portrait of Max. S. N. Behrman. BM(452), SCL(3660), 1961a(198).
Portrait of the Artist as a Young Dog. Dylan Thomas. MCLE(4195), MP4(1019).
Portrait of the Artist as a Young Man, A. James Joyce. MCLE(4198), MEF(687), MP1(769), PO2(110), SGBN (277).
Possessed, The. Fyodor Mikhailovich Dostoevski. MCLE (4200), MEU(596), MP1(771).
Postman, The. Roger Martin du Gard. SCL(3663), 1955a (208).
Postman Always Rings Twice, The. James M. Cain. MCLE (4203), MP4(1021).

Pot of Gold, The. Titus Maccius Plautus. MCLE(4206), MD(653), MP2(849).
Potting Shed, The. Graham Greene. SCL(3666), 1958a(196).
Powdered Eggs. Charles Simmons. SCL(3669), 1965a(223).
Power. Lion Feuchtwanger. MCLE(4208), MEU(599), MP1 (773).
Power and the Glory, The. Graham Greene. MCLE(4211), MEF(689), MP2(851), SGBN(336).
Power of Darkness, The. Count Leo Tolstoy. MCLE(4214), MD(655), MP3(841), POP(360).
Practical Christianity. Rufus Matthew Jones. CHL(819).
Practice of the Presence of God, The. Brother Lawrence (Nicholas Herman). CHL(543).
Pragmatism. William James. MCLE(4217), MN(251), MP3 (843), WP(779).
Prairie, The. James Fenimore Cooper. MAF(503), MCLE (4220), MP1(776).
Praise of Folly, The. Desiderius Erasmus. CAL(501), CHL(326), MCLE(4223), MN(254), MP3(846).
Prayer. George Arthur Buttrick. CHL(1064).
Preces privatae. Lancelot Andrewes. CHL(473).
Precious Bane. Mary Webb. MCLE(4225), MEF(692), MP1 (778).
Preface to Shakespeare. Samuel Johnson. MCLE(4228), MP4(1024).
Prejudices: Six Series. H. L. Mencken. MCLE(4231), MN (256), MP3(847).
Prelude, A. Edmund Wilson. SCL(3672), 1968a(251).
Prelude, The. William Wordsworth. MCLE(4233), MP(303), MP3(849).
Presence of Grace, The. J. F. Powers. SCL(3674), 1957a (209).
Present at the Creation. Dean Acheson. 1971a(256).
President, The. R. V. Cassill. SCL(3677), 1965a(226).
Presidential Lottery. James A. Michener. 1970a(246).
Price, The. Arthur Miller. SCL(3682), 1969a(264).
Price of Glory: Verdun, 1916, The. Alastair Horne. SCL (3686), 1964a(215).
Pricksongs and Descants. Robert Coover. 1970a(250).
Pride and Prejudice. Jane Austen. MCLE(4236), MEF(695), MP1(780), PO(14), PON(324), SGBN(55).
Priest to the Temple, A. George Herbert. CHL(485).
Prime of Miss Jean Brodie, The. Muriel Spark. SCL(3689), 1963a(199).
Prince, The. Niccolò Machiavelli. CAL(523), MCLE(4240), MN(258), MP3(852), WP(354).
Prince and the Pauper, The. Samuel L. Clemens. MAF(506),

MCLE(4243), MP2(854), MPA5(84), PO(200).
Prince Eugen of Savoy. Nicholas Henderson. SCL(3692), 1966a(242).
Prince of Homburg, The. Heinrich von Kleist. MCLE(4246), MD(658), MP3(854).
Prince of Parthia, The. Thomas Godfrey. DGAP(6).
Princess, The. Alfred, Lord Tennyson. MCLE(4248), MP4 (1026).
Princess Casamassima, The. Henry James. MCLE(4251), MP4(1029), MPA3(45).
Princess of Clèves, The. Madame Marie de Lafayette. MCLE(4254), MEU(602), MP2(856), PO2(291).
Principal Doctrines and Letter to Menoeceus. Epicurus. WP(191).
Principia ethica. George Edward Moore. WP(755).
Principle of Individuality and Value, The. Bernard Bosanquet. WP(790).
Principles of Literary Criticism. I. A. Richards. MCLE (4257), MP4(1031).
Principles of Political Economy. John Stuart Mill. MCLE (4260), MP4(1034).
Prisoner of Zenda, The. Anthony Hope. MCLE(4263), MEF (699), MP1(784), PO(109), PON(329).
Private Diaries of Stendhal, The. Stendhal. SCL(3696), 1954a(216).
Private Life of the Master Race, The. Bertolt Brecht. MCLE(4266), MD(660), MP2(858).
Private Lives. Noel Coward. MCLE(4269), MD(663), MP2 (860).
Private Papers of Henry Ryecroft, The. George Gissing. MCLE(4271), MEF(702), MP2(862).
Probable Volume of Dreams, A. Marvin Bell. 1970a(255).
Problem of Christianity, The. Josiah Royce. CHL(878).
Problem of Slavery in Western Culture, The. David Brion Davis. SCL(3699), 1967a(271).
Problems of Ethics. Moritz Schlick. WP(935).
Process and Reality. Alfred North Whitehead. WP(921).
Processional. John Howard Lawson. DGAP(225).
Professor, The. Charlotte Brontë. MCLE(4274), MEF(705), MP2(864).
Professor's House, The. Willa Cather. MAF(509), MCLE (4277), MP2(867).
Profiles in Courage. John F. Kennedy. SCL(3705), 1957a (212).
Progress and Religion. Christopher Dawson. CAL(798).
Prolegomena to Ethics. Thomas Hill Green. WP(681).
Prometheus. Aeschylus. POP(382).

Prometheus Bound. Aeschylus. MCLE(4280), MD(665), MP1 (786).
Prometheus: The Life of Balzac. André Maurois. SCL (3709), 1967a(276).
Prometheus Unbound. Percy Bysshe Shelley. MCLE(4282), MP(306), MP1(788).
Promised Land, The. Henrik Pontoppidan. MCLE(4284), MEU(605), MP2(869).
Promises. Robert Penn Warren. BM(455), SCL(3713), 1958a(198).
Prophet, The. Sholem Asch. SCL(3717), 1955a(211).
Prophet, The. Kahil Gibran. MCLE(4287), MP4(1036).
Proserpine and Ceres. Folk tradition. MCLE(4289), MEU (608), MP1(789).
Proslogion. Saint Anselm of Canterbury. CAL(280), CHL (197).
Prospects Are Pleasing, The. Honor Tracy. SCL(3721), 1959a(207).
Protagoras. Plato. WP(59).
Proud Tower, The. Barbara W. Tuchman. SCL(3724), 1966a(246).
Proust: The Early Years. George D. Painter. BM(459), SCL(3731), 1960a(206).
Proust: The Later Years. George D. Painter. SCL(3735), 1966a(252).
Public Image, The. Muriel Spark. SCL(3739), 1969a(268).
Pudd'nhead Wilson. Samuel L. Clemens. PON(334).
Pulitzer. W. A. Swanberg. SCL(3743), 1968a(254).
Pump House Gang, The. Tom Wolfe. SCL(3747), 1969a(271).
Pure and the Impure, The. Sidonie Gabrielle Claudine Colette. SCL(3750), 1968a(257).
Puritan Carpenter, The. Julia Randall. SCL(3753), 1966a (256).
Puritan Village. Sumner Chilton Powell. SCLs(234).
Purple Dust. Sean O'Casey. MCLE(4291), MD(667), MP3 (857), TCP(247).
Purple Land, The. W. H. Hudson. MCLE(4294), MEF(708), MP1(791).
Puzzleheaded Girl, The. Christina Stead. SCL(3756), 1968a (260).
Pygmalion. George Bernard Shaw. MCLE(4296), MD(670), MP3(859), TCP(355).
Pyramid, The. William Golding. SCL(3760), 1968a(264).

Quadragesimo anno. Pope Pius XI. CAL(812).
Quality Street. James M. Barrie. MCLE(4298), MD(672), MP1(793).

Quare Fellow, The. Brendan Behan. SCL(3764), 1958a(201).
Quarry, The. Richard Eberhart. SCL(3767), 1965a(230).
Quarup. Antonio Callado. SCLs(238).
Queen After Death. Henry de Montherlant. TCP(236).
Queen Alexandra. Georgina Battiscombe. 1970a(259).
Queen and the Rebels, The. Ugo Betti. TCP(69).
Queen Mary. James Pope-Hennessy. BM(463), SCL(3770), 1961a(200).
Queen of France. André Castelot. SCL(3773), 1958a(204).
Queen Victoria. Lytton Strachey. MCLE(4300), MP4(1038).
Queen Victoria: Born to Succeed. Elizabeth, Countess of Longford. SCL(3776), 1966a(259).
Queens and the Hive, The. Edith Sitwell. BM(466), SCL (3780), 1963a(202).
Queen's Necklace, The. Alexandre Dumas (father). MCLE (4304), MEU(610), MP2(871).
Queen's Necklace, The. Frances Mossiker. SCL(3784), 1962a(232).
Quentin Durward. Sir Walter Scott. MCLE(4307), MEF(710), MP1(795).
Quest for Being, The. Sidney Hook. SCL(3788), 1962a(235).
Quest for Certainty, The. John Dewey. WP(907).
Quest of the Historical Jesus, The. Albert Schweitzer. CHL(847).
Questions of Precedence. François Mauriac. SCL(3791), 1960a(209).
Questions of Travel. Elizabeth Bishop. SCL(3795), 1966a (263).
Quiet American, The. Graham Greene. SCL(3798), 1957a (215).
Quiet Enemy, The. Cecil Dawkins. SCL(3801), 1964a(218).
Quo vadis. Henryk Sienkiewicz. MCLE(4310), MEU(613), MP1(797), PO(388), PON(338).
Quoat-Quoat. Jacques Audiberti. TCP(40).

R. E. Lee. Douglas Southall Freeman. MCLE(4381), MN (261), MP3(874).
R. U. R. Karel Čapek. MCLE(4563), MD(720), MP2(927), POP(341), TCP(93).
Rabbit, Run. John Updike. BM(470), MCLE(4313), MP4 (1042), SCL(3804), 1961a(203).
Rack, The. A. E. Ellis. SCL(3807), 1960a(212).
Raditzer. Peter Matthiessen. SCL(3810), 1962a(239).
Rain. John B. Colton and Clemence Randolph. POP(89).
Rainbird, The. Sara Lidman. SCL(3815), 1963a(205).
Rainbow, The. D. H. Lawrence. MCLE(4316), MEF(713), MP1(800).

Rainbow on the Road. Esther Forbes. SCL(3818), 1954a (219).
Raintree County. Ross Lockridge, Jr. MAF(512), MCLE (4319), MP2(874).
Raise High the Roof Beam, Carpenters. J. D. Salinger. SCL(3821), 1964a(220).
Raisin in the Sun, A. Lorraine Hansberry. DGAP(419), SCL(3824), SGAP(301), 1960a(215).
Rakóssy. Cecelia Holland. SCL(3827), 1967a(280).
Ralph Roister Doister. Nicholas Udall. MCLE(4322), MD (674), MP2(876).
Ramayana, The. Aubrey Menen. SCL(3831), 1954a(222).
Ramayana, The. Valmiki. MCLE(4324), MP(308), MP3(861).
Rambler, The. Samuel Johnson. MCLE(4327), MP4(1044).
Rameau's Nephew. Denis Diderot. MCLE(4330), MEU(616), MP3(863).
Ramona. Helen Hunt Jackson. PO(240), PON(342).
Rape of Lucrece, The. William Shakespeare. MCLE(4333), MP(311), MP2(878).
Rape of the Fair Country, The. Alexander Cordell. SCL (3834), 1960a(218).
Rape of the Lock, The. Alexander Pope. MCLE(4335), MP (313), MP1(802).
Rasselas. Samuel Johnson. MCLE(4337), MEF(716), MP1 (804).
Rats, The. Gerhart Hauptmann. TCP(181).
Ravenshoe. Henry Kingsley. MCLE(4340), MEF(719), MP2 (880).
Raw and the Cooked, The. Claude Lévi-Strauss. 1970a(263).
Real Life of Sebastian Knight, The. Vladimir Nabokov. MCLE(4343), MP4(1046), SCL(3837), 1960a(220).
Real Majority, The. Richard M. Scammon. 1971a(262).
Reality of Faith, The. Friedrich Gogarten. CHL(1167).
Realms of Being. George Santayana. WP(895).
Reason and Existenz. Karl Jaspers. WP(1004).
Reason Why, The. Cecil Woodham-Smith. SCL(3840), 1954a (225).
Reasonableness of Christianity, The. John Locke. CHL(551).
Rebecca. Daphne Du Maurier. MCLE(4345), MEF(722), MP1(806).
Rebel, The. Albert Camus. SCL(3843), WP(1127), 1954a (228).
Rebel Generation, The. Johanna van Ammers-Küller. MCLE(4348), MEU(619), MP3(865).
Recognitions, The. William Gaddis. SCLs(243).
Recovery of Confidence, The. John W. Gardner. 1971a(265).
Recruiting Officer, The. George Farquhar. MCLE(4351),

MD(676), MP2(882).
Rector of Justin, The. Louis Auchincloss. SCL(3846), 1965a(234).
Red and the Black, The. Stendhal. MCLE(4354), MEU(622), MP1(808), PO(329), PON(346), SGEN(41).
Red Badge of Courage, The. Stephen Crane. MAF(515), MCLE(4357), MP1(811), MPA1(89), PO(210), PON(351), SGAN(72).
Red Cock Flies to Heaven, The. Miodrag Bulatovic. SCL (3852), 1963a(208).
Red Fort, The. James Leasor. SCL(3855), 1958a(206).
Red Room, The. August Strindberg. MCLE(4360), MEU (625), MP3(868).
Red Rover, The. James Fenimore Cooper. MAF(518), MCLE(4363), MP1(813).
Red Sky at Morning. Richard Bradford. SCL(3858), 1969a (274).
Redburn. Herman Melville. MAF(521), MCLE(4366), MP2 (885), MPA4(87).
Redskins, The. James Fenimore Cooper. MAF(524), MCLE (4369), MP3(870), MPA1(72).
Reflections on the Psalms. C. S. Lewis. SCL(3861), 1959a (209).
Reformation, The. Will Durant. BM(473), SCL(3864), 1958a (209).
Refutation of All Heresies. Saint Hippolytus. CAL(58).
Rehearsal for Reconstruction. Willie Lee Rose. SCL(3868), 1965a(240).
Reinhart in Love. Thomas Berger. SCLs(247).
Reivers, The. William Faulkner. MCLE(4373), MP4(1048), SCL(3871), 1963a(211).
Relapse, The. Sir John Vanbrugh. MCLE(4377), MD(679), MP2(887).
Relearning the Alphabet. Denise Levertov. 1971a(269).
Religio medici. Sir Thomas Browne. CHL(450).
Religion and the American Mind. Alan E. Heimert. SCL (3876), 1967a(283).
Religion in the Making. Alfred North Whitehead. CHL(925).
Religion Within the Limits of Reason Alone. Immanuel Kant. CHL(626).
Religious a priori, The. Ernst Troeltsch. CHL(865).
Remember the House. Santha Rama Rau. SCL(3881), 1957a (218).
Remembered Darkness, A. John Ratti. 1970a(265).
Remembrance of Things Past. Marcel Proust. MCLE(4384), MEU(628), MP1(815).
Remembrance Rock. Carl Sandburg. MAF(528), MCLE

(4387), MP2(889).
Reminiscences. Douglas MacArthur. SCL(3884), 1965a(243).
Renaissance, The. Walter Pater. MCLE(4392), MP4(1052).
Renée Mauperin. Edmond and Jules de Goncourt. MCLE (4395), MEU(631), MP2(894).
Report of the President's Commission on the Assassination of President John F. Kennedy. J. Lee Rankin, Earl Warren and Others. SCL(3888), 1965a(246).
Report to Greco. Nikos Kazantzakis. SCL(3894), 1966a(265).
Representative Men. Ralph Waldo Emerson. MCLE(4398), MP4(1054), MPA1(123).
Republic, The. Plato. MCLE(4402), MN(263), MP3(876), WP(88).
Requiem for a Nun. William Faulkner. MCLE(4405), MP4 (1058).
Rerum novarum. Pope Leo XIII. CAL(699).
Rescue the Dead. David Ignatow. SCL(3898), 1969a(277).
Resistance, Rebellion, and Death. Albert Camus. SCL (3901), 1962a(243).
Responsibilities of the Novelist, The. Frank Norris. MCLE (4408), MP4(1061).
Rest Is Done with Mirrors, The. Carolyn See. 1971a(271).
Restlessness of Shanti Andía, The. Pío Baroja. SCL(3905), 1960a(223).
Resurrection. Count Leo Tolstoy. MCLE(4411), MEU(634), MP3(879).
Retracing the Arts to Theology. Saint Bonaventure. CHL (228).
Return, The. Walter De la Mare. MCLE(4414), MEF(725), MP2(896).
Return of H*Y*M*A*N K*A*P*L*A*N, The. Leo Rosten. SCL(3908), 1960a(226).
Return of Lady Brace, The. Nancy Wilson Ross. SCL(3911), 1958a(212).
Return of the King, The. J. R. R. Tolkien. MCLE(4417), MP4(1063).
Return of the Native, The. Thomas Hardy. MCLE(4420), MEF(728), MP1(818), PO(98), SGBN(167).
Reunion. Merle Miller. SCL(3913), 1954a(231).
Revelation and Reason. Emil Brunner. WP(1058).
Revelations of Divine Love, The. Lady Julian (Juliana) of Norwich. CAL(476), CHL(284).
Revenge of Bussy d'Ambois, The. George Chapman. MCLE (4423), MD(682), MP3(881).
Revenger's Tragedy, The. Cyril Tourneur. MCLE(4426), MD(685), MP3(883).
Revolt in Aspromonte. Corrado Alvaro. SCL(3916), 1963a

(216).
Revolt of Gunner Asch, The. Hans Hellmut Kirst. SCL (3919), 1957a(221).
Revolt of the Angels, The. Anatole France. MCLE(4429), MEU(637), MP1(821).
Revolt of the Masses, The. José Ortega y Gasset. MCLE (4432), MN(266), MP3(886).
Reynard the Fox. Unknown. MCLE(4435), MEU(640), MP2 (899).
Rhadimistus and Zenobia. Prosper Jolyot de Crébillon. MCLE(4439), MD(688), MP3(888).
Rhetoric. Aristotle. WP(169).
Rhinoceros. Eugène Ionesco. MCLE(4441), MP4(1066), TCP (202).
Riceyman's Steps. Arnold Bennett. MCLE(4444), MEF(731), MP1(823).
Rich Nations and the Poor Nations, The. Barbara Ward. SCL(3922), 1963a(218).
Richard the Second. William Shakespeare. MCLE(4446), MD(691), MP2(901).
Richard the Third. William Shakespeare. MCLE(4449), MD (694), MP2(903).
Richard Wagner. Robert W. Gutman. SCL(3925), 1969a(280).
Richelieu. Edward George Earle Bulwer-Lytton. POP(162).
Riddle of the Universe, The. Ernst Heinrich Haeckel. WP (734).
Riders in the Chariot. Patrick White. MCLE(4452), MP4 (1069), SCL(3930), 1962a(246).
Riders to the Sea. John Millington Synge. POP(235), TCP (415).
Right and the Good, The. W. David Ross. WP(929).
Right You Are--If You Think Think You Are. Luigi Pirandello. MCLE(4455), MD(697), MP3(891), TCP(298).
Rime of Petrarch, Le. Francesco Petrarch. MCLE(4458), MP(315), MP3(893).
Rime of the Ancient Mariner, The. Samuel Taylor Coleridge. MCLE(4461), MP(318), MP1(825).
Ring and the Book, The. Robert Browning. MCLE(4463), MP(320), MP1(826).
Ring of Bright Water. Gavin Maxwell. SCL(3934), 1962a (250).
Ring Round the Moon. Jean Anouilh. MCLE(4466), MD(700), MP3(896).
Rip Van Winkle. Washington Irving. MAF(533), MCLE (4469), MP2(905), MPA2(96).
Rip Van Winkle. Joseph Jefferson, Charles Burke, Dion Boucicault. DGAP(90).

Rise and Fall of the Third Reich, The. William L. Shirer. BM(477), SCL(3938), 1961a(206).
Rise of American Civilization, The. Charles A. and Mary R. Beard. MCLE(4471), MP4(1071).
Rise of Silas Lapham, The. William Dean Howells. MAF (535), MCLE(4475), MP1(828), MPA2(86), PO(232), SGAN(54).
Rise of the West, The. William H. McNeill. SCL(3945), 1964a(223).
Rivals, The. Richard Brinsley Sheridan. MCLE(4478), MD (703), MP1(831), POP(170).
River of Earth. James Still. MAF(538), MCLE(4481), MP1 (833).
Rivers and Mountains. John Ashberry. SCL(3948), 1967a (287).
Rivet in Grandfather's Neck, The. James Branch Cabell. MAF(541), MCLE(4484), MP3(898).
Roan Stallion. Robinson Jeffers. MCLE(4487), MP(323), MP1(835).
Roar Lion Roar. Irvin Faust. SCL(3951), 1966a(269).
Rob Roy. Sir Walter Scott. MCLE(4489), MEF(733), MP1 (837).
Robert Bruce and the Community of the Realm of Scotland. G. W. S. Barrow. SCL(3954), 1966a(272).
Robert Frost. Elizabeth Shepley Sergeant. SCL(3957), 1961a(213).
Robin Hood's Adventures. Unknown. MCLE(4492), MEF(736), MP2(907).
Robinson Crusoe. Daniel Defoe. MCLE(4495), MEF(739), MP1(839), PO2(1), PON(356), SGBN(9).
Rochelle; or Virtue Rewarded. David Slavitt. SCL(3961), 1968a(268).
Rock Pool, The. Cyril Connolly. SCL(3965), 1968a(272).
Roderick Hudson. Henry James. MCLE(4498), MP4(1074), MPA3(50).
Roderick Random. Tobias Smollett. MCLE(4502), MEF(742), MP1(841).
Roethke: Collected Poems. Theodore Roethke. SCL(3969), 1967a(290).
Rogue Herries. Hugh Walpole. MCLE(4505), MEF(745), MP1(844).
Roman Actor, The. Philip Massinger. MCLE(4508), MD (706), MP3(901).
Roman Wall. Bryher. SCL(3974), 1954a(234).
Romance of a Schoolmaster, The. Edmondo de Amicis. MCLE(4511), MEU(643), MP2(909).
Romance of Leonardo da Vinci, The. Dmitri Merejkowski.

MCLE(4514), MEU(646), MP2(911).
Romance of the Forest, The. Mrs. Ann Radcliffe. MCLE (4517), MEF(748), MP2(914).
Romance of the Three Kingdoms. Lo Kuan-chung. MCLE (4522), MEU(649), MP3(903).
Romantic Comedians, The. Ellen Glasgow. MAF(544), MCLE(4524), MP1(846).
Romantic Egoists, The. Louis Auchincloss. SCL(3977), 1954a(237).
Romantic Ladies, The. Molière. MCLE(4527), MD(709), MP2(918).
Romany Rye, The. George Henry Borrow. MCLE(4529), MEF(753), MP1(849).
Rome Haul. Walter D. Edmonds. MAF(547), MCLE(4532), MP1(851).
Romeo and Juliet. William Shakespeare. MCLE(4535), MD (711), MP1(853), POP(214).
Romola. George Eliot. MCLE(4538), MEF(756), MP1(856), PO(86), PON(361).
Roof of Tiger Lilies, A. Donald Hall. SCL(3980), 1965a (252).
Room at the Top. John Braine. BM(484), MCLE(4541), MP4(1078), SCL(3984), 1958a(214).
Room with a View, A. E. M. Forster. MCLE(4544), MEF (759), MP3(905).
Roosevelt Family of Sagamore Hill, The. Hermann Hagedorn. SCL(3987), 1954a(240).
Roosevelt Leadership, 1933-1945, The. Edgar Eugene Robinson. SCL(3990), 1955a(214).
Roosevelt: The Lion and the Fox. James MacGregor Burns. SCL(3993), 1957a(224).
Roosevelt: The Soldier of Freedom. James MacGregor Burns. 1971a(276).
Roots of American Communism, The. Theodore Draper. SCL(3996), 1958a(217).
Roots of Heaven, The. Romain Gary. SCL(3999), 1959a(212).
Rory O'More. Samuel Lover. MCLE(4547), MEF(762), MP2(920).
Rosencrantz and Guildenstern Are Dead. Tom Stoppard. SCL(4002), 1968a(275).
Rosmersholm. Henrik Ibsen. MCLE(4550), MD(714), MP2 (922).
Rothschilds, The. Frederic Morton. SCL(4006), 1963a(221).
Roughing It. Samuel Clemens. MCLE(4553), MN(269), MP1 (858), MPA5(89).
Rousseau and Revolution. Will and Ariel Durant. SCL(4010), 1968a(279).

Roxana. Daniel Defoe. MCLE(4555), MEF(765), MP2(924).
Royal Flash. George McDonald Fraser. 1971a(280).
Royal Hunt of the Sun, The. Peter Shaffer. SCL(4014), 1966a(275).
Ruan. Bryher. SCL(4018), 1961a(216).
Rubáiyát of Omar Khayyám, The. Edward FitzGerald. MCLE(4558), MP(325), MP3(907).
Rule a Wife and Have a Wife. John Fletcher. MCLE(4560), MD(717), MP3(909).
Rule and Exercise of Holy Living and Holy Dying, The. Jeremy Taylor. CHL(477).
Rule of St. Benedict, The. Saint Benedict of Nursia. CAL (234), CHL(172).
Rupert Brooke. Christopher Hassall. SCL(4021), 1965a(256).
Ruslan and Lyudmila. Alexander Pushkin. MCLE(4566), MP4(1080).
Russia and the West under Lenin and Stalin. George F. Kennan. BM(487), SCL(4025), 1962a(254).
Russia at War, 1941-1945. Alexander Werth. SCL(4030), 1965a(260).
Russia Leaves the War, Volume I. George F. Kennan. BM (492), SCL(4034), 1957a(227).
Russia, the Atom and the West. George F. Kennan. SCL (4038), 1959a(214).
Russian Empire 1801-1917, The. Hugh Seton-Watson. SCL (4041), 1968a(283).
Russian Revolution, 1917, The. N. N. Sukhanov. SCL(4045), 1955a(217).

Sacred Fount, The. Henry James. MCLE(4569), MP4(1082), MPA3(57).
Sacred Wood: Essays on Poetry and Criticism, The. T. S. Eliot. MCLE(4574), MP4(1086).
Sailor, Sense of Humour, and Other Stories, The. V. S. Pritchett. SCL(4048), 1957a(230).
Saint, The. Antonio Fogazzaro. MCLE(4577), MEU(651), MP2(929).
Saint Bartholomew's Night. Philippe Erlanger. SCL(4051), 1963a(225).
Saint Francis. Nikos Kazantzakis. SCL(4054), 1963a(227).
St. Francis of Assisi. Gilbert Keith Chesterton. CAL(781).
Saint Francis of Assisi. Johannes Jörgensen. CAL(756).
Saint Francis Xavier. James Brodrick, S.J. CAL(990).
Saint Joan. George Bernard Shaw. MCLE(4580), MD(723), MP3(912), TCP(358).
St. Peter's Umbrella. Kálmán Mikszáth. MCLE(4582), MEU (654), MP3(914).

St. Ronan's Well. Sir Walter Scott. MCLE(4585), MEF (768), MP3(916).
Sainte-Beuve. Sir Harold Nicolson. SCL(4058), 1958a(219).
Saints' Everlasting Rest, The. Richard Baxter. CHL(481).
Sakuntala. Kalidasa. MCLE(4589), MD(725), MP2(931).
Sal Si Puedes. Peter Matthiessen. 1971a(283).
Salammbô. Gustave Flaubert. MCLE(4592), MEU(657), MP1 (860), PO2(310).
Salar the Salmon. Henry Williamson. MCLE(4595), MP4 (1088).
Salerno. Hugh Pond. SCL(4061), 1963a(231).
Salvation, 1944-1946. Charles de Gaulle. SCL(4064), 1961a (219).
Samson Agonistes. John Milton. MCLE(4598), MD(728), MP3(920).
Sanctuary. William Faulkner. MAF(550), MCLE(4600), MP1 (862), PO2(237).
Sand Pebbles, The. Richard McKenna. SCL(4067), 1964a (226).
Sandford and Merton. Thomas Day. MCLE(4603), MEF(772), MP2(933).
Sands of Dunkirk, The. Richard Collier. SCL(4070), 1962a (258).
Sanine. Mikhail Artsybashev. MCLE(4606), MEU(660), MP3 (921).
Sappho. Alphonse Daudet. MCLE(4609), MP1(865), PO(276).
Sappho. Franz Grillparzer. MCLE(4611), MD(730), MEU (663), MP3(923).
Saragossa. Benito Pérez Galdós. MCLE(4614), MEU(665), MP2(935).
Sartor Resartus. Thomas Carlyle. MCLE(4617), MN(271), MP3(925).
Sartoris. William Faulkner. MCLE(4619), MP4(1091).
Satanstoe. James Fenimore Cooper. MAF(553), MCLE (4623), MP3(927).
Satin Slipper. Paul Claudel. TCP(102).
Satires. Nicholas Boileau-Despréaux. MCLE(4627), MP4 (1094).
Satires. Juvenal. MCLE(4630), MP(327), MP3(931).
Satires. Lucian. MCLE(4632), MP4(1097).
Satiromastix. Thomas Dekker. MCLE(4635), MD(733), MP3 (933).
Saturday Night and Sunday Morning. Alan Sillitoe. SCL (4073), 1960a(229).
Satyricon, The. Gaius Petronius. MCLE(4638), MEU(668), MP2(938).
Savage Mind, The. Claude Lévi-Strauss. SCLs(251).

Savage State, The. Georges Conchon. SCL(4077), 1966a (278).
Save Every Lamb. Jesse Stuart. SCL(4080), 1965a(263).
Scale of Perfection, The. Walter Hilton. CHL(316).
Scarecrow, The. Percy MacKaye. DGAP(178).
Scarlet Letter, The. Nathaniel Hawthorne. MAF(557), MCLE(4641), MP1(867), MPA2(58), PO(218), PON(365), SGAN(21).
Scarlet Thread, The. Doris Betts. SCL(4083), 1966a(281).
Scepticism and Animal Faith. George Santayana. MCLE (4644), MN(273), MP3(935).
Schatten Affair, The. Frederic Morton. SCL(4086), 1966a (283).
School for Dictators, The. Ignazio Silone. SCL(4089), 1964a(228).
School for Husbands, The. Molière. MCLE(4647), MD(736), MP3(938).
School for Scandal, The. Richard Brinsley Sheridan. MCLE (4650), MD(739), MP1(869), POP(166).
School for Wives, The. Molière. MCLE(4653), MD(742), MP2(940).
Science and Health with Key to the Scriptures. Mary Baker Eddy. CHL(775).
Science, Religion and Christianity. Hans Urs von Balthasar. CAL(1021).
Scornful Lady, The. Francis Beaumont and John Fletcher. MCLE(4655), MD(744), MP3(940).
Scott Fitzgerald. Andrew Turnbull. SCL(4092), 1963a(234).
Scottish Chiefs, The. Jane Porter. MCLE(4658), MEF(775), MP2(942).
Scott's Last Expedition. Captain Robert Falcon Scott. MCLE(4661), MP4(1100).
Scottsboro. Dan T. Carter. 1970a(269).
Screwtape Letters, The. Clive Staples Lewis. CHL(1068).
Scripture-Doctrine of the Trinity, The. Samuel Clarke. CHL(562).
Scrolls from the Dead Sea, The. Edmund Wilson. SCL (4096), 1955a(220).
Sea and the Jungle, The. H. M. Tomlinson. MCLE(4664), MN(276), MP3(942).
Sea Dreamer, The. Gérard Jean-Aubry. SCL(4099), 1958a (222).
Sea Fights and Shipwrecks. Hanson W. Baldwin. SCL(4103), 1955a(223).
Sea of Grass, The. Conrad Richter. MAF(560), MCLE (4667), MP1(872).
Sea Wolf, The. Jack London. MAF(563), MCLE(4670), MP1

(874), PON(369).
Seagull, The. Anton Chekhov. MCLE(4673), MD(747), MP2 (945).
Seamarks. St.-John Perse. BM(496), MCLE(4676), MP4 (1102), SCL(4106), 1959a(216).
Séance and Other Stories, The. Isaac Bashevis Singer. SCL(4109), 1969a(284).
Search, The. C. P. Snow. BM(499), SCL(4113), 1960a(232).
Search for Captain Slocum, The. Walter Magnes Teller. SCL(4116), 1957a(233).
Searchers, The. Alan LeMay. SCL(4120), 1954a(243).
Season in Hell, A. Arthur Rimbaud. MCLE(4678), MP(329), MP3(944).
Seasonable Thoughts on the State of Religion in New England. Charles Chauncy. CHL(586).
Seasons, The. James Thomson. MCLE(4681), MP4(1104).
Seat of Wisdom, The. Louis Bouyer. CAL(1037).
Second Apology, The. Saint Justin Martyr. CAL(19), CHL (19).
Second Chance. Louis Auchincloss. 1971a(287).
Second Mrs. Tanqueray, The. Arthur Wing Pinero. MCLE (4684), MD(750), MP2(947), POP(134).
Second Shepherds' Play, The. Unknown. MCLE(4687), MD (753), MP2(949).
Second Skin. John Hawkes. SCL(4123), 1965a(266).
Second Tree from the Corner, The. E. B. White. SCL (4126), 1954a(246).
Second World War, The. Winston S. Churchill. MCLE(4689), MN(279), MP3(947).
Secret, The. Alba de Céspedes. SCL(4129), 1959a(219).
Secret Agent, The. Joseph Conrad. MCLE(4692), MEF(778), MP3(949).
Secret Diary of Harold L. Ickes: Volume II, The. Harold L. Ickes. SCL(4132), 1954a(249).
Secret of Luca, The. Ignazio Silone. SCL(4135), 1959a(222).
Secret Service. William Gillette. DGAP(136).
Secret Sharer, The. Joseph Conrad. PO2(95).
Seed, The. Pierre Gascar. SCL(4138), 1960a(235).
Seed and the Sower, The. Laurens Van Der Post. SCL (4141), 1964a(231).
Seed Beneath the Snow, The. Ignazio Silone. SCL(4144), 1966a(286).
Seeds of Contemplation. Thomas Merton. CAL(955).
Seedtime on the Cumberland. Harriette Simpson Arnow. SCL(4150), 1961a(222).
Segaki. David Stacton. SCL(4153), 1960a(237).
Segregation. Robert Penn Warren. SCL(4156), 1957a(236).

Seize the Day. Saul Bellow. SCLs(254).
Sejanus. Ben Jonson. MCLE(4695), MD(755), MP3(951).
Selected Letters. Baron Friedrich John von Hügel. CHL (938).
Selected Letters of Dylan Thomas. Dylan Thomas. SCL (4159), 1967a(295).
Selected Letters of Malcolm Lowry. Malcolm Lowry. SCL (4163), 1966a(291).
Selected Letters of Robert Frost. Robert Frost. SCL(4167), 1965a(269).
Selected Poems. A. R. Ammons. SCL(4173), 1968a(287).
Selected Poems. Rubén Darío. SCL(4176), 1966a(295).
Selected Poems. Randall Jarrell. SCL(4182), 1955a(225).
Selected Poems. Thomas Merton. SCL(4185), 1968a(290).
Selected Poems. John Crowe Ransom. MCLE(4698), MP (332), MP3(954), SCLs(262).
Selected Poems. Louis Simpson. SCL(4189), 1966a(300).
Selected Poems: New and Old 1923-1966. Robert Penn Warren. SCL(4192), 1967a(298).
Selected Poems: 1944-1970. Gwendolyn Brooks. SCLs(266).
Selected Poems: 1928-1958. Stanley Kunitz. SCLs(268).
Selected Tales. Nikolai Leskov. SCL(4197), 1962a(261).
Selected Writings on the Spiritual Life. Saint Peter Damian. CHL(190).
Self Condemned. Wyndham Lewis. SCL(4200), 1955a(228).
Self-Tormentor, The. Terence. MCLE(4701), MD(758), MP3(956).
El Señor Presidente. Miguel Ángel Asturias. MCLE(1342), MP4(260).
Sense and Sensibility. Jane Austen. MCLE(4704), MEF(781), MP2(951).
Sense of Beauty, The. George Santayana. WP(718).
Sense of Dark, A. William Malliol. SCL(4203), 1968a(293).
Sense of Reality, A. Graham Greene. SCL(4206), 1964a (234).
Sentimental Education, A. Gustave Flaubert. MCLE(4707), MEU(671), MP1(876).
Sentimental Journey, A. Laurence Sterne. MCLE(4710), MEF(784), MP1(879).
Separate Peace, A. John Knowles. SCL(4208), 1961a(225).
Serious Call to a Devout and Holy Life, A. William Law. CHL(566).
Sermo contra auxentium. Saint Ambrose. CAL(132).
Sermons and Treatises. Johann Eckhart. CHL(245).
Servant in the House, The. Charles Rann Kennedy. POP(49).
Servile State, The. Hilaire Belloc. CAL(754).
Set This House on Fire. William Styron. BM(502), MCLE

(4713), SCL(4211), 1961a(228).
Seven Against Thebes. Aeschylus. MCLE(4716), MD(761), MP2(953).
Seven Books of History Against the Pagans. Paulus Orosius. CAL(178), CHL(145).
Seven Epistles of Ignatius, The. Saint Ignatius, Bishop of Antioch. CHL(7).
Seven Gothic Tales. Isak Dinesen. MCLE(4719), MEU(674), MP3(958).
Seven Islands, The. Jon Godden. SCL(4215), 1957a(238).
Seven Men Among the Penguins. Mario Marret. SCL(4218), 1955a(231).
Seven Pillars of Wisdom. T. E. Lawrence. MCLE(4722), MN(282), MP3(961).
Seven Plays. Bertolt Brecht. BM(506), SCL(4221), 1962a (264).
Seven Short Plays. Lady Gregory. MCLE(4725), MD(764), MP3(963).
Seven Storey Mountain, The. Thomas Merton. CAL(930).
Seven Who Fled, The. Frederic Prokosch. MAF(566), MCLE(4727), MP2(955).
Seven Who Were Hanged, The. Leonid Andreyev. MCLE (4730), MEU(677), MP2(957).
Seven Years in Tibet. Heinrich Harrer. SCL(4224), 1954a (252).
Seventeen. Booth Tarkington. MAF(569), MCLE(4732), MP1 (882).
77 Dream Songs. John Berryman. SCL(4227), 1965a(275).
73 Poems. E. E. Cummings. SCL(4230), 1964a(236).
Severed Head, A. Iris Murdoch. SCL(4233), 1962a(266).
Sexual Politics. Kate Millett. 1971a(290).
Shadow and Act. Ralph Ellison. SCL(4236), 1965a(277).
Shadow Knows, The. David Madden. 1971a(296).
Shadow of Night, The. George Chapman. MCLE(4735), MP4(1110).
Shadows on the Grass. Isak Dinesen. SCL(4239), 1962a(269).
Shadows on the Rock. Willa Cather. MAF(572), MCLE (4738), MP1(884).
Shakespeare and Company. Sylvia Beach. SCL(4242), 1960a (240).
Shaughraun, The. Dion Boucicault. POP(238).
She. H. Rider Haggard. MCLE(4741), MEF(787), MP1(886).
She Stoops to Conquer. Oliver Goldsmith. MCLE(4744), MD(766), MP1(889), POP(173).
She Would Be a Soldier. Mordecai Manuel Noah. DGAP(30).
Sheep Well, The. Lope de Vega. MCLE(4747), MD(769), MP2(960).

SheLa. Aubrey Menen. SCL(4245), 1963a(237).
Shelburne Essays. Paul Elmer More. MCLE(4750), MP4 (1112).
Sheltered Life, The. Ellen Glasgow. MAF(575), MCLE (4753), MP1(891).
Shepheardes Calendar, The. Edmund Spenser. MCLE(4756), MP4(1114).
Shepherd, The. Hermas. CAL(12), CHL(13).
Shepherds of the Night. Jorge Amado. SCL(4248), 1967a (303).
Sherlock Holmes. William Gillette. POP(65).
Shield of Achilles, The. W. H. Auden. BM(509), SCL(4251), 1955a(234).
Shih Ching, The. Confucius. MCLE(4760), MP(335), MP3 (965).
Ship of Fools. Katherine Anne Porter. MCLE(4763), MP4 (1118), SCL(4254), 1963a(240).
Shirley. Charlotte Brontë. MCLE(4769), MEF(790), MP3 (968).
Shoemaker's Holiday, The. Thomas Dekker. MCLE(4772), MD(772), MP2(962), POP(188).
Shoemaker's Prodigious Wife. Federico García Lorca. TCP (149).
Shoes of the Fisherman, The. Morris L. West. SCL(4261), 1964a(238).
Shooting Star, A. Wallace Stegner. SCL(4264), 1962a(272).
Short and Clear Exposition of the Christian Faith, A. Ulrich Zwingli. CHL(363).
Short Friday and Other Stories. Isaac Bashevis Singer. SCL(4267), 1965a(280).
Short Novels of Thomas Wolfe, The. Thomas Wolfe. SCLs (271).
Short Stories of A. E. Coppard, The. A. E. Coppard. MCLE(4775), MP4(1123).
Short Stories of D. H. Lawrence, The. D. H. Lawrence. MCLE(4777), MP4(1125).
Short Stories of E. M. Forster, The. E. M. Forster. MCLE(4780), MP4(1127).
Short Stories of Ernest Hemingway, The. Ernest Hemingway. MCLE(4784), MP4(1130).
Short Stories of Eudora Welty, The. Eudora Welty. MCLE (4787), MP4(1133).
Short Stories of Flannery O'Connor, The. Flannery O'Connor. MCLE(4790), MP4(1136).
Short Stories of John Cheever, The. John Cheever. MCLE (4793), MP4(1139).
Short Stories of John Updike, The. John Updike. MCLE

(4796), MP4(1142).
Short Stories of Katherine Mansfield. Katherine Mansfield. MCLE(4800), MEF(793), MP3(970).
Short Stories of O. Henry. William Sydney Porter. MAF (578), MCLE(4803), MP3(972).
Short Stories of Peter Taylor, The. Peter Taylor. MCLE (4806), MP4(1145).
Short Stories of Saki, The. Saki. MCLE(4809), MP4(1148).
Shorter Rules, The. Saint Basil. CHL(99).
Shropshire Lad, A. A. E. Housman. MCLE(4812), MP(338), MP3(974).
Sibyl, The. Pär Lagerkvist. SCL(4270), 1959a(224).
Sic et non. Peter Abelard. CAL(291).
Sick Fox, The. Paul Brodeur. SCL(4273), 1964a(241).
Sickles the Incredible. W. A. Swanberg. SCL(4276), 1957a (241).
Sickness unto Death, The. Søren Kierkegaard. MCLE(4814), MN(285), MP3(976).
Siege at Peking, The. Peter Fleming. SCL(4279), 1960a (242).
Siege of Rhodes, The. Sir William Davenant. MCLE(4817), MD(775), MP3(979).
Sign in Sidney Brustein's Window, The. Lorraine Hansberry. SCLs(276).
Sign of Four, The. Arthur Conan Doyle. MCLE(4819), MEF (796), MP2(964).
Signs, Language and Behavior. Charles W. Morris. WP (1102).
Silas Marner. George Eliot. MCLE(4821), MEF(798), MP1 (893), PO2(43).
Silence in the Snowy Fields. Robert Bly. SCL(4282), 1963a (247).
Silence of Desire, A. Kamala Markandaya. SCL(4285), 1961a(232).
Silent Spring. Rachel Carson. SCL(4288), 1963a(249).
Silent Woman, The. Ben Jonson. MCLE(4823), MD(777), MP3(980).
Silver Cord, The. Sidney Howard. DGAP(230).
Simple Honorable Man, A. Conrad Richter. MCLE(4826), MP4(1151), SCL(4291), 1963a(251).
Simpleton of the Unexpected Isles, The. George Bernard Shaw. TCP(362).
Simplicissimus the Vagabond. H. J. C. von Grimmelshausen. MCLE(4829), MEU(679), MP2(966).
Sincerely, Willis Wayde. John P. Marquand. SCL(4294), 1955a(237).
Sinclair Lewis. Mark Schorer. BM(512), SCL(4297), 1962a (275).

Singapore: The Japanese Version. Colonel Masanobe Tsuji. SCL(4301), 1962a(279).
Single Pebble, A. John Hersey. SCL(4305), 1957a(244).
Sinister Twilight, A. Noel Barber. SCL(4308), 1969a(288).
Sir Charles Grandison. Samuel Richardson. MCLE(4832), MEF(800), MP3(983).
Sir Gawain and the Green Knight. Unknown. MCLE(4835), MP(340), MP2(969).
Sir John van Olden Barnavelt. John Fletcher. MCLE(4837), MD(780), MP3(985).
Sir Roger de Coverley Papers, The. Joseph Addison. MCLE(4840), MN(288), MP3(988).
Sir Walter Ralegh. A. L. Rowse. SCL(4312), 1963a(254).
Sir William. David Stacton. SCL(4315), 1964a(244).
Sissie. John A. Williams. SCLs(279).
Sister Carrie. Theodore Dreiser. MAF(581), MCLE(4843), MP1(895), PO2(199), SGAN(130).
Sister Philomène. Edmond and Jules de Goncourt. MCLE (4845), MEU(682), MP3(990).
Six Books of the Republic, The. Jean Bodin. CAL(552).
Six Characters in Search of an Author. Luigi Pirandello. MCLE(4848), MD(783), MP3(993), POP(277), TCP(301).
Skin of Our Teeth, The. Thornton Wilder. MCLE(4851), MD(786), MP3(995), SGAP(135), TCP(439).
Skylark, The. Ralph Hodgson. SCL(4319), 1961a(235).
Slaughterhouse-Five. Kurt Vonnegut, Jr. 1970a(273).
Slave, The. Isaac Bashevis Singer. SCL(4322), 1963a(236).
Sleep of Baby Filbertson, The. James Leo Herlihy. SCLs (282).
Sleepwalkers, The. Hermann Broch. MCLE(4854), MEU (685), MP2(970).
Sleepwalkers, The. Arthur Koestler. SCL(4325), 1960a(245).
Slipknot, The. Titus Maccius Plautus. MCLE(4857), MD (789), MP3(997).
Small House at Allington, The. Anthony Trollope. MCLE (4860), MEF(803), MP2(973).
Small Souls. Louis Couperus. MCLE(4864), MEU(688), MP3(1000).
Smoke. Ivan Turgenev. MCLE(4867), MEU(691), MP1(897).
Snake Pit, The. Sigrid Undset. MCLE(4870), MEU(694), MP2(976).
Snow-Bound. John Greenleaf Whittier. MCLE(4873), MP (342), MP1(899), MPA5(125).
Snow Country and Thousand Cranes. Yasunari Kawabata. 1970a(277).
Snow White. Donald Barthelme. SCL(4329), 1968a(296).
So Big. Edna Ferber. MCLE(4875), MP4(1153).

So Human an Animal. René Dubos. SCLs(285).
So Red the Rose. Laurence Stallings, Maxwell Anderson and Edwin Justin Mayer. DGAP(70).
So Red the Rose. Stark Young. MAF(583), MCLE(4878), MP1(901).
Social Contract, The. Robert Ardrey. 1971a(300).
Social Contract, The. Jean Jacques Rousseau. WP(512).
Social Origins of Dictatorship and Democracy. Barrington Moore, Jr. SCL(4334), 1967a(306).
Social Teaching of the Christian Churches, The. Ernst Troeltsch. CHL(873).
Society and Solitude. Ralph Waldo Emerson. MCLE(4881), MP4(1156), MPA1(131).
Sohrab and Rustum. Matthew Arnold. MCLE(4884), MP(344), MP3(1002).
Soirées de Saint-Pétersbourg, Les. Joseph Marie de Maistre. CAL(630).
Soldier. General Matthew B. Ridgway. SCL(4337), 1957a (247).
Soldier with the Arabs, A. Sir John Bagot Glubb. SCL (4340), 1959a(226).
Soldiers and Civilians. Marcus Cunliffe. SCL(4343), 1969a (291).
Soldier's Art, The. Anthony Powell. SCL(4346), 1969a(294).
Soldier's Fortune, The. Thomas Otway. MCLE(4886), MD (792), MP3(1004).
Soliloquy on the Earnest Money of the Soul. Hugh of St. Victor. CHL(209).
Solitary Singer, The. Gay Wilson Allen. BM(516), SCL (4352), 1955a(240).
Some Inner Fury. Kamala Markandaya. SCL(4355), 1957a (250).
Some People. Sir Harold Nicolson. MCLE(4889), MP4(1159).
Something about a Soldier. Mark Harris. SCL(4358), 1958a (225).
Sometimes a Great Notion. Ken Kesey. SCL(4361), 1965a (283).
Son Avenger, The. Sigrid Undset. MCLE(4891), MEU(697), MP2(978).
Son of Dust. H. F. M. Prescott. SCL(4366), 1957a(252).
Son of the Middle Border, A. Hamlin Garland. MCLE(4894), MP4(1160).
Sonezaki Shinjû. Chikamatsu Monzaemon. MCLE(4897), MD (795), MP3(1006).
Song of Bernadette, The. Franz Werfel. MCLE(4899), MEU (700), MP1(903).
Song of Hiawatha, The. Henry Wadsworth Longfellow.

MCLE(4902), MP(346), MP1(905), MPA4(15).
Song of Roland, The. Unknown. MCLE(4904), MEU(703), MP1(907).
Song of Songs, The. Hermann Sudermann. MCLE(4907), MEU(706), MP1(910).
Song of the Lark, The. Willa Cather. MAF(586), MCLE (4910), MP2(981).
Song of the World. Jean Giono. MCLE(4913), MEU(709), MP2(983).
Songs for Eve. Archibald MacLeish. BM(519), SCL(4369), 1954a(255).
Songs of Innocence and of Experience. William Blake. CHL (623).
Sonnets from the Portuguese. Elizabeth Barrett Browning. MCLE(4916), MP(348), MP3(1007).
Sonnets of Shakespeare, The. William Shakespeare. MCLE (4918), MP4(1163).
Sonnets to Orpheus. Rainer Maria Rilke. MCLE(4923), MP4(1167).
Sons and Lovers. D. H. Lawrence. MCLE(4925), MEF(807), MP1(913), PO(124), SGBN(263).
Sons of Darkness, Sons of Light. John A. Williams. 1970a (281).
Sophist. Plato. WP(110).
Sorrows of Young Werther, The. Johann Wolfgang von Goethe. MCLE(4928), MEU(712), MP1(915), PO2(435).
Sotileza. José María de Pereda. MCLE(4930), MEU(714), MP2(985).
Sot-Weed Factor, The. John Barth. MCLE(4933), MP4 (1168), SCL(4372), 1961a(238).
Soul of Wood and Other Stories. Jakov Lind. SCL(4377), 1966a(303).
Soul on Ice. Eldridge Cleaver. SCL(4380), 1968a(301).
Sound and the Fury, The. William Faulkner. MAF(589), MCLE(4937), MP1(917), SGAN(196).
Sound of the Mountain, The. Yasunari Kawabata. 1971a(304).
Sound of Waves, The. Yukio Mishima. MCLE(4940), MP4 (1171), SCL(4385), 1957a(255).
Source of Human Good, The. Henry Nelson Wieman. CHL (1084).
South Wind. Norman Douglas. MCLE(4943), MEF(810), MP2(988), SGBN(285).
Southern Heritage, The. James McBride Dabbs. SCLs(288).
Soviet Russia in China. Chiang Kai-shek. SCL(4388), 1958a (228).
Space, Time and Deity. Samuel Alexander. WP(823).
Spanish Civil War, The. Hugh Thomas. BM(522), SCL

(4391), 1962a(282).
Spanish Friar, The. John Dryden. MCLE(4946), MD(797), MP3(1009).
Spanish Gipsy, The. Thomas Middleton and William Rowley. MCLE(4948), MD(799), MP3(1011).
Spanish Tragedy, The. Thomas Kyd. MCLE(4951), MD(802), MP2(990).
Speak, Memory. Vladimir Nabokov. SCL(4395), 1968a(305).
Specimen Days. Walt Whitman. MCLE(4953), MP4(1173), MPA5(114).
Spectral Boy, The. Donald Petersen. SCL(4399), 1966a(306).
Speculations About Jakob. Uwe Johnson. MCLE(4956), MP4 (1176), SCL(4402), 1964a(247).
Spider King, The. Lawrence Schoonover. SCL(4405), 1954a (258).
Spider's House, The. Paul Bowles. SCL(4408), 1955a(243).
Spinoza of Market Street, The. Isaac Bashevis Singer. SCL(4411), 1962a(285).
Spinster. Sylvia Ashton-Warner. SCL(4414), 1960a(249).
Spire, The. William Golding. SCL(4417), 1965a(287).
Spirit of Catholicism, The. Karl Adam. CAL(778).
Spirit of Mediaeval Philosophy, The. Étienne Gilson. CAL (816), WP(946).
Spirit of Saint Francis of Sales, The. Jean Pierre Camus. CAL(597).
Spirit of the Laws, The. Charles de Montesquieu. MCLE (4959), MP4(1178).
Spiritual Espousals, The. John of Ruysbroeck. CAL(461).
Spiritual Exercises. Saint Ignatius Loyola. CAL(534).
Spiritual Friendship. Saint Aelred. CAL(319).
Spoilers, The. Rex Beach. MAF(592), MCLE(4962), MP1 (919).
Spoils of Poynton, The. Henry James. MAF(595), MCLE (4965), MP3(1013), MPA3(66).
Spoon River Anthology. Edgar Lee Masters. MCLE(4968), MP(350), MP3(1015).
Spring of the Thief. John Logan. SCL(4420), 1964a(250).
Spy, The. James Fenimore Cooper. MAF(598), MCLE(4971), MP1(921), MPA1(79).
Spy in the House of Love, A. Anaïs Nin. SCL(4423), 1954a (261).
Stand Up, Friend, with Me. Edward Field. SCL(4426), 1964a(252).
Star of Seville, The. Unknown. MCLE(4975), MD(804), MP3(1018).
State Fair. Phil Stong. MAF(602), MCLE(4977), MP1(925).
State in Catholic Thought, The. Heinrich Rommen. CAL(897).

Statesman. Plato. WP(116).
Status Seekers, The. Vance Packard. SCL(4429), 1960a(251).
Steagle, The. Irvin Faust. SCL(4432), 1967a(308).
Stephen A. Douglas. Gerald M. Capers. SCL(4434), 1960a (253).
Stephen Crane. R. W. Stallman. SCL(4438), 1969a(299).
Steppenwolf. Hermann Hesse. MCLE(4979), MEU(717), MP2 (992), PO2(459), SGEN(360).
Steps. Jerzy Kosinski. SCL(4442), 1969a(302).
Steps of Humility, The. Saint Bernard. CHL(205).
Stern. Bruce Jay Friedman. SCLs(292).
Stoic, The. Theodore Dreiser. MAF(604), MCLE(4982), MP3(1020).
Stone Angel, The. Margaret Lawrence. SCL(4445), 1965a (290).
Stone Desert. Hugo Wast. MAF(607), MCLE(4985), MP2 (994).
Stones of Venice, The. John Ruskin. MCLE(4988), MP4 (1180).
Stonewall Jackson. Lenoir Chambers. SCL(4448), 1960a(257).
Stop, You're Killing Me. James Leo Herlihy. 1971a(307).
Stop-time. Frank Conroy. SCL(4451), 1968a(308).
Stories and Texts for Nothing. Samuel Beckett. SCL(4455), 1968a(312).
Stories of Liam O'Flaherty, The. Liam O'Flaherty. SCL (4458), 1957a(258).
Stories of William Sansom, The. William Sansom. SCL (4461), 1964a(254).
Storm and Other Poems, The. William Pitt Root. 1970a (284).
Story of a Bad Boy, The. Thomas Bailey Aldrich. MAF (610), MCLE(4991), MP1(927), MPA1(12).
Story of a Country Town, The. Edgar Watson Howe. MAF (613), MCLE(4994), MP1(929).
Story of a Life, The. Konstantin Paustovsky. SCLs(295).
Story of a Soul, The. Saint Therese of Lisieux. CAL(729).
Story of an African Farm, The. Olive Schreiner. MCLE (4997), MEU(720), MP1(932), PO(140).
Story of Burnt Njal, The. Unknown. MCLE(5000), MEU (723), MP2(997).
Story of Gösta Berling. Selma Lagerlöf. MCLE(5003), MEU (726), MP1(934), PO(391).
Story of My Boyhood and Youth, The. John Muir. MCLE (5006), MP4(1183).
Story of the Guitar. Kao Tse-ch'eng. MCLE(5008), MD(806), MP3(1022).
Story Teller's Story, A. Sherwood Anderson. MCLE(5010),

MP4(1184).

Story That Ends with a Scream and Eight Others, A. James Leo Herlihy. SCLs(298).

Stowaway. Lawrence Sargent Hall. SCL(4464), 1962a(288).

Straight and Narrow Path, The. Honor Tracy. SCL(4467), 1957a(261).

Strange Interlude. Eugene O'Neill. MCLE(5013), MD(808), MP2(1000), TCP(280).

Strange Stories from a Chinese Studio. P'u Sung-ling. MCLE(5016), MEU(729), MP3(1024).

Stranger, The. Albert Camus. MCLE(5018), MP4(1187), PO2(359), SGEN(440).

Strangers and Brothers. C. P. Snow. SCL(4470), 1961a (242).

Strangers and Graves. Peter S. Feibleman. SCL(4473), 1967a(311).

Strawberry Statement, The. James Simon Kunen. 1970a (287).

Street Scene. Elmer Rice. DGAP(245), MCLE(5021), MD (811), MP3(1026), SGAP(79), TCP(309).

Streetcar Named Desire, A. Tennessee Williams. MCLE (5023), MP4(1189), SGAP(214), TCP(453).

Strife. John Galsworthy. MCLE(5026), MD(813), MP1(936), POP(106).

Strike the Father Dead. John Wain. SCL(4476), 1963a(259).

String Too Short to Be Saved. Donald Hall. SCL(4479), 1962a(290).

Stromata, or Miscellanies, The. Saint Clement of Alexandria. CHL(43).

Stromateis. Saint Clement of Alexandria. CAL(44).

Students Without Teachers. Harold Taylor. 1970a(291).

Studies in Classic American Literature. D. H. Lawrence. MCLE(5028), MP4(1192).

Studies on Hysteria. Josef Breuer and Sigmund Freud. MCLE(5031), MP4(1195).

Studs Lonigan: A Trilogy. James T. Farrell. MAF(616), MCLE(5034), MP3(1028).

Study in Scarlet, A. Arthur Conan Doyle. MCLE(5036), MEF(813), MP1(938).

Study of History, A. Arnold Toynbee. MCLE(5039), MN (291), MP3(1030).

Study of Religion, A. James Martineau. CHL(802).

Styles of Radical Will. Susan Sontag. 1970a(294).

Subject Was Roses, The. Frank D. Gilroy. SCLs(300).

Sue 'Em. Nancy Bancroft Brosius. DGAP(215).

Suez. Hugh Thomas. SCL(4482), 1968a(315).

Summa contra gentiles. Saint Thomas Aquinas. CAL(385),

CHL(232), WP(314).
Summa de creaturis. Saint Albert the Great. CAL(352).
Summa theologica (or theologiae). Saint Thomas Aquinas. CAL(416), CHL(241), MCLE(5042), MN(294), MP3 (1033), WP(321).
Summa universae theologiae. Alexander of Hales. CAL(382).
Summer Knowledge. Delmore Schwartz. SCL(4486), 1960a (260).
Summing Up, The. W. Somerset Maugham. MCLE(5045), MP4(1198).
Summoned by Bells. John Betjeman. SCL(4490), 1961a(245).
Sun Also Rises, The. Ernest Hemingway. MAF(618), MCLE(5048), MP1(941), SGAN(161).
Sunken Bell, The. Gerhart Hauptmann. MCLE(5051), MD (815), MP3(1035).
Sunrise at Campobello. Dore Schary. DGAP(415).
Suppliants, The. Aeschylus. MCLE(5054), MD(818), MP2 (1002).
Suppliants, The. Euripides. MCLE(5057), MD(821), MP3 (1038).
Suppositi, I. Ludovico Ariosto. MCLE(5059), MD(823), MP3(1039).
Surry of Eagle's-Nest. John Esten Cooke. MAF(621), MCLE(5061), MP3(1042).
Swallow Barn. John P. Kennedy. MAF(624), MCLE(5064), MP2(1004).
Swamp Fox. Robert Duncan Bass. SCLs(303).
Swann's Way. Marcel Proust. PO(319), SGEN(317).
Sweet Bird of Youth. Tennessee Williams. BM(526), SCL (4494), 1960a(263).
Sweet Thursday. John Steinbeck. SCL(4498), 1954a(264).
Swiss Family Robinson, The. Johann Rudolf Wyss. MCLE (5066), MEU(731), MP1(943).
Sword of God, The. René Hardy. SCL(4501), 1954a(267).
Symbolism. Johann Adam Möhler. CAL(640).
Symposium. Plato. WP(74).
Syntagma philosophicum. Pierre Gassendi. WP(404).
System of Doctrines. Samuel Hopkins. CHL(629).
System of Logic, A. John Stuart Mill. WP(606).
Systematic Theology. Charles Hodge. CHL(766).
Systematic Theology. Augustus Hopkins Strong. CHL(797).
Systematic Theology. Paul Tillich. CHL(1135), WP(1138).

Taft Story, The. William Smith White. SCLs(307).
Take a Girl Like You. Kingsley Amis. SCL(4504), 1962a (293).
Tale for Midnight, A. Frederic Prokosch. SCL(4508),

1955a(246).
Tale for the Mirror. Hortense Calisher. SCL(4511), 1963a (262).
Tale of a Tub, A. Jonathan Swift. MCLE(5069), MP4(1201).
Tale of Genji, The. Lady Murasaki Shikibu. MCLE(5073), MEU(734), MP2(1006), PO2(423).
Tale of Two Cities, A. Charles Dickens. MCLE(5075), MEF(816), MP1(945), PO(59), PON(373), SGBN(88).
Tales. LeRoi Jones. SCLs(310).
Tales of Ise. Arihara no Narihira. MCLE(5079), MEU(737), MP3(1044).
Tales of Soldiers and Civilians. Ambrose Bierce. MAF (626), MCLE(5081), MP3(1047), MPA1(22).
Tales of Uncle Remus. Joel Chandler Harris. MAF(629), MCLE(5084), MP3(1049), MPA2(20).
Talisman, The. Sir Walter Scott. MCLE(5087), MEF(819), MP2(1009).
Tamar. Robinson Jeffers. MCLE(5090), MP(353), MP1(948).
Tamburlaine the Great. Christopher Marlowe. MCLE(5092), MD(825), MP1(950), POP(218).
Taming of the Shrew, The. William Shakespeare. MCLE (5095), MD(828), MP2(1011).
Tao Te Ching. Unknown. WP(207).
Taps for Private Tussie. Jesse Stuart. MAF(632), MCLE (5098), MP1(952), 1970a(298).
Taras Bulba. Nikolai V. Gogol. MCLE(5101), MEU(740), MP1(954).
Tarka the Otter. Henry Williamson. MCLE(5104), MP4 (1203).
Tarr. Wyndham Lewis. MCLE(5107), MEF(822), MP3(1051).
Tartarin of Tarascon. Alphonse Daudet. MCLE(5109), MEU (743), MP1(956).
Tartuffe. Molière. MCLE(5113), MD(831), MP1(959), POP (262).
Task, The. William Cowper. MCLE(5116), MP(355), MP3 (1054).
Tea and Sympathy. Robert Anderson. BM(530), SCL(4514), SGAP(265), 1954a(270).
Teaching as a Subversive Activity. Neil Postman and Charles Weingartner. 1970a(303).
Teahouse of the August Moon, The. John Patrick. BM(533), DGAP(390), SCL(4517), 1954a(273).
Teitelbaum's Window. Wallace Markfield. 1971a(311).
Telephone Poles. John Updike. SCL(4520), 1964a(257).
Tell Freedom. Peter Abrahams. SCL(4524), 1954a(276).
Tell Me a Riddle. Tillie Olsen. SCL(4527), 1962a(296).
Tell Me, Tell Me. Marianne Moore. SCL(4529), 1967a(313).
Tell Me That You Love Me, Junie Moon. Marjorie Kellogg.

SCL(4533), 1969a(305).
Temper of Our Time, The. Eric Hoffer. SCL(4537), 1967a (316).
Tempest, The. William Shakespeare. MCLE(5118), MD(833), MP1(961).
Temple, The. George Herbert. MCLE(5121), MP(357), MP3(1056).
Temple Beau, The. Henry Fielding. MCLE(5124), MD(836), MP2(1013).
Temple of the Golden Pavilion, The. Yukio Mishima. SCL (4541), 1960a(266).
Temptation of Saint Anthony, The. Gustave Flaubert. MCLE (5127), MEU(746), MP3(1059).
Ten North Frederick. John O'Hara. SCL(4545), 1955a(249).
Ten Thousand Things, The. Maria Dermoût. SCL(4548), 1959a(229).
Tenant of Wildfell Hall, The. Anne Brontë. MCLE(5130), MEF(825), MP1(963).
Tenants of Moonbloom, The. Edward Lewis Wallant. MCLE (5132), MP4(1205), SCL(4551), 1964a(261).
Tender Is the Night. F. Scott Fitzgerald. MAF(635), MCLE (5135), MP2(1016), PO2(233).
Tenth Man, The. Paddy Chayefsky. SGAP(277).
Terezín Requiem, The. Josef Bor. SCL(4554), 1964a(264).
Terrible Beauty, A. Arthur J. Roth. SCL(4559), 1959a(231).
Teseide, La. Giovanni Boccaccio. MCLE(5138), MP4(1208).
Tess of the d'Urbervilles. Thomas Hardy. MCLE(5141), MEF(827), MP1(965), PO(105), PON(377).
Thackeray: The Age of Wisdom, 1847-1863. Gordon N. Ray. BM(536), SCL(4562), 1959a(234).
Thackeray: The Uses of Adversity. Gordon N. Ray. BM (540), SCL(4566), 1955a(252).
Thaddeus of Warsaw. Jane Porter. MCLE(5144), MEF(830), MP1(967).
Thaddeus Stevens: Scourge of the South. Fawn M. Brodie. SCLs(315).
Thaïs. Anatole France. PO2(323).
That Uncertain Feeling. Kingsley Amis. MCLE(5147), MP4 (1210).
Theaetetus. Plato. WP(98).
Thebais, The. Publius Papinius Statius. MCLE(5150), MP (360), MP3(1062).
them. Joyce Carol Oates. 1970a(307).
Theodicy. Gottfried Wilhelm von Leibniz. WP(454).
Theodore Roosevelt: The Formative Years. Carlton Putnam. SCL(4570), 1959a(237).
Theologica germanica. Unknown. CHL(276).

Theology and Sanity. Francis Joseph Sheed. CAL(906).
Theology as an Empirical Science. Douglas Clyde Macintosh. CHL(899).
Theology for the Social Gospel, A. Walter Rauschenbusch. CHL(886).
Theology of the New Testament. Rudolf Bultmann. CHL (1097).
Theophilus to Autolycus. Saint Theophilus of Antioch. CAL (33), CHL(32).
Theory of Moral Sentiments. Adam Smith. WP(506).
Theory of the Leisure Class, The. Thorsten Veblen. MCLE (5152), MP4(1213).
There Are Crimes and Crimes. August Strindberg. MCLE (5154), MD(839), MP3(1064).
Therefore Be Bold. Herbert Gold. SCL(4574), 1961a(248).
Thérèse. François Mauriac. MCLE(5157), MEU(749), MP3 (1066).
These Lovers Fled Away. Howard Spring. SCL(4577), 1955a(256).
These Thousand Hills. A. B. Guthrie, Jr. SCL(4580), 1957a(263).
Thesmophoriazusae, The. Aristophanes. MCLE(5159), MD (842), MP3(1068).
They Called Him Stonewall. Burke Davis. SCL(4583), 1954a(279).
They Came to Cordura. Glendon Swarthout. SCL(4586), 1959a(241).
They Hanged My Saintly Billy. Robert Graves. SCL(4589), 1958a(231).
They Knew What They Wanted. Sidney Howard. POP(23), SGAP(74).
They Shoot Horses, Don't They? Horace McCoy. MCLE (5161), MP4(1214).
Thieves' Carnival. Jean Anouilh. TCP(32).
Thin Man, The. Dashiell Hammett. MAF(638), MCLE(5164), MP1(970).
Thin Red Line, The. James Jones. SCL(4592), 1963a(265).
Things of This World. Richard Wilbur. SCL(4595), 1957a (266).
Third Book About Achim, The. Uwe Johnson. SCL(4598), 1968a(318).
Third Policeman, The. Flann O'Brien. SCL(4601), 1968a (321).
Thirteenth Apostle, The. Eugene Vale. SCL(4604), 1960a (270).
Thirty-Nine Steps, The. John Buchan. MCLE(5167), MEF (833), MP1(972).

This Above All. Eric Knight. MCLE(5170), MEF(836), MP1 (974).
This Hallowed Ground. Bruce Catton. BM(544), SCL(4607), 1957a(269).
This Way for the Gas, Ladies and Gentlemen. Tadeusz Borowski. SCL(4610), 1968a(324).
Thomas. Shelley Mydans. SCL(4614), 1966a(309).
Thomas Becket. Richard Winston. SCL(4619), 1968a(328).
Thomas Wolfe. Elizabeth Nowell. BM(547), SCL(4622), 1961a(251).
Thoughts on the Interpretation of Nature. Denis Diderot. WP(495).
Thousand Cranes. Yasunari Kawabata. 1970a(277).
Thousand Days, A. Arthur M. Schlesinger. SCL(4626), 1966a(313).
Thread That Runs So True, The. Jesse Stuart. SCLs(318).
Three. Sylvia Ashton-Warner. 1971a(314).
Three Black Pennys, The. Joseph Hergesheimer. MAF(641), MCLE(5172), MP1(976).
Three by Eastlake. William Eastlake. 1971a(318).
Three-Cornered Hat, The. Pedro Antonio de Alarcón. MCLE(5175), MEU(751), MP1(978), PO2(440).
Three Lectures on Aesthetic. Bernard Bosanquet. WP(806).
Three Men in a Boat. Jerome K. Jerome. MCLE(5178), MEF(838), MP2(1018).
Three Men on a Horse. John Cecil Holm and George Abbott. SGAP(172).
Three Musketeers, The. Alexandre Dumas (father). MCLE (5181), MEU(754), MP1(981), PO(279), PON(381).
Three Plays. Harold Pinter. SCL(4631), 1963a(267).
Three Saints and a Sinner. Louise Hall Tharp. SCL(4634), 1957a(272).
Three Sisters, The. Anton Chekhov. MCLE(5185), MD(844), MP2(1020), POP(357).
Three Soldiers. John Dos Passos. MAF(644), MCLE(5188), MP1(984).
Three Tickets to Adventure. Gerald Durrell. SCL(4637), 1955a(259).
Three Travelers. Marie-Claire Blais. SCL(1054), 1968a(63).
Three Ways, The. Saint Bonaventure. CAL(356).
Threepenny Opera, The. Bertolt Brecht. TCP(89).
Three's Company. Alfred Duggan. SCL(4640), 1959a(244).
Threescore and Ten. Walter Allen. SCL(4644), 1960a(272).
Through Streets Broad and Narrow. Gabriel Fielding. SCL (4647), 1961a(255).
Through the Looking Glass. Lewis Carroll. MCLE(5191), MEF(841), MP2(1023), PO2(64).

Thus Spake Zarathustra. Friedrich Wilhelm Nietzsche. MCLE(5194), MN(297), MP3(1069), WP(686).
Thy Tears Might Cease. Michael Farrell. SCL(4650), 1965a(293).
Thyestes. Lucius Annaeus Seneca. MCLE(5197), MD(847), MP2(1026).
Tidings Brought to Mary, The. Paul Claudel. TCP(109).
Tiger at the Gates. Jean Giraudoux. BM(551), MCLE(5199), MP4(1217), SCL(4654), TCP(170), 1955a(262).
Tiger of the Snows. Tenzing Norgay. SCL(4658), 1955a(265).
Till We Have Faces. C. S. Lewis. SCL(4662), 1958a(233).
Timaeus. Plato. WP(125).
Time and a Place, A. William Humphrey. SCL(4665), 1969a(309).
Time and Again. Jack Finney. 1971a(324).
Time and Eternity. Walter T. Stace. CHL(1139).
Time and Free Will. Henri Bergson. WP(703).
Time in Rome, A. Elizabeth Bowen. SCL(4668), 1961a(258).
Time Machine, The. H. G. Wells. MCLE(5202), MEF(844), MP1(986), SGBN(201).
Time of Friendship, The. Paul Bowles. SCL(4670), 1968a (331).
Time of Man, The. Elizabeth Madox Roberts. MAF(647), MCLE(5205), MP1(989).
Time of Your Life, The. William Saroyan. DGAP(325), SGAP(202).
Timon of Athens. William Shakespeare. MCLE(5208), MD (849), MP2(1028).
Tin Can, The. William Jay Smith. SCL(4674), 1967a(320).
Tin Drum, The. Günter Grass. MCLE(5211), MP4(1220), SCL(4679), 1964a(269).
'Tis Pity She's a Whore. John Ford. MCLE(5214), MD(852), MP2(1030).
Titan, The. Theodore Dreiser. MAF(650), MCLE(5218), MP1(991).
Titans, The. André Maurois. SCL(4682), 1959a(248).
Titus Andronicus. William Shakespeare. MCLE(5221), MD (856), MP2(1033).
To an Early Grave. Wallace Markfield. SCL(4685), 1965a (296).
To Appomattox. Burke Davis. SCL(4689), 1960a(275).
To Be a Pilgrim. Joyce Cary. MCLE(5225), MEF(847), MP3(1072).
To Criticize the Critic. T. S. Eliot. SCL(4692), 1967a(324).
To Damascus, Part I. August Strindberg. TCP(401).
To Damascus, Part II. August Strindberg. TCP(405).
To Damascus, Part III. August Strindberg. TCP(408).

To Kill a Mockingbird. Harper Lee. BM(555), SCL(4696), 1961a(260).
To Leave Before Dawn. Julian Green. SCL(4699), 1968a (334).
To Mix with Time. May Swenson. SCL(4703), 1964a(271).
To Teach, To Love. Jesse Stuart. 1971a(327).
To the Lighthouse. Virginia Woolf. MCLE(5228), MEF(850), MP1(993).
Tobacco Road. Erskine Caldwell. MAF(653), MCLE(5231), MP1(996), POP(10).
Tobacco Road. Jack Kirkland. DGAP(265), SGAP(166).
Toilers of the Sea, The. Victor Hugo. MCLE(5233), MEU (758), MP2(1037), PON(385).
Tolstoy. Henri Troyat. SCL(4706), 1969a(312).
Tom Barber. Forrest Reid. SCL(4710), 1955a(269).
Tom Brown's School Days. Thomas Hughes. MCLE(5236), MEF(853), MP2(1039), PON(389).
Tom Burke of Ours. Charles Lever. MCLE(5238), MEF (855), MP2(1041).
Tom Cringle's Log. Michael Scott. MCLE(5243), MEF(860), MP1(997).
Tom Jones. Henry Fielding. MCLE(5246), MEF(863), MP1 (1000), PO(89), PON(393), SGBN(24).
Tom Sawyer. Samuel L. Clemens. MAF(655), MCLE(5250), MP1(1003), MPA5(93), SGAN(40).
Tom Thumb the Great. Henry Fielding. MCLE(5253), MD (860), MP2(1046).
Tome. Saint Leo the Great. CAL(201), CHL(159).
Tomorrow and Yesterday. Heinrich Böll. SCL(4714), 1958a (236).
Tonight We Improvise. Luigi Pirandello. TCP(305).
Tono-Bungay. H. G. Wells. MCLE(5256), MEF(867), MP1 (1006), SGBN(206).
Touch. Thom Gunn. SCL(4717), 1969a(315).
Touch of the Poet, A. Eugene O'Neill. BM(558), SCL(4720), 1958a(239).
Tower of London, The. William Harrison Ainsworth. MCLE (5259), MEF(870), MP1(1008).
Towers of Trebizond, The. Rose Macaulay. SCL(4723), 1958a(242).
Town, The. William Faulkner. BM(561), MAF(658), MCLE (5262), MP3(1074), SCL(4726), 1958a(245).
Town, The. Conrad Richter. MAF(661), MCLE(5265), MP2 (1048).
Toys in the Attic. Lillian Hellman. SCL(4729), 1961a(263).
Track of the Cat, The. Walter Van Tilburg Clark. MAF (664), MCLE(5268), MP2(1051).

Tract Concerning the First Principle, The. John Duns Scotus. WP(329).
Tractatus logico-philosophicus. Ludwig Wittgenstein. WP (829).
Tragedy of Superstition, The. James Nelson Barker. DGAP (37).
Tragic Muse, The. Henry James. MCLE(5271), MP4(1222), MPA3(71).
Tragic Sense of Life in Men and in Peoples, The. Miguel de Unamuno y Jugo. MCLE(5275), MP4(1225).
Train of Powder, A. Rebecca West. SCL(4732), 1955a(272).
Training in Christianity. Søren Kierkegaard. CHL(720).
Traité du libre arbitre. Yves René Marie Simon. CAL(986).
Traitor, The. James Shirley. MCLE(5277), MD(863), MP3 (1077).
Transformation in Christ. Dietrich von Hildebrand. CAL (946).
Transgressor, The. Julian Green. SCL(4736), 1958a(247).
Transient and Permanent in Christianity, The. Theodore Parker. CHL(700).
Trap, The. Dan Jacobson. SCL(4739), 1955a(275).
Traveling Through the Dark. William Stafford. SCLs(325).
Travellers, The. Jean Stubbs. SCL(4742), 1964a(274).
Travels in Arabia Deserta. Charles M. Doughty. MCLE (5280), MN(300), MP3(1079).
Travels of Jaimie McPheeters, The. Robert Lewis Taylor. SCL(4747), 1959a(251).
Travels of Marco Polo. Marco Polo. MCLE(5283), MN(303), MP1(1011).
Travels to the Interior Districts of Africa. Mungo Park. MCLE(5287), MP4(1227).
Travels with a Donkey. Robert Louis Stevenson. MCLE (5290), MN(307), MP1(1014).
Travels with Charley. John Steinbeck. SCL(4751), 1963a (270).
Travels with My Aunt. Graham Greene. 1971a(332).
Treasure Island. Robert Louis Stevenson. MCLE(5292), MEF(873), MP1(1015), PO2(71), PON(398), SGBN(185).
Treatise Concerning Religious Affections, A. Jonathan Edwards. CHL(590).
Treatise Concerning the Principles of Human Knowledge, A. George Berkeley. WP(447).
Treatise Concerning the Pursuit of Learning. Hugh of St. Victor. CAL(300).
Treatise Concerning the Search After Truth. Nicholas Malebranche. CHL(522).
Treatise of Excommunication. Thomas Erastus. CHL(414).

Treatise of Human Nature, A (Book I). David Hume. WP (471).
Treatise of Reformation Without Tarrying for Any. Robert Browne. CHL(400).
Treatise on Christian Liberty, A. Martin Luther. CHL(339).
Treatise on Laws. Francisco Suarez, S. J. CAL(575).
Treatise on the Church. John Huss. CHL(304).
Treatise on the Four Gospels. Joachim of Fiore. CHL(224).
Treatise on the Holy Spirit. Saint Basil. CAL(107).
Treatise on the Laws and Customs of England. Henry of Bracton. CAL(367).
Treatise on the Laws of Ecclesiastical Polity. Richard Hooker. CHL(418).
Treatise on the Mysteries. Saint Hilary of Poitiers. CAL (103).
Treatise on the Passion. Sir Thomas More. CAL(538).
Treatise on the Promises. Saint Dionysius of Alexandria. CAL(78).
Treatises and Sermons of Meister Eckhart, The. Johann Eckhart. CAL(451).
Treatises of Cicero, The. Marcus Tullius Cicero. MCLE (5295), MP4(1229).
Treatises on Marriage. Tertullian. CAL(54).
Treblinka. Jean-Francois Steiner. SCL(4753), 1968a(337).
Tree Grows in Brooklyn, A. Betty Smith. MAF(667), MCLE(5298), MP1(1018).
Tree of Man, The. Patrick White. MCLE(5301), MP4(1232), SCL(4756), 1955a(278).
Tree of the Folkungs, The. Verner von Heidenstam. MCLE (5304), MEU(761), MP2(1053).
Tree on Fire, A. Alan Sillitoe. SCL(4759), 1969a(318).
Trees, The. Conrad Richter. MAF(670), MCLE(5307), MP2(1055).
Trelawney of the Wells. Arthur Wing Pinero. POP(138).
Trial, The. Franz Kafka. MCLE(5310), MEU(764), MP1 (1020), PO2(478), SGEN(352).
Trial by Jury. W. S. Gilbert and Arthur Sullivan. MCLE (5313), MD(866), MP2(1058).
Trialogus. John Wycliffe. CHL(294).
Tribe That Lost Its Head, The. Nicholas Monsarrat. SCL (4763), 1957a(275).
Trick to Catch the Old One, A. Thomas Middleton. MCLE (5315), MD(868), MP2(1059).
Trickster, The. Titus Maccius Plautus. MCLE(5318), MD (871), MP3(1081).
Trilby. George Du Maurier. MCLE(5321), MEF(876), MP1 (1023), PO(70), PON(402).

Trip to Chinatown, A. Charles H. Hoyt. DGAP(125).
Tristan and Isolde. Gottfried von Strassburg. MCLE(5324), MP(362), MP3(1083).
Tristram. Edwin Arlington Robinson. MCLE(5326), MP (364), MP1(1025).
Tristram Shandy. Laurence Sterne. MCLE(5329), MEF(879), MP1(1027), PO2(20), SGBN(40).
Triumph in the West. Sir Arthur Bryant. BM(564), SCL (4767), 1960a(278).
Triumph of Death, The. Gabriele D'Annunzio. MCLE(5332), MEU(767), MP2(1061).
Triumph or Tragedy: Reflections on Vietnam. Richard N. Goodwin. SCL(4770), 1967a(328).
Troilus and Cressida. William Shakespeare. MCLE(5334), MD(874), MP2(1063).
Troilus and Criseyde. Geoffrey Chaucer. MCLE(5337), MP (367), MP1(1030).
Trojan Women, The. Euripides. MCLE(5339), MD(877), MP3(1085), POP(375).
Tropic of Capricorn. Henry Miller. MCLE(5341), MP4(1234).
True Adventures of Huckleberry Finn. John Seeyle. 1970a (313).
True Christianity. Johann Arndt. CHL(422).
True Grit. Charles Portis. SCL(4773), 1969a(321).
True History, The. Lucian. MCLE(5345), MEU(769), MP3 (1087).
True Humanism. Jacques Maritain. CHL(1020).
True Intellectual System of the Universe, The. Ralph Cudworth. CHL(534).
Trustee from the Toolroom. Nevil Shute. SCL(4777), 1961a (266).
Trusting and the Maimed, The. James Plunkett. SCL(4780), 1955a(281).
Truth of the Christian Religion, The. Hugo Grotius. CHL (432).
Truth Suspected. Juan Ruiz de Alarcón. MCLE(5347), MD (879), MP3(1089).
Tunc. Lawrence Durrell. SCL(4783), 1969a(324).
Tunnel of Love, The. Peter De Vries. SCL(4787), 1954a (282).
Turcaret. Alain René Le Sage. MCLE(5349), MD(881), MP3(1091).
Turn of the Screw, The. Henry James. MAF(673), MCLE (5352), MP2(1066), MPA3(77), PO2(186), SGAN(66).
Turn of the Tide, The. Sir Arthur Bryant. BM(567), SCL (4790), 1958a(250).
Twelfth Night. William Shakespeare. MCLE(5355), MD(884),

MP2(1069).
Twelve Pictures, The. Edith Simon. SCL(4793), 1955a(284).
Twenty Letters to a Friend. Svetlana Alliluyeva. SCL (4796), 1968a(340).
Twenty Thousand Leagues Under the Sea. Jules Verne. MCLE(5358), MEU(771), MP1(1031), PON(407), SGEN (188).
Twenty Years After. Alexandre Dumas (father). MCLE (5360), MEU(773), MP2(1071).
Twilight in Italy. D. H. Lawrence. MCLE(5363), MP4 (1238).
Two Adolescents. Alberto Moravia. SGEN(448).
Two Cities, The. Otto of Freising. CAL(316).
Two Deaths of Quincas Wateryell, The. Jorge Amado. SCL (4799), 1966a(319).
Two Discourses on Universal History. Anne Robert Jacques Turgot. CAL(628).
Two-Edged Sword, The. John L. McKenzie, S.J. CAL (1028).
Two Essays on Analytical Psychology. Carl G. Jung. MCLE(5366), MP4(1240).
Two Gentlemen of Verona. William Shakespeare. MCLE (5369), MD(887), MP2(1074).
Two Noble Kinsmen, The. William Shakespeare and John Fletcher. MCLE(5371), MD(889), MP2(1076).
Two Sides of an Island. Martin Halpern. SCL(4803), 1964a (278).
Two Sources of Morality and Religion, The. Henri Bergson. CHL(990), WP(959).
Two Tales. Shmuel Yosef Agnon. SCL(4806), 1967a(331).
Two Towers, The. J. R. R. Tolkien. MCLE(5373), MP4 (1242).
Two Under the Indian Sun. Jon and Rumer Godden. SCL (4809), 1967a(333).
Two Weeks in Another Town. Irvin Shaw. SCL(4813), 1961a (268).
Two Women. Alberto Moravia. MCLE(5376), MP4(1245), SCL(4817), 1959a(254).
Two Years Before the Mast. Richard Henry Dana, Jr. MCLE(5379), MN(309), MP1(1033), MPA1(94).
Typee. Herman Melville. MAF(676), MCLE(5382), MP1 (1035), MPA4(92).

U. S. A. John Dos Passos. MAF(685), MCLE(5436), MP1 (1051), PON(416).
Ubu Roi. Alfred Jarry. TCP(206).
Ugly Duchess, The. Lion Feuchtwanger. MCLE(5385), MEU

(776), MP1(1037).
Ulysses. James Joyce. MCLE(5388), MEF(882), MP1(1040).
Unbearable Bassington, The. Saki. MCLE(5391), MEF(885), MP1(1042).
Uncle Silas. Joseph Sheridan Le Fanu. MCLE(5394), MEF (888), MP2(1078).
Uncle Tom's Cabin. George L. Aiken. DGAP(72).
Uncle Tom's Cabin. Harriet Beecher Stowe. MAF(679), MCLE(5398), MP1(1044), MPA5(31), PO(256), PON (411), POP(72), SGAN(33).
Uncle Vanya. Anton Chekhov. MCLE(5401), MD(891), MP2 (1082).
Uncompleted Past, The. Martin Duberman. 1970a(315).
Under Fire. Henri Barbusse. MCLE(5404), MEU(779), MP1 (1047).
Under Milk Wood: A Play for Voices. Dylan Thomas. BM (570), MCLE(5407), MP4(1247), SCL(4820), 1954a(285).
Under the Greenwood Tree. Thomas Hardy. MCLE(5411), MEF(892), MP2(1084).
Under the Mountain Wall. Peter Matthiessen. SCL(4824), 1963a(272).
Under the Volcano. Malcolm Lowry. MCLE(5414), MP4 (1250).
Under the Yoke. Ivan Vazov. MCLE(5417), MEU(782), MP2 (1086).
Under Two Flags. Ouida. MCLE(5420), MEF(895), MP1 (1049).
Under Western Eyes. Joseph Conrad. MCLE(5423), MEF (898), MP3(1093).
Underdogs, The. Mariano Azuela. MAF(682), MCLE(5425), MP2(1088).
Undine. Friedrich de La Motte-Fouqué. MCLE(5428), MEU (785), MP2(1091).
Une Vie. Guy de Maupassant. PO(315).
Unexpected Universe, The. Loren Eisely. 1970a(320).
Unfinished Woman, An. Lillian Hellman. 1970a(322).
Unfortunate Traveller, The. Thomas Nash. MCLE(5430), MEF(900), MP2(1092).
Unicorn, The. Iris Murdoch. SCL(4828), 1964a(281).
Unitarian Christianity. William Ellery Channing. CHL(650).
Unity, 1942-1944. Charles de Gaulle. SCL(4831), 1960a(281).
Unity of Philosophical Experience, The. Étienne Gilson. CAL(845).
Universal Baseball Association, Inc., J. Henry Waugh, Prop., The. Robert Coover. SCL(4834), 1969a(327).
Unknown of Arras, The. Armand Salacrou. TCP(313).
Unnamable, The. Samuel Beckett. SCL(4838), 1959a(257).

Unofficial Rose, An. Iris Murdoch. SCL(4841), 1963a(276).
Unperfect Society, The. Milovan Djilas. 1970a(326).
Unspeakable Practices, Unnatural Acts. Donald Barthelme. SCL(4845), 1969a(331).
Unspeakable Skipton, The. Pamela Hansford Johnson. SCL (4848), 1960a(284).
Untoward Hills, The. Albert Stewart. SCL(4851), 1963a (279).
Unvanquished, The. William Faulkner. MCLE(5433), MP4 (1253).
Upon the Sweeping Flood. Joyce Carol Oates. SCL(4854), 1967a(336).
Us He Devours. James B. Hall. SCL(4858), 1965a(299).
Uses of Disorder, The. Richard Sennett. 1971a(335).
Utilitarianism. John Stuart Mill. WP(654).
Utopia. Sir Thomas More. CAL(509), MCLE(5439), MN (312), MP3(1095), WP(348).

V. Thomas Pynchon. SCL(4861), 1964a(284).
Valley of Bones, The. Anthony Powell. SCL(4864), 1965a (302).
Vanessa. Hugh Walpole. MCLE(5442), MEF(903), MP1(1054).
Vanished Cities. Herman and Georg Schreiber. SCL(4867), 1958a(252).
Vanity Fair. William Makepeace Thackeray. MCLE(5445), MEF(906), MP1(1056), PO(167), PON(423), SGBN(116).
Varieties of Religious Experience, The. William James. CHL(836).
Variety Photoplays. Edward Field. SCL(4870), 1968a(343).
Vasco. Georges Schéhadé. TCP(333).
Vathek. William Beckford. MCLE(5449), MEF(910), MP2 (1094).
Velvet Horn, The. Andrew Lytle. BM(573), MCLE(5451), MP4(1256), SCL(4873), 1958a(255).
Venetian Glass Nephew, The. Elinor Wylie. MAF(688), MCLE(5454), MP2(1096).
Venetian Red. P. M. Pasinetti. SCL(4877), 1961a(272).
Venice Preserved. Thomas Otway. MCLE(5457), MD(894), MP2(1098).
Venus and Adonis. William Shakespeare. MCLE(5460), MP (369), MP1(1060).
Verdi. George Martin. SCL(4880), 1964a(286).
Very Private Life, A. Michael Frayn. SCL(4884), 1969a (334).
Vicar of Bullhampton, The. Anthony Trollope. MCLE(5462), MEF(912), MP2(1101).
Vicar of Wakefield, The. Oliver Goldsmith. MCLE(5465),

MEF(915), MP1(1061), PO(95), PON(427), SGBN(32).
Vicomte de Bragelonne, The. Alexandre Dumas (father). MCLE(5468), MEU(787), MP1(1063).
Victim, The. Saul Bellow. MCLE(5472), MP4(1259).
Victory. Joseph Conrad. MCLE(5475), MEF(918), MP1 (1067).
Victory. Oliver Warner. BM(577), SCL(4887), 1959a(260).
Victory in the Pacific, 1945. Samuel Eliot Morison. SCL (4890), 1961a(275).
Vida, La. Oscar Lewis. SCL(2460), 1967a(182).
View from Pompey's Head, The. Hamilton Basso. SCL (4893), 1954a(288).
View from the Bridge, A. Arthur Miller. BM(580), SCL (4896), TCP(229), 1955a(287).
View of the Evidences of Christianity, A. William Paley. WP(563).
Vile Bodies. Evelyn Waugh. MCLE(5478), MEF(921), MP2 (1103).
Village, The. Ivan Alexeyevich Bunin. MCLE(5481), MEU (791), MP2(1105).
Village, The. George Crabbe. MCLE(5484), MP(371), MP3 (1097).
Villette. Charlotte Brontë. MCLE(5486), MEF(924), MP2 (1108).
Vindication of Natural Society, A. Edmund Burke. MCLE (5489), MN(315), MP3(1099).
Violated, The. Vance Bourjaily. SCL(4899), 1959a(263).
Violent Bear It Away, The. Flannery O'Connor. MCLE (5492), MP4(1261), SCL(4903), 1961a(278).
Violent Land, The. Jorge Amado. MAF(691), MCLE(5494), MP2(1110).
Virgin of San Gil, The. Paul Olsen. SCL(4906), 1966a(322).
Virgin Soil. Ivan Turgenev. MCLE(5497), MEU(794), MP1 (1069), PO2(390).
Virginia Comedians, The. John Esten Cooke. MAF(694), MCLE(5500), MP2(1113).
Virginian, The. Owen Wister. MAF(697), MCLE(5503), MP1(1072).
Virginians, The. William Makepeace Thackeray. MCLE (5506), MEF(927), MP1(1074).
Visión de Anáhuac. Alfonso Reyes. MCLE(5509), MN(318), MP3(1101).
Vision of God: The Christian Doctrine of the Summum Bonum, The. Kenneth E. Kirk. CHL(977).
Vision of William, Concerning Piers the Plowman, The. William Langland. MCLE(5513), MP(373), MP3(1105).
Visit, The. Friedrich Dürrenmatt. TCP(130).

Vita nuova, The. Dante Alighieri. MCLE(5516), MP(376), MP3(1107).
Vital Parts. Thomas Berger. 1971a(338).
Vive moi! Seán O'Faoláin. SCL(4910), 1965a(305).
Vivian Grey. Benjamin Disraeli. MCLE(5519), MEF(930), MP2(1115), PON(432).
Vocation of Man, The. Johann Gottlieb Fichte. WP(570).
Voice at the Back Door, The. Elizabeth Spencer. SCL (4913), 1957a(278).
Voice of the Desert, The. Joseph Wood Krutch. SCL(4916), 1955a(290).
Voices of Glory, The. Davis Grubb. SCL(4919), 1963a(282).
Voices of Silence, The. André Malraux. MCLE(5522), MP4 (1263).
Volpone. Ben Jonson. MCLE(5525), MD(897), MP1(1076), POP(192).
Voltaire in Love. Nancy Mitford. SCL(4923), 1959a(266).
Volupté. Charles Augustin Sainte-Beuve. MCLE(5528), MEU(797), MP3(1110).
Voss. Patrick White. SCL(4926), 1958a(258).
Voyage of Magellan. Antonio Pigafetta. SCLs(328).
Voyage of the Beagle, The. Charles Darwin. MCLE(5531), MN(322), MP1(1079).
Voyage of the Lucky Dragon, The. Ralph E. Lapp. SCL (4930), 1959a(268).
Voyager: A Life of Hart Crane. John Unterecker. 1970a (328).

Waiting for Godot. Samuel Beckett. BM(583), MCLE(5533), MD(900), MP3(1113), SCL(4933), TCP(59), 1957a(281).
Waiting for Lefty. Clifford Odets. DGAP(285), TCP(257).
Walden. Henry David Thoreau. MCLE(5536), MN(324), MP2 (1117), MPA5(48).
Walk Egypt. Vinnie Williams. SCL(4936), 1961a(281).
Walking to Sleep. Richard Wilbur. 1970a(331).
Wall-Street; or, Ten Minutes Before Three. Richard W. Mead. DGAP(34).
Wallenstein. Johann Christoph Friedrich von Schiller. MCLE(5539), MD(903), MP2(1119).
Waltz of the Toreadors, The. Jean Anouilh. SCL(4939), TCP(34), 1958a(261).
Wanderer, The. Henri Alain-Fournier. MCLE(5542), MEU (800), MP1(1081), PO2(342).
Wandering Jew, The. Eugène Sue. MCLE(5545), MEU(803), MP1(1083), PO(333).
Wandering Scholar from Paradise, The. Hans Sachs. MCLE (5548), MD(906), MP3(1115).

Waning of the Middle Ages, The. Johan Huizinga. MCLE (5550), MP4(1266).
Wapshot Chronicle, The. John Cheever. BM(586), MCLE (5553), MP4(1268), SCL(4942), 1958a(264).
Wapshot Scandal, The. John Cheever. MCLE(5557), MP4 (1271), SCL(4946), 1964a(290).
War and Peace. Count Leo Tolstoy. MCLE(5561), MEU (806), MP1(1085), PO2(402), SGEN(173).
War for the Union, The, Vol. I. Allan Nevins. BM(590), SCL(4953), 1960a(286).
War for the Union, The, Vol. II. Allan Nevins. BM(594), SCL(4957), 1961a(284).
War in Algeria, The. Jules Roy. SCL(4961), 1962a(298).
War Lover, The. John Hersey. SCL(4964), 1960a(290).
War of the Worlds, The. H. G. Wells. MCLE(5566), MEF (933), MP1(1090), PO(178), PON(437).
Warden, The. Anthony Trollope. MCLE(5568), MEF(935), MP1(1092), PO2(51).
Warwick the Kingmaker. Paul Murray Kendall. SCL(4967), 1958a(268).
Washing of the Spears, The. Donald R. Morris. SCL(4970), 1966a(326).
Washington. Constance McLaughlin Green. SCLs(333).
Washington Square. Henry James. MAF(700), MCLE(5570), MP3(1117), MPA3(82), PO2(181).
Wasps, The. Aristophanes. MCLE(5573), MD(908), MP3 (1119).
Waste Land, The. T. S. Eliot. MCLE(5575), MP(379), MP3(1121).
Waste Makers, The. Vance Packard. SCL(4973), 1961a(287).
Watch on the Rhine. Lillian Hellman. DGAP(349).
Watch That Ends the Night, The. Hugh MacLennan. SCL (4976), 1960a(293).
Waterlily Fire. Muriel Rukeyser. SCL(4979), 1963a(285).
Waterloo: Day of Battle. David Howarth. SCL(4982), 1969a(337).
Waters of Kronos, The. Conrad Richter. BM(598), MCLE (5577), MP4(1274), SCL(4986), 1961a(290).
Waverley. Sir Walter Scott. MCLE(5580), MEF(937), MP1 (1094), PON(441).
Waves, The. Virginia Woolf. MCLE(5583), MEF(940), MP2 (1122).
Way of All Flesh, The. Samuel Butler. MCLE(5586), MEF (943), MP1(1097), PO(38), SGBN(159).
Way of Opinion, The. Parmenides of Elea. WP(16).
Way of Perfection, The. Saint Teresa of Ávila. CAL(555).
Way of the World, The. William Congreve. MCLE(5589),

MD(910), MP1(1099), POP(181).
Way of Truth, The and Way of Opinion, The. Parmenides of Elea. WP(16).
Way to Christ, The. Jakob Boehme. CHL(436).
Way to Rainy Mountain, The. N. Scott Momaday. 1970a (335).
We Bombed in New Haven. Joseph Heller. SCL(4989), 1969a (340).
We Have Always Lived in the Castle. Shirley Jackson. SCL(4992), 1963a(288).
We Hold These Truths. John Courtney Murray, S. J. CAL (1098).
Wealth of Nations, The. Adam Smith. MCLE(5591), MN (327), MP3(1122).
Weathers and Edges. Philip Booth. SCL(4994), 1967a(339).
Weavers, The. Gerhart Hauptmann. MCLE(5594), MD(912), MP2(1124), POP(301), TCP(184).
Web and the Rock, The. Thomas Wolfe. MAF(703), MCLE (5597), MP1(1101).
Web of Victory, The. Earl Schenck Miers. BM(601), SCL (4999), 1955a(293).
Wedemeyer Reports! General Albert C. Wedemeyer. SCL (5002), 1959a(271).
Weedkiller's Daughter, The. Harriette Simpson Arnow. 1970a(337).
Week on the Concord and Merrimack Rivers, A. Henry David Thoreau. MCLE(5600), MP4(1277), MPA5(53).
Weekend in Dinlock. Clancy Sigal. SCL(5005), 1961a(293).
Wellington. Elizabeth, Countess of Longford. 1971a(342).
Westward Ho! Charles Kingsley. MCLE(5603), MEF(946), MP1(1103), PO(117), PON(445).
What a Way to Go! Wright Morris. SCL(5008), 1963a(290).
What Comes Next. Jonathan Baumbach. SCL(5013), 1969a (343).
What Every Woman Knows. James M. Barrie. MCLE(5606), MD(915), MP1(1106), TCP(51).
What I Believe. Count Leo Tolstoy. CHL(790).
What I'm Going to Do, I Think. L. Woiwode. 1970a(340).
What Is Art? Count Leo Tolstoy. WP(723).
What Is Christianity? Adolf Harnack. CHL(823).
What Maisie Knew. Henry James. MAF(706), MCLE(5609), MP3(1125), MPA3(87).
What Price Glory? Laurence Stallings and Maxwell Anderson. DGAP(217), POP(31), SGAP(99).
Wheel of Earth, The. Helga Sandburg. SCL(5016), 1959a (274).
Wheel of Love, The. Joyce Carol Oates. 1971a(346).

When My Girl Comes Home. V. S. Pritchett. SCL(5019), 1962a(301).
When She Was Good. Philip Roth. SCL(5022), 1968a(346).
When the Cheering Stopped. Gene Smith. SCL(5025), 1965a (308).
When the Kissing Had to Stop. Constantine FitzGibbon. SCL(5028), 1961a(296).
When the Legends Die. Hal Borland. SCL(5031), 1964a(297).
When the Mountain Fell. Charles-Ferdinand Ramuz. MCLE (5612), MEU(811), MP2(1127).
When the War Is Over. Stephen Becker. 1970a(345).
When We Dead Awaken. Henrik Ibsen. MCLE(5614), MD (918), MP3(1127).
Where Angels Fear to Tread. E. M. Forster. MCLE(5616), MEF(949), MP3(1129).
Where the Air Is Clear. Carlos Fuentes. MCLE(5619), MP4(1279), SCL(5034), 1961a(300).
Where the Light Falls. Chard Powers Smith. SCL(5039), 1966a(329).
Whispering Land, The. Gerald Durrell. SCL(5043), 1963a (295).
White Company, The. Arthur Conan Doyle. MCLE(5623), MEF(952), MP1(1108), PON(450).
White Devil, The. John Webster. MCLE(5626), MD(920), MP3(1131).
White-Jacket. Herman Melville. MAF(709), MCLE(5629), MP2(1128), MPA4(97).
White Nile, The. Alan Moorehead. BM(604), SCL(5045), 1962a(304).
Whitsun Weddings, The. Philip Larkin. SCL(5048), 1966a (333).
Who Took the Gold Away. John Leggett. 1970a(348).
Who's Afraid of Virginia Woolf? Edward Albee. BM(607), MCLE(5632), MP4(1282), SCL(5052), SGAP(288), TCP (15), 1963a(297).
Wicked Pavilion, The. Dawn Powell. SCL(5058), 1954a(291).
Wickford Point. John P. Marquand. MAF(712), MCLE(5637), MP1(1110).
Widows of Thornton, The. Peter Taylor. SCL(5061), 1954a (294).
Wieland. Charles Brockden Brown. MAF(714), MCLE(5639), MP2(1131).
Wild Ass's Skin, The. Honoré de Balzac. MCLE(5642), MEU(813), MP2(1133).
Wild Duck, The. Henrik Ibsen. MCLE(5645), MD(923), MP1 (1113).
"Wild Old Wicked Men, The" and Other Poems. Archibald

MacLeish. SCL(5064), 1969a(346).
Wild Palms, The. William Faulkner. MCLE(5647), MP4 (1287).
Wild Wales. George Henry Borrow. MCLE(5650), MP4 (1289).
Wilderness of Ladies. Eleanor Ross Taylor. SCL(5067), 1961a(304).
Wilhelm Meister. Johann Wolfgang von Goethe. PO(379).
Wilhelm Meister's Apprenticeship. Johann Wolfgang von Goethe. MCLE(5653), MEU(816), MP2(1136).
Wilhelm Meister's Travels. Johann Wolfgang von Goethe. MCLE(5656), MEU(819), MP2(1139).
Will to Believe, The. William James. WP(727).
William Butler Yeats. Harold Bloom. 1971a(349).
William Faulkner. Cleanth Brooks. SCL(5070), 1964a(299).
William Faulkner: The Journey to Self-Discovery. H. Edward Richardson. 1970a(352).
William James: A Biography. Gay Wilson Allen. SCL (5076), 1968a(349).
William Morris. Philip Henderson. SCL(5081), 1968a(353).
William of Ockham: Selections. William of Ockham. WP (337).
William Penn. Catherine Owens Peare. SCL(5085), 1958a (270).
William Tell. Johann Christoph Friedrich von Schiller. MCLE(5659), MD(925), MP1(1115), POP(309).
William the Conqueror. David C. Douglas. SCL(5088), 1965a(311).
Wilson: Confusions and Crises, 1915-1916. Arthur S. Link. SCL(5091), 1966a(337).
Wind in the Willows, The. Kenneth Grahame. MCLE(5662), MEF(955), MP2(1141).
Wind, Sand and Stars. Antoine de Saint-Exupéry. MCLE (5665), MP4(1291), PO2(355).
Windsor Castle. William Harrison Ainsworth. MCLE(5668), MEF(958), MP1(1117).
Winesburg, Ohio. Sherwood Anderson. MAF(717), MCLE (5672), MP1(1121), SGAN(115).
Wings of the Dove, The. Henry James. MAF(720), MCLE (5675), MP2(1143), MPA3(92).
Winners, The. Julio Cortázar. SCL(5095), 1966a(341).
Winter in the Air. Sylvia Townsend Warner. SCL(5098), 1957a(284).
Winter in the Hills, A. John Wain. 1971a(352).
Winter News. John Haines. SCL(5101), 1967a(344).
Winter of Our Discontent, The. John Steinbeck. SCL(5105), 1962a(306).

Winter Quarters. Alfred Duggan. SCL(5108), 1957a(287).
Winter Solstice. Gerald Warner Brace. SCL(5112), 1961a (307).
Winter's Tale, The. William Shakespeare. MCLE(5678), MD(928), MP2(1146).
Winterset. Maxwell Anderson. DGAP(289), MCLE(5681), MD(931), MP1(1123), SGAP(39), TCP(19).
Wisdom of God, The. Sergius Bulgakov. CHL(1035).
Wisdom of the Sands, The. Antoine de Saint-Exupéry. MCLE(5684), MP4(1294).
Wise Blood. Flannery O'Connor. MCLE(5687), MP4(1296).
Witching Hour, The. Augustus Thomas. DGAP(166), POP (53).
With Fire and Sword. Henryk Sienkiewicz. MCLE(5690), MEU(822), MP2(1148).
With Love from Gracie. Grace Hegger Lewis. SCL(5115), 1957a(291).
With Shuddering Fall. Joyce Carol Oates. SCL(5119), 1965a(313).
Within the Gates. Sean O'Casey. MCLE(5693), MD(934), MP3(1134).
Wolf Solent. John Cowper Powys. MCLE(5696), MEF(962), MP3(1136).
Woman at the Washington Zoo, The. Randall Jarrell. BM (613), SCL(5124), 1961a(309).
Woman Hater, The. Francis Beaumont and John Fletcher. MCLE(5699), MD(937), MP3(1138).
Woman in the Dunes, The. Kobo Abé. SCL(5128), 1965a (318).
Woman in White, The. Wilkie Collins. MCLE(5702), MEF (965), MP1(1125), PO(45), PON(454).
Woman Killed with Kindness, A. Thomas Heywood. MCLE (5705), MD(940), MP2(1151).
Woman of Rome, The. Alberto Moravia. MCLE(5708), MEU(825), MP2(1153).
Woman Who Was Poor, The. Léon Bloy. CAL(726).
Woman Within, The. Ellen Glasgow. SCL(5132), 1954a(297).
Woman's Life, A. Guy de Maupassant. MCLE(5711), MEU (828), MP1(1127).
Woman's Prize, The. John Fletcher. MCLE(5714), MD(943), MP3(1141).
Women and Thomas Harrow. John P. Marquand. SCL(5136), 1959a(277).
Women Beware Women. Thomas Middleton. MCLE(5717), MD(946), MP3(1144).
Women in Love. D. H. Lawrence. MCLE(5720), MP4(1298).
Women of Trachis, The. Sophocles. MCLE(5723), MD(949),

MP3(1146).
Woodlanders, The. Thomas Hardy. MCLE(5726), MEF(968), MP2(1156).
Woodrow Wilson. Arthur Walworth. SCL(5139), 1959a(280).
Woodstock. Sir Walter Scott. MCLE(5729), MEF(971), MP2(1158).
Words, The. Jean-Paul Sartre. SCL(5142), 1965a(322).
Words upon the Window-Pane, The. William Butler Yeats. TCP(460).
Works and Days. Hesiod. MCLE(5732), MP(381), MP3(1149).
Works of Jonathan Edwards. Jonathan Edwards. MCLE (5734), MN(330), MP3(1150).
Works of Lyman Beecher, The. Lyman Beecher. CHL(724).
World and the Individual, The. Josiah Royce. WP(739).
World as Will and Idea, The. Arthur Schopenhauer. MCLE (5737), MN(333), MP3(1153), WP(582).
World Enough and Time. Robert Penn Warren. MAF(723), MCLE(5740), MP2(1160).
World of John McNulty, The. John McNulty. SCL(5145), 1958a(273).
World of Love, A. Elizabeth Bowen. SCL(5148), 1955a(296).
World of Profit, A. Louis Auchincloss. SCL(5151), 1969a (349).
World of Silence, The. Max Picard. CAL(936).
World of Strangers, A. Nadine Gordimer. SCL(5154), 1959a(283).
World of the Thibaults, The. Roger Martin du Gard. MCLE (5743), MEU(831), MP1(1130).
World the Slaveholders Made, The. Eugene D. Genovese. 1971a(356).
World We Live In, The. Lincoln Barnett. SCL(5157), 1955a (299).
World's Great Religions, The. The Editors of Life. SCL (5160), 1958a(276).
World's Illusion, The. Jacob Wassermann. MCLE(5746), MEU(834), MP1(1133), PO2(445), SGEN(336).
Worship. Evelyn Underhill. CHL(1024).
Woyzeck. Georg Büchner. MCLE(5749), MD(952), MP2 (1163).
Wreath for Udomo, A. Peter Abrahams. SCL(5163), 1957a (294).
Wreck of the Grosvenor, The. W. Clark Russell. MCLE (5753), MEF(974), MP1(1135).
Wreck of the Thresher and Other Poems, The. William Meredith. SCL(5167), 1965a(324).
Writer's Diary, A. Virginia Woolf. BM(617), SCL(5171), 1954a(301).

Writings of Saint Patrick, The. Saint Patrick. CAL(207).
Wuthering Heights. Emily Brontë. MCLE(5754), MEF(976), MP1(1137), PO(28), PON(457), SGBN(109).

Yard of Sun, A. Christopher Fry. 1971a(363).
Year of My Rebirth, The. Jesse Stuart. BM(620), SCL (5174), 1957a(297).
Year of the Whale, The. Victor B. Scheffer. 1970a(354).
Yearling, The. Marjorie Kinnan Rawlings. MAF(726), MCLE(5757), MP1(1140).
Years, The. Virginia Woolf. MCLE(5760), MEF(979), MP3 (1156).
Years with Ross, The. James Thurber. SCL(5177), 1960a (295).
Yellow Jacket, The. George Cochrane Hazelton and Harry Benrimo. POP(42).
Yemassee, The. William Gilmore Simms. MAF(729), MCLE(5763), MP2(1165).
Yesterday. Maria Dermoût. SCL(5180), 1960a(298).
Yevtushenko Poems. Yevgeny Yevtushenko. SCL(5182), 1967a(347).
Yoke and the Arrows, The. Herbert Lionel Matthews. SCL (5186), 1958a(279).
You Can't Go Home Again. Thomas Wolfe. MAF(732), MCLE(5766), MP1(1142).
You Can't Take It with You. George S. Kaufman and Moss Hart. DGAP(294), POP(5), SGAP(46), TCP(212).
You, Emperors, and Others. Robert Penn Warren. SCL (5189), 1961a(313).
You Know Me Al. Ring Lardner. MAF(735), MCLE(5769), MP3(1159).
You Might as Well Live. John Keats. 1971a(368).
You Must Know Everything. Isaac Emmanuelovich Babel. 1970a(357).
Youma. Lafcadio Hearn. MAF(737), MCLE(5771), MP2 (1167).
Young Lonigan: A Boyhood in Chicago Streets. James T. Farrell. SGAN(240).
Young Sam Johnson. James L. Clifford. BM(623), SCL (5192), 1955a(302).
Yvain. Chrétien de Troyes. MCLE(5774), MP(383), MP3 (1161).

Zadig. Voltaire. MCLE(5778), MEU(837), MP3(1165).
Zaïre. Voltaire. MCLE(5781), MD(955), MP3(1168).
Zapata and the Mexican Revolution. John Womack, Jr. 1970a(360).

Zarco, El. Ignacio Manuel Altamirano. MAF(740), MCLE (5784), MP3(1170).
Zen Buddhism. Daisetz T. Suzuki. WP(1115).
Zen Catholicism. Dom Aelred Graham, O.S.B. CAL(1124).
Zincali, The. George Henry Borrow. MCLE(5787), MP4 (1301).
Zoo Story, The. Edward Albee. SGAP(284).
Zorba the Greek. Nikos Kazantzakis. MCLE(5790), MP4 (1304).
Zuleika Dobson. Max Beerbohm. MCLE(5793), MEF(982), MP2(1169), PO2(98).

AUTHOR INDEX

Abbey, Edward. Desert Solitaire. SCL(1134), 1969a(93).
Abbott, George and John Cecil Holm. Three Men on a Horse. SGAP(172).
Abé, Kobo. Woman in the Dunes, The. SCL(5128), 1965a (318).
Abelard, Peter. Glosses on Porphyry, The. WP(290). Historia calamitatum. CAL(307), MCLE(2039), MN (134), MP3(464). Know Thyself. CHL(212). Sic et non. CAL(291).
About, Edmond François. King of the Mountains, The. MCLE(2459), MEU(410), MP2(531).
Abrahams, Peter. Tell Freedom. SCL(4524), 1954a(276). Wreath for Udomo, A. SCL(5163), 1957a(294).
Acheson, Dean. Present at the Creation. 1971a(256).
Acton, John Emerich Edward Dalberg. History of Freedom and Other Essays, The. CAL(759).
Adam, Karl. Christ of Faith, The. CAL(1000). Spirit of Catholicism, The. CAL(778)
Adamov, Arthur. Ping-Pong. MCLE(3681), MP4(694).
Adams, Henry. Education of Henry Adams, The. MCLE (1328), MN(95), MP1(238). Mont-Saint-Michel and Chartres. MCLE(3158), MP4(614).
Adams, John. Adams Papers, The. BM(8), SCL(42), 1962a(4). Defense of the Constitutions of Government of the United States of America, A. MCLE(1103), MN(77), MP3(263).
Adams, Samuel Hopkins. Grandfather Stories. SCL(1836), 1955a(115).
Adamson, Joy. Born Free. SCL(480), 1961a(26).
Addison, Joseph. Sir Roger de Coverley Papers, The. MCLE(4840), MN(288), MP3(988).
Aelfric. Homilies. CAL(272).
Aelred, Saint. Spiritual Friendship. CAL(319).
Aeschylus. House of Atreus, The. MCLE(2121), MD(363), MP1(378).
Aeschylus. Persians, The. MCLE(3591), MD(615), MP2 (818). Prometheus. POP(382). Prometheus Bound. MCLE(4280), MD(665), MP1(786). Seven Against Thebes. MCLE(4716), MD(761), MP2(953).

Suppliants, The. MCLE(5054), MD(818), MP2(1002).

Aesop. Aesop's Fables. MCLE(39), MEU(7), MP3(15).

Africanus, Sextus Julius. Extant Writings of Julius Africanus, The. CHL(61).

Agee, James. Collected Poems of James Agee, The. SCL (817), 1969a(72). Collected Short Prose of James Agee, The. SCL(827), 1969a(74). Death in the Family, A. BM(117), MCLE(1046), MP4(192), SCL (1088), 1958a(69). Let Us Now Praise Famous Men. BM(313), MCLE(2597), MP4(515), SCL(2570), 1961a (160). Letters of James Agee to Father Flye. SCL (2593), 1963a(122).

Agnon, Shmuel Yosef. Two Tales. SCL(4806), 1967a(331).

Aishinger, Ilse. Herod's Children. SCL(2021), 1964a(126).

Aiken, Conrad. Poetry of Aiken, The. MCLE(3744), MP4 (711).

Aiken, George L. Uncle Tom's Cabin. DGAP(72).

Ainsworth, William Harrison. Jack Sheppard. MCLE(2313), MEF(364), MP2(504). Old St. Paul's. MCLE(3379), MEF(601), MP2(768). Tower of London, The. MCLE(5259), MEF(870), MP1(1008). Windsor Castle. MCLE(5668), MEF(958), MP1(1117).

Alacoque, Saint Margaret Mary. Autobiography of Saint Margaret Mary Alacoque, The. CAL(615).

Alain-Fournier, Henri. Wanderer, The. MCLE(5542), MEU (800), MP1(1081), PO2(342).

Alarcón, Juan Ruiz de. Truth Suspected. MCLE(5347), MD (879), MP3(1089).

Alarcón, Pedro Antonio de. Three-Cornered Hat, The. MCLE(5175), MEU(751), MP1(978), PO2(440).

Albee, Edward. Ballad of the Sad Café, The. SCL(309), 1964a(12). Delicate Balance, A. SCL(1117), 1967a (75). Who's Afraid of Virginia Woolf? BM(607), MCLE(5632), MP4(1282), SCL(5052), SGAP(288), TCP (15), 1963a(297). Zoo Story, The. SGAP(284).

Albert the Great, Saint. Commentary on Aristotle's Deanima. CAL(360). Summa de creaturis. CAL(352).

Alcott, Louisa May. Little Women. MAF(348), MCLE (2707), MP1(515) MPA1(7), PO(188), PON(208).

Alcuin. Concerning Rhetoric and Virtue. CAL(261).

Aldington, Richard. Death of a Hero. MCLE(1052), MEF (140), MP2(223).

Aldrich, Thomas Bailey. Story of a Bad Boy, The. MAF (610), MCLE(4991), MP1(927), MPA1(12).

Alegría, Ciro. Is the World Broad and Alien. MAF(72), MCLE(515), MP2(116).

Alemán, Mateo. Guzmán de Alfarache. MCLE(1895), MEU (349), MP2(393).

Alexander, Samuel. Space, Time and Deity. WP(823).
Alexander of Hales. Summa universae theologiae. CAL(382).
Alfred, William. Hogan's Goat. SCL(2068), 1967a(143).
Alfriend, Edward M. and A. C. Wheeler. Great Diamond Robbery, The. DGAP(131).
Allen, Gay Wilson. Solitary Singer, The. BM(516), SCL (4352), 1955a(240). William James: A Biography. SCL(5076), 1968a(349).
Allen, Hervey. Anthony Adverse. MAF(25), MCLE(194), MP1(34).
Allen, Walter. Threescore and Ten. SCL(4644), 1960a(272).
Alliluyeva, Svetlana. Twenty Letters to a Friend. SCL (4796), 1968a(340).
Altamirano, Ignacio Manuel. Zarco, El. MAF(740), MCLE (5784), MP3(1170).
Alvaro, Corrado. Revolt in Aspromonte. SCL(3916), 1963a (216).
Amado, Jorge. Dona Flor and Her Two Husbands. 1971a (63). Gabriela, Clove and Cinnamon. MCLE(1709), MP4(369), SCL(1687), 1963a(62). Home Is the Sailor. SCL(2090), 1965a(133). Shepherds of the Night. SCL (4248), 1967a(303). Two Deaths of Quincas Wateryell, The. SCL(4799), 1966a(319). Violent Land, The. MAF(691), MCLE(5494), MP2(1110).
Ambrose, Saint. Epistle XXI: To the Most Clement Emperor and Most Blessed Augustus. CAL(127). Hymns of Saint Ambrose, The. CAL(152). On the Christian Faith. CAL(112). On the Duties of the Clergy. CAL(145), CHL(121). Sermo contra auxentium. CAL (132).
Ames, William. Of Conscience, Its Power and Cases. CHL (445).
Amicis, Edmondo de. Romance of a Schoolmaster, The. MCLE(4511), MEU(643), MP2(909).
Amis, Kingsley. Green Man, The. SCLs(121). Lucky Jim. MCLE(2787), MP4(569). One Fat Englishman. SCL (3421), 1965a(219). Take a Girl Like You. SCL(4504), 1962a(293). That Uncertain Feeling. MCLE(5147), MP4(1210).
Ammers-Küller, Johanna van. Rebel Generation, The. MCLE(4348), MEU(619), MP3(865).
Ammons, A. R. Selected Poems. SCL(4173), 1968a(287).
Anacreon. Poetry of Anacreon, The. MCLE(3747), MP4 (714).
Anaxagoras of Clazomenae. Anaxagoras: Fragments. WP (22).
Anaximander of Miletus. Anaximander: Fragments. WP(1).

Andersen, Hans Christian. Andersen's Fairy Tales (Selections). MCLE(164), MEU(23), MP2(27).

Anderson, John Murray. New Faces of 1952. DGAP(382).

Anderson, Maxwell. Winterset. DGAP(289), MCLE(5681), MD(931), MP1(1123), SGAP(39), TCP(19).

Anderson, Maxwell and Laurence Stallings. What Price Glory? DGAP(217), POP(31), SGAP(99).

Anderson, Maxwell, Edwin Justin Mayer and Laurence Stallings. So Red the Rose. DGAP(70).

Anderson, Robert. Tea and Sympathy. BM(530), SCL(4514), SGAP(265), 1954a(270).

Anderson, Sherwood. Dark Laughter. MAF(125), MCLE (1019), MP1(185). Poor White. MAF(496), MCLE (4185), MP1(762). Story Teller's Story, A. MCLE (5010), MP4(1184). Winesburg, Ohio. MAF(717), MCLE(5672), MP1(1121), SGAN(115).

Andrewes, Lancelot. Preces privatae. CHL(473).

Andreyev, Leonid. He Who Gets Slapped. POP(345). Seven Who Were Hanged, The. MCLE(4730), MEU (677), MP2(957).

Andrić, Ivo. Bosnian Chronicle. SCL(486), 1964a(27). Bridge on the Drina, The. MCLE(506), MP4(87), SCL(522), 1960a(30). Devil's Yard. SCL(1156), 1963a(42).

Angelou, Maya. I Know Why the Caged Bird Sings. SCLs (133).

Annunzio, Gabriele D'. Triumph of Death, The. MCLE (5332), MEU(767), MP2(1061).

Anouilh, Jean. Antigone. TCP(23). Becket, or The Honor of God. TCP(26). Ornifle. TCP(29). Ring Round the Moon. MCLE(4466), MD(700), MP3(896). Thieves' Carnival. TCP(32). Waltz of the Toreadors, The. SCL(4939), TCP(34), 1958a(261).

Anselm of Canterbury, Saint. Cur Deus homo. CAL(286), CHL(202). Monologion. CHL(194). Monologion and Proslogion. WP(284). Proslogion. CAL(280), CHL (197).

Ansky, S. Dybbuk, The. POP(364).

Apollinaire, Guillaume. Poetry of Apollinaire, The. MCLE (3751), MP4(718).

Apuleius, Lucius. Golden Ass of Lucius Apuleius, The. MCLE(1784), MEU(332), MP1(309), PO2(418).

Aquinas, Saint Thomas. De veritate. CAL(379). Hymns of Saint Thomas Aquinas, The. CAL(421). On Being and Essence. CAL(364). On Free Choice. CAL(406). On Kingship. CAL(391). On Spiritual Creatures. CAL(402). On the Power of God. CAL(394). On the

Soul. CAL(409). On the Virtues in General. CAL (413). Summa contra gentiles. CAL(385), CHL(232), WP(314). Summa theologica (or theologiae). CAL (416), CHL(241), MCLE(5042), MN(294), MP3(1033), WP(321).
Aragon, Louis. Holy Week. SCL(2079), 1962a(149).
Archer, William. Green Goddess, The. POP(98).
Ardrey, Robert. Social Contract, The. 1971a(300).
Arendt, Hannah. On Revolution. SCL(3393), 1964a(200).
Arent, Arthur. "... one-third of a nation..." DGAP(309), SGAP(178).
Aretino, Pietro. Courtesan, The. MCLE(909), MD(179), MP3(234). Discourses. MCLE(1187), MP4(239).
Arihara no Narihira. Tales of Ise. MCLE(5079), MEU(737), MP3(1044).
Ariosto, Ludovico. Orlando Furioso. MCLE(3433), MP(194), MP2(776). Suppositi, I. MCLE(5059), MD(823), MP3 (1039).
Aristides. Apology of Aristides, The. CAL(10), CHL(9).
Aristophanes. Acharnians, The. MCLE(21), MD(6), MP3(7). Birds, The. MCLE(422), MD(80), MP2(94). Clouds, The. MCLE(779), MD(158), MP1(152). Ecclesiazusae, The. MCLE(1321), MD(237), MP3(322). Frogs, The. MCLE(1698), MD(284), MP1(297). Knights, The. MCLE(2483), MD(429), MP1(480). Lysistrata. MCLE (2809), MD(467), MP2(610), POP(369). Peace, The. MCLE(3538), MD(605), MP3(726). Plutus. MCLE (3718), MD(648), MP2(845). Thesmophoriazusae, The. MCLE(5159), MD(842), MP3(1068). Wasps, The. MCLE(5573), MD(908), MP3(1119).
Aristotle. Ethica Nicomachea. WP(157). Metaphysics. WP(152). On the Soul. WP(147). Organon. WP(137). Physics. WP(143). Poetics. MCLE(3735), MN(248), MP3(774), WP(174). Politics. WP(163). Rhetoric. WP(169).
Armah, Ayi Kwei. Beautyful Ones Are Not Yet Born, The. SCL(346), 1969a(33). Fragments. 1971a(77).
Arminius, Jacobus. Declaration of Sentiments, The. CHL (424).
Arndt, Johann. True Christianity. CHL(422).
Arnold, Matthew. Culture and Anarchy. MCLE(962), MP4 (169). Literature and Dogma. CHL(770). Poetry of Arnold, The. MCLE(3754), MP4(720). Sohrab and Rustum. MCLE(4884), MP(344), MP3(1002).
Arnow, Harriette Simpson. Dollmaker, The. SCL(1206), 1954a(55). Flowering of the Cumberland. SCL(1600), 1964a(93). Seedtime on the Cumberland. SCL(4150),

1961a(222). Weedkiller's Daughter, The. 1970a(337).
Artsybashev, Mikhail. Sanine. MCLE(4606), MEU(660), MP3(921).
Asbury, Francis. Journal of Francis Asbury, The. CHL (654).
Asch, Sholem. Apostle, The. MAF(28), MCLE(211), MP1 (38). Nazarene, The. MAF(439), MCLE(3242), MP1 (645). Prophet, The. SCL(3717), 1955a(211).
Ashberry, John. Rivers and Mountains. SCL(3948), 1967a (287).
Ashmore, Harry S. Epitaph for Dixie, An. SCL(1370), 1959a(73).
Ashton-Warner, Sylvia. Incense to Idols. SCL(2211), 1961a (124). Spinster. SCL(4414), 1960a(249). Three. 1971a(314).
Asser, John. Life of Alfred. CAL(268).
Asturias, Miguel Ángel. Mulata, The. SCL(3128), 1968a (212). El Señor Presidente. MCLE(1342), MP4(260).
Athanasius, Saint. Discourses Against the Arians. CAL(94). Incarnation of the Word of God, The. CAL(84), CHL (83). Life of Antony, The. CHL(95).
Athenagoras. Apology of Athenagoras, The. CHL(29). On the Resurrection of the Dead. CAL(30). Plea for the Christians, The. CAL(27).
Atwood, Margaret. Animals in That Country, The. 1970a (28).
Aubrey, John. Brief Lives. MCLE(509), MP4(89).
Auchincloss, Louis. Embezzler, The. SCL(1317), 1967a (91). House of Five Talents, The. SCL(2124), 1961a (121). Portrait in Brownstone. SCL(3657), 1963a (196). Rector of Justin, The. SCL(3846), 1965a(234). Romantic Egoists, The. SCL(3977), 1954a(237). Second Chance. 1971a(287). World of Profit, A. SCL(5151), 1969a(349).
Auden, W. H. About the House. SCL(5), 1966a(1). City Without Walls and Other Poems. 1971a(38). Dyer's Hand and Other Essays, The. SCL(1258), 1963a(47). Homage to Clio. SCL(2082), 1961a(119). Poetry of Auden, The. MCLE(3757), MP(228), MP3(777). Shield of Achilles, The. BM(509), SCL(4251), 1955a (234).
Auden, W. H. and Christopher Isherwood. Ascent of F6, The. TCP(37).
Audiberti, Jacques. Quoat-Quoat. TCP(40).
Augustine, Saint. City of God. CAL(188), CHL(140), WP (258). Confessions of Saint Augustine, The. CAL (165), CHL(128), MCLE(823), MN(58), MP3(213), WP

(252). De magistro. CAL(140). De trinitate. CAL (173). Enarrations on the Psalms. CAL(196). Enchiridion on Faith, Hope, and Love, The. CHL(149). Faith, Hope, and Charity. CAL(184). First Catechetical Instruction, The. CAL(161). On the Trinity. CHL(134).
Aulén, Gustaf. Christus Victor. CHL(950). Faith of the Christian Church, The. CHL(912).
Aurelius, Marcus. Meditations. MCLE(2980), MN(201), MP3(644), WP(229).
Austen, Jane. Emma. MCLE(1374), MEF(179), MP1(246), PO2(24). Mansfield Park. MCLE(2904), MEF(469), MP1(562). Northanger Abbey. MCLE(3302), MEF (586), MP2(750). Persuasion. MCLE(3596), MEF (652), MP1(734). Pride and Prejudice. MCLE(4236), MEF(695), MP1(780), PO(14), PON(324), SGBN(55). Sense and Sensibility. MCLE(4704), MEF(781), MP2 (951).
Averroës. Incoherence of the Incoherence, The. WP(294).
Avicenna. Book of Salvation, The. WP(278).
Ayer, Alfred Jules. Language, Truth and Logic. WP(1010).
Aymé, Marcel. Green Mare, The. SCL(1877), 1957a(99).
Ayrton, Michael. Maze Maker, The. SCL(2949), 1968a(192).
Azuela, Mariano. Flies, The. MCLE(1622), MP4(342). Underdogs, The. MAF(682), MCLE(5425), MP2(1088).

Babel, Isaac Emmanuelovich. Collected Stories, The. SCL (830), 1955a(62). You Must Know Everything. 1970a (357).
Bacchelli, Riccardo. Mill on the Po, The. MCLE(3053), MEU(495), MP2(664). Nothing New Under the Sun. SCL(3326), 1955a(190).
Bacon, Sir Francis. Advancement of Learning, The. WP (369). Essays. MCLE(1440), MN(110), MP3(357). History of the Reign of King Henry VII. MCLE(2073), MP4(421). New Atlantis. MCLE(3248), MN(212), MP3(685). Novum organum. WP(373).
Bacon, Frank and Winchell Smith. Lightnin'. POP(38).
Bacon, Roger. Opus majus. CAL(398).
Baillie, Donald M. God Was in Christ. CHL(1093).
Bailyn, Bernard. Ideological Origins of the American Revolution, The. SCLs(135).
Baines, Jocelyn. Joseph Conrad. BM(272), SCL(2362), 1961a(132).
Bakeless, John. Background to Glory. SCL(295), 1958a(26).
Baker, Benjamin A. Glance at New York, A. DGAP(68).
Baker, Carlos. Ernest Hemingway. 1970a(112). Friend in

Power, A. SCL(1661), 1959a(92).
Baker, Elliot. Fine Madness, A. SCL(1533), 1965a(95).
Baker, George Melville. Merry Christmas of the Old Woman Who Lived in a Shoe, The. DGAP(102).
Balchin, Nigel. Fall of a Sparrow, The. SCL(1443), 1957a (64).
Bald, R. C. John Donne: A Life. 1971a(148).
Baldwin, Hanson W. Sea Fights and Shipwrecks. SCL(4103), 1955a(223).
Baldwin, James. Fire Next Time, The. SCL(1541), 1964a (88). Go Tell It on the Mountain. MCLE(1770), MP4 (379). Nobody Knows My Name. BM(398), SCL(3290), 1962a(219).
Bale, John. King John. MCLE(2447), MD(412), MP3(543).
Balfour, Patrick, see Kinross, Patrick Balfour, Lord.
Balthasar, Hans Urs von. Anxiety and the Christian. CAL (969). Science, Religion and Christianity. CAL(1021).
Balzac, Honoré de. César Birotteau. MCLE(676), MEU (123), MP2(142). Chouans, The. MCLE(730), MEU (138), MP2(151). Country Doctor, The. MCLE(900), MEU(170), MP2(185). Cousin Bette. MCLE(913), MEU(173), MP1(166). Cousin Pons. MCLE(916), MEU(176), MP2(189), PON(62). Eugénie Grandet. MCLE(1482), MEU(284), MP1(258), PO(272), SGEN(75). Father Goriot. MCLE(1565), MEU(293), MP1(271). Lost Illusions. MCLE(2756), MEU(455), MP2(595). Père Goriot. PO(268), SGEN(78). Wild Ass's Skin, The. MCLE(5642), MEU(813), MP2(1133).
Barber, Noel. Sinister Twilight, A. SCL(4308), 1969a(288).
Barbusse, Henri. Under Fire. MCLE(5404), MEU(779), MP1(1047).
Barclay, John. Argenis. MCLE(233), MEF(31), MP3(59).
Barclay, Robert. Apology for the True Christian Divinity, An. CHL(526).
Barker, George. Poetry of Barker, The. MCLE(3760), MP4(723).
Barker, James Nelson. Indian Princess, The. DGAP(26). Tragedy of Superstition, The. DGAP(37).
Barnabas, Unknown, but attributed to the Apostle. Epistle of Barnabas, The. CHL(3).
Barnett, Lincoln. World We Live In, The. SCL(5157), 1955a(299).
Baroja, Pío. Caesar or Nothing. MCLE(567), MEU(100), MP1(97). King Paradox. MCLE(2462), MEU(413), MP2(533). Restlessness of Shanti Andía, The. SCL (3905), 1960a(223).
Barrie, James M. Admirable Crichton, The. MCLE(28),

MD(8), MP1(10), POP(121), TCP(42). Dear Brutus. MCLE(1041), MD(199), MP1(196), TCP(44). Little Minister, The. MCLE(2704), MEF(439), MP1(513), PO(17), PON(204). Peter Pan. MCLE(3602), MD (617), MP2(820), POP(126), TCP(47). Quality Street. MCLE(4298), MD(672), MP1(793). What Every Woman Knows. MCLE(5606), MD(915), MP1(1106), TCP(51).

Barrios, Eduardo. Brother Ass. MCLE(524), MP4(94).

Barrow, G. W. S. Robert Bruce and the Community of the Realm of Scotland. SCL(3954), 1966a(272).

Barry, Philip. Animal Kingdom, The. SGAP(116). Holiday. DGAP(242). Hotel Universe. TCP(55).

Barth, John. End of the Road, The. MCLE(1379), MP4 (273). Floating Opera, The. SCLs(108). Giles Goat-Boy. SCL(1752), 1967a(126). Lost in the Funhouse. SCL(2784), 1969a(205). Sot-Weed Factor, The. MCLE(4933), MP4(1168), SCL(4372), 1961a(238).

Barth, Karl. Church Dogmatics. CHL(981). Epistle to the Romans, The. CHL(894). Knowledge of God and the Service of God, The. WP(1027).

Barthelme, Donald. City Life. 1971a(36). Snow White. SCL(4329), 1968a(296). Unspeakable Practices, Unnatural Acts. SCL(4845), 1969a(331).

Baruch, Bernard M. Baruch: The Public Years. SCL(320), 1961a(13).

Barzun, Jacques. House of Intellect, The. BM(242), SCL (2128), 1960a(96).

Bashô, Matsuo. Poetry of Bashô, The. MCLE(3762), MP (231), MP3(779).

Basil, Saint. Against Eunomius. CAL(98). Letters of Saint Basil, The. CAL(110). Longer Rules and The Shorter Rules, The. CHL(99). Treatise on the Holy Spirit. CAL(107).

Bass, Robert Duncan. Swamp Fox. SCLs(303).

Bassani, Giorgio. Garden of the Finzi-Continis, The. SCL (1706), 1966a(114). Heron, The. 1971a(115).

Basso, Hamilton. Light Infantry Ball, The. SCL(2671), 1960a(136). View from Pompey's Head, The. SCL (4893), 1954a(288).

Bate, Walter Jackson. John Keats. SCLs(141).

Bates, H. E. Feast of July, The. SCL(1502), 1954a(71).

Battiscombe, Georgina. Queen Alexandra. 1970a(259).

Baudelaire, Charles. Flowers of Evil. MCLE(1629), MP (104), MP3(399).

Baum, Vicki. Grand Hotel. MCLE(1816), MEU(335), MP1 (318), POP(293).

Baumbach, Jonathan. What Comes Next. SCL(5013), 1969a

(343).
Baxter, Richard. Christian Directory, A. CHL(501). Saints' Everlasting Rest, The. CHL(481).
Bayle, Pierre. Historical and Critical Dictionary, The. WP(441).
Beach, Rex. Spoilers, The. MAF(592), MCLE(4962), MP1 (919).
Beach, Sylvia. Shakespeare and Company. SCL(4242), 1960a(240).
Beagel, Peter S. Last Unicorn, The. SCL(2537), 1969a(188).
Beard, Charles A. and Mary R. Rise of American Civilization, The. MCLE(4471), MP4(1071).
Beaumarchais, Pierre A. Caron de. Barber of Seville, The. MCLE(330), MD(58), MP2(70), POP(255). Marriage of Figaro, The. MCLE(2939), MD(499), MP2(637).
Beaumont, Francis. Knight of the Burning Pestle, The. MCLE(2480), MD(426), MP2(542).
Beaumont, Francis and John Fletcher. Coxcomb, The. MCLE(919), MD(181), MP3(236). King and No King, A. MCLE(2441), MP3(541). Maid's Tragedy, The. MCLE(2848), MD(480), MP2(612). Philaster. MCLE (3616), MD(622), MP2(825). Scornful Lady, The. MCLE(4655), MD(744), MP3(940). Woman Hater, The. MCLE(5699), MD(937), MP3(1138).
Beauvoir, Simone de. Mandarins, The. SCL(2878), 1957a (165).
Becker, Stephen. Outcasts, The. SCL(3481), 1968a(237). When the War Is Over. 1970a(345).
Beckett, Samuel. Stories and Texts for Nothing. SCL(4455), 1968a(312). Unnamable, The. SCL(4838), 1959a(257). Waiting for Godot. BM(583), MCLE(5533), MD(900), MP3(1113), SCL(4933), TCP(59), 1957a(281).
Beckford, William. Vathek. MCLE(5449), MEF(910), MP2 (1094).
Beddoes, Thomas Lovell. Poetry of Beddoes, The. MCLE (3765), MP4(725).
Bede, Saint. Ecclesiastical History of the English People. CAL(258), CHL(181).
Beecher, Henry Ward. Evolution and Religion. CHL(793).
Beecher, Lyman. Works of Lyman Beecher, The. CHL (724).
Beerbohm, Max. Essays of Max Beerbohm, The. MCLE (1464), MP4(307). Zuleika Dobson. MCLE(5793), MEF(982), MP2(1169), PO2(98).
Behan, Brendan. Borstal Boy. SCL(483), 1960a(25). Hostage, The. TCP(64). Quare Fellow, The. SCL (3764), 1958a(201).

Behn, Mrs. Aphra. Oroonoko. MCLE(3445), MEF(622), MP2(783).
Behrman, S. N. Biography. DGAP(257), SGAP(92). Burning Glass, The. SCL(558), 1969a(54). End of Summer. TCP(67). Portrait of Max. BM(452), SCL(3660), 1961a(198).
Belasco, David. Girl of the Golden West, The. DGAP(148).
Belasco, David and John Luther Long. Madame Butterfly. DGAP(140).
Belitt, Ben. Nowhere but Light: Poems 1964-1969. 1971a (228).
Bell, Marvin. Probable Volume of Dreams, A. 1970a(255).
Bellamann, Henry. King's Row. MAF(322), MCLE(2476), MP1(478).
Bellamy, Edward. Looking Backward. MAF(356), MCLE (2741), MP1(520), MPA1(17), PO(191), SGAN(77).
Bellarmine, Saint Robert Cardinal. Political Writings. CAL(564).
Belloc, Hilaire. Path to Rome, The. CAL(734), MCLE (3523), MN(228), MP3(722). Servile State, The. CAL(754).
Bellonici, Maria. Life and Times of Lucrezia Borgia, The. SCL(2638), 1954a(147).
Bellow, Saul. Adventures of Augie March, The. MCLE(33), MP4(1), SGAN(337). Henderson the Rain King. MCLE(1979), MP4(408), SCL(1987), 1960a(94). Herzog. SCL(2025), 1965a(127). Last Analysis, The. SCL(2498), 1966a(138). Mr. Sammler's Planet. 1971a(208). Mosby's Memoirs and Other Stories. SCL(3091), 1969a(234). Seize the Day. SCLs(254). Victim, The. MCLE(5472), MP4(1259).
Bemis, Samuel Flagg. John Quincy Adams and the Union. BM(268), SCL(2359), 1957a(138).
Benavente, Jacinto. Bonds of Interest, The. MCLE(455), MD(92), MP2(107), POP(285). Passion Flower, The. MCLE(3509), MD(600), MP3(718).
Benedict of Nursia, Saint. Rule of St. Benedict, The. CAL (234), CHL(172).
Benedictus, David. Fourth of June, The. SCL(1639), 1963a (56).
Benét, Stephen Vincent. John Brown's Body. MCLE(2347), MP(144), MP1(445). Poetry of Stephen Vincent Benét, The. MCLE(4105), MP4(960).
Bengtsson, Frans G. Long Ships, The. SCL(2756), 1954a (159).
Bennett, Arnold. Anna of the Five Towns. MCLE(181), MEF(19), MP2(37). Clayhanger Trilogy, The. MCLE

(763), MEF(109), MP1(148). Old Wives' Tale, The. MCLE(3382), MD(587), MEF(604), MP1(684), PO2(102), PON(274), SGBN(250). Riceyman's Steps. MCLE (4444), MEF(731), MP1(823).
Bennett, John Coleman. Christians and the State. CHL (1175).
Benrimo, Harry and George Cochrane Hazelton. Yellow Jacket, The. POP(42).
Bentham, Jeremy. Introduction to the Principles of Morals and Legislation, An. WP(551).
Berdyaev, Nikolai. Destiny of Man, The. CHL(960), WP (940). Dostoevsky. MCLE(1258), MP4(245). Freedom and the Spirit. CHL(929).
Berger, Thomas. Crazy in Berlin. SCLs(81). Killing Time. SCL(2417), 1968a(169). Little Big Man. SCL (2698), 1965a(176). Reinhart in Love. SCLs(247). Vital Parts. 1971a(338).
Berger, Yves. Garden, The. SCL(1696), 1964a(102).
Bergin, Thomas. Dante. SCL(1001), 1966a(56).
Bergson, Henri. Creative Evolution. WP(767). Introduction to Metaphysics, An. WP(749). Laughter. MCLE(2561), MP4(505). Matter and Memory. MCLE (2962), MP4(599). Time and Free Will. WP(703). Two Sources of Morality and Religion, The. CHL (990), WP(959).
Berkeley, George. Essay Towards a New Theory of Vision, An. MCLE(1438), MP4(292). Treatise Concerning the Principles of Human Knowledge, A. WP(447).
Bernanos, Georges. Diary of a Country Priest, The. MCLE (1167), MEU(234), MP2(251).
Bernard, Saint. Letters of Saint Bernard of Clairvaux, The. CAL(332). On the Necessity of Loving God. CAL (311). On the Steps of Humility and Pride. CAL(296). Steps of Humility, The. CHL(205).
Berney, William and Howard Richardson. Dark of the Moon. DGAP(362).
Berry, John. Krishna Fluting. SCL(2457), 1960a(126).
Berry, Wendell. Broken Ground, The. SCL(530), 1965a(18). Findings. 1970a(129). Long-Legged House, The. SCLs(163). Openings. SCL(3438), 1969a(255). Place on Earth, A. SCL(3586), 1968a(244).
Berryman, John. Berryman's Sonnets. SCL(383), 1968a(28). His Toy, His Dream, His Rest. SCL(2056), 1969a (152). Homage to Mistress Bradstreet. MCLE(2090), MP4(430), SCL(2084), 1957a(119). 77 Dream Songs. SCL(4227), 1965a(275).
Bertin, Célia. Last Innocence, The. SCL(2518), 1955a(141).

Bertocci, Peter Anthony. Introduction to the Philosophy of Religion. CHL(1130).
Besier, Rudolf. Barretts of Wimpole Street, The. POP(81).
Betjeman, John. Collected Poems. BM(93), SCL(794), 1960a(41). High and Low. SCL(2031), 1968a(157). Poetry of Betjeman, The. MCLE(3768), MP4(727). Summoned by Bells. SCL(4490), 1961a(245).
Betti, Ugo. Queen and the Rebels, The. TCP(69).
Betts, Doris. Astronomer and Other Stories, The. SCL (240), 1967a(22). Scarlet Thread, The. SCL(4083), 1966a(281).
Bhattacharya, Bhabani. He Who Rides a Tiger. SCL(1963), 1954a(108).
Bierce, Ambrose. Tales of Soldiers and Civilians. MAF (626), MCLE(5081), MP3(1047), MPA1(22).
Billing, Einar. Our Calling. CHL(857).
Billington, James H. Icon and the Axe, The. SCL(2155), 1967a(154).
Bion. Poetry of Bion, The. MCLE(3771), MP4(729).
Bird, Robert Montgomery. Gladiator, The. DGAP(50). Nick of the Woods. MAF(442), MCLE(3270), MP2 (737).
Bishop, Elizabeth. Complete Poems. 1970a(86). Questions of Travel. SCL(3795), 1966a(263).
Bishop, Jim. Day Lincoln Was Shot, The. SCL(1058), 1955a(81).
Bissell, Richard. High Water. SCL(2046), 1954a(111).
Bjarnhof, Karl. Good Light, The. SCL(1812), 1961a(104).
Björnson, Björnstjerne. Arne. MCLE(239), MEU(37), MP1 (42). Beyond Human Power, II. MCLE(404), MD (77), MP2(90). Fisher Maiden, The. MCLE(1618), MEU(302), MP2(330).
Blackmore, Richard D. Lorna Doone. MCLE(2750), MEF (450), MP1(524), PO(21), PON(216).
Blais, Marie-Claire. Day Is Dark, The. SCL(1054), 1968a(63). Three Travelers. SCL(1054), 1968a(63).
Blake, William. Poetry of Blake, The. MCLE(3773), MP (234), MP3(781). Songs of Innocence and of Experience. CHL(623).
Blanshard, Brand. Nature of Thought, The. WP(1040).
Blok, Aleksandr. Poetry of Blok, The. MCLE(3776), MP4 (731).
Blondel, Maurice. Action, L'. CAL(706).
Bloom, Harold. William Butler Yeats. 1971a(349).
Bloy, Léon. Woman Who Was Poor, The. CAL(726).
Blunden, Edmund Charles. Poetry of Blunden, The. MCLE

(3779), MP4(733).
Bly, Robert. Light Around the Body, The. SCL(2665), 1968a(176). Silence in the Snowy Fields. SCL(4282), 1963a(247).
Blythe, Ronald. Akenfield. 1970a(7).
Boas, Franz. Mind of Primitive Man, The. MCLE(3056), MP4(608).
Boccaccio, Giovanni. Amorosa Fiammetta, L'. MCLE (2525), MEU(424), MP3(550). Decameron, The (Selections). MCLE(1080), MEU(219), MP2(230). Filostrato, Il. MCLE(1607), MP4(340). Teseide, La. MCLE(5138), MP4(1208).
Bodin, Jean. Six Books of the Republic, The. CAL(552).
Boehme, Jakob. Way to Christ, The. CHL(436).
Boethius, Saint Anicius Manlius Severinus. De trinitate. CAL(223). Consolation of Philosophy, The. CAL (229), MCLE(863), MN(67), MP3(225), WP(264). On the Holy Trinity. CHL(169).
Bogan, Louise. Blue Estuaries, The. SCL(457), 1969a(45).
Boiardo, Matteo Maria. Orlando Innamorato. MCLE(3437), MP(198), MP3(703).
Boileau-Despréaux, Nicolas. Dialogues des Héros de Roman. MCLE(1145), MN(79), MP3(275). Satires. MCLE (4627), MP4(1094).
Bojer, Johan. Emigrants, The. MCLE(1362), MEU(279), MP1(244). Last of the Vikings, The. MCLE(2544), MEU(430), MP2(560).
Boker, George Henry. Francesca da Rimini. DGAP(80).
Bokser, Ben Zion. Judaism: Profile of a Faith. SCLs(145).
Böll, Heinrich. Billiards at Half Past Nine. SCLs(31). Clown, The. SCL(779), 1966a(49). Tomorrow and Yesterday. SCL(4714), 1958a(236).
Bolt, David. Adam. SCL(38), 1962a(1).
Bonaventure, Saint. Journey of the Mind to God. CHL(237), WP(308). On the Reduction of the Arts to Theology. WP(305). Mind's Road to God, The. CAL(371). Three Ways, The. CAL(356). Retracing the Arts to Theology. CHL(228).
Bonaventure, Saint and unknown Franciscan Monk. Meditations on the Life of Christ. CAL(455).
Bonhoeffer, Dietrich. Cost of Discipleship, The. CHL(1028). Ethics. CHL(1101).
Boorstin, Daniel Joseph. Americans: The National Experience, The. SCL(157), 1966a(8).
Booth, Philip. Islanders, The. SCL(2275), 1962a(159). Poetry of Booth, The. MCLE(3781), MP4(735). Weathers and Edges. SCL(4994), 1967a(339).

Bor, Josef. Terezín Requiem, The. SCL(4554), 1964a(264).
Borges, Jorge Luis. Aleph and Other Stories: 1933-1969, The. 1971a(10). Ficciones. MCLE(1589), MP4(329), SCL(1511), 1963a(53). Personal Anthology, A. SCL (3547), 1967a(262).
Borland, Hal. High, Wide and Lonesome. SCL(2049), 1957a (113). When the Legends Die. SCL(5031), 1964a(297).
Boros, Eva. Mermaids, The. SCL(3011), 1957a(180).
Borowski, Tadeusz. This Way for the Gas, Ladies and Gentlemen. SCL(4610), 1968a(324).
Borrow, George Henry. Bible in Spain, The. MCLE(407), MP4(69). Lavengro. MCLE(2564), MEF(428), MP1 (501). Romany Rye, The. MCLE(4529), MEF(753), MP1(849). Wild Wales. MCLE(5650), MP4(1289). Zincali, The. MCLE(5787), MP4(1301).
Bosanquet, Bernard. Principle of Individuality and Value, The. WP(790). Three Lectures on Aesthetic. WP (806).
Bossuet, Jacques Bénigne. Discourse on Universita History. CAL(608).
Boswell, James. Boswell for the Defence, 1769-1774. BM (41), SCL(493), 1960a(27). Boswell in Search of a Wife, 1766-1769. BM(44), SCL(496), 1957a(36). Boswell on the Grand Tour. BM(47), SCL(499), 1955a(32). Boswell: The Ominous Years. SCL(503), 1964a(31). Boswell's London Journal: 1762-1763. MCLE(473), MP4(85). Journal of a Tour to the Hebrides. MCLE(2371), MP4(467). Life of Samuel Johnson, LL. D., The. MCLE(2670), MN(186), MP3 (579).
Boucicault, Dion. Octoroon, The. DGAP(85). Shaughraun, The. POP(238).
Boucicault, Dion, Charles Burke and Joseph Jefferson. Rip Van Winkle. DGAP(90).
Boulle, Pierre. Bridge over the River Kwai, The. SCL (525), 1954a(25).
Bourget, Paul. Disciple, The. MCLE(1182), MP1(209).
Bourjaily, Vance. Violated, The. SCL(4899), 1959a(263).
Bouyer, Louis. Christian Humanism. CAL(1058). Liturgical Piety. CAL(1014). Seat of Wisdom, The. CAL(1037).
Bowen, Catherine Drinker. Francis Bacon. SCL(1648), 1964a(99). Lion and the Throne, The. BM(344), SCL(2692), 1958a(150).
Bowen, Elizabeth. Death of the Heart, The. MCLE(1066), MEF(142), MP2(228). Eva Trout. SCL(1392), 1969a (119). Heat of the Day, The. MCLE(1964), MEF(289),

MP2(420). House in Paris, The. MCLE(2118), MEF (318), MP2(463). Little Girls, The. SCL(2705), 1964a(160). Time in Rome, A. SCL(4668), 1961a (258). World of Love, A. SCL(5148), 1955a(296).

Bowers, Claude G. Jefferson and Hamilton: The Struggle for Democracy in America. MCLE(2330), MP4(462).

Bowles, Jane. Collected Works of Jane Bowles, The. SCL (841), 1967a(41).

Bowles, Paul. Spider's House, The. SCL(4408), 1955a(243). Time of Friendship, The. SCL(4670), 1968a(331).

Bowne, Borden Parker. Personalism. CHL(851).

Boyd, James. Drums. MAF(157), MCLE(1288), MP1(228). Marching On. MAF(390), MCLE(2912), MP1(566).

Boyle, Kay. Nothing Ever Breaks Except the Heart. SCL (3320), 1967a(246).

Brace, Gerald Warner. Winter Solstice. SCL(5112), 1961a (307).

Brackenridge, Hugh Henry. Modern Chivalry. MAF(419), MCLE(3125), MP2(693).

Bradford, Gamaliel. Damaged Souls. MCLE(984), MP4(176).

Bradford, Richard. Red Sky at Morning. SCL(3858), 1969a (274).

Bradford, William. Of Plimouth Plantation. MCLE(3343), MP4(639).

Bradley, Francis Herbert. Appearance and Reality. WP (706). Ethical Studies. WP(676).

Braine, John. From the Hand of the Hunter. SCL(1667), 1961a(98). Life at the Top. SCL(2644), 1963a(132). Room at the Top. BM(484), MCLE(4541), MP4(1078), SCL(3984), 1958a(214).

Brainerd, David. Diary of David Brainerd, The. CHL(594).

Brant, Irving. James Madison: 1809-1812. SCL(2292), 1957a(132). James Madison: 1812-1836. SCL(2296), 1962a(162).

Brautigan, Richard. Brautigan's. 1970a(56).

Brecht, Arnold. Political Theory: The Foundations of Twentieth-Century Political Thought. SCLs(228).

Brecht, Bertolt. Baal. MCLE(309), MP4(62), TCP(73). Caucasian Chalk Circle, The. TCP(76). Galileo. TCP(79). Good Woman of Setzuan. TCP(82). Mother Courage and Her Children. TCP(86). Private Life of the Master Race, The. MCLE(4266), MD(660), MP2(858). Seven Plays. BM(506), SCL(4221), 1962a (264). Threepenny Opera, The. TCP(89).

Breton, André. Poetry of André Breton, The. MCLE(3748), MP4(715).

Breton, Nicholas. Poetry of Nicholas Breton, The. MCLE

(4049), MP4(920).
Breuer, Bessie. Actress, The. SCL(35), 1958a(1).
Breuer, Josef and Sigmund Freud. Studies on Hysteria. MCLE(5031), MP4(1195).
Bridgman, Percy Williams. Logic of Modern Physics, The. WP(880).
Brightman, Edgar Sheffield. Philosophy of Religion, A. CHL(1047).
Bring, Ragnar. Commentary on Galatians. CHL(1180).
Brinkley, William. Don't Go Near the Water. SCL(1215), 1957a(58).
Broad, Charlie Dunbar. Mind and Its Place in Nature, The. WP(862).
Broch, Hermann. Death of Virgil, The. MCLE(1069), MEU (213), MP3(258). Sleepwalkers, The. MCLE(4854), MEU(685), MP2(970).
Brodeur, Paul. Sick Fox, The. SCL(4273), 1964a(241).
Brodie, Fawn M. Devil Drives, The. SCL(1145), 1968a (79). Thaddeus Stevens: Scourge of the South. SCLs (315).
Brodrick, James, S.J. Origin of the Jesuits, The. CAL (868). Saint Francis Xavier. CAL(990).
Brome, Richard. Jovial Crew, A. MCLE(2400), MD(400), MP3(531). Northern Lass, The. MCLE(3305), MD (574), MP3(689).
Bromfield, Louis. Green Bay Tree, The. MAF(237), MCLE(1849), MP1(331).
Brontë, Anne. Agnes Grey. MCLE(59), MEF(7), MP3(16). Tenant of Wildfell Hall, The. MCLE(5130), MEF(825), MP1(963).
Brontë, Charlotte. Jane Eyre. MCLE(2319), MEF(367), MP1(432), PO(24), PON(171), SGBN(102). Professor, The. MCLE(4274), MEF(705), MP2(864). Shirley. MCLE(4769), MEF(790), MP3(968). Villette. MCLE (5486), MEF(924), MP2(1108).
Brontë, Emily. Poetry of Emily Brontë, The. MCLE(3878), MP4(803). Wuthering Heights. MCLE(5754), MEF (976), MP1(1137), PO(28), PON(457), SGBN(109).
Brooke, Henry. Fool of Quality, The. MCLE(1643), MEF (216), MP2(333).
Brooke, Rupert. Letters of Rupert Brooke, The. SCL(2608), 1969a(196). Poetry of Brooke, The. MCLE(3784), MP4(737).
Brooks, Cleanth. William Faulkner. SCL(5070), 1964a(299).
Brooks, Gwendolyn. Selected Poems: 1944-1970. SCLs (266).
Brooks, Phillips. Lectures on Preaching. CHL(778).

Brooks, Van Wyck. America's Coming-of-Age. MCLE(140), MP4(38). Days of the Phoenix. SCL(1076), 1958a (66). Dream of Arcadia, The. SCL(1233), 1959a(62).
Brosius, Nancy Bancroft. Sue 'Em. DGAP(215).
Brown, Charles Brockden. Wieland. MAF(714), MCLE (5639), MP2(1131).
Brown, Claude. Manchild in the Promised Land. SCL(2874), 1966a(171).
Brown, Norman O. Love's Body. SCL(2803), 1967a(205).
Brown, William Adams. Christian Theology in Outline. CHL(840).
Browne, Robert. Treatise of Reformation Without Tarrying for Any. CHL(400).
Browne, Sir Thomas. Hydriotaphia: Urn-Burial. MCLE (2171), MP4(432). Religio medici. CHL(450).
Browning, Elizabeth Barrett. Sonnets from the Portuguese. MCLE(4916), MP(348), MP3(1007).
Browning, Robert. Blot in the 'Scutcheon, A. MCLE(446), MD(86), MP2(102). Dramatic Monologues and Lyrics of Browning. MCLE(1274), MP4(247). Dramatis Personae. MCLE(1277), MP4(250). Men and Women. MCLE(3012), MP4(603). Ring and the Book, The. MCLE(4463), MP(320), MP1(826).
Brownson, Orestes Augustus. American Republic, The. CAL(667).
Bruckberger, R. L. Image of America. SCL(2162), 1960a (99).
Brunner, Emil. Divine Imperative, The. CHL(986). Dogmatics. CHL(1076). Revelation and Reason. WP (1058).
Bruno, Giordano. Dialogues Concerning Cause, Principle, and One. WP(365).
Bryan, C. D. B. P. S. Wilkinson. SCLs(231).
Bryant, Sir Arthur. Medieval Foundation of England, The. SCL(2958), 1968a(196). Triumph in the West. BM (564), SCL(4767), 1960a(278). Turn of the Tide, The. BM(567), SCL(4790), 1958a(250).
Bryant, William Cullen. Poetry of Bryant, The. MCLE (3787), MP(237), MP3(784), MPA1(28).
Bryce, James. American Commonwealth, The. MCLE(132), MP4(32).
Bryher. Gate to the Sea. SCL(1713), 1959a(96). Roman Wall. SCL(3974), 1954a(234). Ruan. SCL(4018), 1961a(216).
Buber, Martin. I and Thou. CHL(917), WP(856).
Bucer, Martin. De regno Christi. CHL(396).
Buchan, John. Thirty-Nine Steps, The. MCLE(5167), MEF

(833), MP1(972).
Büchner, Friedrich Karl Christian Ludwig. Force and Matter. WP(633).
Büchner, Georg. Woyzeck. MCLE(5749), MD(952), MP2 (1163).
Buck, Pearl S. Dragon Seed. MAF(154), MCLE(1271), MP1 (226). Good Earth, The. MAF(217), MCLE(1806), MP1(313), PO(195), SGAN(226). Imperial Woman. SCL(2169), 1957a(130). My Several Worlds. SCL (3160), 1954a(186).
Bulatovic, Miodrag. Red Cock Flies to Heaven, The. SCL (3852), 1963a(208).
Bulgakov, Sergius. Wisdom of God, The. CHL(1035).
Bullen, Frank T. Cruise of the Cachalot, The. MCLE(955), MEF(131), MP1(178).
Bullinger, Johann Heinrich. Decades, The. CHL(381).
Bullock, Alan L. C. Hitler. SCL(2064), 1965a(130).
Bultmann, Rudolf. Theology of the New Testament. CHL (1097).
Bulwer-Lytton, Edward George Earle. Eugene Aram. MCLE(1476), MEF(187), MP2(297). Last Days of Pompeii, The. MCLE(2533), MEF(420), MP1(490), PO(31), PON(190), SGBN(71). Last of the Barons, The. MCLE(2538), MEF(425), MP1(492). Richelieu. POP (162).
Bunin, Ivan Alexeyevich. Village, The. MCLE(5481), MEU (791), MP2(1105).
Bunyan, John. Grace Abounding to the Chief of Sinners. CHL(506). Life and Death of Mr. Badman, The. MCLE(2656), MEF(431), MP3(575). Pilgrim's Progress, The. CHL(530), MCLE(3672), MEF(678), MP1 (748), PO(35), PON(304), SGBN(1).
Buonarroti, Michelangelo. Poetry of Michelangelo, The. MCLE(4026), MP4(902).
Burdick, Eugene. Ninth Wave, The. SCL(3279), 1957a(191).
Burgess, Anthony. Enderby. SCL(1356), 1969a(115). Nothing Like the Sun. SCL(3323), 1965a(215).
Burke, Charles, Dion Boucicault and Joseph Jefferson. Rip Van Winkle. DGAP(90).
Burke, Edmund. Vindication of Natural Society, A. MCLE (5489), MN(315), MP3(1099).
Burney, Fanny. Cecilia. MCLE(664), MEF(92), MP3(163). Diary and Letters of Mme. d'Arblay, The. MCLE (1163), MP4(226). Evelina. MCLE(1500), MEF(198), MP2(306).
Burns, James MacGregor. Roosevelt: The Lion and the Fox. SCL(3993), 1957a(224). Roosevelt: The Soldier of

Freedom. 1971a(276).

Burns, Robert. Poems, Chiefly in the Scottish Dialect. MCLE(3729), MP(222), MP3(769).

Burton, Robert. Anatomy of Melancholy, The. MCLE(160), MN(11), MP3(39).

Bushnell, Horace. Christian Nurture. CHL(736). God in Christ. CHL(716).

Butler, Joseph. Analogy of Religion, The. CHL(573). Fifteen Sermons Preached at the Rolls Chapel. WP (465).

Butler, Samuel. Erewhon. MCLE(1421), MEF(182), MP1 (252), SGBN(154). Hudibras. MCLE(2148), MP(131), MP3(492). Way of All Flesh, The. MCLE(5586), MEF(943), MP1(1097), PO(38), SGBN(159).

Buttrick, George Arthur. Prayer. CHL(1064).

Byrne, Donn. Destiny Bay. MCLE(1133), MEF(151), MP2 (249). Hangman's House. MCLE(1925), MEF(272), MP2(403). Messer Marco Polo. MCLE(3026), MEF (502), MP1(584).

Byron, George Gordon, Lord. Cain. MCLE(570), MD(121), MP2(127). Childe Harold's Pilgrimage. MCLE(709), MP4(127). Don Juan. MCLE(1237), MP(66), MP1 (217). Lyric Poetry of Byron, The. MCLE(2793), MP4(571). Manfred. MCLE(2893), MP(179), MP2 (621).

Cabell, James Branch. Cream of the Jest, The. MAF(110), MCLE(927), MP1(168). Jurgen. MAF(317), MCLE (2418), MP1(464), SGAN(123). Rivet in Grandfather's Neck, The. MAF(541), MCLE(4484), MP3(898).

Cable, George W. Grandissimes, The. MAF(220), MCLE (1819), MP1(320), MPA1(34).

Caesar, Gaius Julius. Commentaries. MCLE(808), MN(53), MP3(204).

Cain, James M. Postman Always Rings Twice, The. MCLE (4203), MP4(1021).

Cajetan, Saint. Commentary on the Summa theologica of Saint Thomas. CAL(516).

Calderón de la Barca, Pedro. Devotion of the Cross, The. MCLE(1139), MD(208), MP3(270). It Is Better than It Was. MCLE(2294), MD(389), MP3(517). It Is Worse than It Was. MCLE(2296), MD(391), MP3(519). Life Is a Dream. MCLE(2661), MD(441), MP2(580), POP(289). Mayor of Zalamea, The. MCLE(2972), MD(503), MP2(645). Mock Astrologer, The. MCLE (3123), MD(551), MP3(669).

Caldwell, Erskine. God's Little Acre. SGAN(247). Tobacco

Road. MAF(653), MCLE(5231), MP1(996), POP(10).
Calisher, Hortense. Tale for the Mirror. SCL(4511), 1963a(262).
Callado, Antonio. Quarup. SCLs(238).
Callahan, North. Henry Knox. SCLs(128).
Calvin, John. Institutes of the Christian Religion, The. CHL(358). Necessity of Reforming the Church, The. CHL(371).
Camoëns, Luis Vaz de. Lusiad, The. MCLE(2790), MP (167), MP2(608).
Campbell, Alexander. Christian System, The. CHL(672).
Campbell, John McLeod. Nature of the Atonement, The. CHL(731).
Campion, Thomas. Poetry of Campion, The. MCLE(3790), MP4(740).
Camus, Albert. Exile and the Kingdom. BM(172), MCLE (1515), MP4(311), SCL(1404), 1959a(78). Fall, The. BM(180), MCLE(1537), MP4(316), SCL(1440), 1958a (83). Lyrical and Critical Essays. SCL(2813), 1969a(215). Myth of Sisyphus, The. MCLE(3216), MP4(624). Notebooks: 1935-1942. SCL(3312), 1964a (194). Notebooks: 1942-1951. SCL(3314), 1966a(203). Plague, The. MCLE(3692), MEU(587), MP2(836), PO2(365). Rebel, The. SCL(3843), WP(1127), 1954a (228). Resistance, Rebellion, and Death. SCL(3901), 1962a(243). Stranger, The. MCLE(5018), MP4(1187), PO2(359), SGEN(440).
Camus, Jean Pierre. Spirit of Saint Francis of Sales, The. CAL(597).
Čapek, Karel and Joseph. Insect Comedy. TCP(95).
Čapek, Karel. R. U. R. MCLE(4563), MD(720), MP2(927), POP(341), TCP(93).
Capers, Gerald M. Stephen A. Douglas. SCL(4434), 1960a (253).
Capote, Truman. Breakfast at Tiffany's. SCLs(49). In Cold Blood. SCL(2175), 1967a(158).
Carducci, Giosuè. Poetry of Carducci, The. MCLE(3793), MP(240), MP3(787).
Carew, Thomas. Poetry of Carew, The. MCLE(3796), MP4(743).
Carleton, William. Emigrants of Ahadarra, The. MCLE (1364), MEF(177), MP3(328).
Carlyle, Thomas. French Revolution, The. MCLE(1690), MN(128), MP3(404). History of Frederick II of Prussia. MCLE(2048), MP4(415). On Heroes, Hero-Worship and the Heroic in History. MCLE(3399), MP4(646). Sartor Resartus. MCLE(4617), MN(271),

MP3(925).
Carnap, Rudolf. Introduction to Semantics. WP(1075). Philosophy and Logical Syntax. WP(997).
Carpentier, Alejo. Kingdom of This World, The. SCL (2445), 1958a(130).
Carroll, Lewis. Alice in Wonderland. MCLE(85), MEF(10), MP1(21), PO2(64), PON(14), SGBN(147). Through the Looking Glass. MCLE(5191), MEF(841), MP2(1023), PO2(64).
Carson, Rachel. Edge of the Sea, The. BM(145), SCL (1279), 1955a(89). Silent Spring. SCL(4288), 1963a (249).
Carter, Dan T. Scottsboro. 1970a(269).
Carter, John Stewart. Full Fathom Five. SCL(1676), 1966a (109).
Cary, Joyce. African Witch, The. SCL(68), 1963a(1). American Visitor, An. SCL(154), 1962a(19). Captive and the Free, The. SCL(626), 1960a(33). Charley Is My Darling. SCL(690), 1961a(38). Herself Surprised. MCLE(2021), MEF(298), MP3(459), PO2(127). Horse's Mouth, The. MCLE(2106), MEF(312), MP2(456), PON (148). Not Honour More. SCL(3305), 1955a(187). To Be a Pilgrim. MCLE(5225), MEF(847), MP3 (1072).
Casanova de Seingalt, Giovanni Jacopo. Memoirs. MCLE (2994), MN(203), MP3(646).
Cassian, John. Institutes of the Monastic Life, The. CAL (193).
Cassill, R. V. Father, The. SCL(1481), 1966a(106). Happy Marriage, The. SCL(1921), 1967a(133). President, The. SCL(3677), 1965a(226).
Cassirer, Ernst. Philosophy of Symbolic Forms, The. WP (850).
Cassola, Carlo. Fausto and Anna. SCL(1495), 1961a(75).
Castelot, André. King of Rome, The. BM(287), SCL(2434), 1961a(143). Queen of France. SCL(3773), 1958a(204).
Castiglione, Baldassare. Book of the Courtier, The. MCLE (461), MP4(77).
Castillo, Michel del. Child of Our Time. SCL(709), 1959a (31).
Cather, Willa. Death Comes for the Archbishop, MAF(133), MCLE(1043), MP1(199), PO2(204). Lost Lady, A. MAF(359), MCLE(2759), MP1(529). My Antonia. MAF(430), MCLE(3198), MP1(630), SGAN(108). O Pioneers! MAF(447), MCLE(3324), MP1(663). Professor's House, The. MAF(509), MCLE(4277), MP2

(867). Shadows on the Rock. MAF(572), MCLE (4738), MP1(884). Song of the Lark, The. MAF(586), MCLE(4910), MP2(981).
Catherine of Genoa, Saint. Dialogue Between the Soul and the Body, The. CAL(530).
Catherine of Siena, Saint. Dialogue of Saint Catherine of Siena, The. CAL(473), CHL(280).
Catton, Bruce. Coming Fury, The. SCL(858), 1962a(78). Grant Moves South. BM(208), SCL(1849), 1961a(109). Never Call Retreat. SCL(3197), 1966a(189). This Hallowed Ground. BM(544), SCL(4607), 1957a(269).
Catullus, Gaius Valerius. Carmina. MCLE(625), MP(41), MP3(156).
Cau, Jean. Mercy of God, The. SCL(3000), 1964a(175).
Caudill, Harry M. Night Comes to the Cumberlands. SCL (3229), 1964a(188).
Cavafy, Constantine P. Complete Poems of Cavafy, The. SCL(874), 1962a(84). Poetry of Cavafy, The. MCLE (3800), MP4(746).
Cavendish, George. Life and Death of Cardinal Wolsey, The. MCLE(2653), MP4(546).
Cecil, Lord David. Max. SCL(2941), 1966a(178). Melbourne. BM(364), SCL(2961), 1954a(174).
Cela, Camilio José. Family of Pascual Duarte, The. MCLE(1548), MP4(321), SCL(1459), 1965a(86). Hive, The. MCLE(2076), MP4(424).
Céline, Louis-Ferdinand. Journey to the End of the Night. MCLE(2395), MEU(407), MP1(453).
Cellini, Benvenuto. Autobiography of Benvenuto Cellini, The. MCLE(284), MN(32), MP2(64).
Cervantes Saavedra, Miguel de. Don Quixote de la Mancha. MCLE(1246), MEU(252), MP1(220), PO(372), PON(102), SGEN(15). Exemplary Novels. MCLE(1512), MEU (287), MP3(370).
Céspedes, Alba de. Secret, The. SCL(4129), 1959a(219).
Chalmers, Thomas. On the Adaptation of External Nature to the Moral and Intellectual Constitution of Man. CHL (668).
Chambers, Lenoir. Stonewall Jackson. SCL(4448), 1960a (257).
Chambers, Whittaker. Odyssey of a Friend. 1971a(235).
Channing, William Ellery. Unitarian Christianity. CHL(650).
Chaplin, Charles. My Autobiography. SCL(3140), 1965a(211).
Chapman, George. All Fools. MCLE(90), MD(17), MP3(22). Bussy D'Ambois. MCLE(554), MD(115), MP2(122). Gentleman Usher, The. MCLE(1735), MD(295), MP3

(413). Monsieur d'Olive. MCLE(3149), MD(553), MP3(674). Revenge of Bussy d'Ambois, The. MCLE (4423), MD(682), MP3(881). Shadow of Night, The. MCLE(4735), MP4(1110).

Chapman, George with Ben Jonson and John Marston. Eastward Ho! MCLE(1316), MD(234), MP3(317).

Chappell, Fred. Dagon. SCL(986), 1969a(82). Inkling, The. SCL(2233), 1966a(132).

Charnock, Stephen. Discourses upon the Existence and Attributes of God. CHL(539).

Charrière, Henri. Papillon. 1971a(245).

Chase, Mary Ellen. Edge of Darkness, The. SCL(1268), 1958a(80). Lovely Ambition, The. SCL(2800), 1961a (168).

Chateaubriand, François René de. Atala. MCLE(267), MEU (51), MP2(59).

Chatterton, Thomas. Poetry of Chatterton, The. MCLE (3803), MP4(748).

Chaucer, Geoffrey. Canterbury Tales, The (Selections). MCLE(598), MP(33), MP2(129). Legend of Good Women, The. MCLE(2580), MP(164), MP3(557). Parliament of Fowls, The. MCLE(3501), MP(207), MP3 (716). Troilus and Criseyde. MCLE(5337), MP(367), MP1(1030).

Chauncy, Charles. Seasonable Thoughts on the State of Religion in New England. CHL(586).

Chayefsky, Paddy. Tenth Man, The. SGAP(277).

Cheever, John. Brigadier and the Golf Widow, The. SCL (528), 1965a(16). Bullet Park. 1970a(63). Housebreaker of Shady Hill, The. SCL(2134), 1959a(122). Short Stories of John Cheever, The. MCLE(4793), MP4(1139). Wapshot Chronicle, The. BM(586), MCLE(5553), MP4(1268), SCL(4942), 1958a(264). Wapshot Scandal, The. MCLE(5557), MP4(1271), SCL (4946), 1964a(290).

Chekhov, Anton. Cherry Orchard, The. MCLE(700), MD (146), MP2(144), POP(353). Seagull, The. MCLE (4673), MD(747), MP2(945). Three Sisters, The. MCLE(5185), MD(844), MP2(1020), POP(357). Uncle Vanya. MCLE(5401), MD(891), MP2(1082).

Ch'eng-en, Wu. Monkey. MCLE(3144), MEU(505), MP3(671).

Chesnutt, Charles Waddell. Conjure Woman, The. MAF(97), MCLE(844), MP2(172), MPA1(39).

Chesterton, Gilbert Keith. Essays of G. K. Chesterton, The. MCLE(1457), MP4(302). Everlasting Man, The. CAL(785). Man Who Was Thursday, The. MCLE (2882), MEF(466), MP2(619). Napoleon of Notting

Hill, The. MCLE(3225), MEF(558), MP2(721). Orthodoxy. CAL(744). St. Francis of Assisi. CAL (781).
Chou, Chuang. Chuang Tzu. WP(185).
Chrétien de Troyes. Cligés. MCLE(766), MP(46), MP3(195). Erec and Enide. MCLE(1417), MP(85), MP3(348). Yvain. MCLE(5774), MP(383), MP3(1161).
Chrysostom, Saint John. Discourse on the Priesthood. CAL(123). Homilies of Saint John Chrysostom. CAL (154). Homilies on the Statues. CHL(117).
Chukovskaya, Lydia. Deserted House, The. SCL(1137), 1968a(75).
Church, Richard. Golden Sovereign, The. SCL(1800), 1958a (101).
Churchill, Winston S. Age of Revolution, The. BM(18), SCL(100), 1958a(4). Birth of Britain, The. BM(38), SCL(412), 1957a(26). Crisis, The. MAF(112), MCLE (935), MP1(172), PON(77). Great Democracies, The. BM(212), SCL(1859), 1959a(103). New World, The. BM(391), SCL(3213), 1957a(188). Second World War, The. MCLE(4689), MN(279), MP3(947).
Chute, B. J. Greenwillow. SCL(1883), 1957a(102).
Cibber, Colley. Apology for the Life of Colley Cibber, Comedian, An. MCLE(208), MN(23), MP3(52).
Cicero, Marcus Tullius. Cicero's Orations. MCLE(745), MN(51), MP3(188). Treatises of Cicero, The. MCLE (5295), MP4(1229).
Clare, John. Poetry of Clare, The. MCLE(3809), MP4(751).
Clarendon, Edward Hyde, Earl of. History of the Rebellion and Civil Wars in England. MCLE(2071), MP4(420).
Clark, Eleanor. Baldur's Gate. 1971a(14). Oysters of Locmariaquer, The. SCLs(213).
Clark, General Mark W. From the Danube to the Yalu. BM(202), SCL(1664), 1954a(86).
Clark, Thomas D. Emerging South, The. BM(163), SCL (1323), 1962a(106).
Clark, Walter Van Tilburg. Ox-Bow Incident, The. MAF (470), MCLE(3473), MP1(706), SGAN(275). Track of the Cat, The. MAF(664), MCLE(5268), MP2(1051).
Clark, William and Meriwether Lewis. Journals of Lewis and Clark, The. MCLE(2392), MP4(484).
Clarke, Samuel. Scripture-Doctrine of the Trinity, The. CHL(562).
Claudel, Paul. Break of Noon. TCP(99). Poetry of Claudel, The. MCLE(3812), MP4(754). Satin Slipper. TCP (102). Tidings Brought to Mary, The. TCP(109).
Cleaver, Eldridge. Soul on Ice. SCL(4380), 1968a(301).

Clemens, Samuel L. Adventures of Huckleberry Finn, The. PO2(176), SGAN(45). Adventures of Tom Sawyer, The. PO2(171). Autobiography of Mark Twain, The. SCL(278), 1960a(19). Connecticut Yankee in King Arthur's Court, A. MAF(100), MCLE(847), MP1(154), MPA5(64), PO(203). Huckleberry Finn. MAF(282), MCLE(2145), MP1(387), MPA5(74), PON(158). Letters from the Earth. SCL(2576), 1963a(120). Life on the Mississippi. MCLE(2673), MN(189), MP1(504), MPA5(80). Prince and the Pauper, The. MAF(506), MCLE(4243), MP2(854), MPA5(84), PO(200). Pudd'nhead Wilson. PON(334). Roughing It. MCLE(4553), MN(269), MP1(858), MPA5(89). Tom Sawyer. MAF (655), MCLE(5250), MP1(1003), MPA5(93), SGAN(40).

Clemens, Samuel L. and Charles Dudley Warner. Gilded Age, The. MAF(204), MCLE(1759), MP2(368), MPA5(69).

Clement of Alexandria, Saint. Miscellanies. CHL(43). Stromata, or Miscellanies, The. CHL(43). Stromateis. CAL(44).

Clement of Rome, Saint. First Epistle of Clement to the Corinthians, The. CHL(1).

Clement I, Saint. Letter of the Church of Rome to the Church of Corinth, The. CAL(4).

Clifford, James L. Young Sam Johnson. BM(623), SCL (5192), 1955a(302).

Climacus, Saint John. Ladder of Divine Ascent, The. CAL (254), CHL(179).

Coates, Robert M. Man Just Ahead of You, The. SCL (2857), 1965a(193).

Cocteau, Jean. Holy Terrors, The. MCLE(2087), MEU (367), MP3(483). Infernal Machine, The. TCP(113). Infernal Machine and Other Plays, The. SCL(2222), 1965a(143). Orpheus. TCP(116). Plays of Cocteau, The. MCLE(3709), MP4(699).

Coit, Margaret L. Mr. Baruch. SCL(3051), 1958a(163).

Cole, Hubert. Laval. SCL(2550), 1964a(146).

Coleridge, Samuel Taylor. Aids to Reflection. CHL(663). Biographia Literaria. MCLE(419), MP4(72). Poetry of Coleridge, The. MCLE(3815), MP4(756). Rime of the Ancient Mariner, The. MCLE(4461), MP(318), MP1(825).

Colette, Sidonie Gabrielle Claudine. Chéri. MCLE(697), MEU(131), MP3(176). Other One, The. MCLE(3455), MEU(557), MP3(709). Pure and the Impure, The. SCL(3750), 1968a(257).

Collier, Richard. Sands of Dunkirk, The. SCL(4070), 1962a (258).

Collingwood, Robin George. Essay on Metaphysics, An. WP(1046).
Collins, James D. God in Modern Philosophy. CAL(1071).
Collins, Wilkie. Moonstone, The. MCLE(3167), MEF(546), MP1(623), PO(41), PON(251). No Name. MCLE (3294), MEF(581), MP1(659). Woman in White, The. MCLE(5702), MEF(965), MP1(1125), PO(45), PON(454).
Collins, William. Poetry of Collins, The. MCLE(3819), MP4(760).
Colton, John B. and Clemence Randolph. Rain. POP(89).
Colum, Padraic. Flying Swans, The. SCL(1603), 1958a(94).
Comenius, Johannes Amos. Didactica magna. CHL(489).
Commodianus. Instructions in Favor of Christian Discipline. CHL(71).
Compton, Arthur Holly. Atomic Quest. SCL(258), 1957a(14).
Compton-Burnett, Ivy. Father and His Fate, A. SCL(1485), 1959a(84). God and His Gifts, A. SCL(1773), 1965a (110). Heritage and Its History, A. MCLE(2012), MP4(411), SCL(2017), 1961a(116). Mighty and Their Fall, The. BM(371), MCLE(3045), MP4(606), SCL (3033), 1963a(145). Mr. Bullivant and His Lambs. MCLE(3089), MP4(611). Mother and Son. BM(378), MCLE(3179), MP4(617), SCL(3106), 1955a(163). Pastors and Masters. MCLE(3518), MP4(675).
Comte, Auguste. Course on the Positive Philosophy. WP (588).
Conant, James Bryant. Citadel of Learning, The. SCL(748), 1957a(45).
Conchon, Georges. Savage State, The. SCL(4077), 1966a (278).
Condon, Richard. Infinity of Mirrors, An. SCL(2226), 1965a(146).
Confucius. Analects of Confucius, The (Lun Yü). WP(5). Shih Ching, The. MCLE(4760), MP(335), MP3(965).
Congreve, William. Double-Dealer, The. MCLE(1261), MD(227), MP2(281). Love for Love. MCLE(2764), MD(453), MP2(597). Old Bachelor, The. MCLE (3352), MD(581), MP2(759). Way of the World, The. MCLE(5589), MD(910), MP1(1099), POP(181).
Connell, Evan S., Jr. At the Crossroads. SCL(253), 1966a (19). Diary of a Rapist, The. SCL(1163), 1967a(82). Mr. Bridge. 1970a(212). Notes from a Bottle Found on the Beach at Carmel. MCLE(3317), MP4(636), SCL(3317), 1964a(196).
Connelly, Marc. Green Pastures, The. DGAP(249), POP (20), SGAP(69).
Connelly, Marc and George S. Kaufman. Beggar on Horse-

back. DGAP(208).
Connolly, Cyril. Rock Pool, The. SCL(3965), 1968a(272).
Conquest, Robert. Great Terror, The. SCL(1870), 1969a (140).
Conrad, Joseph. Almayer's Folly. MCLE(118), MEF(13), MP2(20). Chance. PO2(86). Heart of Darkness. MCLE(1952), MEF(280), MP3(447), PO2(91), SGBN (214). Lord Jim. MCLE(2744), MEF(447), MP1(522), PO(48), PON(212), SGBN(219). Nigger of the Narcissus, The. MCLE(3278), MEF(573), MP2(743). Nostromo. MCLE(3311), MEF(589), MP2(752). Secret Agent, The. MCLE(4692), MEF(778), MP3 (949). Secret Sharer, The. PO2(95). Under Western Eyes. MCLE(5423), MEF(898), MP3(1093). Victory. MCLE(5475), MEF(918), MP1(1067).
Conroy, Frank. Stop-time. SCL(4451), 1968a(308).
Conscience, Hendrik. Lion of Flanders, The. MCLE(2691), MEU(448), MP3(583).
Constant, Benjamin. Adolphe. MCLE(30), MEU(4), MP3(12).
Cooke, John Esten. Surry of Eagle's-Nest. MAF(621), MCLE(5061), MP3(1042). Virginia Comedians, The. MAF(694), MCLE(5500), MP2(1113).
Cooper, James Fenimore. Chainbearer, The. MAF(85), MCLE(679), MP3(166). Deerslayer, The. MAF(139), MCLE(1091), MP1(203), MPA1(44), PO2(158), PON(86). Last of the Mohicans, The. MAF(324), MCLE(2541), MP1(494), MPA1(50), PO(207), PON(195), SGAN(3). Leatherstocking Saga, The. SCL(2556), 1954a(141). Pathfinder, The. MAF(473), MCLE(3526), MP1(715), MPA1(56). Pilot, The. MAF(487), MCLE(3678), MP1(750), MPA1(60), PON(310). Pioneers, The. MAF(490), MCLE(3684), MP1(753), MPA1(66). Prairie, The. MAF(503), MCLE(4220), MP1(776). Red Rover, The. MAF(518), MCLE(4363), MP1(813). Redskins, The. MAF(524), MCLE(4369), MP3(870), MPA1(72). Satanstoe. MAF(553), MCLE(4623), MP3(927). Spy, The. MAF(598), MCLE(4971), MP1(921), MPA1(79).
Coover, Robert. Origin of the Brunists, The. SCL(3462), 1967a(255). Pricksongs and Descants. 1970a(250). Universal Baseball Association, Inc., J. Henry Waugh, Prop., The. SCL(4834), 1969a(327).
Coppard, A. E. Short Stories of A. E. Coppard, The. MCLE(4775), MP4(1123).
Corbière, Tristan. Poetry of Corbière, The. MCLE(3822), MP4(763).
Cordell, Alexander. Rape of the Fair Country, The. SCL (3834), 1960a(218).

Corneille, Pierre. Cid, The. MCLE(747), MD(150), MP1 (142), POP(269). Cinna. MCLE(749), MD(152), MP3 (190). Horace. MCLE(2104), MD(361), MP3(490). Menteur, Le. MCLE(3017), MD(513), MP3(656). Polyeucte. MCLE(4176), MD(650), MP3(839).

Corrington, John William. Lonesome Traveler and Other Stories, The. SCL(2742), 1969a(200).

Cortázar, Julio. Hopscotch. SCL(2097), 1967a(146). Winners, The. SCL(5095), 1966a(341).

Coster, Charles de. Legend of Tyl Ulenspiegel, The. MCLE(2588), MEU(439), MP2(573).

Cotton, John. Keys of the Kingdom of Heaven, The. CHL (458).

Couperus, Louis. Small Souls. MCLE(4864), MEU(688), MP3(1000).

Courtney, Marguerite. Laurette. BM(305), SCL(2546), 1955a(144).

Cousins, Paul M. Joel Chandler Harris. SCL(2340), 1969a (177).

Cousteau, Jacques-Yves. Living Sea, The. SCL(2727), 1964a(163).

Coward, Noel. Blithe Spirit. TCP(120). Design for Living. POP(77). Private Lives. MCLE(4269), MD(663), MP2(860).

Cowley, Abraham. Miscellanies. MCLE(3070), MP(187), MP3(663).

Cowley, Malcolm. Blue Juniata. SCL(461), 1969a(48).

Cowper, William. Letters of William Cowper, The. MCLE (2636), MP4(541). Poetry of Cowper, The. MCLE (3826), MP4(766). Task, The. MCLE(5116), MP(355), MP3(1054).

Cozzens, James Gould. By Love Possessed. SCL(577), 1958a(44). Guard of Honor. MAF(244), MCLE(1876), MP3(435). Morning Noon and Night. SCL(3083), 1969a(231).

Crabbe, George. Borough: A Poem in Twenty-Four Letters, The. MCLE(467), MP4(79). Village, The. MCLE (5484), MP(371), MP3(1097).

Crane, Hart. Bridge, The. MCLE(501), MP(28), MP3(131).

Crane, Stephen. Maggie: A Girl of the Streets. MAF(370), MCLE(2831), MP1(543), MPA1(86). Red Badge of Courage, The. MAF(515), MCLE(4357), MP1(811), MPA1(89), PO(210), PON(351), SGAN(72).

Crankshaw, Edward. Fall of the House of Hapsburg, The. SCL(1453), 1964a(77).

Cranmer, Thomas. Defense of the True and Catholic Doctrine of the Sacrament, A. CHL(385).

Crashaw, Richard. Carmen Deo nostro. CAL(600). Poetry of Crashaw, The. MCLE(3829), MP4(768).
Crawford, Joanna. Birch Interval. SCL(405), 1965a(11).
Crébillon, Prosper Jolyot de. Rhadimistus and Zenobia. MCLE(4439), MD(688), MP3(888).
Creeley, Robert. Island, The. SCL(2272), 1964a(138).
Crèvecoeur, Michet-Guillaume Jean de. Letters from an American Farmer. MCLE(2600), MN(169), MP3(560).
Crichton, Michael. Andromeda Strain, The. 1970a(24).
Croce, Benedetto. Aesthetic. MCLE(41), MP4(3), WP(745).
Crockett, David. Narrative of the Life of David Crockett, A. MCLE(3231), MN(209), MP2(724).
Cromwell, Oliver. Oliver Cromwell's Letters and Speeches. CHL(493).
Crouse, Russel and Howard Lindsay. Life with Father. DGAP(317), POP(1), SGAP(58).
Crowley, Mart. Boys in the Band, The. SCL(509), 1969a (51).
Crumley, James. One to Count Cadence. 1970a(231).
Cudworth, Ralph. True Intellectual System of the Universe, The. CHL(534).
Cullmann, Oscar. Christ and Time. CHL(1072).
Cummings, E. E. Enormous Room, The. MAF(166), MCLE(1394), MP1(250). him. TCP(125). 95 Poems. BM(395), SCL(3276), 1959a(177). Poems: 1923-1954. BM(439), SCL(3635), 1954a(210). Poetry of Cummings, The. MCLE(3833), MP4(772). 73 Poems. SCL(4230), 1964a(236).
Cunliffe, Marcus. Soldiers and Civilians. SCL(4343), 1969a (291).
Current, Richard N. and James G. Randall. Lincoln the President. BM(340), SCL(2686), 1955a(147).
Cyprian of Carthage, Saint. On the Unity of the Catholic Church. CAL(75), CHL(73).
Cyril, Saint, Bishop of Jerusalem. Cathechetical Lectures, The. CAL(90), CHL(92).

Dabbs, James McBride. Southern Heritage, The. SCLs(288).
Dahl, Roald. Kiss, Kiss. SCL(2451), 1961a(147).
Daly, Augustin. Horizon. DGAP(95).
Damian, Saint Peter. Selected Writings on the Spiritual Life. CHL(190).
Dana, Richard Henry, Jr. Two Years Before the Mast. MCLE(5379), MN(309), MP1(1033), MPA1(94).
Dane, Clemence. Flower Girls, The. SCL(1593), 1955a(98).
Daniel, Samuel. Poetry of Daniel, The. MCLE(3835), MP4 (774).

Daniélou, Jean, S. J. Lord of History, The. CAL(997).
Daniel-Rops, Henri. Jesus and His Times. CAL(1006).
Dante Alighieri. De monarchia. CAL(438), CHL(255). Divine Comedy, The. CAL(443), CHL(259), MCLE (1192), MP(63), MP1(211). Vita nuova, The. MCLE (5516), MP(376), MP3(1107).
D'Arcy, Martin Cyril, S. J. Meeting of Love and Knowledge, The. CAL(1040). Mind and Heart of Love, The. CAL(909).
Darío, Rubén. Selected Poems. SCL(4176), 1966a(295).
Darwin, Charles. Descent of Man, and Selection in Relation to Sex, The. MCLE(1128), MP4(221). On the Origin of Species. MCLE(3407), MN(220), MP3(700). Voyage of the Beagle, The. MCLE(5531), MN(322), MP1 (1079).
Daudet, Alphonse. Kings in Exile. MCLE(2474), MEU(416), MP2(538). Sappho. MCLE(4609), MP1(865), PO(276). Tartarin of Tarascon. MCLE(5109), MEU(743), MP1 (956).
Davenant, Sir William. Siege of Rhodes, The. MCLE(4817), MD(775), MP3(979).
Davenport, Russell W. Dignity of Man, The. SCL(1176), 1955a(83).
Davidson, Donald. Long Street, The. BM(350), SCL(2759), 1962a(192).
Davis, Burke. Gray Fox. SCL(1853), 1957a(93). Jeb Stuart, The Last Cavalier. SCL(2313), 1958a(120). They Called Him Stonewall. SCL(4583), 1954a(279). To Appomattox. SCL(4689), 1960a(275).
Davis, David Brion. Problem of Slavery in Western Culture, The. SCL(3699), 1967a(271).
Davis, H. L. Distant Music, The. SCL(1186), 1958a(73). Harp of a Thousand Strings, MAF(249), MCLE(1935), MP2(407). Honey in the Horn. MAF(264), MCLE (2098), MP1(371). Kettle of Fire. SCL(2409), 1960a (117).
Dawkins, Cecil. Quiet Enemy, The. SCL(3801), 1964a(218).
Dawson, Christopher. Making of Europe, The. CAL(824). Progress and Religion. CAL(798).
Day, Clarence, Jr. Life with Father. MAF(340), MCLE (2676), MP1(506).
Day, Thomas. Sandford and Merton. MCLE(4603), MEF (772), MP2(933).
Deakin, F. W. Brutal Friendship, The. SCL(541), 1964a (37).
Deal, Borden. Dragon's Wine. SCL(1230), 1961a(61).
Defoe, Daniel. Captain Singleton. MCLE(609), MEF(80),

MP3(154). History of Colonel Jacque, The. MCLE (2042), MEF(307), MP2(451). Journal of the Plague Year, A. MCLE(2374), MP4(469). Memoirs of a Cavalier, The. MCLE(2997), MEF(491), MP3(649). Moll Flanders. MCLE(3137), MEF(538), MP1(614), PO(52). Robinson Crusoe. MCLE(4495), MEF(739), MP1(839), PO2(1), PON(356), SGBN(9). Roxana. MCLE(4555), MEF(765), MP2(924).

De Forest, John William. Miss Ravenel's Conversion. MAF(410), MCLE(3083), MP2(677).

Dekker, Thomas. Gull's Hornbook, The. MCLE(1886), MP4(401). Honest Whore, Part One, The. MCLE (2092), MD(355), MP3(485). Honest Whore, Part Two, The. MCLE(2095), MD(358), MP3(487). Old Fortunatus. MCLE(3361), MD(584), MP3(696). Satiromastix. MCLE(4635), MD(733), MP3(933). Shoemaker's Holiday, The. MCLE(4772), MD(772), MP2(962), POP(188).

De Koninck, George. Hollow Universe, The. CAL(1084).

De la Mare, Walter. Collected Poems. MCLE(790), MP(50), MP3(198). Memoirs of a Midget. MCLE(3003), MEF (497), MP1(577). O Lovely England. SCL(3337), 1957a(197). Return, The. MCLE(4414), MEF(725), MP2(896).

Deledda, Grazia. Mother, The. MCLE(3173), MEU(514), MP2(708).

Deloney, Thomas. Jack of Newberry. MCLE(2311), MEF (361), MP2(501).

Democritus of Abdera. Democritus: Fragments. WP(37).

De Morgan, William. Joseph Vance. MCLE(2368), MEF (388), MP1(450).

Demosthenes. Philippics, The. MCLE(3619), MN(236), MP3(738).

Dennis, Nigel. Cards of Identity. SCL(629), 1955a(44).

Dennis, Patrick. Auntie Mame. SCL(266), 1955a(14).

Denti di Pirajno, Alberto. Ippolita. SCL(2264), 1962a(157).

Denzinger, Heinrich Joseph Dominicus. Enchiridion symbolorum et definitionum. CAL(658).

De Quincey, Thomas. Confessions of an English Opium Eater. MCLE(829), MN(64), MP2(167).

Dermoût, Maria. Ten Thousand Things, The. SCL(4548), 1959a(229). Yesterday. SCL(5180), 1960a(298).

De Santillana, Giorgio. Crime of Galileo, The. SCL(947), 1955a(71).

Descartes, René. Discourse on Method. WP(380). Meditations on First Philosophy. WP(386). Passions of the Soul, The. MCLE(3512), MP4(670).

De Terra, Helmut. Humboldt. SCL(2137), 1955a(128).
De Vries, Peter. Let Me Count the Ways. SCL(2566),
 1966a(141). Mackerel Plaza, The. SCL(2821), 1959a
 (152). Mrs. Wallop. 1971a(213). Tunnel of Love,
 The. SCL(4787), 1954a(282).
Dewey, John. Art as Experience. WP(986). Human Nature
 and Conduct. WP(835). Logic, the Theory of Inquiry.
 WP(1033). Quest for Certainty, The. WP(907).
Dick, Oliver Lawson, Editor. Aubrey's Brief Lives. SCL
 (262), 1958a(22).
Dickens, Charles. Barnaby Rudge. MCLE(335), MEF(38),
 MP2(72). Bleak House. MCLE(437), MEF(57), MP1
 (77). Christmas Carol, A. MCLE(733), MEF(101),
 MP1(139), PO2(32). David Copperfield. MCLE(1023),
 MEF(136), MP1(189), PO(55), PON(81), SGBN(83).
 Dombey and Son. MCLE(1225), MEF(167), MP2(267).
 Great Expectations. MCLE(1827), MEF(248), MP1
 (326), PO2(36), SGBN(94). Hard Times. MCLE(1928),
 MEF(275), MP2(405). Little Dorrit. MCLE(2699),
 MEF(436), MP2(585). Martin Chuzzlewit. MCLE
 (2943), MEF(478), MP2(640). Mystery of Edwin
 Drood, The. MCLE(3213), MEF(555), MP2(717).
 Nicholas Nickleby. MCLE(3267), MEF(570), MP2
 (734). Old Curiosity Shop, The. MCLE(3358), MEF
 (595), MP2(761). Oliver Twist. MCLE(3392), MEF
 (607), MP1(686), PO(63), PON(279). Our Mutual
 Friend. MCLE(3458), MEF(625), MP2(785), PON(282).
 Pickwick Papers. MCLE(3652), MEF(667), MP1(743),
 PO(66), PON(301), SGBN(78). Tale of Two Cities, A.
 MCLE(5075), MEF(816), MP1(945), PO(59), PON(373),
 SGBN(88).
Dickey, James. Buckdancer's Choice. SCL(544), 1966a(38).
 Deliverance. 1971a(58). Drowning with Others.
 SCL(1251), 1963a(44). Eye-Beaters, Blood, Victory,
 Madness, Buckhead and Mercy, The. 1971a(69).
 Helmets. SCL(1984), 1965a(121). Poems: 1957-1967.
 SCL(3631), 1968a(247). Poetry of Dickey, The.
 MCLE(3842), MP4(778).
Dickinson, Emily. Letters of Emily Dickinson, The. BM
 (319), MCLE(2609), MP4(520), SCL(2586), 1959a(144).
 Poems of Emily Dickinson, The. BM(445), SCL(3638),
 1955a(205). Poetry of Emily Dickinson, The. MCLE
 (3881), MP(255), MP3(798), MPA1(99).
Dickson, Lovat. H. G. Wells. 1970a(164).
Diderot, Denis. Rameau's Nephew. MCLE(4330), MEU(616),
 MP3(863). Thoughts on the Interpretation of Nature.
 WP(495).

Didion, Joan. Play It as It Lays. 1971a(253).
Diekmann, Godfrey, O. S. B. Come, Let Us Worship. CAL (1103).
Dillard, R. H. W. Day I Stopped Dreaming About Barbara Steele and Other Poems, The. SCL(1047), 1967a(69).
Dillon, Richard. Meriwether Lewis: A Biography. SCL (3003), 1966a(182).
Dinesen, Isak. Anecdotes of Destiny. SCL(181), 1959a(11). Ehrengard. PO2(497). Last Tales. SCL(2530), 1958a(138). Seven Gothic Tales. MCLE(4719), MEU (674), MP3(958). Shadows on the Grass. SCL(4239), 1962a(269).
Dionysius of Alexandria, Saint. Extant Fragments of the Works of Dionysius. CHL(77). Treatise on the Promises. CAL(78).
Dionysius, the Pseudo-Areopagite. Divine Names, The. CHL(165). Mystical Theology, The. CAL(218). On the Divine Names. CAL(215).
Disraeli, Benjamin. Coningsby. MCLE(841), MEF(118), MP2(170). Vivian Grey. MCLE(5519), MEF(930), MP2(1115), PON(432).
Djilas, Milovan. Land Without Justice. SCL(2492), 1959a (137). New Class, The. SCL(3202), 1958a(169). Unperfect Society, The. 1970a(326).
Dodd, Charles Harold. Parables of the Kingdom, The. CHL(1012).
Doderer, Heimito von. Demons, The. SCL(1124), 1962a (100).
Dodson, Kenneth. Away All Boats. SCL(285), 1954a(7).
Donald, David. Charles Summer and the Coming of the Civil War. BM(69), SCL(687), 1961a(36).
Dondeyne, Albert. Contemporary European Thought and Christian Faith. CAL(1061).
Donleavy, J. P. Beastly Beatitudes of Balthazar B, The. SCL(340), 1969a(30). Ginger Man, The. SCL(1757), 1959a(98).
Donne, John. Death's Duell. MCLE(1075), MP4(202). Devotions upon Emergent Occasions. CHL(441). Ignatius His Conclave. MCLE(2206), MP4(437). Poetry of Donne, The. MCLE(3846), MP(249), MP3 (793).
Donoso Cortés, Juan Francisco Maria de la Saludad. Essay on Catholicism, Liberalism, and Socialism. CAL(650).
Doolittle, Hilda. Bid Me to Live. SCL(396), 1961a(21). Poetry of H. D., The. MCLE(3925), MP4(834).
Dooyeweerd, Herman. New Critique of Theoretical Thought, A. CHL(1016).

Dorner, Isaac August. History of the Development of the Doctrine of the Person of Christ. CHL(692).
Dos Passos, John. 42nd Parallel, The. SGAN(217). Manhattan Transfer. MAF(385), MCLE(2895), MP1(555). Midcentury. SCL(3018), 1962a(205). Most Likely to Succeed. SCL(3103), 1954a(180). Three Soldiers. MAF(644), MCLE(5188), MP1(984). U. S. A. MAF (685), MCLE(5436), MP1(1051), PON(416).
Dostoevski, Fyodor Mikhailovich. Brothers Karamazov, The. MCLE(534), MEU(89), MP1(88), PO(356), SGEN(152). Crime and Punishment. MCLE(929), MEU(179), MP1 (170), PO(352), PON(70), SGEN(145). Diary of a Writer. MCLE(1170), MP4(230). Gambler, The. MCLE(1712), MEU(315), MP2(352). Grand Inquisitor, The. CHL(786). Idiot, The. MCLE(2193), MEU(388), MP1(415), PO2(396). Letters from the Underworld. MCLE(2603), MEU(442), MP2(576). Poor People. MCLE(4182), MEU(593), MP2(847). Possessed, The. MCLE(4200), MEU(596), MP1(771).
Doughty, Charles M. Travels in Arabia Deserta. MCLE (5280), MN(300), MP3(1079).
Douglas, David C. William the Conqueror. SCL(5088), 1965a(311).
Douglas, Ellen. Black Cloud, White Cloud. SCL(430), 1964a(25).
Douglas, George. House with the Green Shutters, The. MCLE(2133), MEF(321), MP2(467).
Douglas, Lloyd C. Magnificent Obsession, The. MAF(372), MCLE(2839), MP1(547).
Douglas, Norman. Old Calabria. MCLE(3355), MP4(641). South Wind. MCLE(4943), MEF(810), MP2(988), SGBN(285).
Dowdey, Clifford. Land They Fought For, The. SCL(2488), 1955a(137).
Dowson, Ernest Christopher. Poems of Ernest Dowson, The. CAL(720). Poetry of Dowson, The. MCLE(3849), MP4(781).
Doyle, Arthur Conan. Hound of the Baskervilles, The. PO2(75). Micah Clarke. MCLE(3031), MEF(504), MP1(585). Sign of Four, The. MCLE(4819), MEF (796), MP2(964). Study in Scarlet, A. MCLE(5036), MEF(813), MP1(938). White Company, The. MCLE (5623), MEF(952), MP1(1108), PON(450).
Draper, Theodore. Abuse of Power. SCL(12), 1968a(4). Roots of American Communism, The. SCL(3996), 1958a(217).
Drayton, Michael. Poetry of Drayton, The. MCLE(3852),

MP(252), MP3(796).
Dreiser, Theodore. American Tragedy, An. MAF(23), MCLE(138), MP1(29), PO(214), PON(19), SGAN(135). Bulwark, The. MAF(75), MCLE(548), MP3(142). Financier, The. MAF(184), MCLE(1610), MP1(280). "Genius," The. MAF(192), MCLE(1729), MP3(409). Jennie Gerhardt. MAF(312), MCLE(2333), MP1(526). Sister Carrie. MAF(581), MCLE(4843), MP1(895), PO2(199), SGAN(130). Stoic, The. MAF(604), MCLE (4982), MP3(1020). Titan, The. MAF(650), MCLE (5218), MP1(991).
Drucker, Peter F. Age of Discontinuity, The. 1971a(7).
Drummond, Henry. Ascent of Man, The. CHL(805).
Drury, Allen. Advise and Consent. SCL(56), 1960a(3). Capable of Honor. SCL(615), 1967a(35).
Dryden, John. Absalom and Achitophel. MCLE(15), MP(1), MP3(5). All for Love. MCLE(92), MD(19), MP2(11). Essay of Dramatic Poesy, An. MCLE(1429), MP4(285). Hind and the Panther, The. CAL(611). Marriage à la Mode. MCLE(2937), MD(497), MP3(634). Poetry of Dryden, The. MCLE(3855), MP4(784). Spanish Friar, The. MCLE(4946), MD(797), MP3(1009).
Du Bellay, Joachim. Poetry of Du Bellay, The. MCLE (3860), MP4(788).
Duberman, Martin. Charles Francis Adams. SCL(683), 1962a(48). James Russell Lowell. SCL(2300), 1967a (171). Uncompleted Past, The. 1970a(315).
Dubos, René. So Human an Animal. SCLs(285).
Ducasse, Curt John. Nature, Mind, and Death. WP(1132).
Dudintsev, Vladimir. Not by Bread Alone. SCL(3297), 1958a(172).
Dugan, Alan. Poems 2. SCLs(225).
Dugan, James and Carroll Stewart. Ploesti. SCL(3604), 1963a(186).
Duggan, Alfred. Cunning of the Dove, The. SCL(979), 1961a(51). King of Pontus. SCL(2431), 1960a(121). Lady for Ransom, The. MCLE(2494), MP4(492), SCL(2473), 1954a(135). Leopards and Lilies. MCLE (2594), MP4(512), SCL(2563), 1954a(144). My Life for My Sheep. SCL(3157), 1955a(166). Three's Company. SCL(4640), 1959a(244). Winter Quarters. SCL(5108), 1957a(287).
Dumas, Alexandre (father). Chevalier of the Maison Rouge, The. MCLE(702), MEU(134), MP3(179). Corsican Brothers, The. MCLE(881), MEU(156), MP2(179). Count of Monte Cristo, The. MCLE(889), MEU(161), MP1(158), PO(282), PON(57), SGEN(101). Countess de

Charny, The. MCLE(895), MEU(167), MP3(230). Memoirs of a Physician. MCLE(3005), MEU(491), MP3(651). Queen's Necklace, The. MCLE(4304), MEU(610), MP2(871). Three Musketeers, The. MCLE(5181), MEU(754), MP1(981), PO(279), PON(381). Twenty Years After. MCLE(5360), MEU(773), MP2 (1071). Vicomte de Bragelonne, The. MCLE(5468), MEU(787), MP1(1063).

Dumas, Alexandre (son). Camille. MCLE(584), MD(124), MP1(105), PO(289), PON(43), POP(247).

Du Maurier, Daphne. Rebecca. MCLE(4345), MEF(722), MP1(806).

Du Maurier, George. Peter Ibbetson. MCLE(3599), MEF (655), MP1(736), PO(75). Trilby. MCLE(5321), MEF(876), MP1(1023), PO(70), PON(402).

Dumitriu, Petru. Extreme Occident, The. SCL(1419), 1967a (104). Incognito. MCLE(2235), MP4(446), SCL(2215), 1965a(139).

Duncan, John. Colloquia peripatetica. CHL(762).

Dunlap, William. André. DGAP(23).

du Noüy, Pierre Lecomte. Human Destiny. CAL(913).

Duns Scotus, John. De primo principio. CAL(423). Opus oxoniense. CAL(427). Ordinatio: Oxford Commentary on the Sentences of Peter Lombard. CHL(251). Tract Concerning the First Principle, The. WP(329).

Durant, Will. Reformation, The. BM(473), SCL(3864), 1958a(209).

Durant, Will and Ariel. Age of Louis XIV, The. SCL(92), 1964a(6). Age of Reason Begins, The. BM(14), SCL (96), 1962a(15). Age of Voltaire, The. SCL(115), 1966a(5). Rousseau and Revolution. SCL(4010), 1968a(279).

Durrell, Gerald. Birds, Beasts, and Relatives. 1970a(53). Three Tickets to Adventure. SCL(4637), 1955a(259). Whispering Land, The. SCL(5043), 1963a(295).

Durrell, Lawrence. Acte. SCL(31), 1967a(1). Alexandria Quartet, The. MCLE(75), MP4(14). Balthazar. BM (31), SCL(313), 1959a(20). Bitter Lemons. SCL(428), 1959a(26). Clea. BM(83), SCL(765), 1961a(44). Collected Poems. SCL(798), 1961a(49). Dark Labyrinth, The. SCL(1017), 1963a(35). Justine. BM (282), SCL(2395), 1958a(125). Mountolive. BM(381), SCL(3112), 1960a(174). Nunquam. 1971a(232). Tunc. SCL(4783), 1969a(324).

Dürrenmatt, Friedrich. Physicists. TCP(128). Pledge, The. SCL(3600), 1960a(195). Visit, The. TCP(130).

Duun, Olav. People of Juvik, The. MCLE(3572), MEU(579), MP2(809).

Earl, Lawrence. Crocodile Fever. SCL(951), 1954a(46).
Eastlake, William. Bamboo Bed, The. 1970a(49). Castle Keep. SCL(635), 1966a(46). Three by Eastlake. 1971a(318).
Ebeling, Gerhard. Nature of Faith, The. CHL(1184).
Eberhart, Richard. Poetry of Eberhart, The. MCLE(3864), MP4(792). Quarry, The. SCL(3767), 1965a(230).
Eça de Queiroz, José Maria. Maias, The. SCL(2824), 1966a(157).
Echegaray, José. Great Galeoto, The. MCLE(1830), MD (311), MP2(381).
Eckermann, Johann Peter. Conversations of Goethe with Eckermann and Soret. MCLE(868), MP4(158).
Eckhart, Johann. Sermons and Treatises. CHL(245). Treatises and Sermons of Meister Eckhart, The. CAL(451).
Eddy, Mary Baker. Science and Health with Key to the Scriptures. CHL(775).
Edel, Leon. Henry James. SCL(2002), 1963a(81).
Edgeworth, Maria. Absentee, The. MCLE(17), MEF(1), MP2(1). Castle Rackrent. MCLE(643), MEF(88), MP1(126).
Edmonds, Walter D. Drums Along the Mohawk. MAF(160), MCLE(1291), MP1(230). Rome Haul. MAF(547), MCLE(4532), MP1(851).
Edwards, Jonathan. Freedom of the Will. CHL(598), WP (501). Great Christian Doctrine of Original Sin Defended, The. CHL(602). Treatise Concerning Religious Affections, A. CHL(590). Works of Jonathan Edwards. MCLE(5734), MN(330), MP3(1150).
Egan, Pierce. Life in London. MCLE(2658), MEF(433), MP2(578).
Eggleston, Edward. Hoosier Schoolmaster, The. MAF(267), MCLE(2101), MP1(373), MPA1(105).
Eichendorff, Josef von. Poetry of Eichendorff, The. MCLE (3869), MP4(795).
Einhard. Life of Charlemagne, The. CAL(265).
Eiseley, Loren. Firmament of Time, The. SCL(1550), 1961a(80). Unexpected Universe, The. 1970a(320).
Eisenhower, Dwight D. Mandate for Change, 1953-1956. SCL(2881), 1964a(172).
Elder, Lonne, III. Ceremonies in Dark Old Men. 1970a(72).
Eliot, George. Adam Bede. MCLE(23), MEF(5), MP1(8), PO(78), PON(6), SGBN(132). Daniel Deronda. MCLE (1009), MEF(133), MP3(249). Felix Holt, Radical. MCLE(1581), MEF(207), MP3(388). Middlemarch. MCLE(3039), MEF(507), MP1(588), PO2(47). Mill on

the Floss, The. MCLE(3050), MEF(510), MP1(593), PO(82). Romola. MCLE(4538), MEF(756), MP1(856), PO(86), PON(361). Silas Marner. MCLE(4821), MEF(798), MP1(893), PO2(43).

Eliot, T. S. After Strange Gods. MCLE(48), MP4(9). Ash Wednesday. MCLE(259), MP(12), MP3(72). Cocktail Party, The. MCLE(781), MD(160), MP2(158). Confidential Clerk, The. BM(111), MCLE(838), MP4(150), SCL(897), 1954a(34). Dante. MCLE(1012), MP4(188). Elder Statesman, The. BM(152), MCLE(1344), MP4 (262), SCL(1297), 1960a(67). Family Reunion, The. MCLE(1551), MD(272), MP2(321). Four Quartets. MCLE(1672), MP(106), MP3(401). John Dryden: The Poet, the Dramatist, the Critic. MCLE(2350), MP4 (465). Idea of a Christian Society, The. CHL(1043). Murder in the Cathedral. MCLE(3192), MD(564), MP2(714), TCP(133). On Poetry and Poets. BM(408), SCL(3391), 1958a(175). Poems Written in Early Youth. SCL(3641), 1967a(268). Sacred Wood: Essays on Poetry and Criticism, The. MCLE(4574), MP4(1086). To Criticize the Critic. SCL(4692), 1967a(324). Waste Land, The. MCLE(5575), MP(379), MP3(1121).

Elizabeth, Countess of Longford. Queen Victoria: Born to Succeed. SCL(3776), 1966a(259). Wellington. 1971a (342).

Elkin, Stanley. Bad Man, A. SCL(299), 1968a(19). Boswell. SCL(490), 1965a(13).

Elliott, George P. Among the Dangs. SCL(161), 1962a(22).

Ellis, A. E. Rack, The. SCL(3807), 1960a(212).

Ellison, Ralph. Invisible Man. MCLE(2272), MP4(457), SGAN(330). Shadow and Act. SCL(4236), 1965a(277).

Ellmann, Richard. James Joyce. SCL(2289), 1960a(105).

Elsner, Gisela. Giant Dwarfs, The. SCL(1740), 1966a(118).

Elwin, Malcolm. Lord Byron's Wife. SCL(2777), 1964a(165).

Emerson, Ralph Waldo. Divinity School Address, The. CHL(684). Essays: First and Second Series. MCLE (1443), MN(113), MP3(359), MPA1(110). Poetry of Emerson, The. MCLE(3874), MP4(800), MPA1(116). Representative Men. MCLE(4398), MP4(1054), MPA1 (123). Society and Solitude. MCLE(4881), MP4(1156), MPA1(131).

Empedocles of Acragas. Empedocles: Fragments. WP(26).

Empiricus, Sextus. Outlines of Pyrrhonism. WP(234).

England, Barry. Figures in a Landscape. SCL(1528), 1968a (108).

Ephraem the Syrian. Hymns of Ephraem the Syrian, The. CHL(103).

Epictetus. Discourses and Manual. WP(224).
Epicurus. Principal Doctrines and Letter to Menoeceus. WP(191).
Epiphanius of Salamis, Saint. Panarion. CHL(111).
Epstein, Jason. Great Conspiracy Trial, The. 1971a(105).
Epstein, Seymour. Caught in That Music. SCL(651), 1968a (37).
Erasmus, Desiderius. Enchiridion militis Christiani. CAL (498), CHL(321). Paraclesis, The. CAL(505). Praise of Folly, The. CAL(501), CHL(326), MCLE (4223), MN(254), MP3(846).
Erastus, Thomas. Treatise of Excommunication. CHL(414).
Erikson, Erik H. Gandhi's Truth. 1971a(91).
Erlanger, Philippe. Saint Bartholomew's Night. SCL(4051), 1963a(225).
Eschenbach, Wolfram von. Parzival. MCLE(3503), MP(209), MP2(795).
Esenin, Sergei. Poetry of Esenin, The. MCLE(3884), MP4 (806).
Etherege, Sir George. Man of Mode, The. MCLE(2879), MD(491), MP2(617).
Euripides. Alcestis. MCLE(67), MD(12), MP1(16). Andromache. MCLE(171), MD(33), MP3(40). Bacchae, The. MCLE(315), MD(52), MP2(68). Children of Herakles, The. MCLE(718), MD(148), MP3(182). Cyclops, The. MCLE(969), MD(189), MP3(245). Electra. MCLE(1350), MD(245), MP1(243), POP(372). Helen. MCLE(1977), MD(326), MP3(452). Herakles Mad. MCLE(2005), MD(348), MP3(454). Hippolytus. MCLE(2036), MD(350), MP2(449). Ion. MCLE(2280), MD(381), MP3(513). Iphigenia in Aulis. MCLE(2283), MD(384), MP2(495). Iphigenia in Tauris. MCLE(2285), MD(386), MP2(497). Medea. MCLE(2978), MD(509), MP1(573). Phoenician Women, The. MCLE(3643), MD(628), MP3(753). Suppliants, The. MCLE(5057), MD(821), MP3(1038). Trojan Women, The. MCLE (5339), MD(877), MP3(1085), POP(375).
Eusebius of Caesarea. Ecclesiastical History. CHL(87).
Eusebius of Pamphili. Ecclesiastical History. CAL(88).
Eustis, Helen. Fool Killer, The. SCL(1610), 1954a(80).
Evelyn, John. Diary. MCLE(1158), MN(86), MP3(281).

Fairbairn, Ann. Five Smooth Stones. SCL(1568), 1967a(115).
Falkner, Murry C. Falkners of Mississippi: A Memoir, The. SCL(1437), 1968a(97).
Farquhar, George. Beaux' Stratagem, The. MCLE(362), MD(63), MP2(86), POP(184). Recruiting Officer, The.

MCLE(4351), MD(676), MP2(882).
Farrell, James T. Studs Lonigan: A Trilogy. MAF(616), MCLE(5034), MP3(1028). Young Lonigan: A Boyhood in Chicago Streets. SGAN(240).
Farrell, Michael. Thy Tears Might Cease. SCL(4650), 1965a(293).
Fast, Howard. Freedom Road. SCLs(111).
Faulkner, John. Cabin Road, The. 1970a(66).
Faulkner, William. Absalom, Absalom! MAF(1), MCLE(12), MP1(5). As I Lay Dying. MAF(39), MCLE(255), MP2(52). Big Woods. SCL(399), 1955a(20). Fable, A. BM(176), MAF(174), MCLE(1521), MP3(375), SCL (1427), 1954a(61). Go Down, Moses. MCLE(1766), MP4(375). Hamlet, The. MCLE(1909), MP2(398). Intruder in the Dust. MAF(298), MCLE(2270), MP3 (511). Light in August. MAF(345), MCLE(2681), MP1(509), PO2(242), SGAN(206). Mansion, The. BM(360), MCLE(2907), MP4(591), SCL(2900), 1960a (152). Reivers, The. MCLE(4373), MP4(1048), SCL (3871), 1963a(211). Requiem for a Nun. MCLE(4405), MP4(1058). Sanctuary. MAF(550), MCLE(4600), MP1 (862), PO2(237). Sartoris. MCLE(4619), MP4(1091). Sound and the Fury, The. MAF(589), MCLE(4937), MP1(917), SGAN(196). Town, The. BM(561), MAF (658), MCLE(5262), MP3(1074), SCL(4726), 1958a(245). Unvanquished, The. MCLE(5433), MP4(1253). Wild Palms, The. MCLE(5647), MP4(1287).
Faust, Irvin. File on Stanley Patton Buchta, The. SCLs (102). Roar Lion Roar. SCL(3951), 1966a(269). Steagle, The. SCL(4432), 1967a(308).
Fei, Han. Han Fei Tzu. WP(201).
Feibleman, Peter S. Strangers and Graves. SCL(4473), 1967a(311).
Felix, Minucius. Octavius. CAL(50), CHL(51).
Ferber, Edna. So Big. MCLE(4875), MP4(1153).
Ferguson, Charles W. Naked to Mine Enemies. SCL(3168), 1959a(174).
Fermor, Patrick Leigh. Mani. SCL(2891), 1961a(173).
Fernández de Lizardi, José Joaquín. Itching Parrot, The. MAF(303), MCLE(2304), MP2(499).
Ferré, Nels. Christian Understanding of God, The. CHL (1124).
Ferreira, António. Inês de Castro. MCLE(2247), MD(374), MP3(506).
Ferreira de Castro, José Maria. Emigrants, The. SCL (1327), 1963a(51).
Feuchtwanger, Lion. Power. MCLE(4208), MEU(599), MP1

(773). Ugly Duchess, The. MCLE(5385), MEU(776), MP1(1037).
Feuerbach, Ludwig. Essence of Christianity, The. CHL (697).
Fichte, Johann Gottlieb. Vocation of Man, The. WP(570).
Field, Edward. Stand Up, Friend, with Me. SCL(4426), 1964a(252). Variety Photoplays. SCL(4870), 1968a (343).
Fielding, Gabriel. Birthday King, The. SCL(415), 1964a (22). Brotherly Love. SCL(538), 1962a(33). In the Time of Greenbloom. SCL(2202), 1958a(111). Through Streets Broad and Narrow. SCL(4647), 1961a(255).
Fielding, Henry. Amelia. MCLE(127), MEF(16), MP1(24). Jonathan Wild. MCLE(2359), MEF(379), MP2(516). Joseph Andrews. MCLE(2365), MEF(385), MP1(448), PO2(12). Temple Beau, The. MCLE(5124), MD(836), MP2(1013). Tom Jones. MCLE(5246), MEF(863), MP1(1000), PO(89), PON(393), SGBN(24). Tom Thumb the Great. MCLE(5253), MD(860), MP2(1046).
Filas, Francis L., S.J. Joseph: The Man Closest to Jesus. CAL(1115).
Findley, Timothy. Last of the Crazy People, The. SCL (2521), 1968a(173).
Finney, Charles Grandison. Lectures on Revivals of Religion. CHL(675).
Finney, Jack. Time and Again. 1971a(324).
Firbank, Arthur Annesley Ronald. Complete Ronald Firbank, The. SCL(877), 1962a(87).
Fischer, Louis. Life of Lenin, The. SCL(2654), 1965a(170).
Fisher, Vardis. Children of God. MAF(89), MCLE(715), MP1(137).
Fitch, Clyde. City, The. POP(57). Climbers, The. DGAP (143).
FitzGerald, Edward. Rubáiyát of Omar Khayyám, The. MCLE(4558), MP(325), MP3(907).
Fitzgerald, F. Scott. Afternoon of an Author. SCL(81), 1959a(3). Great Gatsby, The. MAF(228), MCLE (1832), MP1(329), PO2(229), SGAN(155). Last Tycoon, The. MAF(330), MCLE(2553), MP3(552). Letters of F. Scott Fitzgerald, The. MCLE(2612), MP4(523), SCL(2589), 1964a(149). Tender Is the Night. MAF (635), MCLE(5135), MP2(1016), PO2(233).
Fitzgerald, Robert. In the Rose of Time. SCL(2200), 1958a (109).
FitzGibbon, Constantine. Life of Dylan Thomas, The. SCL (2647), 1966a(148). When the Kissing Had to Stop.

SCL(5028), 1961a(296).
Flacius, Matthias (and others). Magdeburg Centuries, The. CHL(388).
Flaubert, Gustave. Bouvard and Pécuchet. MCLE(478), MEU(80), MP3(121). Madame Bovary. MCLE(2821), MEU(461), MP1(539), PO(293), PON(220), SGEN(113). Salammbô. MCLE(4592), MEU(657), MP1(860), PO2 (310). Sentimental Education, A. MCLE(4707), MEU (671), MP1(876). Temptation of Saint Anthony, The. MCLE(5127), MEU(746), MP3(1059).
Flecker, James Elroy. Poetry of Flecker, The. MCLE (3887), MP4(808).
Fleming, Peter. Siege at Peking, The. SCL(4279), 1960a (242).
Fletcher, John. Faithful Shepherdess, The. MCLE(1535), MD(270), MP3(383). Rule a Wife and Have a Wife. MCLE(4560), MD(717), MP3(909). Sir John van Olden Barnavelt. MCLE(4837), MD(780), MP3(985). Woman's Prize, The. MCLE(5714), MD(943), MP3(1141).
Fletcher, John and Francis Beaumont. Coxcomb, The. MCLE(919), MD(181), MP3(236). King and No King, A. MCLE(2441), MP3(541). Maid's Tragedy, The. MCLE(2848), MD(480), MP2(612). Philaster. MCLE (3616), MD(622), MP2(825). Scornful Lady, The. MCLE(4655), MD(744), MP3(940). Woman Hater, The. MCLE(5699), MD(937), MP3(1138).
Fletcher, John and Philip Massinger. Beggars' Bush, The. MCLE(368), MD(69), MP3(96).
Fletcher, John and William Shakespeare. Two Noble Kinsmen, The. MCLE(5371), MD(889), MP2(1076).
Fogazzaro, Antonio. Patriot, The. MCLE(3532), MEU(563), MP2(800). Saint, The. MCLE(4577), MEU(651), MP2(929).
Folk Tradition. Cadmus. MCLE(562), MEU(98), MP1(96). Cupid and Psyche. MCLE(965), MEU(187), MP1(180). Hercules and His Twelve Labors. MCLE(2007), MEU (359), MP1(366). Jason and the Golden Fleece. MCLE(2322), MEU(402), MP1(435). Orpheus and Eurydice. MCLE(3450), MEU(555), MP1(700). Proserpine and Ceres. MCLE(4289), MEU(608), MP1 (789).
Fontane, Theodore. Effi Briest. MCLE(1334), MEU(273), MP3(323).
Foote, Shelby. Civil War: A Narrative, The, Vol. I. SCL (759), 1959a(37). Civil War: A Narrative, The, Vol. II. SCL(763), 1964a(55).
Forbes, Esther. Mirror for Witches, A. MAF(404), MCLE

(3065), MP2(671). Rainbow on the Road. SCL(3818), 1954a(219).
Ford, Ford Madox. Fifth Queen, The. MCLE(1601), MP4 (337), SCL(1518), 1964a(83). Parade's End. MCLE (3489), MEF(634), MP2(792).
Ford, Jesse Hill. Feast of St. Barnabas, The. 1970a(123). Fishes, Birds and Sons of Men. SCL(1565), 1968a (111). Liberation of Lord Byron Jones, The. SCL (2627), 1966a(144).
Ford, John. 'Tis Pity She's a Whore. MCLE(5214), MD (852), MP2(1030).
Forester, C. S. Captain Horatio Hornblower. MCLE(606), MEF(77), MP1(109). Good Shepherd, The. SCL (1818), 1955a(112).
Forster, E. M. Howards End. MCLE(2139), MEF(327), MP2(469). Longest Journey, The. MCLE(2731), MEF (444), MP3(593). Marianne Thornton. SCL(2904), 1957a(170). Passage to India, A. MCLE(3506), MEF (638), MP1(713), PO2(147), SGBN(292). Room with a View, A. MCLE(4544), MEF(759), MP3(905). Short Stories of E. M. Forster, The. MCLE(4780), MP4 (1127). Where Angels Fear to Tread. MCLE(5616), MEF(949), MP3(1129).
Forsyth, Peter Taylor. Person and Place of Jesus Christ, The. CHL(861).
Fortune, The Editors of. Exploding Metropolis, The. SCL (1413), 1959a(81).
Foster, Ruel E. Jesse Stuart. SCL(2334), 1969a(172).
Fouqué, Friedrich De la Motte. Undine. MCLE(5428), MEU (785), MP2(1091).
Fowles, John. Collector, The. SCL(846), 1964a(59). French Lieutenant's Woman, The. 1970a(139). Magus, The. SCLs(174).
Fox, George. Journal of George Fox, The. CHL(546).
France, Anatole. At the Sign of the Reine Pédauque. MCLE (264), MEU(48), MP2(57). Crime of Sylvestre Bonnard, The. MCLE(932), MEU(182), MP2(196), SGEN(215). Gods Are Athirst, The. MCLE(1776), MEU(329), MP3 (420). Penguin Island. MCLE(3566), MEU(576), MP1 (729), SGEN(219). Revolt of the Angels, The. MCLE (4429), MEU(637), MP1(821). Thaïs. PO2(323).
Francis, Robert. Come Out into the Sun. SCL(849), 1967a (45).
Francis de Sales, Saint. Introduction to the Devout Life. CAL(568), CHL(428). Love of God, The. CAL(584).
Francis of Assisi, Saint. Extant Writings of Saint Francis of Assisi, The. CAL(349).

Franklin, Benjamin. Autobiography of Benjamin Franklin, The. MCLE(278), MN(29), MP3(74). Papers of Benjamin Franklin, The. SCL(3507), 1960a(184).
Fraser, Lady Antonia. Mary Queen of Scots. 1970a(198).
Fraser, George McDonald. Royal Flash. 1971a(280).
Frayn, Michael. Very Private Life, A. SCL(4884), 1969a (334).
Frazer, Sir James George. Golden Bough, The. MCLE (1787), MP4(384).
Frederic, Harold. Copperhead, The. MAF(103), MCLE(872), MP3(227). Damnation of Theron Ware, The. MAF (122), MCLE(989), MP2(214), MPA2(7).
Freeman, Douglas Southall. R. E. Lee. MCLE(4381), MN (261), MP3(874).
Freeman, Mary E. Wilkins-. Jerome: A Poor Man. PON (176).
Frémont, John Charles. Narratives of Exploration and Adventure. SCL(3178), 1957a(185).
Freneau, Philip. Poetry of Freneau, The. MCLE(3889), MP(258), MP3(801).
Freud, Sigmund. General Introduction to Psychoanalysis, A. MCLE(1726), MP4(371). Interpretation of Dreams, The. MCLE(2267), MN(163), MP3(508).
Freud, Sigmund and Josef Breuer. Studies on Hysteria. MCLE(5031), MP4(1195).
Freytag, Gustav. Debit and Credit. MCLE(1077), MEU(216), MP3(261).
Friedenthal, Richard. Goethe. SCL(1780), 1966a(120).
Friedman, Bruce Jay. Dick, The. 1971a(61). Mother's Kisses, A. SCL(3109), 1965a(205). Stern. SCLs (292).
Friend, Theodore. Between Two Empires. SCLs(28).
Froissart, Jean. Chronicles of Froissart. MCLE(739), MN (48), MP3(185).
Fromentin, Eugène. Dominique. MCLE(1228), MEU(246), MP3(294).
Frost, Robert. In the Clearing. BM(245), SCL(2185), 1963a (95). Letters of Robert Frost, The. MCLE(2623), MP4(532). Letters of Robert Frost to Louis Untermeyer, The. SCL(2603), 1964a(152). Poetry of Frost, The. MCLE(3892), MP(261), MP3(803). Selected Letters of Robert Frost. SCL(4167), 1965a(269).
Fry, Christopher. Dark is Light Enough, The. SCL(1014), 1954a(150). Lady's Not for Burning, The. MCLE (2507), MD(436), MP2(549), TCP(136). Light Is Dark Enough, The. 1954a(150). Yard of Sun, A. 1971a(363).

Fuchida, Mitsuo and Masatake Okumiya. Midway. SCL (3029), 1955a(160).
Fuentes, Carlos. Change of Skin, A. SCL(676), 1969a(65). Death of Artemio Cruz, The. MCLE(1057), MP4(195), SCL(1096), 1965a(63). Where the Air Is Clear. MCLE(5619), MP4(1279), SCL(5034), 1961a(300).
Fuller, Thomas. Holy State and the Profane State, The. MCLE(2084), MP4(428).
Fülöp-Miller, René. Night of Time, The. SCL(3242), 1955a (175).
Furnas, J. C. Goodbye to Uncle Tom. SCL(1830), 1957a (87).

Gaboriau, Émile. File No. 113. MCLE(1604), MEU(299), MP1(278), PON(121). Monsieur Lecoq. MCLE(3152), MEU(508), MP2(703).
Gaddis, William. Recognitions, The. SCLs(243).
Gaines, Ernest J. Bloodline. SCL(452), 1969a(41). Catherine Carmier. SCLs(61).
Galbraith, John Kenneth. Affluent Society, The. SCL(65), 1959a(1). Ambassador's Journal. 1970a(18).
Galdós, Benito Pérez. Angel Guerra. MCLE(175), MEU (28), MP3(42). Doña Perfecta. MCLE(1256), MEU (256), MP3(298). Fortunata and Jacinta. MCLE(1660), MEU(309), MP2(336). Saragossa. MCLE(4614), MEU (665), MP2(935).
Galilei, Galileo. Dialogue Concerning the Two Chief World Systems. CAL(593). Letter to the Grand Duchess Christina. CAL(579).
Gallant, Mavis. Fairly Good Time, A. SCLs(91).
Gallegos, Rómulo. Doña Barbara. MAF(151), MCLE(1253), MP2(277).
Galsworthy, John. Country House, The. MCLE(903), MEF (121), MP3(232). Forsyte Saga, The. MCLE(1652), MEF(219), MP1(284). Fraternity. MCLE(1681), MEF (237), MP2(343). Justice. MCLE(2421), MD(407), MP1(466), POP(102), TCP(139). Loyalties. MCLE (2779), MD(465), MP1(533). Man of Property, The. PO(92), SGBN(242). Modern Comedy, A. MCLE (3128), MEF(536), MP1(612). Patrician, The. MCLE (3530), MEF(641), MP3(724). Strife. MCLE(5026), MD(813), MP1(936), POP(106).
Galt, John. Annals of the Parish. MCLE(188), MEF(22), MP2(39).
Gardner, John W. Recovery of Confidence, The. 1971a(265).
Gardner, Leonard. Fat City. 1970a(120).
Garland, Hamlin. Main-Travelled Roads. MAF(378), MCLE

(2857), MP3(615), MPA2(12). Son of the Middle Border, A. MCLE(4894), MP4(1160).
Garnett, David. Golden Echo, The. SCL(1790), 1954a(95). Lady into Fox. MCLE(2500), MEF(416), MP1(486).
Garrett, George. Cold Ground Was My Bed Last Night. SCL(788), 1965a(47). Do, Lord, Remember Me. SCL(1190), 1966a(74). For a Bitter Season. SCL (1613), 1968a(118). Poetry of Garrett, The. MCLE (3898), MP4(812).
Gary, Romain. Roots of Heaven, The. SCL(3999), 1959a(212).
Gascar, Pierre. Beasts and Men. SCL(343), 1957a(20). Seed, The. SCL(4138), 1960a(235).
Gascoigne, George. Poetry of Gascoigne, The. MCLE (3901), MP4(814).
Gaskell, Mrs. Elizabeth. Cranford. MCLE(925), MEF(123), MP2(194). Mary Barton. MCLE(2947), MP4(594).
Gasquet, Francis Neil Aidan, Cardinal. Parish Life in Mediaeval England. CAL(736).
Gass, William H. In the Heart of the Country. SCL(2196), 1969a(164). Omensetter's Luck. SCLs(209).
Gassendi, Pierre. Syntagma philsophicum. WP(404).
Gaston, Paul M. New South Creed, The. 1971a(225).
Gaulle, Charles de. Call to Honour, The. SCL(604), 1955a (38). Salvation, 1944-1946. SCL(4064), 1961a(219). Unity, 1942-1944. SCL(4831), 1960a(281).
Gautier, Théophile. Mademoiselle de Maupin. MCLE(2824), MEU(464), MP1(542), PO(296), SGEN(86). Poetry of Gautier, The. MCLE(3907), MP4(820).
Gay, John. Beggar's Opera, The. MCLE(371), MD(72), MP1(59), POP(177).
Gay, Peter. Enlightenment: An Interpretation, The. SCL (1363), 1967a(94). Enlightenment: An Interpretation, The, Vol. II. 1970a(109).
Gazzo, Michael Vincente. Hatful of Rain, A. DGAP(399).
Geismar, Maxwell. Mark Twain: An American Prophet. 1971a(200).
Gelb, Arthur and Barbara. O'Neill. BM(415), SCL(3429), 1963a(162).
Gelber, Jack. Connection, The. SGAP(295).
Genêt, Jean. Blacks, The. TCP(152).
Genovese, Eugene D. World the Slaveholders Made, The. 1971a(356).
George, Stefan. Poetry of Stefan George, The. MCLE(4101), MP(294), MP3(831).
Gerard, John. Autobiography of a Hunted Priest, The. CAL(571).
Gershwin, George and Ira and DuBose Heyward. Porgy and Bess. DGAP(277).

Gershwin, George and Ira, George S. Kaufman, and Morrie Ryskind. Of Thee I Sing. DGAP(253), SGAP(53).
Gershwin, Ira, Moss Hart and Kurt Weill. Lady in the Dark. DGAP(334).
Gershwin, Ira, see also George and Ira Gershwin.
Gerson, John. On Ecclesiastical Unity. CHL(299).
Ghelderode, Michel de. Chronicles of Hell. TCP(155).
Ghiselin, Brewster. Country of the Minotaur. 1971a(51).
Gibbon, Edward. History of the Decline and Fall of the Roman Empire, The. MCLE(2062), MN(146), MP3(474).
Gibbons, Stella. Cold Comfort Farm. MCLE(784), MP4 (139).
Gibney, Frank. Operators, The. SCL(3441), 1961a(191).
Gibran, Kahil. Prophet, The. MCLE(4287), MP4(1036).
Gibson, William. Mass for the Dead, A. SCL(2927), 1969a (222).
Gide, André. Counterfeiters, The. MCLE(892), MEU(164), MP1(160), PO2(336), SGEN(273). Immoralist, The. PO2(330), SGEN(267). Journals of André Gide, The. MCLE(2386), MP4(478).
Gilbert, W. S. and Arthur Sullivan. Gondoliers, The. MCLE(1798), MD(307), MP2(377). H. M. S. Pinafore. MCLE(2082), MD(353), MP1(370). Iolanthe. MCLE (2278), MD(379), MP2(493). Mikado, The. MCLE (3048), MD(530), MP1(591). Patience. MCLE(3528), MD(603), MP2(798). Pirates of Penzance, The. MCLE(3687), MD(636), MP2(834). Trial by Jury. MCLE(5313), MD(866), MP2(1058).
Gill, Brendan. Day the Money Stopped, The. SCL(1067), 1958a(63).
Gillette, William. Secret Service. DGAP(136). Sherlock Holmes. POP(65).
Gilroy, Frank D. Subject Was Roses, The. SCLs(300).
Gilson, Étienne. Philosopher and Theology, The. CAL(1088). Spirit of Mediaeval Philosophy, The. CAL(816), WP (946). Unity of Philosophical Experience, The. CAL (845).
Giono, Jean. Horseman on the Roof, The. SCL(2112), 1954a(114). Song of the World. MCLE(4913), MEU (709), MP2(983).
Giraudoux, Jean. Amphitryon 38. MCLE(149), MD(28), MP3(30). Electra. TCP(158). Enchanted, The. TCP(160). Madwoman of Chaillot, The. MCLE(2828), MD(474), MP3(606), TCP(163). Ondine. SCL(3409), TCP(167), 1954a(201). Tiger at the Gates. BM(551), MCLE(5199), MP4(1217), SCL(4654), TCP(170), 1955a (262).

Gironella, José María. Cypresses Believe in God, The. MCLE(974), MP4(172), SCL(983), 1955a(78).
Gissing, George. New Grub Street, The. MCLE(3253), MEF(564), MP1(647). Private Papers of Henry Ryecroft, The. MCLE(4271), MEF(702), MP2(862).
Gittings, Robert. John Keats: The Living Year. SCL(2352), 1954a(120).
Gladden, Washington. Christian Pastor, The. CHL(812).
Glasgow, Ellen. Barren Ground. MAF(44), MCLE(342), MP1(57). Collected Stories of Ellen Glasgow, The. SCL(833), 1964a(57). Romantic Comedians, The. MAF(544), MCLE(4524), MP1(846). Sheltered Life, The. MAF(575), MCLE(4753), MP1(891). Woman Within, The. SCL(5132), 1954a(297).
Glubb, Sir John Bagot. Soldier with the Arabs, A. SCL (4340), 1959a(226).
Godden, Jon. Seven Islands, The. SCL(4215), 1957a(238).
Godden, Jon and Rumer. Two Under the Indian Sun. SCL (4809), 1967a(333).
Godden, Rumer. Episode of Sparrows, An. SCL(1367), 1955a(95). Greengage Summer, The. SCL(1880), 1959a(106).
Godfrey, Thomas. Prince of Parthia, The. DGAP(6).
Godwin, William. Caleb Williams. MCLE(575), MEF(75), MP1(101). Inquiry Concerning Political Justice, An. MCLE(2261), MP4(454).
Goethe, Johann Wolfgang von. Egmont. MCLE(1337), MD (242), MP2(288). Elective Affinities. MCLE(1347), MEU(276), MP3(326). Faust. MCLE(1574), MD(278), MP1(276), POP(305). Poetry and Truth from My Own Life. MCLE(3738), MP4(706). Sorrows of Young Werther, The. MCLE(4928), MEU(712), MP1(915), PO2(435). Wilhelm Meister. PO(379). Wilhelm Meister's Apprenticeship. MCLE(5653), MEU(816), MP2(1136). Wilhelm Meister's Travels. MCLE(5656), MEU(819), MP2(1139).
Goetzmann, William H. Exploration and Empire. SCL(1416), 1967a(101).
Gogarten, Friedrich. Reality of Faith, The. CHL(1167).
Gogol, Nikolai V. Dead Souls. MCLE(1038), MEU(202), MP1(194), PO2(384), SGEN(94). Inspector General, The. MCLE(2264), MD(376), MP2(491). Overcoat, The. MCLE(3470), MEU(560), MP2(790). Taras Bulba. MCLE(5101), MEU(740), MP1(954).
Gold, Herbert. Fathers. SCL(1488), 1968a(105). Great American Jackpot, The. 1970a(143). Therefore Be Bold. SCL(4574), 1961a(248).

Gold, Ivan. Nickel Miseries. SCLs(202).
Golden, Harry. Only in America. SCL(3435), 1959a(190).
Golding, William. Free Fall. BM(198), MCLE(1684), MP4 (361), SCL(1654), 1961a(94). Inheritors, The. MCLE (2255), MP4(452), SCL(2229), 1963a(101). Lord of the Flies. MCLE(2747), MP4(566), SGBN(350). Pyramid, The. SCL(3760), 1968a(264). Spire, The. SCL(4417), 1965a(287).
Goldman, Eric G. Crucial Decade, The. SCL(965), 1957a (51).
Goldoni, Carlo. Mistress of the Inn, The. MCLE(3114), MD(545), MP2(691), POP(280).
Goldsmith, Oliver. Poetry of Goldsmith, The. MCLE(3910), MP4(823). She Stoops to Conquer. MCLE(4744), MD (766), MP1(889), POP(173). Vicar of Wakefield, The. MCLE(5465), MEF(915), MP1(1061), PO(95), PON(427), SGBN(32).
Goncharov, Ivan Alexandrovich. Oblomov. MCLE(3326), MEU(549), MP2(755), SGEN(121).
Goncourt, Edmond and Jules de. Charles Demailly. MCLE (686), MEU(124), MP3(171). Germinie Lacerteux. MCLE(1746), MEU(324), MP2(363), SGEN(137). Goncourt Journals, The. MCLE(1795), MP4(387). Manette Salomon. MCLE(2890), MEU(469), MP3(628). Renée Mauperin. MCLE(4395), MEU(631), MP2(894). Sister Philomène. MCLE(4845), MEU(682), MP3(990).
Goncourt, Jules de, see Edmond and Jules de Goncourt.
Goodman, Mitchell. End of It, The. SCL(1343), 1962a(112).
Goodman, Paul. New Reformation. 1971a(223).
Goodrich, Frances and Albert Hackett. Diary of Anne Frank, The. DGAP(395).
Goodwin, Richard N. Triumph or Tragedy: Reflections on Vietnam. SCL(4770), 1967a(328).
Gordimer, Nadine. Not for Publication. SCL(3301), 1966a (200). World of Strangers, A. SCL(5154), 1959a(283).
Gordon, Caroline. Aleck Maury, Sportsman. MAF(10), MCLE(72), MP1(17). Malefactors, The. SCLs(176). Old Red and Other Stories. SCL(3376), 1964a(198).
Gore, Charles. Christ and Society. CHL(942).
Gorki, Maksim. Artamonov Business, The. MCLE(252), MEU(42), MP3(69). Foma Gordyeeff. MCLE(1637), MEU(306), MP2(331). Lower Depths, The. MCLE (2776), MD(462), MP2(604), POP(349), TCP(174). Mother, The. MCLE(3176), MEU(517), MP3(676), PO(359).
Gottfried von Strassburg. Tristan and Isolde. MCLE(5324), MP(362), MP3(1083).

Gourmont, Remy de. Night in the Luxembourg, A. MCLE (3284), MEU(547), MP1(655).
Gouzenko, Igor. Fall of a Titan, The. SCL(1446), 1954a (68).
Goyen, William. Fair Sister, The. SCL(1434), 1964a(75).
Goytisolo, Juan. Fiestas. SCL(1514), 1961a(77).
Graham, Dom Aelred, O. S. B. Zen Catholicism. CAL(1124).
Grahame, Kenneth. Wind in the Willows, The. MCLE (5662), MEF(955), MP2(1141).
Granville-Barker, Harley. Madras House, The. MCLE(2826), MD(472), MP3(604).
Grass, Günter. Cat and Mouse. MCLE(647), MP4(113), SCL(641), 1964a(46). Dog Years. SCL(1202), 1966a (78). Local Anaesthetic. 1971a(170). Tin Drum, The. MCLE(5211), MP4(1220), SCL(4679), 1964a(269).
Gratian, Johannes. Decretum Gratiani. CAL(324).
Grau, Shirley Ann. Black Prince, The. SCL(436), 1955a (26). Hard Blue Sky, The. SCL(1925), 1959a(111). Keepers of the House, The. SCL(2403), 1965a(159).
Graves, John. Goodbye to a River. SCL(1827), 1961a(107).
Graves, Robert. Claudius the God. MCLE(761), MEF(107), MP1(146). Collected Poems, 1955. SCL(809), 1955a (56). Collected Poems, 1961. SCL(813), 1962a(74). I, Claudius. MCLE(2181), MEF(337), MP1(406). Poetry of Graves, The. MCLE(3914), MP4(826). They Hanged My Saintly Billy. SCL(4589), 1958a(231).
Gray, Thomas. Letters of Thomas Gray, The. MCLE(2626), MP4(535). Poetry of Gray, The. MCLE(3917), MP (264), MP3(805).
Green, Constance McLaughlin. Washington. SCLs(333).
Green, Gerald. Last Angry Man, The. SCL(2501), 1958a (136).
Green, Henry. Loving. MCLE(2773), MEF(456), MP2(602).
Green, Julian. Closed Garden, The. MCLE(773), MEU(144), MP2(155). Dark Journey, The. MCLE(1016), MEU (197), MP2(219). To Leave Before Dawn. SCL(4699), 1968a(334). Transgressor, The. SCL(4736), 1958a (247).
Green, Paul and Richard Wright. Native Son. DGAP(344).
Green, Peter. Kenneth Grahame: A Biography. SCL(2406), 1960a(114).
Green, Thomas Hill. Prolegomena to Ethics. WP(681).
Greene, Graham. Burnt-Out Case, A. MCLE(551), MP4 (99), SCL(568), 1962a(36). Comedians, The. SCL (853), 1967a(49). Complaisant Lover, The. SCL(866), 1962a(82). End of the Affair, The. PO2(154). Heart of the Matter, The. MCLE(1958), MEF(286), MP2

(418), PO2(150). Living Room, The. SCL(2724), 1954a(156). May We Borrow Your Husband? SCL (2945), 1968a(188). Ministry of Fear, The. MCLE (3059), MEF(513), MP2(666). Our Man in Havana. SCL(3469), 1959a(196). Potting Shed, The. SCL (3666), 1958a(196). Power and the Glory, The. MCLE(4211), MEF(689), MP2(851), SGBN(336). Quiet American, The. SCL(3798), 1957a(215). Sense of Reality, A. SCL(4206), 1964a(234). Travels with My Aunt. 1971a(332).

Greene, Robert. Friar Bacon and Friar Bungay. MCLE (1693), MD(281), MP2(345). Greene's Groatsworth of Wit Bought with a Million of Repentance. MCLE(1862), MP4(397).

Gregor-Dellin, Martin. Lamp Post, The. SCL(2485), 1965a (167).

Gregory, Horace. Collected Poems. SCL(801), 1965a(50).

Gregory, Lady. Seven Short Plays. MCLE(4725), MD(764), MP3(963).

Gregory of Nazianzus, Saint. Five Theological Orations. CAL(116), CHL(113).

Gregory of Nyssa, Saint. Great Catechism, The. CAL(120), CHL(125). Lord's Prayer, The. CAL(136).

Gregory of Tours, Saint. History of the Franks. CAL(244).

Gregory Thaumaturgus, Saint. Oration and Panegyric Addressed to Origen, The. CAL(69).

Gregory the Great, Saint. Dialogues, The. CAL(241). Pastoral Care. CAL(237), CHL(176).

Grieg, Nordahl. Defeat, The. TCP(178).

Griffin, Gerald. Collegians, The. MCLE(796), MEF(115), MP2(160).

Griffin, John Howard. Black Like Me. SCLs(34). Devil Rides Outside, The. SCLs(88).

Grillparzer, Franz. Jewess of Toledo, The. MCLE(2341), MD(395), MP3(528). Sappho. MCLE(4611), MD(730), MEU(663), MP3(923).

Grimmelshausen, H. J. C. von. Simplicissimus the Vagabond. MCLE(4829), MEU(679), MP2(966).

Groote, Gerhard (Geert de). Following of Christ, The. CHL(291).

Grotius, Hugo. On the Law of War and Peace. MCLE(3404), MP4(648). Truth of the Christian Religion, The. CHL(432).

Grubb, Davis. Dream of Kings, A. SCL(1237), 1955a(86). Night of the Hunter, The. SCL(3236), 1954a(192). Voices of Glory, The. SCL(4919), 1963a(282).

Guardini, Romano. Humanity of Christ, The. CAL(1064).

Lord, The. CAL(849).
Guest, Barbara. Poems. SCL(3614), 1963a(189).
Guillén, Jorge. Cántice. SCL(612), 1966a(43).
Güiraldes, Ricardo. Don Segundo Sombra. MAF(148), MCLE(1250), MP2(277).
Guitton, Jean. Essay on Human Love. CAL(923).
Gunn, Thom. Touch. SCL(4717), 1969a(315).
Gunnarsson, Gunnar. Guest the One-Eyed. MCLE(1878), MEU(347), MP3(437).
Gunther, John. Inside Africa. SCL(2243), 1955a(131). Inside Russia Today. SCL(2246), 1959a(125).
Guthrie, A. B., Jr. Big Sky, The. MAF(57), MCLE(410), MP1(70). These Thousand Hills. SCL(4580), 1957a (263).
Gutman, Robert W. Richard Wagner. SCL(3925), 1969a(280).
Guzmán, Martín Luis. Eagle and the Serpent, The. MCLE (1305), MP4(253).
Gwyther, John. Captain Cook and the South Pacific. SCL (621), 1955a(41).

H. D., see Doolittle, Hilda.
Hachiya, Michihiko. Hiroshima Diary. BM(234), SCL(2052), 1955a(121).
Hackett, Albert and Frances Goodrich. Diary of Anne Frank, The. DGAP(395).
Haeckel, Ernst Heinrich. Riddle of the Universe, The. WP(734).
Hāfiz, Haifiz. Divan, The. MCLE(1190), MP(61), MP3(285).
Hagedorn, Hermann. Roosevelt Family of Sagamore Hill, The. SCL(3987), 1954a(240).
Haggard, H. Rider. King Solomon's Mines. MCLE(2465), MEF(410), MP1(475). She. MCLE(4741), MEF(787), MP1(886).
Haight, Gordon S. George Eliot: A Biography. SCL(1729), 1969a(130).
Haines, John. Winter News. SCL(5101), 1967a(344).
Haines, William Wister. Command Decision. DGAP(370).
Hakluyt, Richard. Hakluyt's Voyages. MCLE(1906), MN (346), MP1(346).
Hale, Edward Everett. Man Without a Country, The. MAF (383), MCLE(2888), MP1(553), MPA2(16), PO2(167).
Halecki, Oscar. Millennium of Europe, The. CAL(1128).
Halévy, Ludovic. Abbé Constantin, The. MCLE(1), MEU(1), MP1(1), PON(1).
Hall, Donald. Alligator Bride, The. SCLs(5). Poetry of Hall, The. MCLE(3919), MP4(829). Roof of Tiger Lilies, A. SCL(3980), 1965a(252). String Too Short

to Be Saved. SCL(4479), 1962a(290).
Hall, James B. Us He Devours. SCL(4858), 1965a(299).
Hall, James Norman and Charles Nordhoff. Mutiny on the Bounty. MAF(427), MCLE(3195), MP1(628), SGAN (233).
Hall, Lawrence Sargent. Stowaway. SCL(4464), 1962a(288).
Halpern, Martin. Two Sides of an Island. SCL(4803), 1964a(278).
Halsband, Robert. Life of Lady Mary Wortley Montagu, The. SCL(2651), 1958a(147).
Hamilton, Alexander, James Madison and John Jay. Federalist, The. MCLE(1577), MN(124), MP3(384).
Hammarskjold, Dag. Markings. SCL(2910), 1965a(195).
Hammerstein, Oscar and Richard Rodgers. Oklahoma. DGAP(353).
Hammett, Dashiell. Glass Key, The. MAF(207), MCLE (1762), MP1(307). Maltese Falcon, The. MAF(380), MCLE(2868), MP1(551). Thin Man, The. MAF(638), MCLE(5164), MP1(970).
Hamsun, Knut. Growth of the Soil. MCLE(1870), MEU(341), MP1(338), SGEN(329). Hunger. MCLE(2163), MEU (380), MP1(400), SCL(2141), 1968a(160).
Hansberry, Lorraine. Raisin in the Sun, A. DGAP(419), SCL(3824), SGAP(301), 1960a(215). Sign in Sidney Brustein's Window, The. SCLs(276).
Harding, Walter. Days of Henry Thoreau, The. SCL(1073), 1966a(63).
Hardy, René. Sword of God, The. SCL(4501), 1954a(267).
Hardy, Thomas. Dynasts, The. MCLE(1302), MD(231), MP1(234). Far from the Madding Crowd. MCLE (1557), MEF(204), MP1(266), PO(101), PON(111). Jude the Obscure. MCLE(2402), MEF(391), MP1(455), PO2(60), SGBN(177). Mayor of Casterbridge, The. MCLE(2969), MEF(485), MP1(571), SGBN(172). Poetry of Hardy, The. MCLE(3922), MP4(831). Return of the Native, The. MCLE(4420), MEF(728), MP1(818), PO(98), SGBN(167). Tess of the d'Urbervilles. MCLE(5141), MEF(827), MP1(965), PO(105), PON(377). Under the Greenwood Tree. MCLE(5411), MEF(892), MP2(1084). Woodlanders, The. MCLE (5726), MEF(968), MP2(1156).
Harnack, Adolf. What Is Christianity? CHL(823).
Harrer, Heinrich. Seven Years in Tibet. SCL(4224), 1954a (252).
Harrigan, Edward. Mulligan Guard Ball, The. DGAP(105).
Harris, Joel Chandler. Tales of Uncle Remus. MAF(629), MCLE(5084), MP3(1049), MPA2(20).

Harris, Mark. Something about a Soldier. SCL(4358), 1958a(225).
Harrison, William. In a Wild Sanctuary. 1970a(174).
Hart, Moss. Act One. SCL(28), 1960a(1).
Hart, Moss and George S. Kaufman. You Can't Take It with You. DGAP(294), POP(5), SGAP(46), TCP(212).
Hart, Moss, Ira Gershwin and Kurt Weill. Lady in the Dark. DGAP(334).
Harte, Bret. Luck of Roaring Camp and Other Sketches, The. MAF(364), MCLE(2784), MP3(597), MPA2(25).
Hartley, L. P. Go-Between, The. SCL(1770), 1954a(92).
Hartmann, Eduard von. Philosophy of the Unconscious, The. WP(660).
Hartmann, Nicolai. Ethics. WP(868).
Hartmann von Aue. Arme Heinrich, Der. MCLE(237), MP (10), MP3(63).
Hartog, Jan de. Inspector, The. SCL(2256), 1961a(130).
Hartshorne, Charles. Divine Relativity, The. CHL(1088).
Hašek, Jaroslav. Good Soldier: Schweik, The. MCLE (1809), MP4(390).
Hassall, Christopher. Rupert Brooke. SCL(4021), 1965a (256).
Hauptmann, Gerhart. Beaver Coat, The. MCLE(365), MD (66), MP3(94). Rats, The. TCP(181). Sunken Bell, The. MCLE(5051), MD(815), MP3(1035). Weavers, The. MCLE(5594), MD(912), MP2(1124), POP(301), TCP(184).
Hawgood, John A. America's Western Frontiers. SCLs(9).
Hawkes, John. Cannibal, The. MCLE(592), MP4(105). Innocent Party, The. SCL(2240), 1967a(165). Lime Twig, The. MCLE(2686), MP4(551), SCL(2678), 1962a(186). Lunar Landscapes. 1970a(190). Second Skin. SCL(4123), 1965a(266).
Hawkins, Sir John, Knt. Life of Samuel Johnson, LL. D., The. SCL(2659), 1962a(184).
Hawthorne, Nathaniel. American Notebooks, The. MCLE (135), MP4(35), MPA2(31). Blithedale Romance, The. MAF(66), MCLE(440), MP2(97), MPA2(38). English Notebooks, The. MCLE(1389), MP4(277), MPA2(43). House of the Seven Gables, The. MAF(276), MCLE (2130), MP1(383), MPA2(49), PO(222), PON(153), SGAN(26). Marble Faun, The. MAF(388), MCLE (2910), MP1(564), MPA2(54), PO(225), PON(227). Scarlet Letter, The. MAF(557), MCLE(4641), MP1 (867), MPA2(58), PO(218), PON(365), SGAN(21).
Haydn, Richard. Journal of Edwin Carp, The. SCL(2368), 1954a(123).

Haydon, Benjamin Robert. Autobiography of Benjamin Robert Haydon, The. MCLE(281), MP4(48).
Hayes, Carlton J. H. Nationalism: A Religion. CAL(1091).
Hazel, Robert. American Elegies. 1970a(21). Poems: 1951-1961. BM(442), SCL(3628), 1962a(229).
Hazelton, George Cochrane and Harry Benrimo. Yellow Jacket, The. POP(42).
Hazlitt, William. Critical Essays of William Hazlitt, The. MCLE(943), MP4(166). Familiar Essays of William Hazlitt, The. MCLE(1542), MP4(319). Liber amoris. MCLE(2644), MN(180), MP3(570).
Hazzard, Shirley. Bay of Noon, The. 1971a(17). Evening of the Holiday, The. SCL(1395), 1967a(98).
Hearn, Lafcadio. Chita. MAF(92), MCLE(727), MP2(149), MPA2(64). Youma. MAF(737), MCLE(5771), MP2 (1167).
Hebbel, Friedrich. Maria Magdalena. MCLE(2922), MD (494), MP2(628).
Hecht, Anthony. Hard Hours, The. SCL(1928), 1968a(140).
Hecht, Ben and Charles MacArthur. Front Page, The. DGAP(234), SGAP(104).
Hefele, Karl Joseph von. History of the Councils. CAL (686).
Hegel, Georg Wilhelm Friedrich. Early Theological Writings. CHL(633). Logic. WP(577). Phenomenology of Spirit, The. CHL(645). Philosophy of History, The. WP(593).
Heggen, Thomas. Mister Roberts. MAF(413), MCLE(3099), MP1(605).
Heidegger, Martin. Being and Time. WP(886).
Heidenstam, Verner von. Tree of the Folkungs, The. MCLE(5304), MEU(761), MP2(1053).
Heim, Karl. Jesus the Lord. CHL(1008).
Heimert, Alan E. Religion and the American Mind. SCL (3876), 1967a(283).
Heine, Heinrich. Book of Songs. MCLE(458), MP(25), MP3 (118).
Heinrich, Willi. Cross of Iron, The. SCL(954), 1957a(48).
Heller, Joseph. Catch-22. MCLE(653), MP4(117), PO2(285), SCL(647), 1962a(44). We Bombed in New Haven. SCL(4989), 1969a(340).
Hellman, Lillian. Children's Hour, The. TCP(189). Little Foxes, The. DGAP(321), MCLE(2702), MD(451), MP3(588), SGAP(196), TCP(191). Toys in the Attic. SCL(4729), 1961a(263). Unfinished Woman, An. 1970a(322). Watch on the Rhine. DGAP(349).
Hemenway, Robert. Girl Who Sang with the Beatles and

Other Stories. 1971a(99).
Hemingway, Ernest. Farewell to Arms, A. MAF(179), MCLE(1560), MP1(269), PO(229), SGAN(166). Fifth Column, The. 1970a(125). For Whom the Bell Tolls. MAF(186), MCLE(1649), MP1(282), PO2(251). Islands in the Stream. 1971a(135). Moveable Feast, A. MCLE(3187), MP4(621), SCL(3116), 1965a(208). Old Man and the Sea, The. MAF(457), MCLE(3367), MP2 (764), PO2(257), SGAN(171). Short Stories of Ernest Hemingway, The. MCLE(4784), MP4(1130). Sun Also Rises, The. MAF(618), MCLE(5048), MP1(941), SGAN(161).
Hémon, Louis. Maria Chapdelaine. MAF(396), MCLE(2919), MP2(626).
Henderson, Archibald. George Bernard Shaw. SCL(1718), 1957a(84).
Henderson, Nicholas. Prince Eugen of Savoy. SCL(3692), 1966a(242).
Henderson, Philip. William Morris. SCL(5081), 1968a(353).
Henley, William Ernest. Poetry of Henley, The. MCLE (3928), MP4(836).
Henry, O., see Porter, William Sydney.
Henry of Bracton. Treatise on the Laws and Customs of England. CAL(367).
Hepburn, Ronald W. Christianity and Paradox. CHL(1171).
Heraclitus of Ephesus. Heraclitus: Fragments. WP(11).
Herbert, Edward, First Lord of Cherbury. De religione laici. CHL(467).
Herbert, George. Priest to the Temple, A. CHL(485). Temple, The. MCLE(5121), MP(357), MP3(1056).
Herbert, Victor and Rida Johnson Young. Naughty Marietta. DGAP(173).
Hérédia, José María de. Poetry of Hérédia, The. MCLE (3930), MP4(838).
Hergesheimer, Joseph. Java Head. MAF(309), MCLE(2324), MP1(437). Three Black Pennys, The. MAF(641), MCLE(5172), MP1(976).
Herlihy, James Leo. All Fall Down. MCLE(88), MP4(21), SCL(135), 1961a(7). Midnight Cowboy. SCL(3026), 1966a(186). Sleep of Baby Filbertson, The. SCLs (282). Stop, You're Killing Me. 1971a(307). Story That Ends with a Scream and Eight Others, A. SCLs (298).
Herlihy, James Leo and William Noble. Blue Denim. SCLs (41).
Herman, Nicholas, see Lawrence, Brother.
Hermas. Shepherd, The. CAL(12), CHL(13).

Hernández, José. Gaucho: Martín Fierro, The. MCLE (1724), MP(111), MP2(358).
Herne, James A. Margaret Fleming. DGAP(117).
Herodotus. History of the Persian Wars, The. MCLE (2068), MN(152), MP3(479).
Herold, J. Christopher. Mistress to an Age. BM(374), SCL(3061), 1959a(167).
Herrick, Robert. Hesperides. MCLE(2024), MP(128), MP3 (461).
Herrligkoffer, Karl M. Nanga Parbat. SCL(3175), 1954a (189).
Hersey, John. Algiers Motel Incident, The. SCL(131), 1969a(1). Bell for Adano, A. MAF(49), MCLE(380), MP1(64). Child Buyer, The. SCL(703), 1961a(41). Single Pebble, A. SCL(4305), 1957a(244). War Lover, The. SCL(4964), 1960a(290).
Hersh, Seymour M. My Lai 4. 1971a(216).
Hesiod. Works and Days. MCLE(5732), MP(381), MP3 (1149).
Hesse, Hermann. Demian. SCL(1121), 1966a(66). Steppenwolf. MCLE(4979), MEU(717), MP2(992), PO2(459), SGEN(360).
Heyerdahl, Thor. Aku-Aku. SCL(119), 1959a(6).
Heyward, Dorothy and DuBose Heyward. Porgy. MAF(498), MCLE(4190), MP1(764), SGAP(64).
Heyward, DuBose and George and Ira Gershwin. Porgy and Bess. DGAP(277).
Heywood, Thomas. Woman Killed with Kindness, A. MCLE (5705), MD(940), MP2(1151).
Hibbert, Christopher. Making of Charles Dickens, The. SCL(2834), 1968a(182).
Hick, John. Faith and Knowledge. CHL(1156).
Hicks, George Dawes. Philosophical Bases of Theism, The. CHL(1031).
Hicks, Granville. Part of the Truth: An Autobiography. SCL(3516), 1966a(227).
Highet, Gilbert. Poets in a Landscape. SCL(3644), 1958a (193).
Hilary of Poitiers, Saint. On the Trinity. CHL(106). Treatise on the Mysteries. CAL(103).
Hildebrand, Dietrich von. Liturgy and Personality. CAL (835). Transformation in Christ. CAL(946).
Hill, Frank Ernest and Allan Nevins. Ford: Decline and Rebirth, 1933-1962. SCL(1619), 1964a(96). Ford: Expansion and Challenge, 1915-1933. SCL(1622), 1958a(96).
Hilton, James. Goodbye, Mr. Chips. MCLE(1812), MEF

(246), MP1(316). Lost Horizon. MCLE(2753), MEF (453), MP1(527), PO2(138), SGBN(329).
Hilton, Walter. Ladder of Perfection, The. CAL(494). Scale of Perfection, The. CHL(316).
Himmelfarb, Gertrude. Darwin and the Darwinian Revolution. SCL(1020), 1960a(51).
Hippolytus, Saint. Apostolic Tradition, The. CHL(54). Refutation of All Heresies. CAL(58).
Hjortsberg, William. Alp. 1970a(14).
Hobbes, Thomas. De corpore. WP(399). Leviathan. MCLE(2641), MN(177), MP3(567), WP(392).
Hochhuth, Rolf. Deputy, The. SCL(1127), 1965a(71).
Hocking, William Ernest. Meaning of God in Human Experience, The. CHL(869).
Hodge, Charles. Systematic Theology. CHL(766).
Hodgson, Ralph. Poetry of Hodgson, The. MCLE(3932), MP4(840). Skylark, The. SCL(4319), 1961a(235).
Höffding, Harald. Philosophy of Religion, The. CHL(828).
Hoffer, Eric. Temper of Our Time, The. SCL(4537), 1967a(316).
Hoffman, William. Days in the Yellow Leaf. SCL(1070), 1959a(50).
Hoffmann, Ernst Theodor Amadeus. Devil's Elixir, The. MCLE(1136), MEU(227), MP3(267).
Hofmannsthal, Hugo von. Poetry of Hofmannsthal, The. MCLE(3934), MP4(842).
Hofstadter, Richard. Age of Reform, The. SCLs(1). Anti-Intellectualism in American Life. SCLs(11).
Hölderlin, Johann Christian Friedrich. Poetry of Hölderlin, The. MCLE(3937), MP4(845).
Holland, Cecelia. Rakóssy. SCL(3827), 1967a(280).
Holm, John Cecil and George Abbott. Three Men on a Horse. SGAP(172).
Holmes, Oliver Wendell. Autocrat of the Breakfast-Table, The. MCLE(293), MN(35), MP3(76), MPA2(69).
Holroyd, Michael. Lytton Strachey. SCL(2817), 1969a(218).
Homer. Illiad, The. MCLE(2209), MP(138), MP1(423), PON(163). Odyssey, The. MCLE(3331), MP(191), MP1(665), PON(264).
Hook, Sidney. Quest for Being, The. SCL(3788), 1962a(235).
Hooker, Richard. Treatise on the Laws of Ecclesiastical Polity. CHL(418).
Hoover, J. Edgar. Masters of Deceit. SCL(2937), 1959a (158).
Hope, A. D. New Poems: 1965-1969. 1971a(220). Poems. SCL(3617), 1963a(191).
Hope, Anthony. Prisoner of Zenda, The. MCLE(4263), MEF

(699), MP1(784), PO(109), PON(329).
Hopkins, Gerard Manley. Poems of Gerard Manley Hopkins, The. CAL(760). Poetry of Hopkins, The. MCLE (3940), MP(266), MP3(807).
Hopkins, Samuel. System of Doctrines. CHL(629).
Horace. Ars poetica. MCLE(246), MN(26), MP3(65). Epistles of Horace, The. MCLE(1411), MP4(282). Poetry of Horace, The. MCLE(3943), MP(269), MP3 (810).
Horgan, Paul. Centuries of Santa Fe, The. SCL(666), 1957a(39). Great River. BM(216), SCL(1866), 1954a (98).
Horne, Alistair. Fall of Paris, The. SCL(1449), 1967a (107). Price of Glory: Verdun, 1916, The. SCL (3686), 1964a(215).
Horton, Walter Marshall. Christian Theology: An Ecumenical Approach. CHL(1148).
Hotchner, A. E. Papa Hemingway. SCL(3501), 1967a(259).
Housman, A. E. Shropshire Lad, A. MCLE(4812), MP (338), MP3(974).
Howard, Bronson. Henrietta, The. DGAP(190).
Howard, Sidney. Silver Cord, The. DGAP(230). They Knew What They Wanted. POP(23), SGAP(74).
Howarth, David. Waterloo: Day of Battle. SCL(4982), 1969a(337).
Howe, Edgar Watson. Story of a Country Town, The. MAF (613), MCLE(4994), MP1(929).
Howe, Mark DeWolfe. Justice Oliver Wendell Holmes. BM (278), SCL(2391), 1958a(122).
Howells, William Dean. Albany Depot, The. DGAP(128). Hazard of New Fortunes, A. MAF(252), MCLE(1944), MP2(412), MPA2(76). Indian Summer. MAF(295), MCLE(2242), MP2(482), MPA2(81). Modern Instance, A. MAF(422), MCLE(3130), MP2(695). Rise of Silas Lapham, The. MAF(535), MCLE(4475), MP1 (828), MPA2(86), PO(232), SGAN(54).
Howes, Barbara. Looking Up at Leaves. SCL(2773), 1967a (201).
Hoyt, Charles H. Trip to Chinatown, A. DGAP(125).
Hudson, W. H. Far Away and Long Ago. MCLE(1554), MN(121), MP2(323). Green Mansions. MCLE(1855), MEF(251), MP1(333), PO(113), SGBN(235). Hampshire Days. MCLE(1914), MP4(406). Purple Land, The. MCLE(4294), MEF(708), MP1(791).
Hügel, Baron Friedrich John von. Mystical Element of Religion, The. CAL(749). Selected Letters. CHL(938).
Hugh of St. Victor. Noah's Ark. CAL(304). Soliloquy on

the Earnest Money of the Soul. CHL(209). Treatise Concerning the Pursuit of Learning. CAL(300).
Hughes, Hatcher. Hell-Bent for Heaven. DGAP(211).
Hughes, Richard. Fox in the Attic, The. SCL(1645), 1963a (59). Innocent Voyage, The. MCLE(2258), MEF(346), MP2(488).
Hughes, Thomas. Tom Brown's School Days. MCLE(5236), MEF(853), MP2(1039), PON(389).
Hugo, Victor. Hernani. POP(251). Hunchback of Notre Dame, The. MCLE(2159), MEU(376), MP1(397), PO (304), SGEN(65). Man Who Laughs, The. PO(308). Misérables, Les. MCLE(3074), MEU(498), MP1(597), PO(300), PON(235), SGEN(58). Poetry of Hugo, The. MCLE(3946), MP4(848). Toilers of the Sea, The. MCLE(5233), MEU(758), MP2(1037), PON(385).
Huizinga, Johan. Waning of the Middle Ages, The. MCLE (5550), MP4(1266).
Hulme, Kathryn. Nun's Story, The. SCL(3334), 1957a(195).
Hume, David. Dialogues Concerning Natural Religion. CHL (615), WP(525). Enquiry Concerning Human Understanding, An. MCLE(1397), MN(101), MP3(339). Enquiry Concerning the Principles of Morals, An. WP(488). Treatise of Human Nature, A (Book I). WP(471).
Humes, H. L. Men Die. SCL(2994), 1960a(165).
Humphrey, William. Home from the Hill. SCL(2087), 1959a(119). Ordways, The. SCL(3456), 1966a(221). Time and a Place, A. SCL(4665), 1969a(309).
Hunt, John. Conquest of Everest, The. SCL(900), 1954a (37).
Hunt, Leigh. Autobiography of Leigh Hunt, The. MCLE (287), MP4(51).
Huss, John. Treatise on the Church. CHL(304).
Husserl, Edmund. Ideas: General Introduction to Pure Phenomenology. WP(795).
Hutchinson, A. S. M. If Winter Comes. MCLE(2203), MEF(340), MP1(421).
Huxley, Aldous. Brave New World. MCLE(490), MEF(63), MP1(79), PO2(135), SGBN(313). Crome Yellow. MCLE(951), MEF(127), MP1(177). Essay of Aldous Huxley, The. MCLE(1449), MP4(297). Island. SCL (2269), 1963a(105). Point Counter Point. MCLE (4173), MEF(684), MP1(760), PO2(130), SGBN(308).
Huxley, Elspeth. Flame Trees of Thika, The. SCL(1575), 1960a(77).
Huxley, Julian. Essays of a Biologist. MCLE(1446), MP4 (294).

Huxley, Thomas Henry. Collected Essays. WP(712). Physical Basis of Life, The. MCLE(3649), MN(245), MP3(754).
Huysmans, Joris Karl. Against the Grain. MCLE(50), MEU(9), MP2(4). Down There. MCLE(1263), MEU (258), MP3(300). En Route. CAL(716).
Hyman, Mac. No Time for Sergeants. SCL(3287), 1954a (195).

Ibáñez, Vicente Blasco. Cabin, The. MCLE(559), MEU(95), MP2(125). Four Horsemen of the Apocalypse, The. PO(375), PON(125).
Ibsen, Henrik. Brand. MCLE(487), MD(103), MP3(126). Doll's House, A. MCLE(1223), MD(216), MP1(216), POP(321). Enemy of the People, An. MCLE(1383), MD(253), MP2(292). Ghosts. MCLE(1752), MD(298), MP1(301). Hedda Gabler. MCLE(1970), MD(324), MP1(359), POP(317). Lady from the Sea, The. MCLE(2497), MD(431), MP2(544). Master Builder, The. MCLE(2950), MD(501), MP2(643). Peer Gynt. MCLE(3551), MD(607), MP1(722), POP(325). Pillars of Society, The. MCLE(3675), MD(633), MP2(831). Rosmersholm. MCLE(4550), MD(714), MP2(922). When We Dead Awaken. MCLE(5614), MD(918), MP3 (1127). Wild Duck, The. MCLE(5645), MD(923), MP1(1113).
Icaza, Jorge. Huasipungo. MAF(279), MCLE(2142), MP2 (472).
Ickes, Harold L. Secret Diary of Harold L. Ickes: Volume II, The. SCL(4132), 1954a(249).
Ignatius, Saint, Bishop of Antioch. Epistles of Saint Ignatius of Antioch, The. CAL(7). Seven Epistles of Ignatius, The. CHL(7).
Ignatow, David. Rescue the Dead. SCL(3898), 1969a(277).
Ikku, Jippensha. Hiza-Kurige. MCLE(2080), MEU(365), MP3(481).
Inge, William. Bus Stop. SCLs(52). Come Back, Little Sheba. SGAP(227). Dark at the Top of the Stairs, The. SCL(1011), 1959a(48). Picnic. DGAP(386).
Inge, William Ralph. Christian Mysticism. CHL(816).
Ingoldsby, Thomas. Ingoldsby Legends, The. MCLE(2252), MP4(449).
Innocent III, Pope. De contemptu mundi. CAL(342). De sacro altaris mysterio. CAL(345).
Ionesco, Eugene. Amédée or How to Get Rid of It. TCP (195). Chairs, The. TCP(197). Lesson, The. TCP (200). Rhinoceros. MCLE(4441), MP4(1066), TCP(202).

Irenaeus, Saint. Against Heresies. CAL(37), CHL(35). Demonstration of Apostolic Teaching, The. CAL(47).
Irvine, William. Apes, Angels, and Victorians. BM(22), SCL(199), 1955a(11).
Irving, Washington. Chronicle of the Conquest of Granada, A. MCLE(736), MN(45), MP3(183). History of New York by Diedrich Knickerbocker, A. MCLE(2056), MN(140), MP3(469). Legend of Sleepy Hollow, The. MAF(335), MCLE(2583), MP2(569), MPA2(92), PO (236), PON(199). Legend of the Moor's Legacy. MAF(337), MCLE(2585), MP2(571). Rip Van Winkle. MAF(533), MCLE(4469), MP2(905), MPA2(96).
Isherwood, Christopher. Berlin Stories, The. SCL(374), 1954a(13).
Isherwood, Christopher and W. H. Auden. Ascent of F6, The. TCP(37).
Isidore of Seville, Saint. Etymologies, The. CAL(248).

Jackson, Charles. Lost Weekend, The. MAF(362), MCLE (2762), MP1(531).
Jackson, Helen Hunt. Ramona. PO(240), PON(342).
Jackson, Shirley. We Have Always Lived in the Castle. SCL(4992), 1963a(288).
Jacobsen, Jens Peter. Niels Lyhne. MCLE(3275), MEU (541), MP2(741).
Jacobson, Dan. Beginners, The. SCL(355), 1967a(28). Dance in the Sun, A. SCL(990), 1957a(55). Trap, The. SCL(4739), 1955a(275).
James, Henry. Ambassadors, The. MAF(18), MCLE(124), MP2(22), MPA3(7). American, The. DGAP(121), MAF(21), MCLE(130), MP1(27), MPA3(12). Awkward Age, The. MCLE(300), MP4(56), MPA3(17). Bostonians, The. MCLE(470), MP4(82), MPA3(25). Daisy Miller. MAF(120), MCLE(982), MP1(182), MPA3(31). Golden Bowl, The. MAF(211), MCLE(1790), MP2 (374), MPA3(34), PO2(189). Henry James: Autobiography. 1957a(110). Portrait of a Lady, The. MAF(500), MCLE(4192), MP1(766), MPA3(39), PO (243), PON(318), SGAN(61). Princess Casamassima, The. MCLE(4251), MP4(1029), MPA3(45). Roderick Hudson. MCLE(4498), MP4(1074), MPA3(50). Sacred Fount, The. MCLE(4569), MP4(1082), MPA3(57). Spoils of Poynton, The. MAF(595), MCLE(4965), MP3(1013), MPA3(66). Tragic Muse, The. MCLE (5271), MP4(1222), MPA3(71). Turn of the Screw, The. MAF(673), MCLE(5352), MP2(1066), MPA3(77), PO2(186), SGAN(66). Washington Square. MAF(700),

MCLE(5570), MP3(1117), MPA3(82), PO2(181). What Maisie Knew. MAF(706), MCLE(5609), MP3(1125), MPA3(87). Wings of the Dove, The. MAF(720), MCLE(5675), MP2(1143), MPA3(92).

James, William. Meaning of Truth, The. WP(784). Pragmatism. MCLE(4217), MN(251), MP3(843), WP(779). Varieties of Religious Experience, The. CHL(836). Will to Believe, The. WP(727).

Jarrell, Randall. Lost World, The. SCL(2790), 1966a(154). Pictures from an Institution. SCL(3570), 1954a(207). Poetry of Jarrell, The. MCLE(3949), MP4(851). Selected Poems. SCL(4182), 1955a(225). Woman at the Washington Zoo, The. BM(613), SCL(5124), 1961a(309).

Jarry, Alfred. Ubu Roi. TCP(206).

Jaspers, Karl. Future of Mankind, The. SCL(1684), 1962a (132). Reason and Existenz. WP(1004).

Jay, John, Alexander Hamilton and James Madison. Federalist, The. MCLE(1577), MN(124), MP3(384).

Jean-Aubry, Gérard. Sea Dreamer, The. SCL(4099), 1958a (222).

Jeffers, Robinson. Cawdor. MCLE(662), MP(44), MP1(130). Hungerfield and Other Poems. SCLs(130). Poetry of Jeffers, The. MCLE(3952), MP4(853). Roan Stallion. MCLE(4487), MP(323), MP1(835). Tamar. MCLE (5090), MP(353), MP1(948).

Jefferson, Joseph, Charles Burke, and Dion Boucicault. Rip Van Winkle. DGAP(90).

Jefferson, Thomas. Notes on the State of Virginia. MCLE (3319), MN(214), MP3(692).

Jenkins, Elizabeth. Elizabeth the Great. BM(156), SCL (1305), 1960a(70).

Jenkins, Roy. Asquith. SCL(235), 1966a(12).

Jensen, Johannes V. Long Journey, The. MCLE(2724), MEU(451), MP2(589).

Jerome, Jerome K. Passing of the Third Floor Back, The. POP(113). Three Men in a Boat. MCLE(5178), MEF (838), MP2(1018).

Jerome, Saint. De viris illustribus. CAL(148). Letters of Saint Jerome, The. CAL(180), CHL(108).

Jewett, Sarah Orne. Country Doctor, A. MAF(106), MCLE (898), MP2(183), MPA3(97). Country of the Pointed Firs, The. MAF(108), MCLE(905), MP1(163), MPA3 (101). Deephaven. MAF(136), MCLE(1088), MP2(238).

Jhabvala, R. Prawer. Amrita. SCL(164), 1957a(4). Nature of Passion, The. SCL(3181), 1958a(166).

Jiménez, Juan Ramón. Platero and I. BM(436), MCLE(3704),

MEU(590), MP3(764), SCL(3595), 1958a(188). Poetry of Jiménez, The. MCLE(3955), MP4(856).
Joachim, Harold Henry. Nature of Truth, The. WP(773).
Joachim of Fiore. Treatise on the Four Gospels. CHL(224).
Job, Thomas. Giants in the Earth. DGAP(238).
John of Damascus, Saint. Fountain of Wisdom, The. CHL (186).
John of Paris. De potestate regia et papali. CAL(432).
John of St. Thomas. Ars logica. CAL(589). Cursus theologicus. CAL(605).
John of Salisbury. Metalogicon. CAL(335). Policraticus. CAL(335), CHL(216).
John of the Cross, Saint. Ascent of Mount Carmel and The Dark Night of the Soul. CAL(558). Dark Night of the Soul, The. CAL(558), CHL(406).
John XXIII, Pope. Mater et magistra. CAL(1106). Pacem in terris. CAL(1131).
Johnson, James Weldon. Autobiography of an Ex-Coloured Man, The. SCLs(14).
Johnson, Pamela Hansford. Unspeakable Skipton, The. SCL(4848), 1960a(284).
Johnson, Samuel. Idler, The. MCLE(2196), MP4(434). Life of Richard Savage. MCLE(2667), MP4(549). Lives of the Poets. MCLE(2716), MP4(558). Poetry of Johnson, The. MCLE(3957), MP4(857). Preface to Shakespeare. MCLE(4228), MP4(1024). Rambler, The. MCLE(4327), MP4(1044). Rasselas. MCLE (4337), MEF(716), MP1(804).
Johnson, Thomas H. Emily Dickinson. SCL(1330), 1955a (92).
Johnson, Uwe. Speculations About Jakob. MCLE(4956), MP4(1176), SCL(4402), 1964a(247). Third Book About Achim, The. SCL(4598), 1968a(318).
Johnston, Denis. Nine Rivers from Jordan. SCL(3270), 1955a(184).
Johnston, Mary. Great Valley, The. MAF(234), MCLE (1843), MP3(428).
Joinville, Jean de. Life of Saint Louis, The. CAL(435).
Jókai, Maurus. Modern Midas, A. MCLE(3133), MEU(501), MP2(697).
Jones, David. In Parenthesis. SCL(2182), 1963a(93).
Jones, Ernest, M.D. Life and Work of Sigmund Freud, The. SCL(2641), 1958a(144).
Jones, Henry Arthur. Liars, The. POP(130). Michael and His Lost Angel. MCLE(3034), MD(522), MP2(660). Mrs. Dane's Defence. MCLE(3111), MD(542), MP2 (688).

Jones, James. Thin Red Line, The. SCL(4592), 1963a(265).
Jones, LeRoi. Tales. SCLs(310).
Jones, Madison. Buried Land, A. SCL(554), 1964a(39). Forest of the Night. SCL(1628), 1961a(87). Innocent, The. SCL(2237), 1958a(114).
Jones, Rufus Matthew. Practical Christianity. CHL(819).
Jones, Tom and Harvey Schmidt. Fantasticks, The. SCLs (94).
Jonson, Ben. Alchemist, The. MCLE(69), MD(14), MP2(8). Bartholomew Fair. MCLE(348), MD(60), MP2(80). Catiline. MCLE(657), MD(135), MP3(161). Every Man in His Humour. MCLE(1503), MD(258), MP2 (309). Every Man Out of His Humour. MCLE(1506), MD(261), MP2(312). Poetry of Jonson, The. MCLE (3960), MP4(860). Sejanus. MCLE(4695), MD(755), MP3(951). Silent Woman, The. MCLE(4823), MD(777), MP3(980). Volpone. MCLE(5525), MD(897), MP1 (1076), POP(192).
Jonson, Ben, George Chapman and John Marston. Eastward Ho! MCLE(1316), MD(234), MP3(317).
Jörgensen, Johannes. Autobiography of Johannes Jörgensen, The. CAL(801). Saint Francis of Assisi. CAL(756).
Josephson, Matthew. Edison: A Biography. BM(148), SCL (1288), 1960a(63).
Josephy, Alvin M., Jr. Nez Perce Indians and the Opening of the Northwest, The. SCL(3217), 1966a(193).
Journet, Charles. Church of the Word Incarnate, The. CAL(875).
Joyce, James. Exiles. MCLE(1518), MD(267), MP3(373). Finnegans Wake. MCLE(1615), MEF(213), MP3(395). Letters of James Joyce. SCL(2597), 1958a(141). Portrait of the Artist as a Young Man, A. MCLE (4198), MEF(687), MP1(769), PO2(110), SGBN(277). Ulysses. MCLE(5388), MEF(882), MP1(1040).
Joyce, Stanislaus. My Brother's Keeper. SCL(3144), 1959a (171).
Juana Inés de la Cruz, Sor. Poetry of Sor Juana Inés de la Cruz, The. MCLE(4095), MP4(958).
Judah, Aaron. Clown on Fire. SCL(782), 1968a(45).
Julian (Juliana) of Norwich, Lady. Revelations of Divine Love, The. CAL(476), CHL(284).
Jung, Carl G. Two Essays on Analytical Psychology. MCLE (5366), MP4(1240).
Jungmann, Josef Andreas, S.J. Good News Yesterday and Today, The. CAL(843). Mass of the Roman Rite, The. CAL(949).
Justice, Donald. Night Light. SCL(3233), 1968a(221).

Justin Martyr, Saint. First Apology. CAL(19), CHL(19). Second Apology, The. CAL(19), CHL(19).
Juvenal. Satires. MCLE(4630), MP(327), MP3(931).

Kafka, Franz. Castle, The. MCLE(636), MEU(113), MP1 (122), SGEN(345). Diaries of Kafka: 1910-1923, The. MCLE(1155), MP4(224). Trial, The. MCLE(5310), MEU(764), MP1(1020), PO2(478), SGEN(352).
Kagawa, Toyohiko. Love, the Law of Life. CHL(921).
Kaiser, Georg. From Morn to Midnight. TCP(209).
Kai-shek, Chiang. Soviet Russia in China. SCL(4388), 1958a(228).
Kalidasa. Sakuntala. MCLE(4589), MD(725), MP2(931).
Kaneko, Hisakazu. Manjiro. SCL(2894), 1957a(168).
Kanin, Garson. Born Yesterday. SGAP(221).
Kant, Immanuel. Critique of Judgment. WP(556). Critique of Practical Reason. WP(545). Critique of Pure Reason. MCLE(946), MN(72), MP3(240), WP(531). Religion Within the Limits of Reason Alone. CHL (626).
Kantor, MacKinlay. Andersonville. SCL(177), 1955a(7).
Kaplan, Justin. Mr. Clemens and Mark Twain. SCL(3054), 1967a(221).
Karmel, Ilona. Estate of Memory, An. 1970a(117).
Kaufman, George S. and Marc Connelly. Beggar on Horseback. DGAP(208).
Kaufman, George S. and Moss Hart. You Can't Take It with You. DGAP(294), POP(5), SGAP(46), TCP(212).
Kaufman, George S., Morrie Ryskind, Ira and George Gershwin. Of Thee I Sing. DGAP(253), SGAP(53).
Kawabata, Yasunari. Snow Country and Thousand Cranes. 1970a(277). Sound of the Mountain, The. 1971a(304). Thousand Cranes. 1970a(277).
Kaye-Smith, Sheila. Joanna Godden. MCLE(2344), MEF(370), MP2(509).
Kazantzakis, Nikos. Freedom or Death. MCLE(1687), MP4 (364), SCL(1658), 1957a(76). Greek Passion, The. MCLE(1846), MP4(395), SCL(1874), 1954a(102). Last Temptation of Christ, The. SCL(2533), SGEN(458), 1961a(153). Odyssey: A Modern Sequel, The. SCLs (205). Report to Greco. SCL(3894), 1966a(265). Saint Francis. SCL(4054), 1963a(227). Zorba the Greek. MCLE(5790), MP4(1304).
Keats, John. Eve of St. Agnes, The. MCLE(1498), MP(95), MP1(263). Insolent Chariots, The. BM(252), SCL (2253), 1959a(128). Letters of John Keats, The.

MCLE(2615), MP4(525). You Might As Well Live. 1971a(368).
Keene, Donald, Ed. Old Woman, the Wife, and the Archer, The. SCL(3381), 1962a(224).
Keller, Gottfried. Grüne Heinrich, Der. MCLE(1873), MEU (344), MP3(432).
Kellogg, Marjorie. Tell Me That You Love Me, Junie Moon. SCL(4533), 1969a(305).
Kelly, George. Craig's Wife. SGAP(1).
Kemal, Yashar. Memed, My Hawk. SCL(2964), 1962a(202).
Kendall, Paul Murray. Warwick the Kingmaker. SCL(4967), 1958a(268).
Kennan, George F. Decision to Intervene, The. BM(125), SCL(1106), 1959a(54). Memoirs: 1925-1950. SCL (2975), 1968a(198). Russia and the West under Lenin and Stalin. BM(487), SCL(4025), 1962a(254). Russia Leaves the War, Volume I. BM(492), SCL(4034), 1957a(227). Russia, the Atom and the West. SCL (4038), 1959a(214).
Kennedy, Charles Rann. Servant in the House, The. POP (49).
Kennedy, John F. Profiles in Courage. SCL(3705), 1957a (212).
Kennedy, John P. Horseshoe Robinson. MAF(270), MCLE (2109), MP1(376). Swallow Barn. MAF(624), MCLE (5064), MP2(1004).
Kennedy, Margaret. Act of God. SCL(22), 1955a(1).
Kennedy, X. J. Growing into Love. 1970a(154).
Kerouac, Jack. On the Road. SCL(3398), 1958a(179).
Kesey, Ken. One Flew over the Cuckoo's Nest. SCL(3423), 1963a(160). Sometimes a Great Notion. SCL(4361), 1965a(283).
Kierkegaard, Søren. Attack on Christendom. CHL(728). Christian Discourses. CAL(709). Concluding Unscientific Postscript. CHL(704), WP(626). Either/Or. WP(612). Philosophical Fragments. WP(619). Sickness unto Death, The. MCLE(4814), MN(285), MP3 (976). Training in Christianity. CHL(720).
Kim, Richard E. Martyred, The. SCL(2924), 1965a(199).
Kingsley, Charles. Hereward the Wake. MCLE(2009), MEF (295), MP1(367). Hypatia. MCLE(2174), MEF(333), MP1(402). Westward Ho! MCLE(5603), MEF(946), MP1(1103), PO(117), PON(445).
Kingsley, Henry. Ravenshoe. MCLE(4340), MEF(719), MP2 (880).
Kingsley, Sidney. Dead End. DGAP(273), SGAP(190).
Kinnell, Galway. Body Rags. SCL(470), 1968a(31). Flower

Herding on Mount Monadnock. SCL(1596), 1965a(101).
Kinross, Patrick Balfour, Lord. Ataturk. SCL(255), 1966a (21).
Kinsella, Thomas. Nightwalker and Other Poems. SCL (3261), 1969a(243).
Kipling, Rudyard. Brushwood Boy, The. MCLE(540), MEF (71), MP2(120). Captains Courageous. MCLE(612), MEF(83), MP1(111), PON(52). Jungle Books, The. MCLE(2413), MEF(397), MP1(461). Kim. MCLE (2438), MD(409), MEF(404), MP1(473), PO2(79), SGBN(227). Light That Failed, The. PO(120). Poetry of Kipling, The. MCLE(3965), MP4(865).
Kirk, Kenneth E. Vision of God: The Christian Doctrine of the Summum Bonum, The. CHL(977).
Kirkland, Jack. Tobacco Road. DGAP(265), SGAP(166).
Kirkwood, James. Good Times/Bad Times. SCL(1821), 1969a(138).
Kirst, Hans Hellmut. Revolt of Gunner Asch, The. SCL (3919), 1957a(221).
Klein-Haparash, J. He Who Flees the Lion. SCL(1960), 1964a(124).
Kleist, Heinrich von. Broken Jug, The. MCLE(518), MD (109), MP3(135). Prince of Homburg, The. MCLE (4246), MD(658), MP3(854).
Knapton, Ernest John. Empress Josephine. SCL(1337), 1965a(80).
Knight, Eric. This Above All. MCLE(5170), MEF(836), MP1(974).
Knowles, Dom David, O. S. B. Monastic Order in England, The. CAL(870).
Knowles, John. Morning in Antibes. SCL(3080), 1963a(148). Separate Peace, A. SCL(4208), 1961a(225).
Knox, John. History of the Reformation in Scotland. CHL (409).
Knox, Ronald. Enthusiasm. CAL(961).
Kober, Arthur. "Having Wonderful Time." SGAP(149).
Koestler, Arthur. Act of Creation, The. SCL(19), 1965a(1). Darkness at Noon. MCLE(1021), MEU(200), MP1(187), PO2(484), SGEN(432). Invisible Writing, The. SCL (2261), 1954a(117). Sleepwalkers, The. SCL(4325), 1960a(245).
Kopit, Arthur. Indians. 1970a(177).
Kosinski, Jerzy. Painted Bird, The. SCL(3491), 1966a(224). Steps. SCL(4442), 1969a(302).
Kozol, Jonathan. Death at an Early Age. SCL(1079), 1968a (67).
Kraemer, Hendrik. Christian Message in a Non-Christian

World, The. CHL(1038).
Kronenberger, Louis. Marlborough's Duchess. SCL(2914), 1959a(155).
Krutch, Joseph Wood. Measure of Man, The. SCLs(182). Voice of the Desert, The. SCL(4916), 1955a(290).
Kuan-chung, Lo. Romance of the Three Kingdoms. MCLE (4522), MEU(649), MP3(903).
Kunen, James Simon. Strawberry Statement, The. 1970a (287).
Küng, Hans. Council, Reform and Reunion, The. CAL (1110).
Kunhardt, Philip B., Jr. My Father's House. SCLs(194).
Kunitz, Stanley. Selected Poems: 1928-58. SCLs(268).
Kuyper, Abraham. Lectures on Calvinism. CHL(969).
Kyd, Thomas. Spanish Tragedy, The. MCLE(4951), MD (802), MP2(990).
Kyôden, Santô. Inazuma-Byôshi. MCLE(2232), MEU(394), MP3(503).

Laclos, Pierre Choderlos de. Dangerous Acquaintances. MCLE(1006), MEU(192), MP3(246).
Lactantius, Lucius Caecilius Firmianus. Divine Institutes, The. CAL(81), CHL(79).
LaFargo, John, S.J. Manner Is Ordinary, The. CAL(1010).
Lafayette, Madame Marie de. Princess of Clèves, The. MCLE(4254), MEU(602), MP2(856), PO2(291).
La Fontaine, Jean de. Fables. MCLE(1527), MP(97), MP3 (378).
Laforgue, Jules. Poetry of Laforgue, The. MCLE(3968), MP4(868).
Lagerkvist, Pär. Barabbas. MCLE(327), MEU(62), MP3(85). Sibyl, The. SCL(4270), 1959a(224).
Lagerlöf, Selma. Gösta Berling's Saga. SGEN(228). Story of Gösta Berling. MCLE(5003), MEU(726), MP1(934), PO(391).
Lall, Anand. House at Adampur, The. SCL(2115), 1957a (126).
Lamartine, Alphonse de. Poetry of Lamartine, The. MCLE (3971), MP4(870).
Lamb, Charles. Essays of Elia and Last Essays of Elia. MCLE(1455), MN(116), MP3(362). Letters of Charles Lamb, The. MCLE(2606), MP4(517).
Lamennais, Félicité Robert de. Essay on Indifference in Matters of Religion. CAL(632).
La Mettrie, Julien Offray de. Man a Machine. WP(482).
Lampedusa, Giuseppe di. Leopard, The. BM(309), MCLE (2591), MP4(510), SCL(2559), 1961a(156).

Landor, Walter Savage. Imaginary Conversations. MCLE (2212), MN(158), MP3(499). Poetry of Landor, The. MCLE(3974), MP4(873).

Lane, Margaret. Night at Sea, A. SCL(3225), 1966a(196).

Lanfranc. Liber de corpore et sanguine domini. CAL(283).

Langland, William. Vision of William, Concerning Piers the Plowman, The. MCLE(5513), MP(373), MP3(1105).

Lanier, Sidney. Poetry of Lanier, The. MCLE(3978), MP (272), MP3(812).

Lapp, Ralph E. Voyage of the Lucky Dragon, The. SCL (4930), 1959a(268).

Lardner, Ring. You Know Me Al. MAF(735), MCLE(5769), MP3(1159).

Larkin, Oliver W. Daumier: Man of His Time. SCL(1038), 1967a(66).

Larkin, Philip. Girl in Winter, A. SCL(1760), 1963a(67). Poetry of Larkin, The. MCLE(3981), MP4(876). Whitsun Weddings, The. SCL(5048), 1966a(333).

La Rochefoucauld, François, Duc de. Maxims, The. MCLE (2967), MN(199), MP3(642).

Latter, Albert L. and Edward Teller. Our Nuclear Future. SCL(3472), 1959a(198).

Laurents, Arthur. Home of the Brave. SGAP(271).

Law, William. Serious Call to a Devout and Holy Life, A. CHL(566).

Lawrence, Brother (Nicholas Herman). Practice of the Presence of God, The. CHL(543).

Lawrence, D. H. Collected Letters of D. H. Lawrence, The. MCLE(787), MP4(141), SCL(791), 1963a(26). Lady Chatterley's Lover. PO2(123), SCL(2468), 1960a(129). Plumed Serpent, The. MCLE(3715), MEF(681), MP2(843). Poetry of Lawrence, The. MCLE(3983), MP4(877). Rainbow, The. MCLE(4316), MEF(713), MP1(800). Short Stories of D. H. Lawrence, The. MCLE(4777), MP4(1125). Sons and Lovers. MCLE(4925), MEF(807), MP1(913), PO(124), SGBN(263). Studies in Classic American Literature. MCLE(5028), MP4(1192). Twilight in Italy. MCLE (5363), MP4(1238). Women in Love. MCLE(5720), MP4(1298).

Lawrence, Jerome and Robert E. Lee. Inherit the Wind. DGAP(403), SGAP(238).

Lawrence, Margaret. Stone Angel, The. SCL(4445), 1965a (290).

Lawrence, T. E. Seven Pillars of Wisdom. MCLE(4722), MN(282), MP3(961).

Lawson, John Howard. Processional. DGAP(225).

Laxness, Halldór. Independent People. MCLE(2239), MEU (397), MP1(425). Paradise Reclaimed. SCL(3509), 1963a(171).
Layamon. Brut, The. MCLE(542), MP(30), MP3(140).
Lea, Tom. King Ranch, The. SCL(2442), 1958a(127).
Leasor, James. Red Fort, The. SCL(3855), 1958a(206).
Léautaud, Paul. Child of Montmartre, The. SCL(706), 1960a(39).
Lee, Harper. To Kill a Mockingbird. BM(555), SCL(4696), 1961a(260).
Lee, Laurie. As I Walked Out One Midsummer Morning. 1970a(34). Edge of Day, The. SCL(1271), 1961a(67).
Lee, Robert E. and Jerome Lawrence. Inherit the Wind. DGAP(403), SGAP(238).
Leech, Margaret. In the Days of McKinley. SCL(2192), 1960a(102).
Le Fanu, Joseph Sheridan. House by the Churchyard, The. MCLE(2112), MEF(315), MP2(458). Uncle Silas. MCLE(5394), MEF(888), MP2(1078).
Leggett, John. Who Took the Gold Away. 1970a(348).
Leibniz, Gottfried Wilhelm von. Monadology. WP(601). New Essays on the Human Understanding. WP(518). Theodicy. WP(454).
LeMay, Alan. Searchers, The. SCL(4120), 1954a(243).
Leo XIII, Pope. Aeterni patris. CAL(691). Immortale Dei. CAL(695). Rerum novarum. CAL(699).
Leo the Great, Saint. Letters and Sermons of Saint Leo the Great, The. CAL(211). Tome. CAL(201), CHL(159).
Leonardo da Vinci. Notebooks of Leonardo da Vinci, The. MCLE(3314), MP4(633).
Leopardi, Giacomo. Poetry of Leopardi, The. MCLE(3986), MP4(880).
Lermontov, Mikhail Yurievich. Demon: An Eastern Tale, The. MCLE(1122), MP4(216). Hero of Our Time, A. MCLE(2015), MEU(361), MP3(456). Novice, The. MCLE(3322), MP4(637).
Lerner, Alan Jay. My Fair Lady. BM(385), SCL(3148), 1957a(182).
Lerner, Max. America as a Civilization. SCL(147), 1958a (17).
Le Sage, Alain René. Diable Boiteux, Le. MCLE(1141), MEU(230), MP3(271). Gil Blas de Santillane. MCLE (1757), MEU(327), MP1(305), PO(311), PON(129). Turcaret. MCLE(5349), MD(881), MP3(1091).
Leskov, Nikolai. Selected Tales. SCL(4197), 1962a(261).
Lessing, Doris. Children of Violence: Vols. I and II. SCL(723), 1965a(40). Children of Violence: Vols. III

and IV. SCL(728), 1967a(38). Four-Gated City, The. 1970a(135). Golden Notebook, The. SCL(1796), 1963a(72). Man and Two Women, A. SCL(2851), 1964a(169).

Lessing, Gotthold Ephraim. Emilia Galotti. MCLE(1369), MD(247), MP3(333). Minna von Barnhelm. MCLE (3062), MD(532), MP2(668). Nathan the Wise. MCLE (3234), MD(567), MP3(683), POP(312).

Lever, Charles. Charles O'Malley. MCLE(689), MEF(95), MP1(133). Tom Burke of Ours. MCLE(5238), MEF (855), MP2(1041).

Levertov, Denise. Jacob's Ladder, The. SCL(2278), 1964a (140). O Taste and See. SCL(3340), 1965a(217). Relearning the Alphabet. 1971a(269).

Levine, Philip. Not This Pig. SCL(3308), 1969a(248).

Lévi-Strauss, Claude. Raw and the Cooked, The. 1970a (263). Savage Mind, The. SCLs(251).

Lewis, Anthony. Gideon's Trumpet. SCL(1743), 1965a(107).

Lewis, Arthur H. Lament for the Molly Maguires. SCL (2482), 1965a(164).

Lewis, C. S. Allegory of Love, The. MCLE(107), MP4 (26). Four Loves, The. BM(191), SCL(1635), 1961a (91). Letters of C. S. Lewis. SCL(2582), 1967a(187). Poems. SCL(3620), 1966a(238). Reflections on the Psalms. SCL(3861), 1959a(209). Till We Have Faces. SCL(4662), 1958a(233).

Lewis, Cecil Day. Poetry of Lewis, The. MCLE(3989), MP(275), MP3(815).

Lewis, Clarence Irving. Analysis of Knowledge and Valuation, An. WP(1096). Mind and the World Order. WP(914).

Lewis, Clive Staples. Screwtape Letters, The. CHL(1068).

Lewis, Grace Hegger. With Love from Gracie. SCL(5115), 1957a(291).

Lewis, H. D. Our Experience of God. CHL(1189).

Lewis, Matthew Gregory. Monk, The. MCLE(3141), MEF (540), MP2(701).

Lewis, Meriwether and William Clark. Journals of Lewis and Clark, The. MCLE(2392), MP4(484).

Lewis, Oscar. Children of Sánchez, The. BM(72), SCL (718), 1962a(55). Death in the Sanchez Family, A. 1970a(101). Pedro Martínez. SCL(3534), 1965a(221). Vida, La. SCL(2460), 1967a(182).

Lewis, Sinclair. Arrowsmith. MAF(36), MCLE(241), MP1 (44), PO(247), SGAN(147). Babbitt. MAF(41), MCLE (312), MP1(50), PO2(218), SGAN(142). Cass Timberlane. MAF(83), MCLE(631), MP1(120). Dodsworth.

MAF(145), MCLE(1220), MP2(265). Elmer Gantry. MCLE(1355), MP4(268). Main Street. MAF(375), MCLE(2854), MP1(549), PO2(212).
Lewis, Wyndham. Self Condemned. SCL(4200), 1955a(228). Tarr. MCLE(5107), MEF(822), MP3(1051).
Lidman, Sara. Rainbird, The. SCL(3815), 1963a(205).
Lie, Jonas. Family at Gilje, The. MCLE(1545), MEU(290), MP2(318).
Life, The Editors of. World's Great Religions, The. SCL (5160), 1958a(276).
Lifton, Robert Jay. Death in Life: Survivors of Hiroshima. SCLs(84).
Liguori, Saint Alphonsus Mary de'. Glories of Mary. CAL (624).
Lilburne, John. Foundations of Freedom, The. CHL(470).
Lincoln, Abraham. Addresses. MCLE(25), MN(4), MP3(9).
Lind, Jakov. Soul of Wood and Other Stories. SCL(4377), 1966a(303).
Lindbergh, Anne Morrow. Gift from the Sea. SCL(1749), 1955a(107).
Lindsay, Howard and Russel Crouse. Life with Father. DGAP(317), POP(1), SGAP(58).
Lindsay, Vachel. Poetry of Lindsay, The. MCLE(3992), MP(278), MP3(817).
Lingard, John. History of England, The. CAL(638).
Link, Arthur S. Wilson: Confusions and Crises, 1915-1916. SCL(5091), 1966a(337).
Lippmann, Walter. Communist World and Ours, The. SCL (863), 1960a(45).
Livy. Annals of the Roman People. MCLE(191), MN(17), MP3(47).
Llewellyn, Richard. How Green Was My Valley. MCLE (2136), MEF(324), MP1(385).
Llosa, Mario Vargas. Green House, The. 1970a(150).
Lobeira, Vasco de. Amadís de Gaul. MCLE(121), MEU(18), MP3(27).
Locke, John. Essay Concerning Human Understanding, An. MCLE(1426), MN(107), MP3(354), WP(428). Of Civil Government: The Second Treatise. WP(436). Reasonableness of Christianity, The. CHL(551).
Lockridge, Ross, Jr. Raintree County. MAF(512), MCLE (4319), MP2(874).
Lofts, Norah. Bless This House. SCL(448), 1954a(22).
Logan, John. Spring of the Thief. SCL(4420), 1964a(250).
Loisy, Alfred. Gospel and the Church, The. CHL(832).
Lombard, Peter. Book of Sentences, The. CAL(328).
London, Jack. Call of the Wild, The. MAF(80), MCLE(581),

MP1(103), PO2(208), SGAN(96). Sea Wolf, The. MAF(563), MCLE(4670), MP1(874), PON(369).
Lonergan, Bernard J. F., S.J. Insight. CAL(1043).
Long, John Luther and David Belasco. Madame Butterfly. DGAP(140).
Longfellow, Henry Wadsworth. Courtship of Miles Standish, The. MCLE(911), MP(59), MP1(165), MPA4(7). Evangeline. MCLE(1495), MP(92), MP1(261), MPA4 (10). Song of Hiawatha, The. MCLE(4902), MP(346), MP1(905), MPA4(15).
Longus, Attributed to. Daphnis and Chloë. MCLE(1014), MEU(195), MP1(183).
Longinus, Unknown, long attributed to. On the Sublime. MCLE(3409), MP4(650).
Longstreet, Augustus Baldwin. Georgia Scenes. MAF(195), MCLE(1738), MP3(416).
Lönnrot, Elias. Kalevala, The. MCLE(2423), MP(147), MP3(535).
Lopez, Calude-Anne. Mon Cher Papa. SCL(3065), 1967a (214).
Lorca, Federico García. Blood Wedding. MCLE(443), MD (83), MP2(99), TCP(143). House of Bernarda Alba. TCP(146). Shoemaker's Prodigious Wife. TCP(149).
Lord, Walter. Day of Infamy. BM(114), SCL(1061), 1958a (60). Night to Remember, A. SCL(3245), 1955a(178).
Loti, Pierre. Iceland Fisherman, An. MCLE(2187), MEU (385), MP1(410).
Lott, Milton. Last Hunt, The. SCL(2511), 1954a(138).
Lotze, Rudolf Hermann. Microcosmus. WP(638).
Lovelace, Richard. Poetry of Lovelace, The. MCLE(3994), MP(280), MP3(819).
Lover, Samuel. Handy Andy. MCLE(1922), MEF(269), MP2(400). Rory O'More. MCLE(4547), MEF(762), MP2(920).
Low, David. Low's Autobiography. SCL(2807), 1958a(155).
Lowell, James Russell. Biglow Papers, The. MCLE(413), MP(22), MP3(111), MPA4(19). Fable for Critics, A. MCLE(1524), MP4(313), MPA4(25). Lyric Poetry of Lowell, The. MCLE(2796), MP4(574), MPA4(31).
Lowell, Robert. For the Union Dead. SCL(1617), 1965a (105). Imitations. SCLs(137). Life Studies. BM (329), SCL(2662), 1960a(133). Near the Ocean. SCL (3184), 1967a(234). Notebook 1967-68. 1970a(225). Old Glory, The. SCL(3369), 1966a(209).
Lowell, Robert, Jr. Poetry of Robert Lowell, The. MCLE (4067), MP4(936).
Lowry, Malcolm. Dark as the Grave Wherein My Friend Is

Laid. SCL(1008), 1969a(86). Hear Us O Lord from Heaven Thy Dwelling Place. BM(220), SCL(1966), 1962a(145). Selected Letters of Malcolm Lowry. SCL(4163), 1966a(291). Under the Volcano. MCLE (5414), MP4(1250).

Loyola, Saint Ignatius. Spiritual Exercises. CAL(534).

Lubac, Henri de, S.J. Catholicism. CAL(856). Discovery of God, The. CAL(1025).

Lucian. Satires. MCLE(4632), MP4(1097). True History, The. MCLE(5345), MEU(769), MP3(1087).

Lucretius. De rerum natura. MCLE(1033), MN(75), MP3 (252), WP(218).

Luke, Peter. Hadrian VII. 1970a(161).

Lung, Kung-sun. Kung-sun Lung Tzu. WP(195).

Luther, Martin. Babylonian Captivity of the Church, The. CHL(334). Bondage of the Will, The. CHL(347). Open Letter to the Christian Nobility of the German Nation, An. CHL(330). Treatise on Christian Liberty, A. CHL(339).

Lyly, John. Campaspe. MCLE(586), MD(126), MP3(148). Endymion. MCLE(1381), MD(251), MP3(337). Euphues and His England. MCLE(1487), MEF(190), MP3(366). Euphues, the Anatomy of Wit. MCLE (1489), MEF(192), MP3(368).

Lytle, Andrew. Bedford Forrest and His Critter Company. SCL(349), 1961a(16). Long Night, The. MAF(350), MCLE(2728), MP2(593). Novel, A Novella and Four Stories, A. SCL(3330), 1959a(179). Velvet Horn, The. BM(573), MCLE(5451), MP4(1256), SCL(4873), 1958a(255).

MacArthur, Charles and Ben Hecht. Front Page, The. DGAP(234), SGAP(104).

MacArthur, Douglas. Reminiscences. SCL(3884), 1965a(243).

Macaulay, Rose. Towers of Trebizond, The. SCL(4723), 1958a(242).

Macaulay, Thomas Babington. History of England, The. MCLE(2045), MN(137), MP3(466).

McCarthy, Cormac. Orchard Keeper, The. SCL(3448), 1966a(218). Outer Dark. SCL(3484), 1969a(258).

McCarthy, Justin Huntly. If I Were King. POP(117).

McCarthy, Mary. Charmed Life, A. SCL(693), 1955a(50). Group, The. SCL(1887), 1964a(119). Memories of a Catholic Girlhood. SCL(2991), 1958a(158).

McConkey, James. Crossroads. SCL(962), 1968a(60).

McCoy, Horace. They Shoot Horses, Don't They? MCLE (5161), MP4(1214).

McCullers, Carson. Clock Without Hands. SCL(771), 1962a (67). Heart Is a Lonely Hunter, The. MAF(255), MCLE(1949), MP2(416), SGAN(282). Member of the Wedding, The. MAF(401), MCLE(2988), MP2(655), SGAP(259).

MacDonald, Dwight. Against the American Grain. SCL(88), 1963a(3).

McFee, William. Casuals of the Sea. MCLE(645), MEF(90), MP1(128).

Mach, Ernst. Analysis of the Sensations, The. WP(691).

Machado, Antonio. Poetry of Machado, The. MCLE(3997), MP4(883).

Machado de Assis, Joaquim Maria. Epitaph of a Small Winner. MAF(169), MCLE(1414), MP2(294). Esau and Jacob. SCL(1382), 1966a(93). Philosopher or Dog? MCLE(3625), MP4(686), SCL(3561), 1954a(204).

Machen, Arthur. Hill of Dreams, The. MCLE(2030), MEF (301), MP2(445).

Machen, John Gresham. Christianity and Liberalism. CHL (908).

Machiavelli, Niccolo. Prince, The. CAL(523), MCLE(4240), MN(258), MP3(852), WP(354).

Macintosh, Douglas Clyde. Theology as an Empirical Science. CHL(899).

MacKaye, Percy. Scarecrow, The. DGAP(178).

McKenna, Richard. Sand Pebbles, The. SCL(4067), 1964a (226).

Mackenzie, Henry. Man of Feeling, The. MCLE(2876), MEF(463), MP2(615).

McKenzie, John L., S.J. Two-Edged Sword, The. CAL (1028).

MacLeish, Archibald. Conquistador. MCLE(850), MP(56), MP3(223). Herakles. SCL(2005), 1968a(152). J. B. BM(255), DGAP(410), SCL(2307), SGAP(85), 1959a(131). Poetry of MacLeish, The. MCLE(4000), MP4(885). Songs for Eve. BM(519), SCL(4369), 1954a(255). "Wild Old Wicked Men, The" and Other Poems. SCL (5064), 1969a(346).

MacLennan, Hugh. Watch That Ends the Night, The. SCL (4976), 1960a(293).

Macmillan, Harold. Blast of War, The. SCL(442), 1969a (36).

Macmurray, John. Form of the Personal, The. CHL(1162).

McMurtry, Larry. Last Picture Show, The. SCLs(154). Moving On. SCLs(188).

MacNeice, Louis. Poetry of MacNeice, The. MCLE(4003), MP4(887).

McNeill, William H. Rise of the West, The. SCL(3945), 1964a(223).
McNulty, John. World of John McNulty, The. SCL(5145), 1958a(273).
Madden, David. Cassandra Singing. 1970a(69). Shadow Knows, The. 1971a(296).
Madison, James, Alexander Hamilton and John Jay. Federalist, The. MCLE(1577), MN(124), MP3(384).
Maeterlinck, Maurice. Pélléas and Mélisande. MCLE(3558), MD(609), MP2(806), POP(273).
Magarshack, David. Dostoevsky. SCL(1219), 1964a(67).
Magee, Bryan. One in Twenty. SCL(3426), 1967a(252).
Magnus, Philip. King Edward the Seventh. SCL(2424), 1965a(161).
Mailer, Norman. Armies of the Night, The. SCL(220), 1969a(21). Naked and the Dead, The. SCLs(199), SGAN(305).
Maimonides. Guide for the Perplexed. WP(300).
Maistre, Joseph Marie de. Soirées de Saint-Pétersbourg, Les. CAL(630).
Majdalany, Fred. Battle of Casino, The. SCL(326), 1958a (30).
Malamud, Bernard. Assistant, The. SCL(238), SGAN(350), 1958a(19). Fixer, The. SCL(1571), 1967a(118). Idiots First. SCL(2159), 1964a(135). Magic Barrel, The. SCLs(171). New Life, A. SCL(3207), 1962a (217). Pictures of Fidelman. 1970a(238).
Malcolm X. Autobiography of Malcolm X, The. SCLs(17).
Malebranche, Nicolas de. Dialogues on Metaphysics and on Religion. WP(422). Treatise Concerning the Search After Truth. CHL(522).
Mallarmé, Stéphane. Poetry of Mallarmé, The. MCLE (4005), MP(283), MP3(821).
Mallea, Eduardo. All Green Shall Perish. SCL(138), 1967a (8). Bay of Silence, The. MAF(47), MCLE(354), MP3(89). Fiesta in November. MCLE(1598), MP4 (335).
Mallet-Joris, François. House of Lies. SCL(2131), 1958a (107).
Malliol, William. Sense of Dark, A. SCL(4203), 1968a(293).
Malone, Dumas. Jefferson and the Ordeal of Liberty. SCL (2316), 1963a(108). Jefferson the President. 1971a (140).
Malory, Sir Thomas. Morte d'Arthur, Le. MCLE(3170), MEF(549), MP1(625).
Malraux, André. Anti-Memoirs. SCL(190), 1969a(14). Man's Fate. MCLE(2901), MEU(475), MP1(559), PO2

(375), SGEN(403). Voices of Silence, The. MCLE (5522), MP4(1263).
Manfred, Frederick F. Lord Grizzly. SCL(2781), 1954a (162).
Mankowitz, Wolf. Old Soldiers Never Die. SCL(3378), 1957a(200).
Mann, Thomas. Black Swan, The. MCLE(431), MP4(74), SCL(439), 1954a(19). Buddenbrooks. MCLE(545), MEU(92), MP1(91), SGEN(236). Confessions of Felix Krull, Confidence Man, The. BM(107), MCLE(832), MEU(150), MP3(218), SCL(889), 1955a(65). Death in Venice. MCLE(1049), MEU(205), MP2(221). Doctor Faustus. MCLE(1199), MEU(240), MP2(258). Joseph and His Brothers. SGEN(252). Magic Mountain, The. MCLE(2833), MEU(466), MP1(545), PO2(451), SGEN (245).
Manners, J. Hartley. Peg O' My Heart. DGAP(186).
Mansfield, Katherine. Short Stories of Katherine Mansfield. MCLE(4800), MEF(793), MP3(970).
Manvell, Roger. Ellen Terry. SCL(1309), 1969a(106).
Manzoni, Alessandro. Betrothed, The. MCLE(392), MEU (74), MP2(88).
Maran, René. Batouala. MCLE(351), MEU(68), MP3(87).
Marcel, Gabriel. Being and Having. CHL(1003). Homo viator. CAL(893). Mystery of Being, The. CAL (966), WP(1120).
March, William. Bad Seed, The. SCL(302), 1954a(10).
Marchand, Leslie A. Byron. BM(56), SCL(583), 1958a(47).
Marie de France. Lais of Marie de France, The. MCLE (2516), MP4(497).
Maritain, Jacques. Art and Scholasticism. CAL(766). Degrees of Knowledge. CAL(828), WP(963). Man and the State. CAL(973). Moral Philosophy. CAL (1094). True Humanism. CHL(1020).
Marius, Richard. Coming of Rain, The. 1970a(82).
Marivaux, Pierre Carlet de Chamblain de. Marianne. MCLE(2925), MEU(478), MP3(631).
Markandaya, Kamala. Nectar in a Sieve. SCL(3190), 1955a (169). Silence of Desire, A. SCL(4285), 1961a(232). Some Inner Fury. SCL(4355), 1957a(250).
Markfield, Wallace. Teitelbaum's Window. 1971a(311). To an Early Grave. SCL(4685), 1965a(296).
Marlowe, Christopher. Doctor Faustus. MCLE(1202), MD (210), MP2(261). Edward the Second. MCLE(1331), MD(239), MP2(286). Jew of Malta, The. MCLE(2339), MD(393), MP1(444). Tamburlaine the Great. MCLE (5092), MD(825), MP1(950), POP(218).

Marot, Clément. Poetry of Marot, The. MCLE(4010), MP4 (890).
Marquand, John P. Late George Apley, The. MAF(332), MCLE(2555), MP1(499), PO2(223), SGAN(260). Point of No Return. PON(314). Sincerely, Willis Wayde. SCL(4294), 1955a(237). Wickford Point. MAF(712), MCLE(5637), MP1(1110). Women and Thomas Harrow. SCL(5136), 1959a(277).
Marquez, Gabriel Garcia. One Hundred Years of Solitude. 1971a(240).
Marret, Mario. Seven Men Among the Penguins. SCL(4218), 1955a(231).
Marryat, Frederick. Mr. Midshipman Easy. MCLE(3096), MEF(524), MP1(602), PON(239). Peter Simple. MCLE(3605), MEF(658), MP2(822).
Marston, John. Malcontent, The. MCLE(2865), MD(486), MP3(619).
Marston, John, George Chapman and Ben Jonson. Eastward Ho! MCLE(1316), MD(234), MP3(317).
Martensen, Hans Lassen. Christian Dogmatics. CHL(712).
Martial. Epigrams of Martial. MCLE(1403), MP(80), MP3 (344).
Martin, George. Verdi. SCL(4880), 1964a(286).
Martin du Gard, Roger. Postman, The. SCL(3663), 1955a (208). World of the Thibaults, The. MCLE(5743), MEU(831), MP1(1130).
Martineau, James. Study of Religion, A. CHL(802).
Marvell, Andrew. Poetry of Marvell, The. MCLE(4013), MP(286), MP3(823).
Marx, Karl. Das Kapital. MCLE(2429), MN(166), MP3(538).
Massie, Robert K. Nicholas and Alexandra. SCL(3220), 1968a(217).
Massinger, Philip. Bondman, The. MCLE(452), MD(89), MP3(116). Maid of Honour, The. MCLE(2845), MD (477), MP3(613). New Way to Pay Old Debts, A. MCLE(3259), MD(569), MP2(732). Roman Actor, The. MCLE(4508), MD(706), MP3(901).
Massinger, Philip and John Fletcher. Beggars' Bush, The. MCLE(368), MD(69), MP3(96).
Masters, Edgar Lee. Spoon River Anthology. MCLE(4968), MP(350), MP3(1015).
Masters, John. Bhowani Junction. SCL(393), 1954a(16).
Mather, Cotton. Magnalia Christi Americana. CHL(557), MCLE(2836), MN(196), MP3(608).
Mathews, Jack. Hanger Stout, Awake! SCL(1911), 1968a (137).
Mathews, Shailer. Growth of the Idea of God, The. CHL

(965).
Matthews, Herbert Lionel. Yoke and the Arrows, The. SCL(5186), 1958a(279).
Matthews, Jack. Beyond the Bridge. 1971a(24).
Matthiessen, Peter. At Play in the Fields of the Lord. SCL(249), 1966a(15). Cloud Forest, The. BM(89), MCLE(776), MP4(136), SCL(775), 1962a(71). Partisans. SCLs(216). Raditzer. SCL(3810), 1962a(239). Sal Si Puedes. 1971a(283). Under the Mountain Wall. SCL(4824), 1963a(272).
Mattingly, Garrett. Armada, The. BM(25), SCL(217), 1960a(13).
Maturin, Charles Robert. Melmoth the Wanderer. MCLE (2985), MEF(488), MP2(653).
Maugham, W. Somerset. Cakes and Ale. MCLE(573), MEF (73), MP1(99). Circle, The. TCP(215). Liza of Lambeth. MCLE(2719), MEF(442), MP2(587). Moon and Sixpence, The. MCLE(3164), MEF(543), MP1 (621). Mystery-Bouffe. TCP(219). Of Human Bondage. MCLE(3338), MEF(592), MP1(670), PO2(105), PON(267), SGBN(270). Summing Up, The. MCLE (5045), MP4(1198).
Maupassant, Guy de. Bel-Ami. MCLE(374), MEU(71), MP1 (62). Mont-Oriol. MCLE(3155), MEU(511), MP1(618). Une Vie. PO(315). Woman's Life, A. MCLE(5711), MEU(828), MP1(1127).
Mauriac, Claude. Dinner Party, The. MCLE(1179), MP4 (235), SCL(1179), 1961a(58). Marquise Went Out at Five, The. SCL(2918), 1963a(139).
Mauriac, François. Frontenacs, The. SCL(1673), 1962a (130). Lamb, The. SCL(2479), 1957a(141). Maltaverne. 1971a(192). Questions of Precedence. SCL (3791), 1960a(209). Thérèse. MCLE(5157), MEU (749), MP3(1066).
Maurice, Frederick Denison. Kingdom of Christ, The. CHL(688).
Maurois, André. Adrienne. SCL(45), 1962a(8). Olympio. SCL(3384), 1957a(203). Prometheus: The Life of Balzac. SCL(3709), 1967a(276). Titans, The. SCL (4682), 1959a(248).
Maximus the Confessor, Saint. Ascetic Life, The. CAL (252).
Maxwell, Gavin. Ring of Bright Water. SCL(3934), 1962a (250).
Maxwell, William. Château, The. SCL(696), 1962a(51).
May, Rollo. Love and Will. 1970a(187).
Mayakovsky, Vladimir. Poetry of Mayakovsky, The. MCLE

(4016), MP4(893).
Mayer, Edwin Justin, Laurence Stallings and Maxwell Anderson. So Red the Rose. DGAP(70).
Mayfield, Sara. Constant Circle, The. SCL(909), 1968a (57).
Meacham, Harry. Caged Panther, The. SCL(595), 1968a (34).
Mead, George Herbert. Mind, Self, and Society. WP(992).
Mead, Richard W. Wall-Street; or, Ten Minutes Before Three. DGAP(34).
Mehnert, Klaus. Peking and Moscow. SCL(3540), 1964a(211).
Melanchthon, Philipp. Loci communes rerum theologicarum. CHL(343).
Meleager. Epigrams of Meleager, The. MCLE(1405), MP4 (280).
Melville, Herman. Benito Cereno. MAF(54), MCLE(385), MP3(98), MPA4(38). Billy Budd, Foretopman. MAF (60), MCLE(416), MP2(92), MPA4(43), PO2(162), SGAN(10). Confidence Man, The. MAF(94), MCLE (835), MP3(221), MPA4(48), PO2(472). Israel Potter. MAF(300), MCLE(2291), MP3(515), MPA4(53). Mardi. MAF(393), MCLE(2915), MP2(623), MPA4(58). Moby Dick. MAF(416), MCLE(3120), MP1(609), MPA4(63), PO(251), PON(244), SGAN(13). Omoo. MAF(467), MCLE(3396), MP1(689), MPA4(69). Pierre. MAF (484), MCLE(3659), MP2(829), MPA4(74). Poetry of Melville, The. MCLE(4019), MP4(896), MPA4(79). Redburn. MAF(521), MCLE(4366), MP2(885), MPA4 (87). Typee. MAF(676), MCLE(5382), MP1(1035), MPA4(92). White-Jacket. MAF(709), MCLE(5629), MP2(1128), MPA4(97).
Menander. Arbitration, The. MCLE(224), MD(44), MP3(54).
Mencius. Meng Tzu. WP(180).
Mencken, H. L. Prejudices: Six Series. MCLE(4231), MN(256), MP3(847).
Menen, Aubrey. Fig Tree, The. SCL(1522), 1960a(74). Ramayana, The. SCL(3831), 1954a(222). SheLa. SCL(4245), 1963a(237).
Meng-lung, Feng. Lieh Kuo Chih. MCLE(2650), MEU(445), MP3(572).
Menotti, Gian-Carlo. Medium, The. DGAP(366).
Meredith, George. Beauchamp's Career. MCLE(343), MEF (48), MP2(83). Diana of the Crossways. MCLE (1152), MEF(154), MP1(206), PO(133). Egoist, The. MCLE(1340), MEF(175), MP1(241), PO2(55), PON(106). Evan Harrington. MCLE(1492), MEF(195), MP2(304). Ordeal of Richard Feverel, The. MCLE(3421), MEF

(611), MP1(692), PO(129), SGBN(139). Poetry of Meredith, The. MCLE(4023), MP4(899).
Meredith, William. Earth Walk. 1971a(66). Wreck of the Thresher and Other Poems, The. SCL(5167), 1965a (324).
Merejkowski, Dmitri. Death of the Gods, The. MCLE (1063), MEU(210), MP1(201). Romance of Leonardo da Vinci, The. MCLE(4514), MEU(646), MP2(911).
Mérimée, Prosper. Carmen. MCLE(623), MEU(108), MP1 (116). Colomba. MCLE(799), MEU(147), MP2(162).
Meriwether, James B. and Michael Millgate, Eds. Lion in the Garden. SCL(2695), 1968a(179).
Merk, Frederick. Monroe Doctrine and American Expansionism, 1843-1849, The. SCL(3068), 1967a(217).
Merrill, James. (Diblos) Notebook, The. SCL(1173), 1966a (69). Fire Screen, The. 1971a(73). Nights and Days. SCL(3257), 1967a(243).
Merton, Thomas. Ascent to Truth. CAL(979). Seeds of Contemplation. CAL(955). Selected Poems. SCL (4185), 1968a(290). Seven Storey Mountain, The. CAL(930).
Merwin, W. S. Moving Target, The. SCL(3123), 1964a(177).
Mewshaw, Michael. Man in Motion. 1971a(195).
Meynell, Alice. Poems of Alice Meynell, The. CAL(775).
Michaels, Sidney. Dylan. SCL(1262), 1965a(74).
Michener, James A. Bridge at Andau, The. SCL(519), 1958a(42). Hawaii. SCL(1956), 1960a(85). Presidential Lottery. 1970a(246).
Middleton, Thomas. Chaste Maid in Cheapside, A. MCLE (694), MD(143), MP3(174). Trick to Catch the Old One, A. MCLE(5315), MD(868), MP2(1059). Women Beware Women. MCLE(5717), MD(946), MP3(1144).
Middleton, Thomas and William Rowley. Changeling, The. MCLE(683), MD(140), MP3(169). Spanish Gipsy, The. MCLE(4948), MD(799), MP3(1011).
Miers, Earl Schenck. Web of Victory, The. BM(601), SCL(4999), 1955a(293).
Mikszáth, Kálmán. St. Peter's Umbrella. MCLE(4582), MEU(654), MP3(914).
Mill, John Stuart. Essay on Liberty. WP(644). On Liberty. MCLE(3401), MN(217), MP3(698). Principles of Political Economy. MCLE(4260), MP4(1034). System of Logic, A. WP(606). Utilitarianism. WP(654).
Millar, George. Crossbowman's Story, A. SCL(958), 1955a (74).
Millay, Edna St. Vincent. Harp-Weaver and Other Poems, The. MCLE(1938), MP(122), MP3(445).

Miller, Arthur. After the Fall. SCL(76), 1965a(3). Crucible, The. SGAP(251), TCP(223). Death of a Salesman. DGAP(378), MCLE(1054), MD(201), MP2 (225), SGAP(244), TCP(226). I Don't Need You Any More. SCL(2149), 1968a(164). Price, The. SCL (3682), 1969a(264). View from the Bridge, A. BM (580), SCL(4896), TCP(229), 1955a(287).
Miller, Heather Ross. Edge of the Woods, The. SCL(1285), 1965a(77). Gone a Hundred Miles. SCL(1809), 1969a (135).
Miller, Henry. Tropic of Capricorn. MCLE(5341), MP4 (1234).
Miller, Merle. Day in Late September, A. SCL(1050), 1964a(61). Reunion. SCL(3913), 1954a(231).
Miller, Perry. Life of the Mind in America, The. SCLs (160).
Miller, Vassar. My Bones Being Wiser. SCLs(191).
Millett, Kate. Sexual Politics. 1971a(290).
Millgate, Michael and James B. Meriwether, Eds. Lion in the Garden. SCL(2695), 1968a(179).
Millis, Walter. Arms and Men. SCL(225), 1957a(10).
Milton, John. Areopagitica. MCLE(230), MP4(42). Comus. MCLE(817), MD(168), MP3(210). Lyric Poetry of Milton, The. MCLE(2800), MP4(577). Paradise Lost. CHL(511), MCLE(3493), MP(202), MP1(711). Paradise Regained. MCLE(3495), MP(204), MP3(711). Samson Agonistes. MCLE(4598), MD(728), MP3(920).
Mishima, Yukio. Death in Midsummer and Other Stories. SCL(1084), 1967a(71). Sound of Waves, The. MCLE (4940), MP4(1171), SCL(4385), 1957a(255). Temple of the Golden Pavilion, The. SCL(4541), 1960a(266).
Mistral, Gabriela. Poetry of Gabriela Mistral, The. MCLE (3895), MP4(810).
Mitchell, Broadus. Alexander Hamilton. SCL(125), 1958a (14).
Mitchell, Langdon. New York Idea, The. DGAP(161).
Mitchell, Margaret. Gone with the Wind. MAF(214), MCLE (1800), MP3(424), PO2(260).
Mitchell, Silas Weir. Hugh Wynne, Free Quaker. MAF(285), MCLE(2151), MP1(390).
Mitford, Mary Russell. Our Village. MCLE(3464), MEF (628), MP2(788).
Mitford, Nancy. Voltaire in Love. SCL(4923), 1959a(266).
Mivart, St. George Jackson. On the Genesis of the Species. CAL(682).
Möhler, Johann Adam. Symbolism. CAL(640).
Molière. Bourgeois Gentleman, The. MCLE(476), MD(98),

MP2(111). Doctor in Spite of Himself, The. MCLE (1205), MD(213), MP3(289). Don Juan. MCLE(1240), MD(221), MP3(296). Hypochondriac, The. MCLE (2178), MD(369), MP2(474). Misanthrope, The. MCLE(3068), MD(535), MP1(595), POP(259). Miser, The. MCLE(3072), MD(537), MP2(673). Romantic Ladies, The. MCLE(4527), MD(709), MP2(918). School for Husbands, The. MCLE(4647), MD(736), MP3(938). School for Wives, The. MCLE(4653), MD(742), MP2(940). Tartuffe. MCLE(5113), MD(831), MP1(959), POP(262).

Molnár, Ferenc. Guardsman, The. POP(333). Liliom. MCLE(2684), MD(444), MP1(511), POP(337), TCP (232).

Momaday, N. Scott. House Made of Dawn. SCL(2119), 1969a(156). Way to Rainy Mountain, The. 1970a(335).

Monsarrat, Nicholas. Tribe That Lost Its Head, The. SCL (4763), 1957a(275).

Montagu, Ewen. Man Who Never Was, The. SCL(2868), 1954a(168).

Montaigne, Michel Eyquem de. Apology for Raimond Sebond. WP(359). Essais. MCLE(1423), MN(104), MP3(352).

Montesquieu, Charles de. Persian Letters. MCLE(3589), MN(234), MP3(736). Spirit of the Laws, The. MCLE (4959), MP4(1178).

Montgomery, Viscount. Memoirs of Field-Marshal Montgomery, The. SCL(2983), 1959a(162).

Montherlant, Henry de. Bachelors, The. SCL(288), 1962a (24). Queen After Death. TCP(236).

Montini, Giovanni Battista Cardinal (Pope Paul VI). Church, The. CAL(1118).

Monzaemon, Chikamatsu. Sonezaki Shinjû. MCLE(4897), MD(795), MP3(1006).

Moody, William Vaughn. Great Divide, The. DGAP(157).

Moore, Barrington, Jr. Social Origins of Dictatorship and Democracy. SCL(4334), 1967a(306).

Moore, Brian. Answer from Limbo, An. SCL(188), 1963a (7). Emperor of Ice-Cream, The. SCL(1334), 1966a (85). Feast of Lupercal, The. SCL(1505), 1958a(86). I Am Mary Dunne. SCL(2145), 1969a(160). Lonely Passion of Judith Hearne, The. SCL(2739), 1957a (159). Luck of Ginger Coffey, The. SCL(2810), 1961a (171).

Moore, Doris Langley. Late Lord Byron, The. BM(301), SCL(2542), 1962a(180).

Moore, George. Esther Waters. MCLE(1468), MEF(184), MP1(254), PO2(83).

Moore, George Edward. Philosophical Studies. WP(842). Principia ethica. WP(755).
Moore, Marianne. Complete Poems. SCL(369), 1968a(47). (Translator) Fables of La Fontaine, The. SCL(1431), 1954a(65). Like a Bulwark. BM(332), SCL(2675), 1957a(156). O to Be a Dragon. BM(401), SCL(3345), 1960a(177). Poetry of Marianne Moore, The. MCLE (4008), MP4(889). Tell Me, Tell Me. SCL(4529), 1967a(313).
Moore, Thomas. Irish Melodies. MCLE(2288), MP4(460). Lalla Rookh. MCLE(2522), MP(154), MP3(548).
Moorehead, Alan. Blue Nile, The. SCL(464), 1963a(12). Cooper's Creek. SCL(919), 1965a(52). Fatal Impact, The. SCL(1477), 1967a(111). Gallipoli. BM(205), SCL(1690), 1957a(81). White Nile, The. BM(604), SCL(5045), 1962a(304).
Moraes, Frank. India Today. SCL(2219), 1961a(127).
Morante, Elsa. Arturo's Island. SCL(229), 1960a(16).
Moravia, Alberto. Bitter Honeymoon. SCL(425), 1957a(29). Empty Canvas, The. SCL(1340), 1962a(110). Ghost at Noon, A. SCL(1734), 1955a(104). Lie, The. SCL (2634), 1967a(194). Two Adolescents. SGEN(448). Two Women. MCLE(5376), MP4(1245), SCL(4817), 1959a(254). Woman of Rome, The. MCLE(5708), MEU(825), MP2(1153).
More, Paul Elmer. Shelburne Essays. MCLE(4750), MP4 (1112).
More, Sir Thomas. Dialogue of Comfort Against Tribulation, A. CHL(354). History of King Richard III. MCLE (2051), MP4(417). Treatise on the Passion. CAL (538). Utopia. CAL(509), MCLE(5439), MN(312), MP3(1095), WP(348).
Morgan, Charles. Burning Glass, The. SCL(562), 1954a (28).
Morier, James. Hajji Baba of Ispahan. MCLE(1903), MEF (260), MP1(343).
Mörike, Eduard. Poetry of Mörike, The. MCLE(4030), MP4(904).
Morison, Samuel Eliot. Christopher Columbus, Mariner. BM(76), SCL(738), 1955a(53). John Paul Jones: A Sailor's Biography. BM(264), SCL(2355), 1960a(111). Leyte: June 1944-January 1945. BM(326), SCL(2624), 1959a(147). "Old Bruin." SCL(3366), 1968a(234). Victory in the Pacific, 1945. SCL(4890), 1961a(275).
Morris, Charles W. Signs, Language and Behavior. WP (1102).
Morris, Desmond. Naked Ape, The. SCL(3163), 1969a(239).

Morris, Donald R. Washing of the Spears, The. SCL(4970), 1966a(326).
Morris, James. Islam Inflamed. SCL(2266), 1958a(117). Pax Britannica. SCL(3526), 1969a(260).
Morris, Richard B. Peacemakers, The. SCL(3530), 1966a (230).
Morris, William. Defence of Guenevere and Other Poems, The. MCLE(1094), MP4(204). Earthly Paradise, The. MCLE(1311), MP4(255).
Morris, Willie. North Toward Home. SCL(3292), 1968a(227).
Morris, Wright. Cause for Wonder. SCL(655), 1964a(49). Ceremony in Lone Tree. BM(66), MCLE(672), MP4 (121), SCL(670), 1961a(33). Field of Vision, The. MCLE(1591), MP4(331), SCLs(98). One Day. SCL (3412), 1966a(213). What a Way to Go! SCL(5008), 1963a(290).
Mortimer, Lillian. No Mother to Guide Her. DGAP(152).
Morton, Frederic. Rothschilds, The. SCL(4006), 1963a(221). Schatten Affair, The. SCL(4086), 1966a(283).
Moschus. Poetry of Moschus, The. MCLE(4033), MP4(907).
Mosley, Leonard. On Borrowed Time. 1970a(228).
Mossiker, Frances. Queen's Necklace, The. SCL(3784), 1962a(232).
Mo Ti. Mo Tzu. WP(31).
Motley, Willard. Knock on Any Door. SCLs(151). Let No Man Write My Epitaph. SCLs(157).
Mounier, Emmanuel. Character of Man, The. CAL(902).
Mouroux, Jean. Meaning of Man, The. CAL(933).
Mowat, Farley. Dog Who Wouldn't Be, The. SCL(1199), 1958a(76).
Mühlenberg, Henry Melchior. Journals of Henry Melchior Mühlenberg, The. CHL(620).
Muir, John. Story of My Boyhood and Youth, The. MCLE (5006), MP4(1183).
Mulock, Dinah Maria. John Halifax, Gentleman. MCLE (2353), MEF(373), MP2(511).
Multatuli. Max Havelaar. MCLE(2964), MEU(485), MP3 (639).
Mumford, Lewis. Brown Decades, The. MCLE(537), MP4 (97). City in History, The. SCL(756), 1962a(64).
Murdoch, Frank Hitchcock. Davy Crockett. DGAP(99).
Murdoch, Iris. Bell, The. BM(35), MCLE(377), MP4(67), SCL(362), 1959a(23). Flight from the Enchanter, The. SCL(1584), 1957a(70). Severed Head, A. SCL(4233), 1962a(266). Unicorn, The. SCL(4828), 1964a(281). Unofficial Rose, An. SCL(4841), 1963a(276).
Murger, Henri. Bohemians of the Latin Quarter, The.

MCLE(449), MEU(77), MP2(104).
Murray, John Courtney, S.J. We Hold These Truths. CAL (1098).
Murray, Marris. Fire-Raisers, The. SCL(1544), 1954a(74).
Musil, Robert. Man Without Qualities: Volume II, The. SCL(2871), 1954a(171).
Musset, Alfred de. No Trifling with Love. MCLE(3297), MD(571), MP2(748). Poetry of Musset, The. MCLE (4035), MP4(908).
Mydans, Shelley. Thomas. SCL(4614), 1966a(309).
Myrdal, Jan. Confessions of a Disloyal European. SCL (885), 1969a(76).
Myrivilis, Stratis. Mermaid Madonna, The. SCL(3008), 1960a(168).

Nabokov, Vladimir. Ada or Ardor: A Family Chronicle. 1970a(1). Defense, The. SCL(1114), 1965a(69). Despair. SCL(1141), 1967a(78). Gift, The. SCL (1746), 1964a(110). King, Queen, Knave. SCL(2438), 1969a(181). Lolita. SCL(2733), 1959a(150). Mary. 1971a(202). Pale Fire. BM(418), MCLE(3476), MP4 (662), SCL(3497), 1963a(165). Pnin. SCL(3611), 1958a(191). Real Life of Sebastian Knight, The. MCLE(4343), MP4(1046), SCL(3837), 1960a(220). Speak, Memory. SCL(4395), 1968a(305).
Nai-an, Shih. All Men Are Brothers. MCLE(98), MEU(12), MP3(24).
Naipaul, V. S. Loss of El Dorado, The. 1971a(178).
Narayan, R. K. Financial Expert, The. SCLs(105). Guide, The. MCLE(1880), MP4(399), SCL(1893), 1959a(109). Man-Eater of Malgudi, The. SCL(2888), 1962a(199).
Nash, Thomas. Unfortunate Traveller, The. MCLE(5430), MEF(900), MP2(1092).
Nathan, Leonard. Day the Perfect Speakers Left, The. 1970a(94).
Nehls, Edward, Editor. D. H. Lawrence: A Composite Biography. BM(129), SCL(1159), 1960a(60).
Nekrasov, Nikolai. Poetry of Nekrasov, The. MCLE(4038), MP4(911).
Nemerov, Howard. Mirrors & Windows: Poems. SCL (3043), 1959a(165).
Neruda, Pablo. Heights of Macchu Picchu, The. SCL(1974), 1968a(149). Poetry of Neruda, The. MCLE(4041), MP4(913).
Nerval, Gérard de. Poetry of Nerval, The. MCLE(4044), MP4(916).
Nestorius. Bazaar of Heraclides, The. CHL(162).

Nevins, Allan. Ford: The Times, The Man, The Company. SCL(1625), 1954a(83). War for the Union, The, Vol. I. BM(590), SCL(4953), 1960a(286). War for the Union, The, Vol. II. BM(594), SCL(4957), 1961a(284).

Nevins, Allan and Frank Ernest Hill. Ford: Decline and Rebirth, 1933-1962. SCL(1619), 1964a(96). Ford: Expansion and Challenge, 1915-1933. SCL(1622), 1958a(96).

Newby, P. H. Guest and His Going, A. SCL(1890), 1961a (113). Picnic at Sakkara, The. SCL(3567), 1955a (202).

Newman, John Henry, Cardinal. Apologia pro vita sua. CAL (661), CHL(743), MCLE(205), MN(20), MP3(49). Essay on the Development of Christian Doctrine, An. CAL(644). Grammar of Assent, A. CAL(678), WP (666). Idea of a University, The. CAL(653).

Newton, Sir Isaac. Philosophiae naturalis principia mathematica. MCLE(3628), MN(239), MP3(743).

Nexö, Martin Andersen. Pelle the Conqueror. MCLE(3555), MEU(571), MP3(730), SGEN(304).

Nicholas of Cusa. Of Learned Ignorance. CAL(482), CHL (312), WP(343).

Nichols, Anne. Abie's Irish Rose. DGAP(199), POP(35).

Nicolson, Sir Harold. Harold Nicolson: Diaries and Letters, 1930-1939. SCL(1936), 1967a(138). Harold Nicolson: Diaries and Letters, 1939-1945. SCL(1941), 1968a (145). Harold Nicolson: Diaries and Letters, 1945-1962. SCL(1945), 1969a(144). Sainte-Beuve. SCL (4058), 1958a(219). Some People. MCLE(4889), MP4 (1159).

Niebuhr, H. Richard. Christ and Culture. CHL(1121). Meaning of Revelation, The. CHL(1054).

Niebuhr, Reinhold. Faith and History. CHL(1104). Nature and Destiny of Man, The. CHL(1059), WP(1064).

Nietzsche, Friedrich Wilhelm. Beyond Good and Evil. MCLE(401), MN(39), MP3(108), WP(696). Thus Spake Zarathustra. MCLE(5194), MN(297), MP3(1069), WP (686).

Nievo, Ippolito. Castle of Fratta, The. MCLE(638), MEU (115), MP3(158), SCL(638), 1959a(28).

Nin, Anaïs. Diary of Anaïs Nin: 1931-1934, The. SCL (1166), 1967a(84). Diary of Anaïs Nin: 1934-1939, The. SCL(1170), 1968a(83). Spy in the House of Love, A. SCL(4423), 1954a(261).

Noah, Mordecai Manuel. She Would Be a Soldier. DGAP(30).

Noble, William and James Leo Herlihy. Blue Denim. SCLs (41).

Nordhoff, Charles and James Norman Hall. Mutiny on the Bounty. MAF(427), MCLE(3195), MP1(628), SGAN(233).
Norgay, Tenzing. Tiger of the Snows. SCL(4658), 1955a (265).
Norris, Frank. McTeague. MAF(367), MCLE(2818), MP1 (537), MPA4(102). Octopus, The. SGAN(85). Pit, The. MAF(493), MCLE(3689), MP1(756), MPA4(107). Responsibilities of the Novelist, The. MCLE(4408), MP4(1061).
Norton, Thomas and Thomas Sackville. Gorboduc. MCLE (1814), MD(309), MP2(379).
Nowell, Elizabeth. Thomas Wolfe. BM(547), SCL(4622), 1961a(251).
Nugent, Elliott and James Thurber. Male Animal, The. DGAP(330), SGAP(110).
Nygren, Anders. Agape and Eros. CHL(946).

Oates, Joyce Carol. Anonymous Sins and Other Poems. 1970a(31). By the North Gate. SCL(580), 1964a(43). Expensive People. SCL(1408), 1969a(122). Garden of Earthly Delights, A. SCL(1702), 1968a(122). Love and Its Derangements. 1971a(181). them. 1970a(307). Upon the Sweeping Flood. SCL(4854), 1967a(336). Wheel of Love, The. 1971a(346). With Shuddering Fall. SCL(5119), 1965a(313).
O'Brien, Flann. Third Policeman, The. SCL(4601), 1968a (321).
O'Brien, Kate. Last of Summer, The. MCLE(2535), MEF (422), MP2(558).
O'Casey, Sean. Bishop's Bonfire, The. SCL(418), 1955a(23). Drums of Father Ned, The. SCL(1255), 1961a(64). Cock-a-Doodle Dandy. TCP(239). Juno and the Paycock. MCLE(2416), MD(405), MP3(533), POP(227), TCP(241). Plough and the Stars, The. MCLE(3712), MD(645), MP2(840), TCP(244). Purple Dust. MCLE (4291), MD(667), MP3(857), TCP(247). Within the Gates. MCLE(5693), MD(934), MP3(1134).
O'Connor, Edwin. Edge of Sadness, The. SCL(1275), 1962a (103). Last Hurrah, The. BM(294), SCL(2514), 1957a(144).
O'Connor, Flannery. Everything That Rises Must Converge. SCL(1398), 1966a(97). Good Man Is Hard to Find, A. SCL(1815), 1955a(109). Mystery and Manners. SCLs (196). Short Stories of Flannery O'Connor, The. MCLE(4790), MP4(1136). Violent Bear It Away, The. MCLE(5492), MP4(1261), SCL(4903), 1961a(278). Wise Blood. MCLE(5687), MP4(1296).

O'Connor, Frank. Domestic Relations. SCL(1213), 1958a (78). My Father's Son. 1970a(215). Only Child, An. SCL(3432), 1962a(227).
O'Dea, Thomas. American Catholic Dilemma. CAL(1066).
Odets, Clifford. Awake and Sing! SGAP(183), TCP(251). Flowering Peach, The. TCP(253). Golden Boy. MCLE(1793), MD(305), MP3(422), TCP(255). Waiting for Lefty. DGAP(285), TCP(257).
O'Faoláin, Seán. Finest Stories of Seán O'Faoláin, The. SCL(1538), 1958a(88). I Remember! I Remember! SCL(2152), 1963a(86). Nest of Simple Folk, A. MCLE(3245), MEF(561), MP2(728). Vive moi! SCL (4910), 1965a(305).
O'Flaherty, Liam. Informer, The. MCLE(2249), MEF(343), MP2(486). Stories of Liam O'Flaherty, The. SCL (4458), 1957a(258).
O'Hara, John. And Other Stories. SCL(173), 1969a(10). Appointment in Samarra. MAF(33), MCLE(216), MP2 (46), SGAN(253). Cape Cod Lighter, The. SCL(619), 1963a(18). From the Terrace. SCL(1670), 1959a(94). Hat on the Bed, The. SCL(1953), 1964a(121). Horse Knows the Way, The. SCL(2105), 1965a(136). Instrument, The. SCL(2258), 1968a(166). Ourselves to Know. SCL(3478), 1961a(195). Ten North Frederick. SCL(4545), 1955a(249).
Okumiya, Masatake and Mitsuo Fuchida. Midway. SCL (3029), 1955a(160).
Oldenbourg, Zoé. Cornerstone, The. MCLE(878), MP4(162), SCL(926), 1955a(68). Crusades, The. SCL(969), 1967a(59). Massacre at Montségur. SCL(2934), 1963a(142).
Olsen, Paul. Country of Old Men. SCL(937), 1967a(56). Virgin of San Gil, The. SCL(4906), 1966a(322).
Olsen, Tillie. Tell Me a Riddle. SCL(4527), 1962a(296).
Oman, John Wood. Natural and the Supernatural, The. CHL(973).
O'Neill, Eugene. Ah, Wilderness! DGAP(260), SGAP(20). Anna Christie. DGAP(195), MCLE(177), MD(37), MP2(35). Desire Under the Elms. DGAP(221), MCLE(1131), MD(206), MP2(247), SGAP(7), TCP(259). Emperor Jones, The. MCLE(1377), MD(249), MP2 (291), POP(27). Great God Brown, The. TCP(261). Hairy Ape, The. DGAP(202). Iceman Cometh, The. SGAP(24), TCP(265). Long Day's Journey into Night. BM(347), DGAP(339), MCLE(2731), SCL(2753), SGAP (30), 1957a(162). Mourning Becomes Electra. MCLE (3184), MD(559), MP2(710), SGAP(12), TCP(273).

Strange Interlude. MCLE(5013), MD(808), MP2(1000), TCP(280). Touch of the Poet, A. BM(558), SCL (4720), 1958a(239).
Ong, Walter J., S.J. American Catholic Crossroads. CAL (1076).
Ooka, Shohei. Fires on the Plain. SCL(1547), 1958a(91).
Oppen, George. Of Being Numerous. SCL(3349), 1969a(252).
Origen. Against Celsus. CHL(66). Contra Celsum. CAL (71). De primcipiis. WP(240). On First Principles. CAL(65), CHL(57).
Orosius, Paulus. Seven Books of History Against the Pagans. CAL(178), CHL(145).
Ortega y Gasset, José. Revolt of the Masses, The. MCLE (4432), MN(266), MP3(886).
Orwell, George. Nineteen Eighty-Four. MCLE(3291), MEF (578), MP2(746), PO2(143), SGBN(343).
Osaragi, Jiro. Journey, The. SCL(2371), 1961a(137).
Osborne, John. Inadmissible Evidence. SCL(2205), 1966a (129). Look Back in Anger. BM(354), MCLE(2734), MP4(563), SCL(2771), TCP(288), 1958a(153). Luther. TCP(290).
Otloh of St. Emmeram. Book of Proverbs. CAL(276).
Otto, Rudolf. Idea of the Holy, The. CHL(882), WP(810).
Otto of Freising. Two Cities, The. CAL(316).
Otway, Thomas. Orphan, The. MCLE(3448), MD(592), MP3(707). Soldier's Fortune, The. MCLE(4886), MD(792), MP3(1004). Venice Preserved. MCLE(5457), MD(894), MP2(1098).
Ouida. Under Two Flags. MCLE(5420), MEF(895), MP1 (1049).
Ovid. Amores. MCLE(144), MP4(41). Ars amatoria. MCLE(244), MP4(45). Heroides. MCLE(2019), MP4 (413). Metamorphoses, The. MCLE(3028), MP(184), MP3(658).
Owen, Guy. Journey for Joedel. 1971a(152).
Owen, John. Discourse Concerning the Holy Spirit. CHL (518).
Owen, Wilfred. Poetry of Owen, The. MCLE(4051), MP4 (922).
Oxford/Cambridge University Presses. New English Bible, The. SCL(3205), 1962a(215).

Packard, Vance. Hidden Persuaders, The. BM(231), SCL (2028), 1958a(104). Status Seekers, The. SCL(4429), 1960a(251). Waste Makers, The. SCL(4973), 1961a (287).
Page, Thomas Nelson. Marse Chan. MAF(399), MCLE

(2941), MP2(638).
Paine, Thomas. Age of Reason, The. MCLE(56), MP4(11). Crisis, The. MCLE(938), MN(69), MP3(238).
Painter, George D. Proust: The Early Years. BM(459), SCL(3731), 1960a(206). Proust: The Later Years. SCL(3735), 1966a(252).
Paley, William. Natural Theology. CHL(641). View of the Evidences of Christianity, A. WP(563).
Paris, Matthew. Chronica majora. CAL(376).
Park, Mungo. Travels to the Interior Districts of Africa. MCLE(5287), MP4(1227).
Parker, De Witt Henry. Experience and Substance. WP (1070).
Parker, Louis Napoleon. Disraeli. POP(109).
Parker, Theodore. Transient and Permanent in Christianity, The. CHL(700).
Parkinson, C. Northcote. Evolution of Political Thought, The. SCL(1401), 1959a(75).
Parkman, Francis. Count Frontenac and New France Under Louis XIV. MCLE(886), MP4(164). Old Regime in Canada, The. MCLE(3376), MP4(643). Oregon Trail, The. MCLE(3425), MN(222), MP1(695).
Parmenides of Elea. Way of Opinion, The. WP(16). Way of Truth, The. WP(16).
Parrington, Vernon Louis. Main Currents in American Thought. MCLE(2851), MP4(586).
Pascal, Blaise. Pensées. CHL(515), MCLE(3569), MN(231), MP3(732), WP(410).
Pasinetti, P. M. Venetian Red. SCL(4877), 1961a(272).
Pasternak, Boris. Doctor Zhivago. BM(133), MCLE(1216), MP4(241), PON(96), SCL(1194), SGEN(467), 1959a(57). Poems. SCL(3624), 1960a(199). Poetry of Pasternak, The. MCLE(4053), MP4(924).
Paston Family. Paston Letters, The. MCLE(3515), MP4 (673).
Pastor, Ludwig von. History of the Popes from the Close of the Middle Ages, The. CAL(796).
Pater, Walter. Marius the Epicurean. MCLE(2928), MEF (472), MP2(630). Renaissance, The. MCLE(4392), MP4(1052).
Paton, Alan. Cry, The Beloved Country. MCLE(957), MEU (185), MP2(202), PO2(490).
Patrick, John. Teahouse of the August Moon, The. BM (533), DGAP(390), SCL(4517), 1954a(273).
Patrick, Saint. Writings of Saint Patrick, The. CAL(207).
Paulding, James Kirke. Bucktails, The; or, Americans in England. DGAP(64).

Paustovsky, Konstantin. Story of a Life, The. SCLs(295).
Paz, Octavio. Labyrinth of Solitude, The. MCLE(2491), MP4(489), SCL(2462), 1963a(117). Poetry of Paz, The. MCLE(4055), MP4(926).
Peacock, Thomas Love. Crotchet Castle. MCLE(953), MEF (129), MP2(201). Headlong Hall. MCLE(1947), MEF (278), MP2(414). Nightmare Abbey. MCLE(3289), MEF(576), MP1(657), PO2(28).
Peare, Catherine Owens. William Penn. SCL(5085), 1958a (270).
Pearson, Hasketh. Merry Monarch. BM(367), SCL(3014), 1961a(177).
Peattie, Donald Culross. Almanac for Moderns, An. MCLE (115), MP4(30).
Peele, George. Old Wives' Tale, The. MCLE(3385), MP2 (771).
Péguy, Charles. Basic Verities. CAL(879). Poetry of Péguy, The. MCLE(4058), MP4(928).
Peirce, Charles Sanders. Collected Papers. WP(952).
Pepys, Samuel. Diary. MCLE(1161), MN(89), MP3(283).
Percy, Walker. Last Gentleman, The. SCL(2508), 1967a (184). Moviegoer, The. SCL(3119), 1962a(212).
Pereda, José María de. Pedro Sánchez. MCLE(3549), MEU(569), MP3(728). Peñas arriba. MCLE(3561), MEU(574), MP3(730). Sotileza. MCLE(4930), MEU (714), MP2(985).
Perry, Ralph Barton. General Theory of Value. WP(874).
Petersen, Donald. Spectral Boy, The. SCL(4399), 1966a (306).
Petrakis, Harry Mark. Dream of Kings, A. SCL(1240), 1968a(86). Pericles on 31st Street. SCLs(219).
Petrarch, Francesco. On His Own Ignorance. CAL(469). Rime of Petrarch, Le. MCLE(4458), MP(315), MP3 (893).
Petronius, Gaius. Satyricon, The. MCLE(4638), MEU(668), MP2(938).
Phillips, R. Hart. Cuba: Island of Paradox. SCL(976), 1960a(48).
Picard, Max. World of Silence, The. CAL(936).
Pick, Robert. Escape of Socrates, The. SCL(1386), 1954a (58).
Pico della Mirandola, Giovanni. Oration on the Dignity of Man. CAL(487), MCLE(3416), MP4(655).
Pieper, Josef. Belief and Faith. CAL(1121). End of Time, The. CAL(964). Leisure the Basis of Culture. CAL (940).
Pierce, Ovid Williams. On a Lonesome Porch. SCL(3387),

1961a(188).
Piercy, Marge. Dance the Eagle to Sleep. 1971a(55).
Pigafetta, Antonio. Voyage of Magellan. SCLs(328).
Pilnyak, Boris. Naked Year, The. MCLE(3219), MEU(526), MP2(719).
Pindar. Epinicia, The. MCLE(1408), MP(82), MP3(346).
Pinero, Arthur Wing. Mid-Channel. MCLE(3037), MD(525), MP3(661). Second Mrs. Tanqueray, The. MCLE (4684), MD(750), MP2(947), POP(134). Trelawney of the Wells. POP(138).
Pinter, Harold. Caretaker, The. MCLE(620), MP4(110). Three Plays. SCL(4631), 1963a(267).
Pirandello, Luigi. Henry IV. TCP(293). Late Mattia Pascal, The. MCLE(2558), MEU(433), MP2(562). Naked. TCP(296). Old and the Young, The. MCLE (3349), MEU(552), MP1(676). Right You Are - If You Think You Are. MCLE(4455), MD(697), MP3(891), TCP(298). Six Characters in Search of an Author. MCLE(4848), MD(783), MP3(993), POP(277), TCP(301). Tonight We Improvise. TCP(305).
Pitt, Barrie. 1918: The Last Act. SCL(3273), 1964a(191).
Pius XI, Pope. Atheistic Communism. CAL(858). Casti connubii. CAL(808). Christian Education of Youth, The. CAL(801). Mit brennender Sorge. CAL(860). Quadragesimo anno. CAL(812).
Pius XII, Pope. Divino afflante Spiritu. CAL(883). Mediator Dei. CAL(915). Mystical Body of Christ, The. CAL(886).
Plath, Sylvia. Ariel. SCL(208), 1967a(17). Colossus and Other Poems, The. SCLs(77).
Plato. Apology. WP(42). Crito. WP(54). Dialogues of Plato, The. MCLE(1148), MN(82), MP3(277). Euthyphro. WP(49). Gorgias. WP(70). Laws. WP (131). Meno. WP(64). Parmenides. WP(106). Phaedo. WP(81). Phaedrus. WP(95). Philebus. WP(120). Protagoras. WP(59). Republic, The. MCLE(4402), MN(263), MP3(876), WP(88). Sophist. WP(110). Statesman. WP(116). Symposium. WP (74). Theaetetus. WP(98). Timaeus. WP(125).
Plautus, Titus Maccius. Amphitryon. MCLE(146), MD(25), MP2(24). Braggart Soldier, The. MCLE(484), MD (100), MP3(123). Captives, The. MCLE(618), MD (130), MP2(134). Menaechmi, The. MCLE(3015), MD(511), MP3(654), POP(387). Pot of Gold, The. MCLE(4206), MD(653), MP2(849). Slipknot, The. MCLE(4857), MD(789), MP3(997). Trickster, The. MCLE(5318), MD(871), MP3(1081).

Plievier, Theodor. Berlin. SCL(371), 1958a(33). Moscow. SCL(3096), 1954a(177).
(Pliny), Gaius Plinius Caecilius Secundus. Letters of Pliny the Younger, The. MCLE(2620), MP4(530).
Plomer, William. Museum Pieces. SCL(3133), 1954a(183).
Plotinus. Enneads. WP(245).
Plunkett, James. Trusting and the Maimed, The. SCL (4780), 1955a(281).
Plutarch. Parallel Lives. MCLE(3498), MN(225), MP3(713).
Plutzik, Hyam. Horatio. SCL(2102), 1962a(152).
Poe, Edgar Allan. Essays of Edgar Allan Poe, The. MCLE (1452), MP4(299), MPA5(7). Fall of the House of Usher, The. MAF(177), MCLE(1540), MP2(316), MPA5(14). Gold Bug, The. MAF(209), MCLE(1779), MP2(373), MPA5(18). Ligeia. MAF(343), MCLE (2679), MP2(583), MPA5(22). Narrative of Arthur Gordon Pym, The. MAF(433), MCLE(3228), MP1(640), MPA5(26).
Pogue, Forrest C. George C. Marshall: Education of a General. SCL(1722), 1964a(107). George C. Marshall: Ordeal and Hope, 1939-1942. SCL(1725), 1967a(122).
Politian. Orfeo. MCLE(3428), MD(590), MP3(702).
Polo, Marco. Travels of Marco Polo. MCLE(5283), MN(303), MP1(1011).
Polycarp of Smyrna, Saint. Epistle to the Philippians. CHL (17). Epistles. CAL(16). Martyrdom of Saint Polycarp, The. CAL(16).
Pomerius, Julianus. Contemplative Life, The. CAL(220).
Poncins, Gontran de. Ghost Voyage, The. SCL(1737), 1954a(89).
Pond, Hugh. Salerno. SCL(4061), 1963a(231).
Pontoppidan, Henrik. Promised Land, The. MCLE(4284), MEU(605), MP2(869).
Pope, Alexander. Dunciad, The. MCLE(1299), MP(72), MP3(310). Essay on Criticism. MCLE(1432), MP4 (287). Essay on Man. MCLE(1435), MP4(290). Rape of the Lock, The. MCLE(4335), MP(313), MP1 (802).
Pope, Dudley. Decision at Trafalgar. BM(121), SCL(1102), 1961a(55).
Pope-Hennessy, James. Queen Mary. BM(463), SCL(3770), 1961a(200).
Porter, Cole and Samuel and Bella Spewack. Kiss Me, Kate. DGAP(374).
Porter, Jane. Scottish Chiefs, The. MCLE(4658), MEF(775), MP2(942). Thaddeus of Warsaw. MCLE(5144), MEF

(830), MP1(967).
Porter, Katherine Ann. Collected Stories of Katherine Anne Porter, The. SCL(835), 1966a(51). Old Mortality. MAF(460), MCLE(3370), MEF(598), MP2(766). Pale Horse, Pale Rider. MCLE(3479), MP4(665). Ship of Fools. MCLE(4763), MP4(1118), SCL(4254), 1963a (240).
Porter, William Sydney. Short Stories of O. Henry. MAF (578), MCLE(4803), MP3(972).
Portis, Charles. True Grit. SCL(4773), 1969a(321).
Postman, Neil and Charles Weingartner. Teaching as a Subversive Activity. 1970a(303).
Potok, Chaim. Chosen, The. SCL(731), 1968a(41).
Pottle, Frederick A. James Boswell: The Earlier Years, 1740-1769. SCL(2281), 1967a(168).
Pound, Ezra. Cantos. MCLE(603), MP(38), MP3(151). Personae. MCLE(3593), MP4(681).
Powell, Anthony. Acceptance World, The. BM(4), SCL(15), 1957a(1). Afternoon Men. SCL(78), 1964a(4). At Lady Molly's. BM(28), SCL(246), 1959a(17). Casanova's Chinese Restaurant. BM(60), SCL(632), 1961a (30). Dance to the Music of Time, A. MCLE(995), MP4(178), SCL(993), 1963a(28). Dance to the Music of Time: Second Movement, A. MCLE(1000), MP4 (183). Kindly Ones, The. SCL(2421), 1963a(115). Military Philosophers. 1970a(207). Soldier's Art, The. SCL(4346), 1969a(294). Valley of Bones, The. SCL(4864), 1965a(302).
Powell, Dawn. Golden Spur, The. SCL(1803), 1963a(76). Wicked Pavilion, The. SCL(5058), 1954a(291).
Powell, Sumner Chilton. Puritan Village. SCLs(234).
Powers, J. F. Morte d'Urban. SCL(3087), 1963a(151). Presence of Grace, The. SCL(3674), 1957a(209).
Powys, John Cowper. Wolf Solent. MCLE(5696), MEF(962), MP3(1136).
Powys, Llewelyn. Ebony and Ivory. MCLE(1319), MEF(173), MP3(320).
Powys, T. F. Mr. Weston's Good Wine. MCLE(3105), MEF(530), MP2(686).
Pratt, James Bissett. Personal Realism. WP(1016).
Prescott, H. F. M. Once to Sinai. SCL(3406), 1959a(187). Son of Dust. SCL(4366), 1957a(252).
Prescott, William Hickling. History of the Conquest of Mexico. MCLE(2059), MN(143), MP3(471).
Prévost, Abbé. Manon Lescaut. MCLE(2898), MEU(472), MP1(557), PO2(297).
Price, Henry Habberley. Perception. WP(968).

Price, Reynolds. Generous Man, A. SCLs(115). Long and Happy Life, A. MCLE(2721), MP4(561), SCL(2748), 1963a(135). Love and Work. SCL(2793), 1969a(208). Names and Faces of Heroes, The. SCL(3172), 1964a (185). Permanent Errors. 1971a(250).

Priestley, J. B. Good Companions, The. MCLE(1803), MEF(243), MP1(311).

Prior, Matthew. Poetry of Prior, The. MCLE(4061), MP4 (930).

Pritchett, V. S. Cab at the Door, A. SCL(587), 1969a(57). George Meredith and English Comedy. 1971a(96). Sailor, Sense of Humour, and Other Stories, The. SCL(4048), 1957a(230). When My Girl Comes Home. SCL(5019), 1962a(301).

Prokosch, Frederic. Missolonghi Manuscript, The. SCL (3048), 1969a(228). Seven Who Fled, The. MAF(566), MCLE(4727), MP2(955). Tale for Midnight, A. SCL (4508), 1955a(246).

Propertius, Sextus. Elegies of Propertius, The. MCLE (1352), MP4(265).

Prosper of Aquitaine, Saint. Call of All Nations, The. CAL(204).

Proust, Marcel. Jean Santeuil. SCL(2310), 1957a(135). Remembrance of Things Past. MCLE(4384), MEU(628), MP1(815). Swann's Way. PO(319), SGEN(317).

Purdy, James. Cabot Wright Begins. SCL(591), 1965a(25). Children Is All. SCL(715), 1963a(23). Color of Darkness. MCLE(802), MP4(144), SCLs(74). Jeremy's Version. 1971a(144). Malcolm. MCLE(2862), MP4 (588), SCL(2847), 1960a(149). Nephew, The. SCL (3194), 1961a(185).

Pusey, Edward B. Eirenicon, An. CHL(751).

Pushkin, Alexander. Boris Godunov. MCLE(464), MD(95), MP2(109). Bronze Horseman: A Petersburg Tale, The. MCLE(521), MP4(91). Captain's Daughter, The. MCLE(615), MEU(105), MP1(113). Eugene Onegin. MCLE(1479), MP(89), MP2(299). Ruslan and Lyudmila. MCLE(4566), MP4(1080).

Putnam, Carlton. Theodore Roosevelt: The Formative Years. SCL(4570), 1959a(237).

Pynchon, Thomas. Crying of Lot 49, The. SCL(973), 1967a(63). V. SCL(4861), 1964a(284).

Quennell, Peter. Alexander Pope. 1970a(10). Hogarth's Progress. SCL(2072), 1955a(124).

Rabelais, François. Gargantua and Pantagruel. MCLE (1721), MEU(318), MP1(298), SGEN(3).
Racine, Jean Baptiste. Andromache. MCLE(173), MD(35), MP2(33). Bérénice. MCLE(390), MD(75), MP3(101). Britannicus. MCLE(512), MD(106), MP3(133). Mithridate. MCLE(3117), MD(548), MP3(667). Phaèdra (Phedre). MCLE(3611), MD(620), MP1(741), POP(265). Plaideurs, Les. MCLE(3695), MD(638), MP3(763).
Radcliffe, Mrs. Ann. Italian, The. MCLE(2298), MEF(352), MP3(521). Mysteries of Udolpho, The. MCLE(3207), MEF(552), MP1(635). Romance of the Forest, The. MCLE(4517), MEF(748), MP2(914).
Radhakrishnan, Sarvepalli. Idealist View of Life, An. WP (974).
Radin, Edward D. Lizzie Borden. SCL(2730), 1962a(189).
Rahner, Karl. On the Theology of Death. CAL(1047).
Raine, Kathleen. Collected Poems. SCL(803), 1958a(53).
Rakosi, Carl. Amulet. SCL(167), 1969a(8).
Raleigh, Sir Walter. Poetry of Raleigh, The. MCLE(4064), MP4(933).
Rama Rau, Santha. Remember the House. SCL(3881), 1957a (218).
Ramsey, Paul. Basic Christian Ethics. CHL(1117).
Ramuz, Charles-Ferdinand. When the Mountain Fell. MCLE (5612), MEU(811), MP2(1127).
Randall, James G. and Richard N. Current. Lincoln the President. BM(340), SCL(2686), 1955a(147).
Randall, Julia. Adam's Dream. 1970a(4). Puritan Carpenter, The. SCL(3753), 1966a(256).
Randolph, Alexander. Mail Boat, The. SCL(2828), 1954a (165).
Randolph, Clemence and John B. Colton. Rain. POP(89).
Rankin, J. Lee, Earl Warren and Others. Report of the President's Commission on the Assassination of President John F. Kennedy. SCL(3888), 1965a(246).
Ransom, John Crowe. New Criticism, The. MCLE(3250), MP4(626). Selected Poems. MCLE(4698), MP(332), MP3(954), SCLs(262).
Raphael, Frederic. Lindmann. SCL(2690), 1965a(174).
Raspe, Rudolph Erich. Baron Münchausen's Narrative. MCLE(339), MEU(65), MP2(76).
Ratti, John. Remembered Darkness, A. 1970a(265).
Rauschenbusch, Walter. Theology for the Social Gospel, A. CHL(886).
Raven, Charles E. Natural Religion and Christian Theology. CHL(1143).
Rawlings, Marjorie Kinnan. Yearling, The. MAF(726),

MCLE(5757), MP1(1140).

Ray, Gordon N. Thackeray: The Age of Wisdom, 1847-1863. BM(536), SCL(4562), 1959a(234). Thackeray: The Uses of Adversity. BM(540), SCL(4566), 1955a (252).

Read, Evelyn. My Lady Suffolk. SCL(3151), 1964a(183).

Read, Kenneth E. High Valley, The. SCL(2043), 1966a(127).

Reade, Charles. Cloister and the Hearth, The. MCLE(770), MEF(112), MP1(150), PO(136). Peg Woffington. MCLE(3553), MEF(643), MP1(724), PON(291).

Rêgo, José Lins do. Dead Fires. MAF(130), MCLE(1035), MP3(254). Plantation Boy. MCLE(3700), MP4(696), SCL(3590), 1967a(264).

Reich, Charles. Greening of America, The. 1971a(108).

Reid, Forrest. Bracknels, The. MCLE(481), MEF(60), MP2(113). Tom Barber. SCL(4710), 1955a(269).

Reid, Thomas. Essays on the Intellectual Powers of Man and Essays on the Active Powers of the Human Mind. WP(538).

Remarque, Erich Maria. All Quiet on the Western Front. MCLE(102), MEU(16), MP2(13), PO(384), SGEN(397). Black Obelisk, The. SCL(433), 1958a(36).

Rembar, Charles. End of Obscenity, The. SCL(1346), 1969a(110).

Renan, Ernest. Life of Jesus, The. CHL(739).

Renault, Mary. Bull from the Sea, The. SCL(549), 1963a (14). Fire from Heaven. 1970a(132). King Must Die, The. BM(284), SCL(2427), 1959a(133). Last of the Wine, The. BM(298), MCLE(2547), MP4(503), SCL(2527), 1957a(147).

Reyes, Alfonso. Visión de Anáhuac. MCLE(5509), MN(318), MP3(1101).

Reymont, Ladislas. Peasants, The. MCLE(3540), MEU(566), MP1(720).

Rhys, Jean. Good Morning, Midnight. 1971a(102).

Rice, Elmer. Street Scene. DGAP(245), MCLE(5021), MD (811), MP3(1026), SGAP(79), TCP(309).

Rich, Adrienne. Necessities of Life: Poems, 1962-1965. SCL(3187), 1967a(237).

Richard of St. Victor. Benjamin Major. CAL(339). Benjamin Minor. CHL(220). Benjamin Minor and Benjamin Major. CAL(339).

Richards, I. A. Principles of Literary Criticism. MCLE (4257), MP4(1031).

Richardson, Dorothy M. Pilgrimage. MCLE(3665), MEF (674), MP3(757).

Richardson, H. Edward. William Faulkner: The Journey to

Self-Discovery. 1970a(352).
Richardson, Henry Handel. Fortunes of Richard Mahony, The. MCLE(1666), MEF(230), MP2(341).
Richardson, Howard and William Berney. Dark of the Moon. DGAP(362).
Richardson, Samuel. Clarissa Harlowe. MCLE(758), MEF (104), MP1(143). Pamela. MCLE(3486), MEF(631), MP1(708), PO2(5). Sir Charles Grandison. MCLE (4832), MEF(800), MP3(983).
Richter, Conrad. Aristocrat, The. SCL(213), 1969a(18). Awakening Land, The. SCLs(21). Fields, The. MAF(181), MCLE(1595), MP2(327). Grandfathers, The. SCL(1840), 1965a(115). Lady, The. SCL(2465), 1958a(133). Sea of Grass, The. MAF(560), MCLE (4667), MP1(872). Simple Honorable Man, A. MCLE (4826), MP4(1151), SCL(4291), 1963a(251). Town, The. MAF(661), MCLE(5265), MP2(1048). Trees, The. MAF(670), MCLE(5307), MP2(1055). Waters of Kronos, The. BM(598), MCLE(5577), MP4(1274), SCL(4986), 1961a(290).
Richter, Werner. Bismarck. SCL(422), 1966a(32).
Ridgway, General Matthew B. Soldier. SCL(4337), 1957a (247).
Riggs, Lynn. Green Grow the Lilacs. MCLE(1852), MD (313), MP3(430).
Rilke, Rainer Maria. Duino Elegies. MCLE(1296), MP(69), MP3(307). Sonnets to Orpheus. MCLE(4923), MP4 (1167).
Rimanelli, Giose. Day of the Lion, The. SCL(1064), 1954a (49).
Rimbaud, Arthur. Season in Hell, A. MCLE(4678), MP (329), MP3(944).
Ritchie, Anna Cora Mowatt. Fashion. DGAP(59).
Ritschl, Albrecht. Christian Doctrine of Justification and Reconciliation, The. CHL(758).
Robbe-Grillet, Alain. Erasers, The. SCL(1379), 1965a(83).
Roberts, Elizabeth Madox. Great Meadow, The. MAF(231), MCLE(1835), MP2(383). Time of Man, The. MAF (647), MCLE(5205), MP1(989).
Roberts, Kenneth. Boon Island. SCL(476), 1957a(32). Northwest Passage. MCLE(3308), MP4(631).
Robertson, Robert B. Of Whales and Men. SCL(3356), 1954a(198).
Robertson, Thomas William. Caste. MCLE(633), MD(132), MP2(135), POP(158).
Robin, Louis D., Jr. Faraway Country, The. SCL(1471), 1964a(80).

Robinson, Edgar Eugene. Roosevelt Leadership, 1933-1945, The. SCL(3990), 1955a(214).
Robinson, Edwin Arlington. Man Against the Sky, The. MCLE(2871), MP(173), MP3(622). Tristram. MCLE (5326), MP(364), MP1(1025).
Robinson, Henry Crabb. Diary of Henry Crabb Robinson, The. MCLE(1173), MP4(232).
Roche, Mazo de la. Jalna. MAF(306), MCLE(2316), MP2 (506).
Rodgers, Richard and Oscar Hammerstein. Oklahoma. DGAP(353).
Roethke, Theodore. Far Field, The. SCL(1469), 1965a(89). Poetry of Roethke, The. MCLE(4072), MP4(940). Roethke: Collected Poems. SCL(3969), 1967a(290).
Rogers, Major Robert. Ponteach; or The Savages of America. DGAP(1).
Rogow, Arnold A. James Forrestal. SCL(2285), 1965a(148).
Rojas, Fernando de. Celestina. MCLE(667), MEU(120), MP2(139).
Rolland, Romain. Jean-Christophe. MCLE(2327), MEU(404), MP1(439), PO(323), SGEN(285).
Rölvaag, O. E. Giants in the Earth. MAF(201), MCLE (1754), MP1(303), SGAN(184). Peder Victorious. MAF(478), MCLE(3543), MP2(802).
Romains, Jules. Death of a Nobody, The. PO2(371).
Rommen, Heinrich. State in Catholic Thought, The. CAL (897).
Ronsard, Pierre de. Poetry of Ronsard, The. MCLE(4077), MP(289), MP3(826).
Root, William Pitt. Storm and Other Poems, The. 1970a (284).
Roper, William. Lyfe of Sir Thomas More, Knighte. CAL (543).
Rosa, João Guimarães. Devil to Pay in the Backlands, The. SCL(1150), 1964a(65).
Rose, Willie Lee. Rehearsal for Reconstruction. SCL(3868), 1965a(240).
Ross, Ishbel. First Lady of the South. SCL(1562), 1959a (89).
Ross, Nancy Wilson. Return of Lady Brace, The. SCL (3911), 1958a(212).
Ross, W. David. Right and the Good, The. WP(929).
Rossetti, Christina. Poetry of Christina Rossetti, The. MCLE(3806), MP(243), MP3(789).
Rossetti, Dante Gabriel. Poetry of Dante Gabriel Rossetti, The. MCLE(3839), MP(246), MP3(791).
Rossiter, Clinton. Alexander Hamilton and the Constitution.

SCL(128), 1965a(5).
Rostand, Edmond. Aiglon, L'. MCLE(2509), MD(438), MP2 (551). Cyrano de Bergerac. MCLE(976), MD(194), MP2(210), POP(243).
Rosten, Leo. Return of H*Y*M*A*N K*A*P*L*A*N, The. SCL(3908), 1960a(226).
Roth, Arthur J. Terrible Beauty, A. SCL(4559), 1959a(231).
Roth, Henry. Call It Sleep. MCLE(577), MP4(102), SCL (599), 1965a(28).
Roth, Philip. Goodbye, Columbus. SCLs(117). Letting Go. SCL(2620), 1963a(129). Portnoy's Complaint. 1970a (242). When She Was Good. SCL(5022), 1968a(346).
Rousseau, Jean Jacques. Confessions. MCLE(826), MN(61), MP3(215). Creed of a Savoyard Priest, The. CHL (605). Discourse on the Origin of Inequality. MCLE (1185), MP4(237). Émile. MCLE(1366), MEU(281), MP3(330). New Héloïse, The. MCLE(3256), MEU (535), MP2(730). Social Contract, The. WP(512).
Roussin, André. Little Hut, The. SCL(2708), 1954a(153).
Rovit, Earl. Far Cry, A. SCL(1463), 1968a(100). Player King, The. SCL(3598), 1966a(236).
Rowley, William and Thomas Middleton. Changeling, The. MCLE(683), MD(140), MP3(169). Spanish Gipsy, The. MCLE(4948), MD(799), MP3(1011).
Rowse, A. L. Churchills, The. SCL(745), 1959a(34). Sir Walter Ralegh. SCL(4312), 1963a(254).
Roy, Jules. Battle of Dienbienphu, The. SCL(330), 1966a (24). War in Algeria, The. SCL(4961), 1962a(298).
Royce, Josiah. Problem of Christianity, The. CHL(878). World and the Individual, The. WP(739).
Rubin, Louis. Golden Weather, The. SCL(1805), 1962a(138).
Rufinus of Aquileia. Commentary on the Apostles' Creed, A. CAL(169).
Rukeyser, Muriel. Waterlily Fire. SCL(4979), 1963a(285).
Rulfo, Juan. Pedro Páramo. BM(425), MCLE(3546), MP4 (678), SCL(3537), 1960a(186).
Ruskin, John. King of the Golden River, The. MCLE(2456), MEF(407), MP2(529). Stones of Venice, The. MCLE (4988), MP4(1180).
Russell, Bertrand. Autobiography of Bertrand Russell: 1872-1914, The. SCL(269), 1968a(15). Autobiography of Bertrand Russell: 1914-1944, The. SCL(273), 1969a(26). Autobiography of Bertrand Russell: 1944-1969, The. 1970a(45). Inquiry into Meaning and Truth, An. WP(1052). Introduction to Mathematical Philosophy. WP(816). Nightmares of Eminent Persons. SCL(3253), 1955a(181). Our Knowledge of the

External World. WP(799).
Russell, George William. Poetry of "A. E.," The. MCLE (3741), MP4(709).
Russell, W. Clark. Wreck of the Grosvenor, The. MCLE (5753), MEF(974), MP1(1135).
Rutherford, Samuel. Lex rex. CHL(462).
Ruysbroeck, John of. Adornment of the Spiritual Marriage, The. CHL(272). Spiritual Espousals, The. CAL (461).
Ryan, Cornelius. Longest Day: June 6, 1944, The. SCL (2768), 1960a(146).
Rydberg, Viktor. Last Athenian, The. MCLE(2528), MEU (427), MP2(553).
Ryer, George W. and Denman Thompson. Old Homestead, The. DGAP(112), POP(68).
Ryle, Gilbert. Concept of Mind, The. WP(1109).
Ryskind, Morrie, George S. Kaufman and George and Ira Gershwin. Of Thee I Sing. DGAP(253), SGAP(53).

Sachs, Hans. Wandering Scholar from Paradise, The. MCLE(5548), MD(906), MP3(1115).
Sachs, Nelly. O the Chimneys. SCL(3342), 1968a(231).
Sackler, Howard. Great White Hope, The. 1970a(146).
Sackville, Thomas and Thomas Norton. Gorboduc. MCLE (1814), MD(309), MP2(379).
Sackville-West, V. Daughter of France. SCL(1023), 1960a (54).
Sagan, Françoise. Bonjour Tristesse. SCL(473), 1955a(29). Certain Smile, A. SCL(673), 1957a(42).
Saikaku, Ibara. Five Women Who Loved Love. MCLE(1620), MEU(304), MP3(398).
Saint-Exupéry, Antoine de. Little Prince, The. PO2(351). Night Flight. MCLE(3281), MEU(544), MP3(687). Wind, Sand and Stars. MCLE(5665), MP4(1291), PO2 (355). Wisdom of the Sands, The. MCLE(5684), MP4(1294).
St.-John Perse. Anabasis. MCLE(152), MP(6), MP3(32). Chronique. BM(80), MCLE(742), MP4(134), SCL(742), 1962a(58). Èloges and Other Poems. BM(160), MCLE(1359), MP4(271), SCL(1314), 1957a(61). Seamarks. BM(496), MCLE(4676), MP4(1102), SCL(4106), 1959a(216).
Saint-Pierre, Bernardin de. Paul and Virginia. PO(326), PON(286).
Sainte-Beuve, Charles Augustin. Monday Conversations. MCLE(3139), MP4(612). Volupté. MCLE(5528), MEU (797), MP3(1110).

Saki. Short Stories of Saki, The. MCLE(4809), MP4(1148). Unbearable Bassington, The. MCLE(5391), MEF(885), MP1(1042).
Salacrou, Armand. Unknown of Arras, The. TCP(313).
Salinger, J. D. Catcher in the Rye, The. SCLs(58), SGAN (316). Franny and Zooey. BM(195), MCLE(1679), MP4(359), SCL(1651), 1962a(127). Raise High the Roof Beam, Carpenters. SCL(3821), 1964a(220).
Salisbury, Harrison E. 900 Days, The. 1970a(221).
Salten, Felix. Bambi. MCLE(324), MEU(59), MP1(52).
Samuels, Ernest. Henry Adams: 1877-1890. BM(228), SCL(1990), 1959a(114). Henry Adams: 1890-1918. SCL(1993), 1965a(124).
Sáñchez, Florencio. Gringa, La. MCLE(1867), MD(316), MP2(389).
Sand, George. Consuelo. MCLE(865), MEU(153), MP1(156). Indiana. MCLE(2245), MEU(400), MP2(485).
Sandburg, Carl. Abraham Lincoln. BM(1), MCLE(9), MN (1), MP3(2), SCL(9), 1954a(1). Chicago Poems. MCLE(706), MP4(124). Letters of Carl Sandburg, The. SCL(2578), 1969a(193). People, Yes, The. MCLE(3577), MP(214), MP3(734). Remembrance Rock. MAF(528), MCLE(4387), MP2(889).
Sandburg, Helga. Measure My Love. SCL(2954), 1960a(158). Wheel of Earth, The. SCL(5016), 1959a(274).
S'añkara. Crest Jewel of Wisdom. WP(268).
Sansom, William. Blue Skies, Brown Studies. SCL(467), 1962a(30). Goodbye. SCL(1824), 1967a(131). Stories of William Sansom, The. SCL(4461), 1964a(254).
Santayana, George. Idea of Christ in the Gospels, The. CHL(1080). Last Puritan, The. MAF(327), MCLE (2550), MP1(497). Life of Reason, The. WP(761). Realms of Being. WP(895). Scepticism and Animal Faith. MCLE(4644), MN(273), MP3(935). Sense of Beauty, The. WP(718).
Sappho. Ode to Aphrodite. MCLE(3329), MP(189), MP3 (694).
Saroyan, William. Human Comedy, The. MAF(288), MCLE (2154), MP1(392), SGAN(289). My Heart's in the Highlands. TCP(316). Time of Your Life, The. DGAP(325), SGAP(202).
Sarraute, Nathalie. Golden Fruits, The. SCL(1793), 1965a (112). Martereau. SCL(2921), 1960a(156).
Sartre, Jean-Paul. Being and Nothingness. WP(1079). Devil and the Good Lord, The. TCP(319). Dirty Hands. MEU(237), TCP(326). Flies, The. MCLE (1626), MP4(346). Nausea. MCLE(3239), MEU(532),

MP2(726), SGEN(423). No Exit. TCP(329). Words, The. SCL(5142), 1965a(322).
Sassoon, Siegfried. Memoirs of a Fox-Hunting Man. MCLE (3000), MEF(494), MP1(575). Memoirs of an Infantry Officer. MCLE(3009), MEF(499), MP1(579).
Scammon, Richard M. Real Majority, The. 1971a(262).
Scarisbrick, J. J. Henry VIII. SCL(1997), 1969a(148).
Schary, Dore. Sunrise at Campobello. DGAP(415).
Scheeben, Matthias Joseph. Mysteries of Christianity, The. CAL(672).
Scheffer, Victor B. Year of the Whale, The. 1970a(354).
Schéhadé, Georges. Vasco. TCP(333).
Scheler, Max. On the Eternal in Man. CHL(904).
Schiller, Johann Christoph Friedrich von. Don Carlos. MCLE(1231), MD(218), MP2(270). Wallenstein. MCLE(5539), MD(903), MP2(1119). William Tell. MCLE(5659), MD(925), MP1(1115), POP(309).
Schlegel, Friedrich von. Lectures on the Philosophy of Life. CAL(635).
Schleiermacher, Friedrich. Christian Faith, The. CHL(657). On Religion: Speeches to its Cultured Despisers. CHL(637).
Schlesinger, Arthur M. Age of Roosevelt, The, Vol. I. SCL(104), 1958a(7). Age of Roosevelt, The, Vol. II. SCL(107), 1960a(7). Age of Roosevelt, The, Vol. III. SCL(111), 1961a(4). Thousand Days, A. SCL(4626), 1966a(313).
Schlick, Moritz. Problems of Ethics. WP(935).
Schmidt, Harvey and Tom Jones. Fantasticks, The. SCLs (94).
Schnitzler, Arthur. Anatol. POP(297).
Schoonover, Lawrence. Spider King, The. SCL(4405), 1954a (258).
Schopenhauer, Arthur. World as Will and Idea, The. MCLE (5737), MN(333), MP3(1153), WP(582).
Schorer, Mark. Sinclair Lewis. BM(512), SCL(4297), 1962a (275).
Schreiber, Herman and Georg. Vanished Cities. SCL(4867), 1958a(252).
Schreiner, Olive. Story of an African Farm, The. MCLE (4997), MEU(720), MP1(932), PO(140).
Schwartz, Delmore. Summer Knowledge. SCL(4486), 1960a (260).
Schwarz-Bart, André. Last of the Just, The. SCL(2524), 1961a(149).
Schweitzer, Albert. Out of My Life and Thought. MCLE (3467), MP4(660). Quest of the Historical Jesus, The.

CHL(847).
Sciacca, Michele Federico. Act and Being. CAL(1031). Death and Immortality. CAL(1078).
Scott, Michael. Tom Cringle's Log. MCLE(5243), MEF (860), MP1(997).
Scott, Paul. Corrida at San Feliu, The. SCL(929), 1965a (56).
Scott, Captain Robert Falcon. Scott's Last Expedition. MCLE(4661), MP4(1100).
Scott, Sir Walter. Antiquary, The. MCLE(199), MEF(25), MP2(41). Bride of Lammermoor, The. MCLE(495), MEF(65), MP3(128). Fair Maid of Perth, The. MCLE(1532), MEF(201), MP3(380). Fortunes of Nigel, The. MCLE(1663), MEF(227), MP2(338). Guy Mannering. MCLE(1889), MEF(257), MP2(391). Heart of Midlothian, The. MCLE(1955), MEF(283), MP1(355), PO(152), PON(138). Ivanhoe. MCLE(2307), MEF(358), MP1(430), PO(145), PON(167), SGBN(63). Kenilworth. MCLE(2434), MEF(400), MP1(469), PO(148), PON(181). Lady of the Lake, The. MCLE(2502), MP(151), MP2 (547). Lay of the Last Minstrel, The. MCLE(2570), MP(157), MP2(564). Marmion. MCLE(2934), MP(181), MP2(635). Old Mortality. MCLE(3373), MP1(681). Quentin Durward. MCLE(4307), MEF(710), MP1(795). Rob Roy. MCLE(4489), MEF(733), MP1(837). St. Ronan's Well. MCLE(4585), MEF(768), MP3(916). Talisman, The. MCLE(5087), MEF(819), MP2(1009). Waverley. MCLE(5580), MEF(937), MP1(1094), PON (441). Woodstock. MCLE(5729), MEF(971), MP2 (1158).
Scott, Winfield Townley. Change of Weather. SCL(680), 1965a(34).
Scotus Erigena, Johannes. On the Division of Nature. WP (273).
Scudéry, Madeleine de. Artamène. MCLE(249), MEU(39), MP3(67).
Seay, James. Let Not Your Hart. 1971a(164).
See, Carolyn. Rest Is Done with Mirrors, The. 1971a(271).
Seeley, Sir John Robert. Ecce homo. CHL(747).
Seeyle, John. True Adventures of Huckleberry Finn. 1970a (313).
Segal, Erich. Love Story. 1971a(189).
Seidel, Frederick. Final Solutions. SCL(1531), 1964a(86).
Sellars, Roy Wood. Philosophy of Physical Realism, The. WP(980).
Semprun, Jorge. Long Voyage, The. SCL(2763), 1965a(188).
Seneca, Lucius Annaeus. Philosophical Treatises and Moral

Reflections of Seneca. MCLE(3631), MP4(688).
Thyestes. MCLE(5197), MD(847), MP2(1026).

Sennett, Richard. Uses of Disorder, The. 1971a(335).

Sergeant, Elizabeth Shepley. Robert Frost. SCL(3957), 1961a(213).

Serling, Rod. Patterns. DGAP(407).

Sertillanges, Antonin Gilbert. Intellectual Life, The. CAL (771).

Servan-Schreiber, Jean-Jacques. American Challenge, The. SCL(150), 1969a(5).

Servetus, Michael. On the Errors of the Trinity. CHL(351).

Seton, Anya. Katherine. SCL(2400), 1954a(132).

Seton-Watson, Hugh. Russian Empire 1801-1917, The. SCL(4041), 1968a(283).

Settle, Mary Lee. Fight Night on a Sweet Saturday. SCL (1525), 1965a(92).

Severus, Sulpicius. Dialogues of Sulpicius Severus, The. CAL(157). Life of St. Martin, The. CHL(137).

Sévigné, Madame Marie de. Letters from Madame La Marquise de Sévigné. SCL(2573), 1957a(150). Letters of Madame de Sévigné, The. MCLE(2618), MP4(528).

Sewall, Jonathan. Americans Roused, The. DGAP(9).

Sexton, Anne. Live or Die. SCL(2719), 1967a(197). Love Poems. SCL(2797), 1969a(212).

Shaffer, Peter. Royal Hunt of the Sun, The. SCL(4014), 1966a(275).

Shaftesbury, Earl of, Anthony Ashley Cooper. Characteristics. WP(459).

Shakespeare, William. All's Well That Ends Well. MCLE (112), MD(22), MP2(18). Antony and Cleopatra. MCLE(202), MD(41), MP2(43). As You Like It. MCLE(257), MD(47), MP1(46), POP(208). Comedy of Errors, The. MCLE(805), MD(163), MP2(164). Coriolanus. MCLE(875), MD(174), MP2(176). Cymbeline. MCLE(971), MD(191), MP2(207). Hamlet, Prince of Denmark. MAF(246), MCLE(1912), MD(319), MP1(348), POP(201). Henry the Fourth, Part One. MCLE(1990), MD(333), MP2(430). Henry the Fourth, Part Two. MCLE(1993), MD(336), MP2(432). Henry the Fifth. MCLE(1988), MD(331), MP1(364). Henry the Sixth, Part One. MCLE(1996), MD(339), MP2 (434). Henry the Sixth, Part Two. MCLE(1999), MD (342), MP2(437). Henry the Sixth, Part Three. MCLE(2002), MD(345), MP2(439). Henry the Eighth. MCLE(1985), MD(328), MP2(427). Julius Caesar. MCLE(2408), MD(402), MP2(522), POP(204). King John. MCLE(2450), MD(415), MP2(524). King Lear.

MCLE(2453), MD(418), MP2(526). Love's Labour's Lost. MCLE(2770), MD(459), MP2(599). Macbeth. MCLE(2815), MD(469), MP1(534), POP(197). Measure for Measure. MCLE(2975), MD(506), MP2(648). Merchant of Venice, The. MCLE(3020), MD(516), MP1(581), POP(211). Merry Wives of Windsor, The. MCLE(3023), MD(519), MP2(657). Midsummer Night's Dream, A. MCLE(3042), MD(527), MP2(662). Much Ado about Nothing. MCLE(3190), MD(562), MP2(712). Othello. MCLE(3452), MD(594), MP1(701). Pericles, Prince of Tyre. MCLE(3586), MD(612), MP2(816). Rape of Lucrece, The. MCLE(4333), MP(311), MP2 (878). Richard the Second. MCLE(4446), MD(691), MP2(901). Richard the Third. MCLE(4449), MD(694), MP2(903). Romeo and Juliet. MCLE(4535), MD(711), MP1(853). POP(214). Sonnets of Shakespeare, The. MCLE(4918), MP4(1163). Taming of the Shrew, The. MCLE(5095), MD(828), MP2(1011). Tempest, The. MCLE(5118), MD(833), MP1(961). Timon of Athens. MCLE(5208), MD(849), MP2(1028). Titus Andronicus. MCLE(5221), MD(856), MP2(1033). Troilus and Cressida. MCLE(5334), MD(874), MP2(1063). Twelfth Night. MCLE(5355), MD(884), MP2(1069). Two Gentlemen of Verona. MCLE(5369), MD(887), MP2(1074). Venus and Adonis. MCLE(5460), MP (369), MP1(1060). Winter's Tale, The. MCLE(5678), MD(928), MP2(1146).

Shakespeare, William and John Fletcher. Two Noble Kinsmen, The. MCLE(5371), MD(889), MP2(1076).

Shapiro, Karl. Poetry of Shapiro, The. MCLE(4079), MP4 (944).

Shaplen, Robert. Lost Revolution, The. SCL(2787), 1966a (151).

Sharp, Frank Chapman. Ethics. WP(901).

Shaw, Felicity. Happy Exiles, The. SCL(1915), 1957a(105).

Shaw, George Bernard. Back to Methuselah. MCLE(321), MD(55), MP3(82), TCP(337). Bernard Shaw. SCL (377), 1966a(27). Caesar and Cleopatra. MCLE(564), MD(118), MP3(145). Candida. MCLE(588), MD(128), MP3(150), TCP(342). Heartbreak House. MCLE(1961), MD(321), MP3(449), TCP(345). Major Barbara. MCLE(2859), MD(483), MP3(617), TCP(349). Man and Superman. MCLE(2874), MD(489), MP3(624), TCP(352). Pygmalion. MCLE(4296), MD(670), MP3 (859), TCP(355). Saint Joan. MCLE(4580), MD(723), MP3(912), TCP(358). Simpleton of the Unexpected Isles, The. TCP(362).

Shaw, Irwin. Bury the Dead. SGAP(233). Two Weeks in Another Town. SCL(4813), 1961a(268).
Shea, John Dawson Gilmary. History of the Catholic Church in the United States, A. CAL(702).
Sheed, Francis Joseph. Theology and Sanity. CAL(906).
Sheed, Wilfrid. Max Jamison. 1971a(206). Office Politics. SCL(3359), 1967a(248).
Sheen, Fulton J. Communism and the Conscience of the West. CAL(944). God and Intelligence in Modern Philosophy. CAL(788). Peace of Soul. CAL(958).
Sheherazade, Princess. Arabian Nights, The. PON(29).
Sheldon, Charles M. In His Steps. CHL(808).
Sheldon, Edward. Boss, The. DGAP(182).
Shelley, Mary Godwin. Frankenstein. MCLE(1677), MEF (235), MP1(295), PO(155).
Shelley, Percy Bysshe. Cenci, The. MCLE(670), MD(138), MP1(131). Defence of Poetry, A. MCLE(1100), MP4 (208). Prometheus Unbound. MCLE(4282), MP(306), MP1(788).
Sheridan, Richard Brinsley. Critic, The. MCLE(941), MD (187), MP2(199). Rivals, The. MCLE(4478), MD (703), MP1(831), POP(170). School for Scandal, The. MCLE(4650), MD(739), MP1(869), POP(166).
Sherriff, Robert Cedric. Journey's End. MCLE(2398), MD (398), MP2(520), POP(86), TCP(366).
Sherwood, Robert E. Abe Lincoln in Illinois. DGAP(304), MCLE(4), MD(1), MP1(3). Idiot's Delight. SGAP(123). Petrified Forest, The. DGAP(269), POP(15), TCP (369).
Shikibu, Lady Murasaki. Tale of Genji, The. MCLE(5073), MEU(734), MP2(1006), PO2(423).
Shirer, William L. Collapse of the Third Republic, The. 1970a(75). Rise and Fall of the Third Reich, The. BM(477), SCL(3938), 1961a(206).
Shirley, James. Hyde Park. MCLE(2168), MD(366), MP3 (497). Traitor, The. MCLE(5277), MD(863), MP3 (1077).
Sholokhov, Mikhail. And Quiet Flows the Don. MCLE(162), MEU(21), MP1(30), SGEN(371). Don Flows Home to the Sea, The. MCLE(1234), MEU(249), MP2(272). Harvest on the Don. SCL(1950), 1962a(142).
Shorthouse, Joseph Henry. John Inglesant. MCLE(2356), MEF(376), MP2(513).
Shudraka. Little Clay Cart, The. MCLE(2696), MD(448), MP3(586).
Shute, Nevil. On the Beach. SCL(3396), 1958a(177). Trustee from the Toolroom. SCL(4777), 1961a(266).

Sidney, Sir Philip. Arcadia. MCLE(227), MEF(28), MP3(56). Defence of Poesie. MCLE(1097), MP4(206). Poetry of Sidney, The. MCLE(4082), MP4(947).
Sidwick, Henry. Methods of Ethics, The. WP(671).
Sienkiewicz, Henryk. Quo vadis. MCLE(4310), MEU(613), MP1(797), PO(388), PON(338). With Fire and Sword. MCLE(5690), MEU(822), MP2(1148).
Sierra, Gregorio Martínez. Cradle Song, The. MCLE(922), MD(184), MP2(192). Kingdom of God, The. MCLE (2471), MD(423), MP3(545).
Sigal, Clancy. Going Away. SCL(1787), 1963a(70). Week-end in Dinlock. SCL(5005), 1961a(293).
Sillanpää, Frans Eemil. Meek Heritage. MCLE(2982), MEU (488), MP2(650).
Sillitoe, Alan. Guzman, Go Home. 1970a(157). Loneliness of the Long-Distance Runner, The. SCL(2736), 1961a (165). Saturday Night and Sunday Morning. SCL (4073), 1960a(229). Tree on Fire, A. SCL(4759), 1969a(318).
Silone, Ignazio. Bread and Wine. MCLE(492), MEU(83), MP1(81), SGEN(412). Fontamara. BM(187), MCLE (1640), MP4(353), SCL(1606), 1966a(83). Fox and the Camellias, The. SCL(1642), 1962a(125). School for Dictators, The. SCL(4089), 1964a(228). Secret of Luca, The. SCL(4135), 1959a(222). Seed Beneath the Snow, The. SCL(4144), 1966a(286).
Simmons, Charles. Powdered Eggs. SCL(3669), 1965a(223).
Simmons, Ernest J. Chekhov. SCL(700), 1963a(20).
Simms, William Gilmore. Yemassee, The. MAF(729), MCLE(5763), MP2(1165).
Simon, Claude. Palace, The. SCL(3494), 1964a(206).
Simon, Edith. Twelve Pictures, The. SCL(4793), 1955a (284).
Simon, Yves René Marie. Philosophy of Democratic Government. CAL(982). Traité du Libre arbitre. CAL(986).
Simons, Menno. Foundation of Christian Doctrine. CHL(367).
Simpson, Louis. Selected Poems. SCL(4189), 1966a(300).
Sinclair, Andrew. Gog. SCL(1783), 1968a(126).
Sinclair, May. Divine Fire, The. MCLE(1195), MEF(160), MP2(256).
Sinclair, Upton. Jungle, The. MAF(315), MCLE(2411), MP1 (459).
Singer, Isaac Bashevis. Family Moskat, The. SCL(1456), 1966a(103). Friend of Kafka, A. 1971a(80). In My Father's Court. SCL(2179), 1967a(162). Manor, The. SCL(2897), 1968a(186). Séance and Other Stories, The. SCL(4109), 1969a(284). Short Friday and Other Stories.

SCL(4267), 1965a(280). Slave, The. SCL(4322), 1963a(256). Spinoza of Market Street, The. SCL (4411), 1962a(285).
Singer, Israel Joshua. Brothers Ashkenazi, The. MCLE (531), MEU(86), MP2(118).
Singmaster, Elsie. Gettysburg. MAF(198), MCLE(1749), MP2(365). High Wind Rising, A. MAF(261), MCLE (2027), MP2(442). I Speak for Thaddeus Stevens. MCLE(2184), MN(155), MP1(408).
Sitwell, Edith. Collected Poems. BM(97), SCL(806), 1955a (59). Poetry of Edith Sitwell, The. MCLE(3866), MP4(793). Queens and the Hive, The. BM(466), SCL(3780), 1963a(202).
Sitwell, Sacheverell. Arabesque and Honeycomb. SCL(202), 1959a(14).
Skelton, John. Poetry of Skelton, The. MCLE(4087), MP4 (951).
Slavitt, David. Day Sailing. 1970a(90). Rochelle; or Virtue Rewarded. SCL(3961), 1968a(268).
Smart, Christopher. Poetry of Smart, The. MCLE(4092), MP4(955).
Smith, Adam. Theory of Moral Sentiments. WP(506). Wealth of Nations, The. MCLE(5591), MN(327), MP3 (1122).
Smith, Betty. Tree Grows in Brooklyn, A. MAF(667), MCLE(5298), MP1(1018).
Smith, Chard Powers. Where the Light Falls. SCL(5039), 1966a(329).
Smith, Gene. When the Cheering Stopped. SCL(5025), 1965a (308).
Smith, Homer W. Kamongo. MCLE(2427), MP4(486).
Smith, Lee. Last Day the Dogbushes Bloomed, The. SCL (2504), 1969a(185).
Smith, Lillian. Journey, The. SCL(2374), 1954a(126).
Smith, Marian Spencer. American Grandfather, An. DGAP (206).
Smith, Page. John Adams. SCL(2344), 1963a(112).
Smith, Pauline. Little Karoo, The. SCL(2711), 1960a(144).
Smith, William H. Drunkard, The; or The Fallen Saved. DGAP(55).
Smith, William Jay. Tin Can, The. SCL(4674), 1967a(320).
Smith, Winchell and Frank Bacon. Lightnin'. POP(38).
Smollett, Tobias. Expedition of Humphry Clinker. PO2(16). Humphry Clinker. MCLE(2156), MEF(330), MP1(394), SGBN(47). Peregrine Pickle. MCLE(3582), MEF(648), MP1(731). Roderick Random. MCLE(4502), MEF(742), MP1(841).

Snodgrass, W. D. After Experience. SCL(71), 1968a(7). Heart's Needle. BM(224), SCL(1970), 1960a(88).
Snow, C. P. Affair, The. BM(11), MCLE(44), MP4(6), SCL(59), 1961a(1). Conscience of the Rich, The. MCLE(853), MP4(152), SCL(903), 1959a(40). Corridors of Power. SCL(933), 1965a(59). Homecoming. SCL(2093), 1957a(123). Last Things. 1971a(161). Masters, The. MCLE(2955), MP4(596). New Men, The. BM(388), SCL(3210), 1955a(172). Search, The. BM(499), SCL(4113), 1960a(232). Strangers and Brothers. SCL(4470), 1961a(242).
Snyder, Gary. Back Country, The. SCLs(25).
Söderblom, Nathan. Living God, The. CHL(994).
Sologub, Fyodor. Petty Demon, The. SCL(3550), 1963a(177).
Solovyev, Vladimir. Lectures on Godmanhood. CHL(782).
Solzhenitsyn, Aleksandr I. Cancer Ward, The. SCL(608), 1969a(61). First Circle, The. SCL(1556), 1969a(126). Love-Girl and the Innocent, The. 1971a(186). One Day in the Life of Ivan Denisovich. SCL(3418), 1964a(203).
Somerlott, Robert. Inquisitor's House, The. 1970a(181).
Sontag, Susan. Against Interpretation. SCL(84), 1967a(5). Benefactor, The. SCL(365), 1964a(16). Death Kit. SCL(1092), 1968a(72). Styles of Radical Will. 1970a (294).
Sophocles. Ajax. MCLE(62), MD(10), MP2(6). Antigone. MCLE(197), MD(39), MP1(37). Oedipus at Colonus. MCLE(3334), MD(577), MP2(757). Oedipus Tyrannus. MCLE(3336), MD(579), MP1(668), POP(379). Philoctetes. MCLE(3622), MD(625), MP3(741). Women of Trachis, The. MCLE(5723), MD(949), MP3 (1146).
Sorge, Rheinhard Johannes. Beggar, The. TCP(372).
Southey, Robert. Life of Nelson. MCLE(2664), MN(183), MP3(576).
Spark, Muriel. Bachelors, The. MCLE(318), MP4(64), SCL(291), 1962a(27). Ballad of Peckham Rye, The. SCL(305), 1961a(10). Collected Poems: I. SCL(823), 1969a(69). Girls of Slender Means, The. SCL(1763), 1964a(112). Mandelbaum Gate, The. SCL(2885), 1966a(175). Memento Mori. MCLE(2991), MP4(601). Prime of Miss Jean Brodie, The. SCL(3689), 1963a (199). Public Image, The. SCL(3739), 1969a(268).
Speer, Albert. Inside the Third Reich. 1971a(128).
Spencer, Elizabeth. Light in the Piazza, The. SCL(2668), 1961a(163). Voice at the Back Door, The. SCL(4913), 1957a(278).

Spencer, Herbert. First Principles. WP(649).
Spender, Stephen. Poetry of Spender, The. MCLE(4098), MP(291), MP3(828).
Spengler, Oswald. Decline of the West, The. SCL(1110), 1963a(38).
Spenser, Edmund. Faerie Queene, The. MCLE(1529), MP (99), MP1(264). Lyric Poetry of Spenser, The. MCLE(2804), MP4(581). Mother Hubberd's Tale. MCLE(3181), MP4(619). Shepheardes Calendar, The. MCLE(4756), MP4(1114).
Sperber, Manes. Journey Without End. SCL(2384), 1954a (129).
Spewack, Samuel and Bella. Boy Meets Girl. SGAP(143).
Spewack, Samuel and Bella and Cole Porter. Kiss Me, Kate. DGAP(374).
Spinoza, Benedictus de. Ethics. MCLE(1473), MN(118), MP3(364), WP(416).
Spring, Howard. These Lovers Fled Away. SCL(4577), 1955a(256).
Spurgeon, Charles Haddon. John Ploughman's Talks. CHL (755).
Stace, Walter T. Time and Eternity. CHL(1139).
Stacton, David. Dancer in Darkness, A. SCL(997), 1963a (32). People of the Book. SCL(3544), 1966a(233). Segaki. SCL(4153), 1960a(237). Sir William. SCL (4315), 1964a(244).
Staël, Madame de. Considerations on the Principal Events of the French Revolution. MCLE(859), MP4(155). Delphine. MCLE(1110), MEU(224), MP2(243).
Stafford, Jean. Collected Stories of Jean Stafford, The. SCLs(72).
Stafford, William. Traveling Through the Dark. SCLs(325).
Stallings, Laurence and Maxwell Anderson. What Price Glory? DGAP(217), POP(31), SGAP(99).
Stallings, Laurence, Maxwell Anderson and Edwin Justin Mayer. So Red the Rose. DGAP(70).
Stallman, R. W. Stephen Crane. SCL(4438), 1969a(299).
Stampp, Kenneth M. Era of Reconstruction, 1865-1877, The. SCL(1373), 1966a(87).
Stanhope, Philip Dormer, Lord Chesterfield. Letters to His Son. MCLE(2639), MN(175), MP3(565).
Starkie, Enid. Flaubert. SCL(1579), 1968a(114).
Statius, Publius Papinius. Thebais, The. MCLE(5150), MP (360), MP3(1062).
Statler, Oliver. Japanese Inn. SCL(2304), 1962a(165).
Stead, Christina. Man Who Loved Children, The. SCL (2865), 1966a(168). Puzzleheaded Girl, The. SCL

(3756), 1968a(260).
Steegmuller, Francis. Cocteau: A Biography. 1971a(42). Grand Mademoiselle, The. SCL(1833), 1957a(90).
Steele, Sir Richard. Conscious Lovers, The. MCLE(856), MD(171), MP2(174). Funeral, The. MCLE(1706), MD(286), MP2(350).
Stegner, Wallace. All the Little Live Things. SCL(143), 1968a(11). Shooting Star, A. SCL(4264), 1962a(272).
Steinbeck, John. East of Eden. MAF(163), MCLE(1313), MP3(315). Grapes of Wrath, The. MAF(225), MCLE (1824), MP1(324), PO2(276), SGAN(267). In Dubious Battle. MAF(293), MCLE(2219), MP2(478). Of Mice and Men. DGAP(300), MAF(449), MCLE(3341), MP1 (672), PO2(272), SGAP(160). Sweet Thursday. SCL (4498), 1954a(264). Travels with Charley. SCL(4751), 1963a(270). Winter of Our Discontent, The. SCL (5105), 1962a(306).
Steiner, Jean-Francois. Treblinka. SCL(4753), 1968a(337).
Stendhal. Charterhouse of Parma, The. MCLE(692), MEU (129), MP1(135), PO2(303), SGEN(48). Lucien Leuwen. MCLE(2781), MEU(458), MP2(606). Private Diaries of Stendhal, The. SCL(3696), 1954a(216). Red and the Black, The. MCLE(4354), MEU(622), MP1(808), PO (329), PON(346), SGEN(41).
Stephens, James. Crock of Gold, The. MCLE(949), MEF (125), MP1(175), PO2(115), SGBN(257). Deirdre. MCLE(1105), MEF(148), MP2(240).
Sterne, Laurence. Journal to Eliza. MCLE(2380), MP4(474). Sentimental Journey, A. MCLE(4710), MEF(784), MP1(879). Tristram Shandy. MCLE(5329), MEF(879), MP1(1027), PO2(20), SGBN(40).
Stevens, James. Paul Bunyan. MAF(475), MCLE(3535), MP1(717).
Stevens, Wallace. Collected Poems of Wallace Stevens, The. BM(100), SCL(820), 1954a(31). Harmonium. MCLE (1931), MP(118), MP3(442). Letters of Wallace Stevens. SCL(2616), 1967a(190). Opus posthumous. SCL(3444), 1958a(182). Poetry of Stevens, The. MCLE(4107), MP4(962).
Stevenson, Charles Leslie. Ethics and Language. WP(1089).
Stevenson, Elizabeth. Lafcadio Hearn. SCL(2476), 1962a (175).
Stevenson, Fanny and Robert Louis. Our Samoan Adventure. SCL(3475), 1955a(196).
Stevenson, Robert Louis. Beach of Falesá, The. MCLE(356), MEF(45), MP3(91). Black Arrow, The. MCLE(425), MEF(54), MP1(72). Dr. Jekyll and Mr. Hyde. MCLE

(1208), MEF(162), MP1(214), PO(159), PON(90), POP (151). Kidnapped. MCLE(2436), MEF(402), MP1(471), PON(186). Master of Ballantrae, The. MCLE(2952), MEF(482), MP1(568), PON(231). Travels with a Donkey. MCLE(5290), MN(307), MP1(1014). Treasure Island. MCLE(5292), MEF(873), MP1(1015), PO2 (71), PON(398), SGBN(185).

Stevenson, Robert Louis, see also Fanny and Robert Louis Stevenson.

Stewart, Albert. Untoward Hills, The. SCL(4851), 1963a (279).

Stewart, Carroll and James Dugan. Ploesti. SCL(3604), 1963a(186).

Stewart, George R. Pickett's Charge. SCL(3564), 1960a (192).

Stewart, Sidney. Give Us This Day. SCL(1767), 1958a(99).

Still, James. River of Earth. MAF(538), MCLE(4481), MP1(833).

Stock, Noel. Life of Ezra Pound, The. 1971a(167).

Stoker, Bram. Dracula. MCLE(1269), MEF(170), MP2(283).

Stone, Irving. Men to Match My Mountains. SCL(2997), 1957a(177).

Stone, John Augustus. Metamora; or, The Last of the Wampanoags. DGAP(45).

Stone, Robert. Hall of Mirrors, A. SCL(1907), 1968a(134).

Stong, Phil. State Fair. MAF(602), MCLE(4977), MP1(925).

Stoppard, Tom. Rosencrantz and Guildenstern Are Dead. SCL(4002), 1968a(275).

Stowe, Harriet Beecher. Oldtown Folks. MAF(463), MCLE (3388), MP2(773). Uncle Tom's Cabin. MAF(679), MCLE(5398), MP1(1044), MPA5(31), PO(256), PON (411), POP(72), SGAN(33).

Strachey, Lytton. Eminent Victorians. MCLE(1371), MN (98), MP3(335). Queen Victoria. MCLE(4300), MP4 (1038).

Strauss, David Friedrich. Life of Jesus Critically Examined, The. CHL(679).

Strindberg, August. Charles XII. TCP(376). Comrades. MCLE(815), MD(166), MP3(208). Dance of Death, The. MCLE(992), MD(196), MP2(217), TCP(379). Dream Play, A. TCP(383). Father, The. MCLE(1562), MD(275), MP2(325), POP(329), TCP(388). Ghost Sonata. TCP(391). Great Highway, The. TCP(394). Link, The. MCLE(2689), MD(446), MP3(581). Miss Julie. MCLE(3077), MD(539), MP2(675), TCP(397). Red Room, The. MCLE(4360), MEU(625), MP3(868). There Are Crimes and Crimes. MCLE(5154), MD(839),

MP3(1064). To Damascus, Part I. TCP(401). To Damascus, Part II. TCP(405). To Damascus, Part III. TCP(408).

Strode, Hudson. Jefferson Davis: American Patriot. BM (258), SCL(2320), 1955a(134). Jefferson Davis: Confederate President. BM(261), SCL(2323), 1960a(108). Jefferson Davis: Private Letters, 1823-1889. SCL (2326), 1967a(175). Jefferson Davis: Tragic Hero. SCL(2330), 1965a(152).

Strong, Augustus Hopkins. Systematic Theology. CHL(797).

Strong, L. A. G. Garden, The. MCLE(1715), MEF(240), MP2(354).

Stuart, Dabney. Particular Place, A. 1970a(234).

Stuart, Jesse. Come Gentle Spring. 1970a(78). Daughter of the Legend. SCL(1031), 1966a(60). God's Oddling. SCL(1776), 1961a(101). Hold April. SCL(2076), 1963a(84). Man with a Bull-Tongue Plow. MCLE (2885), MP(176), MP3(626). Mr. Gallion's School. SCL(3058), 1968a(209). My Land Has a Voice. SCL (3154), 1967a(231). Plowshare in Heaven. SCL(3607), 1959a(204). Save Every Lamb. SCL(4080), 1965a (263). Taps for Private Tussie. MAF(632), MCLE (5098), MP1(952), 1970a(298). Thread That Runs So True, The. SCLs(318). To Teach, To Love. 1971a (327). Year of My Rebirth, The. BM(620), SCL (5174), 1957a(297).

Stubbs, Jean. Travellers, The. SCL(4742), 1964a(274).

Sturluson, Snorri. Heimskringla, The. MCLE(1972), MEU (354), MP2(423).

Sturzo, Luigi. Church and State. CAL(864).

Styron, William. Confessions of Nat Turner, The. SCL (893), 1968a(53). Lie Down in Darkness. MCLE (2647), MP4(544), SGAN(322). Long March, The. SCLs(168). Set This House on Fire. BM(502), MCLE (4713), SCL(4211), 1961a(228).

Suarez, Francisco, S.J. Treatise on Laws. CAL(575).

Suckling, Sir John. Poetry of Suckling, The. MCLE(4110), MP4(965).

Suckow, Ruth. Folks, The. MCLE(1631), MP4(349).

Sudermann, Hermann. Dame Care. MCLE(986), MEU(189), MP2(212). Song of Songs, The. MCLE(4907), MEU (706), MP1(910).

Sue, Eugène. Mysteries of Paris, The. MCLE(3204), MEU (520), MP1(632), PON(255). Wandering Jew, The. MCLE(5545), MEU(803), MP1(1083), PO(333).

Suhard, Emmanuel, Cardinal. Growth or Decline?: The Church Today. CAL(920).

Sukhanov, N. N. Russian Revolution, 1917, The. SCL(4045), 1955a(217).
Sullivan, Arthur, see W. S. Gilbert and Arthur Sullivan.
Summers, Hollis. Day After Sunday, The. SCL(1042), 1969a(89).
Sumner, William Graham. Folkways, The. MCLE(1634), MP4(351).
Sung-ling, P'u. Strange Stories from a Chinese Studio. MCLE(5016), MEU(729), MP3(1024).
Surrey, Henry Howard, Earl of, and Sir Thomas Wyatt. Poetry of Wyatt and Surrey, The. MCLE(4165), MP4 (1010).
Surtees, Robert Smith. Handley Cross. MCLE(1919), MEF (266), MP1(352). Hillingdon Hall. MCLE(2033), MEF(304), MP2(447). Jorrocks' Jaunts and Jollities. MCLE(2362), MEF(382), MP2(518). Mr. Facey Romford's Hounds. MCLE(3091), MEF(519), MP2(679). Mr. Sponge's Sporting Tour. MCLE(3102), MEF(527), MP2(684).
Suso, Blessed Henry, O. P. Little Book of Eternal Wisdom, The. CAL(458).
Suzuki, Daisetz T. Zen Buddhism. WP(1115).
Svevo, Italo. Confessions of Zeno. PO2(472).
Swanberg, W. A. Citizen Hearst. SCL(752), 1962a(61). Dreiser. SCL(1247), 1966a(81). First Blood: The Story of Fort Sumter. SCL(1553), 1959a(87). Pulitzer. SCL(3743), 1968a(254). Sickles the Incredible. SCL(4276), 1957a(241).
Swarthout, Glendon. Bless the Beasts and Children. SCLs (37). They Came to Cordura. SCL(4586), 1959a(241).
Swedenborg, Emanuel. Divine Love and Wisdom. MCLE (1197), MN(91), MP3(287).
Swenson, May. Half Sun Half Sleep. SCL(1903), 1968a(130). Iconographs. 1971a(119). To Mix with Time. SCL (4703), 1964a(271).
Swift, Jonathan. Gulliver's Travels. MCLE(1883), MEF(254), MP1(341), PO(163), PON(134), SGBN(16). Journal to Stella. MCLE(2383), MP4(476). Poetry of Swift, The. MCLE(4113), MP4(968). Tale of a Tub, A. MCLE (5069), MP4(1201).
Swinburne, Algernon Charles. Atalanta in Calydon. MCLE (270), MP(14), MP2(61). Poems and Ballads. MCLE (3726), MP4(704).
Swinnerton, Frank. Nocturne. MCLE(3300), MEF(584), MP1(661).
Sykes, Christopher. Orde Wingate. SCL(3452), 1960a(181).
Synge, John Millington. Deirdre of the Sorrows. MCLE

(1108), MD(204), MP3(265). Playboy of the Western World, The. MCLE(3707), MD(643), MP1(758), POP (231), TCP(412). Riders to the Sea. POP(235), TCP(415).

Tacitus, Cornelius. Annals of Tacitus, The. MCLE(184), MN(13), MP3(44).

Taine, Hippolyte. Philosophy of Art. MCLE(3635), MN(242), MP3(745).

Tarkington, Booth. Alice Adams. MAF(13), MCLE(83), MP1(20). Kate Fennigate. MAF(320), MCLE(2432), MP1(467). Monsieur Beaucaire. MAF(425), MCLE (3147), MP1(616), POP(61). Seventeen. MAF(569), MCLE(4732), MP1(882).

Tasso, Torquato. Jerusalem Delivered. CAL(548), MCLE (2337), MP(141), MP1(441).

Tate, Allen. Fathers, The. BM(183), MCLE(1568), MP4 (324), SCL(1491), 1961a(71). Poetry of Tate, The. MCLE(4118), MP4(972).

Tatian. Address of Tatian to the Greeks. CHL(26). Discourse Against the Greeks, The. CAL(23).

Taylor, Alfred Edward. Faith of a Moralist, The. CHL (954).

Taylor, Edward. Poetical Works of Edward Taylor, The. MCLE(3732), MP(225), MP3(771).

Taylor, Eleanor Ross. Wilderness of Ladies. SCL(5067), 1961a(304).

Taylor, Elizabeth. In a Summer Season. SCL(2172), 1962a (155).

Taylor, Harold. Students Without Teachers. 1970a(291).

Taylor, Henry. Horse Show at Midnight, The. SCL(2108), 1967a(150).

Taylor, Jeremy. Ductor dubitantium. CHL(497). Rule and Exercise of Holy Living and Holy Dying, The. CHL (477).

Taylor, Peter. Collected Stories of Peter Taylor, The. 1971a(46). Happy Families Are All Alike. SCL(1918), 1960a(80). Miss Leonora When Last Seen. SCL(3045), 1965a(202). Short Stories of Peter Taylor, The. MCLE(4806), MP4(1145). Widows of Thornton, The. SCL(5061), 1954a(294).

Taylor, Robert Lewis. Journey to Matecumbe, A. SCL (2380), 1962a(168). Travels of Jaimie McPheeters, The. SCL(4747), 1959a(251).

Teale, Edwin Way. Autumn Across America. SCL(282), 1957a(17). Journey into Summer. SCL(2377), 1961a (140).

Tegnér, Esaias. Frithiof's Saga. MCLE(1696), MP(109), MP2(348).
Teilhard de Chardin, Pierre, S. J. Divine Milieu, The. CAL(1054), CHL(1152). Phenomenon of Man, The. CAL(1017), MCLE(3613), MP4(683), SCL(3557), 1960a (189).
Teller, Edward and Albert L. Latter. Our Nuclear Future. SCL(3472), 1959a(198).
Teller, Walter Magnes. Search for Captain Slocum, The. SCL(4116), 1957a(233).
Temple, William. Nature, Man and God. CHL(999).
Tennant, Frederick Robert. Philosophical Theology. CHL (933).
Tennyson, Alfred, Lord. Enoch Arden. MCLE(1392), MP (75), MP1(249). Idylls of the King, The. MCLE (2199), MP(134), MP1(417). In Memoriam. MCLE (2221), MP4(439). Poems. MCLE(3723), MP4(702). Princess, The. MCLE(4248), MP4(1026).
Terence. Andria. MCLE(169), MD(31), MP2(31). Brothers, The. MCLE(528), MD(112), MP3(138). Eunuch, The. MCLE(1485), MD(256), MP2(302). Phormio. MCLE (3645), MD(630), MP2(827). Self-Tormentor, The. MCLE(4701), MD(758), MP3(956).
Teresa of Ávila, Saint. Interior Castle, The. CAL(561). Life of St. Teresa of Ávila, The. CHL(392). Way of Perfection, The. CAL(555).
Terkel, Studs. Hard Times. 1971a(112).
Tertullian. Apology of Tertullian, The. CAL(41), CHL(39). Treatises on Marriage. CAL(54).
Tertz, Abram. Makepeace Experiment, The. SCL(2831), 1966a(161).
Thackeray, William Makepeace. Barry Lyndon. MCLE(345), MEF(42), MP2(78). Henry Esmond. MCLE(1982), MEF(292), MP1(361), PO(171), PON(143). Newcomes, The. MCLE(3261), MEF(567), MP1(650). Pendennis. MCLE(3563), MEF(645), MP1(726), PO2(39), PON(297). Vanity Fair. MCLE(5445), MEF(906), MP1(1056), PO (167), PON(423), SGBN(116). Virginians, The. MCLE(5506), MEF(927), MP1(1074).
Tharp, Louise Hall. Three Saints and a Sinner. SCL(4634), 1957a(272).
Thaumaturges, Gregory. Declaration of Faith (and Other Writings), A. CHL(64).
Theocritus. Poetry of Theocritus, The. MCLE(4121), MP (298), MP3(834).
Theodoret of Cyrus. Dialogues, The. CHL(156).
Theophilus of Antioch, Saint. Theophilus to Autolycus. CAL

(33), CHL(32).
Therese of Lisieux, Saint. Story of a Soul, The. CAL(729).
Thesiger, Wilfred. Arabian Sands. SCL(205), 1960a(10).
Thomas, Augustus. Witching Hour, The. DGAP(166), POP (53).
Thomas, Brandon. Charley's Aunt. POP(147).
Thomas, Dylan. Adventures in the Skin Trade. SCL(50), 1955a(4). Collected Poems, 1934-1952. MCLE(793), MP(53), MP3(201). Portrait of the Artist as a Young Dog. MCLE(4195), MP4(1019). Selected Letters of Dylan Thomas. SCL(4159), 1967a(295). Under Milk Wood: A Play for Voices. BM(570), MCLE(5407), MP4(1247), SCL(4820), 1954a(285).
Thomas, Elizabeth Marshall. Harmless People, The. SCL (1933), 1960a(82). Herdsmen, The. SCL(2010), 1966a(123).
Thomas, Hugh. Spanish Civil War, The. BM(522), SCL (4391), 1962a(282). Suez. SCL(4482), 1968a(315).
Thomas, John L. Liberator, The. SCL(2631), 1964a(157).
Thomas, Norman. Ask at the Unicorn. SCL(232), 1964a(10).
Thomas à Kempis. Imitation of Christ, The. CAL(491), CHL(308), MCLE(2215), MN(161), MP3(501).
Thompson, Daniel Pierce. Green Mountain Boys, The. MAF(240), MCLE(1858), MP2(385).
Thompson, Denman and George W. Ryer. Old Homestead, The. DGAP(112), POP(68).
Thompson, Francis. Hound of Heaven, The. CAL(709). Poetry of Thompson, The. MCLE(4123), MP4(974).
Thomson, James. Seasons, The. MCLE(4681), MP4(1104).
Thoreau, Henry David. Consciousness in Concord. SCL (906), 1959a(43). Essays of Henry David Thoreau, The. MCLE(1461), MP4(305), MPA5(37). Journal of Thoreau, The. MCLE(2377), MP4(471), MPA5(43). Poetry of Thoreau, The. MCLE(4125), MP4(976). Walden. MCLE(5536), MN(324), MP2(1117), MPA5 (48). Week on the Concord and Merrimack Rivers, A. MCLE(5600), MP4(1277), MPA5(53).
Thucydides. History of the Peloponnesian War. MCLE(2065), MN(149), MP3(476).
Thurber, James. Further Fables for Our Time. SCL(1681), 1957a(79). Lanterns and Lances. SCL(2496), 1962a (178). My Life and Hard Times. MCLE(3201), MN (206), MP3(678). Years with Ross, The. SCL(5177), 1960a(295).
Thurber, James and Elliott Nugent. Male Animal, The. DGAP(330), SGAP(110).
Tillich, Paul. Courage to Be, The. WP(1146). Eternal

Now, The. SCL(1389), 1964a(72). Systematic Theology. CHL(1135), WP(1138).
Tindal, Matthew. Christianity as Old as the Creation. CHL (569).
Tindall, George Brown. Emergence of the New South, 1913-1945, The. SCL(1320), 1968a(94).
Tocqueville, Alexis de. Democracy in America. MCLE (1116), MP4(211).
Toffler, Alvin. Future Shock. 1971a(82).
Toland, John. Battle. SCL(323), 1960a(22). But Not in Shame. BM(51), SCL(572), 1962a(39). Christianity Not Mysterious. CHL(554).
Tolkien, J. R. R. Fellowship of the Ring, The. MCLE (1584), MP4(326). Return of the King, The. MCLE (4417), MP4(1063). Two Towers, The. MCLE(5373), MP4(1242).
Toller, Ernst. Man and the Masses. TCP(417).
Tolstoy, Count Leo. Anna Karénina. MCLE(179), MEU(30), MP1(32), PO(363), PON(25), SGEN(164). Childhood, Boyhood, Youth. MCLE(712), MP4(129). Cossacks, The. MCLE(884), MEU(159), MP2(181). Death of Ivan Ilyich, The. MCLE(1061), MEU(208), MP3(256). Kreutzer Sonata, The. MCLE(2485), MEU(418), MP1 (481), PO2(412). Power of Darkness, The. MCLE (4214), MD(655), MP3(841), POP(360). Resurrection. MCLE(4411), MEU(634), MP3(879). War and Peace. MCLE(5561), MEU(806), MP1(1085), PO2(402), SGEN (173). What I Believe. CHL(790). What Is Art? WP(723).
Tomlinson, H. M. Sea and the Jungle, The. MCLE(4664), MN(276), MP3(942).
Toomer, Jean. Cane. SCLs(55).
Tourgée, Albion W. Fool's Errand, A. MCLE(1646), MP4 (356), MPA5(57).
Tourneur, Cyril. Revenger's Tragedy, The. MCLE(4426), MD(685), MP3(883).
Toynbee, Arnold. Christianity among the Religions of the World. SCL(735), 1958a(50). East to West. BM (142), SCL(1265), 1959a(68). Hellenism. SCL(1981), 1960a(91). Historian's Approach to Religion, An. BM(238), SCL(2060), 1957a(116). Study of History, A. MCLE(5039), MN(291), MP3(1030).
Trachtenberg, Alan. Brooklyn Bridge: Fact and Symbol. SCL(534), 1966a(35).
Tracy, Honor. Butterflies of the Province, The. 1971a(27). First Day of Friday, The. SCL(1560), 1964a(91). Prospects Are Pleasing, The. SCL(3721), 1959a(207).

Straight and Narrow Path, The. SCL(4467), 1957a (261).
Traherne, Thomas. Poetry of Traherne, The. MCLE(4127), MP4(978).
Tranquillus, Gaius Suetonius. Concerning Illustrious Men. MCLE(820), MP4(148). Lives of the Caesars. MCLE (2712), MN(192), MP3(590).
Traven, B. Death Ship, The. MCLE(1072), MP4(199). Night Visitor and Other Stories, The. SCL(3249), 1967a(239).
Traver, Robert. Anatomy of a Murder. SCL(170), 1959a(9).
Treece, Henry. Great Captains, The. SCL(1856), 1957a(96).
Trevelyan, George Macaulay. England Under the Stuarts. MCLE(1386), MP4(275).
Troeltsch, Ernst. Religious a priori, The. CHL(865). Social Teaching of the Christian Churches, The. CHL (873).
Trollope, Anthony. Autobiography, An. MCLE(275), MP4 (46). Barchester Towers. MCLE(332), MEF(35), MP1(55), PO(174), SGBN(124). Doctor Thorne. MCLE(1213), MEF(164), MP2(263). Framley Parsonage. MCLE(1675), MEF(233), MP1(293). Last Chronicle of Barset, The. MCLE(2531), MEF(418), MP2 (556). Orley Farm. MCLE(3441), MEF(618), MP2 (780). Phineas Finn. MCLE(3637), MEF(661), MP3 (748). Phineas Redux. MCLE(3640), MEF(664), MP3 (750). Small House at Allington, The. MCLE(4860), MEF(803), MP2(973). Vicar of Bullhampton, The. MCLE(5462), MEF(912), MP2(1101). Warden, The. MCLE(5568), MEF(935), MP1(1092), PO2(51).
Trowbridge, John Townsend. Cudjo's Cave. MAF(115), MCLE(959), MP2(205).
Troyat, Henri. Tolstoy. SCL(4706), 1969a(312).
Tryon, W. S. Parnassus Corner. SCL(3513), 1964a(208).
Truman, Harry S. Memoirs, Volume I. SCL(2967), 1955a (156). Memoirs, Volume II. SCL(2971), 1957a(173).
Tsao Hsueh-chin. Dream of the Red Chamber. BM(138), MCLE(1281), MEU(263), MP3(302), PO2(429), SCL (1243), 1959a(65).
Tse-ch'eng, Kao. Story of the Guitar. MCLE(5008), MD (806), MP3(1022).
Tseng Tzu or Tzu Sau, Attributed to. Great Learning, The. WP(212).
Tsuji, Colonel Masanobe. Singapore: The Japanese Version. SCL(4301), 1962a(279).
Tucci, Niccolò. Before My Time. SCL(352), 1963a(9).
Tuchman, Barbara W. Guns of August, The. SCL(1896),

1963a(78). Proud Tower, The. SCL(3724), 1966a(246).
Tucker, Glenn. Chickamauga. SCLs(68). High Tide at Gettysburg. SCL(2040), 1959a(117).
Turgenev, Ivan. Fathers and Sons. MCLE(1571), MEU(296), MP1(273), PO(366), PON(116), SGEN(128). House of Gentlefolk, A. MCLE(2124), MEU(373), MP2(465). Month in the Country, A. MCLE(3161), MD(556), MP2(705). Smoke. MCLE(4867), MEU(691), MP1 (897). Virgin Soil. MCLE(5497), MEU(794), MP1 (1069), PO2(390).
Turgot, Anne Robert Jacques. Two Discourses on Universal History. CAL(628).
Turnbull, Andrew. Scott Fitzgerald. SCL(4092), 1963a(234).
Turner, Frederick Jackson. Frontier in American History, The. MCLE(1700), MP4(366).
Tutuola, Amos. Brave African Huntress, The. SCLs(46). Palm-Wine Drinkard, The. MCLE(3483), MP4(668).
Twain, Mark, see Clemens, Samuel Langhorne.
Tyler, Royall. Contrast, The. DGAP(15).
Tyrrell, George. Much Abused Letter, A. CHL(844).

Udall, Nicholas. Ralph Roister Doister. MCLE(4322), MD (674), MP2(876).
Unamuno y Jugo, Miguel de. Tragic Sense of Life in Men and in Peoples, The. MCLE(5275), MP4(1225).
Underhill, Evelyn. Worship. CHL(1024).
Undset, Sigrid. Axe, The. MCLE(304), MEU(56), MP2(66). In the Wilderness. MCLE(2229), MEU(391), MP2 (480). Kristin Lavransdatter. MCLE(2488), MEU (421), MP1(483), PO2(464), SGEN(381). Snake Pit, The. MCLE(4870), MEU(694), MP2(976). Son Avenger, The. MCLE(4891), MEU(697), MP2(978).
Unger, Irwin. Greenback Era, The. SCLs(125).
Unknown. Abraham and Isaac. MCLE(7), MD(4), MP3(1). Arabian Nights' Entertainments, The (Selections). MCLE(219), MEU(32), MP2(48). Aucassin and Nicolette. MCLE(273), MEU(54), MP1(48). Beowulf. MCLE(388), MP(17), MP1(68). Bevis of Hampton. MCLE(398), MP(19), MP3(105). Circle of Chalk, The. MCLE(755), MD(155), MP3(193). Cloud of Unknowing, The. CAL(466), CHL(288). Didache or The Teaching of the Twelve Apostles, The. CAL(1), CHL(23). Epic of Gilgamesh, The. MCLE(1400), MP(77), MP3 (342). Epistle to Diognetus, The. CAL(62), CHL(48). Everyman. MCLE(1509), MD(264), MP2(314), POP (221). Finn Cycle, The. MCLE(1612), MEF(210), MP3(392). Grettir the Strong. MCLE(1864), MEU

(338), MP1(335). Guy of Warwick. MCLE(1892), MP(115), MP3(439). Havelok the Dane. MCLE(1941), MP(125), MP2(410). Huon de Bordeaux. MCLE(2165), MEU(382), MP3(494). King Horn. MCLE(2444), MP4 (487). Lay of Igor's Campaign, The. MCLE(2567), MP4(507). Lazarillo de Tormes. MCLE(2573), MEU (436), MP2(567). Little Flowers of Saint Francis, The. CAL(448), CHL(264). Mabinogion, The. MCLE (2811), MEF(459), MP3(600). Mahabharata, The. MCLE(2842), MP(170), MP3(611). Nibelungenlied, The. MCLE(3264), MEU(538), MP1(652). Occurrences of the Times; or, The Transactions of Four Days. DGAP(20). Pilgrimage of Charlemagne, The. MCLE(3669), MP(216), MP3(760). Poem of the Cid. MCLE(3720), MP(219), MP3(766). Reynard the Fox. MCLE(4435), MEU(640), MP2(899). Robin Hood's Adventures. MCLE(4492), MEF(736), MP2(907). Second Shepherds' Play, The. MCLE(4687), MD(753), MP2(949). Sir Gawain and the Green Knight. MCLE (4835), MP(340), MP2(969). Song of Roland, The. MCLE(4904), MEU(703), MP1(907). Star of Seville, The. MCLE(4975), MD(804), MP3(1018). Story of Burnt Njal, The. MCLE(5000), MEU(723), MP2(997). Tao Te Ching. WP(207). Theologica germanica. CHL(276).

Unterecker, John. Voyager: A Life of Hart Crane. 1970a (328).

Updike, John. Bech: A Book. 1971a(21). Centaur, The. SCL(662), 1964a(52). Couples. SCL(941), 1969a(80). Of the Farm. SCL(3353), 1966a(206). Midpoint and Other Poems. 1970a(203). Music School, The. SCL (3136), 1967a(228). Pigeon Feathers. SCL(3577), 1963a(182). Poorhouse Fair, The. BM(448), MCLE (4187), MP4(1016), SCL(3653), 1960a(202). Rabbit, Run. BM(470), MCLE(4313), MP4(1042), SCL(3804), 1961a(203). Short Stories of John Updike, The. MCLE(4796), MP4(1142). Telephone Poles. SCL (4520), 1964a(257).

Vailland, Roger. Fête. SCL(1508), 1962a(123). Law, The. SCL(2553), 1959a(141).

Vale, Eugene. Thirteenth Apostle, The. SCL(4604), 1960a (270).

Valera, Juan. Pepita Jimenez. MCLE(3579), MEU(584), MP2(813).

Valéry, Paul. Poetry of Valéry, The. MCLE(4130), MP4 (981).

Valmiki. Ramayana, The. MCLE(4324), MP(308), MP3(861).
Vanbrugh, Sir John. Relapse, The. MCLE(4377), MD(679), MP2(887).
Van Der Post, Laurens. Seed and the Sower, The. SCL (4141), 1964a(231).
Vandiver, Frank E. Mighty Stonewall. SCL(3036), 1958a (161).
Van Druten, John. I Remember Mama. SGAP(154).
Vane, Sutton. Outward Bound. POP(94).
Vann, Gerald, O. P. Heart of Man, The. CAL(889).
Van Vechten, Carl. Peter Whiffle. MAF(481), MCLE(3608), MP1(739).
Vaughan, Henry. Poetry of Vaughan, The. MCLE(4133), MP4(984).
Vazov, Ivan. Under the Yoke. MCLE(5417), MEU(782), MP2(1086).
Veblen, Thorsten. Theory of the Leisure Class, The. MCLE(5152), MP4(1213).
Vega, Lope de. Gardener's Dog, The. MCLE(1718), MD (289), MP2(356). King, The Greatest Alcalde, The. MCLE(2469), MD(421), MP2(536). Sheep Well, The. MCLE(4747), MD(769), MP2(960).
Venezis, Ilias. Beyond the Aegean. SCL(389), 1957a(23).
Verga, Giovanni. Cavalleria Rusticana. MCLE(660), MEU (118), MP2(137). House by the Medlar Tree, The. MCLE(2115), MEU(370), MP2(460). Mastro-don Gesualdo. MCLE(2958), MEU(481), MP3(636).
Vergerio, Pier Paolo. On the Education of A Gentleman. CAL(479).
Vergilius Maro, Publius. Eclogues. MCLE(1323), MP4(257). Georgics. MCLE(1741), MP4(373).
Verlaine, Paul. Fêtes galantes and Other Poems. MCLE (1587), MP(102), MP3(390).
Vermigli, Peter Martyr. Disputation of the Sacrament of the Eucharist, A. CHL(376).
Verne, Jules. Around the World in Eighty Days. PO2(317). Mysterious Island, The. MCLE(3210), MEU(523), MP3(681). Twenty Thousand Leagues Under the Sea. MCLE(5358), MEU(771), MP1(1031), PON(407), SGEN (188).
Veuillot, Louis. Life of Our Lord Jesus Christ, The. CAL (665).
Vico, Giovanni Battista. New Science, The. CAL(618), WP(477).
Vidal, Gore. Best Man, The. SCL(386), 1961a(19). Julian. SCL(2387), 1965a(155).
Vigny, Alfred de. Cinq-Mars. MCLE(752), MEU(141), MP2

(153). Poetry of Vigny, The. MCLE(4137), MP4(987).
Villon, François. Great Testament, The. MCLE(1841), MP (113), MP3(426). Lais, Le. MCLE(2512), MP4(494).
Vincent of Lérins, Saint. Commonitory, A. CAL(198), CHL(153).
Virgil. Aeneid, The. MCLE(36), MP(3), MP1(11), PON(11).
Vishnevski, Vsevolod. Optimistic Tragedy, The. TCP(421).
Vittorini, Elio. Dark and the Light, The. SCL(1005), 1962a(90).
Vives, Juan Luis. On Education. CAL(519).
Voltaire. Candide. MCLE(590), MEU(103), MP1(107), PO (339), PON(48), SGEN(29). Zadig. MCLE(5778), MEU(837), MP3(1165). Zaïre. MCLE(5781), MD(955), MP3(1168).
Vonier, Dom Anscar, O. S. B. Key to the Doctrine of the Eucharist, A. CAL(793).
Vonnegut, Kurt, Jr. Cat's Cradle. SCLs(65). Mother Night. SCLs(185). Slaughterhouse-Five. 1970a(273).
Voznesensky, Andrei. Antiworlds. SCL(194), 1967a(12).

Wagoner, David. New and Selected Poems. 1970a(217).
Wain, John. Contenders, The. SCL(916), 1959a(45). Strike the Father Dead. SCL(4476), 1963a(259). Winter in the Hills, A. 1971a(352).
Wakoski, Diane. Discrepancies and Apparitions. SCL (1183), 1966a(72). Inside the Blood Factory. SCL (2250), 1969a(169).
Wallace, Lew. Ben Hur: A Tale of the Christ. MAF(51), MCLE(382), MP1(66), PO(260), PON(34).
Wallant, Edward Lewis. Children at the Gate, The. SCL (712), 1965a(37). Tenants of Moonbloom, The. MCLE(5132), MP4(1205), SCL(4551), 1964a(261).
Waller, Edmund. Poetry of Waller, The. MCLE(4140), MP4(989).
Waller, George. Kidnap. SCL(2413), 1962a(172).
Walpole, Horace. Castle of Otranto, The. MCLE(641), MEF(86), MP1(124). Letters of Walpole, The. MCLE(2633), MN(172), MP3(563).
Walpole, Hugh. Fortitude. MCLE(1655), MEF(222), MP1 (286). Fortress, The. MCLE(1657), MEF(224), MP1 (288). Judith Paris. MCLE(2405), MEF(394), MP1 (457). Rogue Herries. MCLE(4505), MEF(745), MP1 (844). Vanessa. MCLE(5442), MEF(903), MP1(1054).
Walter, Eugene. Easiest Way, The. DGAP(170), POP(46).
Walters, Raymond, Jr. Albert Gallatin. SCL(122), 1958a (10).

Walton, Izaak. Compleat Angler, The. MCLE(812), MN(55), MP3(206). Lives. MCLE(2709), MP4(555).
Walworth, Arthur. Woodrow Wilson. SCL(5139), 1959a(280).
Ward, Aileen. John Keats. SCL(2348), 1964a(143).
Ward, Barbara. Rich Nations and the Poor Nations, The. SCL(3922), 1963a(218).
Warfield, Benjamin. Plan of Salvation, The. CHL(890).
Warner, Charles Dudley and Samuel L. Clemens. Gilded Age, The. MAF(204), MCLE(1759), MP2(368), MPA5 (69).
Warner, Oliver. Victory. BM(577), SCL(4887), 1959a(260).
Warner, Sylvia Townsend. Flint Anchor, The. SCL(1587), 1954a(77). Winter in the Air. SCL(5098), 1957a(284).
Warren, Earl, J. Lee Rankin and Others. Report of the President's Commission on the Assassination of President John F. Kennedy. SCL(3888), 1965a(246).
Warren, Mercy. Group, The. DGAP(12).
Warren, Robert Penn. All the King's Men. MAF(15), MCLE(104), MP2(15), PO2(281), SGAN(297). Audubon: A Vision. 1970a(39). Band of Angels. SCL(317), 1955a(17). Cave, The. SCL(658), 1960a(35). Flood. SCL(1590), 1965a(99). Incarnations. SCL(2208), 1969a(167). Night Rider. MCLE(3286), MP4(628). Poetry of Warren, The. MCLE(4143), MP4(992). Promises. BM(455), SCL(3713), 1958a(198). Segregation. SCL(4156), 1957a(236). Selected Poems: New and Old 1923-1966. SCL(4192), 1967a(298). World Enough and Time. MAF(723), MCLE(5740), MP2(1160). You, Emperors, and Others. SCL(5189), 1961a(313).
Wasserman, Dale. Man of La Mancha. SCL(2860), 1967a (209).
Wassermann, Jacob. World's Illusion, The. MCLE(5746), MEU(834), MP1(1133), PO2(445), SGEN(336).
Wast, Hugo. Black Valley. MAF(63), MCLE(434), MP3(113). Stone Desert. MAF(607), MCLE(4985), MP2(994).
Waterhouse, Keith. Billy Liar. SCL(402), 1961a(24).
Watkins, Vernon. Affinities. SCL(62), 1964a(1).
Watson, James D. Double Helix, The. SCL(1222), 1969a (98).
Watson, Robert. Paper Horse, A. SCL(3504), 1963a(168).
Waugh, Evelyn. Brideshead Revisited. MCLE(498), MEF (68), MP1(83). Decline and Fall. MCLE(1085), MEF (145), MP2(235), SGBN(321). Edmund Campion. CAL (838), MCLE(1326), MN(93), MP1(237). End of the Battle, The. BM(167), SCL(1351), 1962a(115). Handful of Dust, A. MCLE(1916), MEF(263), MP1(350).

Little Learning, A. SCL(2714), 1965a(183). Monsignor Ronald Knox. SCL(3073), 1961a(181). Officers and Gentlemen. BM(405), SCL(3363), 1955a(193). Ordeal of Gilbert Pinfold, The. MCLE(3418), MP4 (657). Vile Bodies. MCLE(5478), MEF(921), MP2 (1103).

Webb, Mary. Precious Bane. MCLE(4225), MEF(692), MP1 (778).

Webb, Walter Prescott. Great Plains, The. MCLE(1838), MP4(393).

Webster, Harvey Curtis. After the Trauma. 1971a(1).

Webster, John. Duchess of Malfi, The. MCLE(1294), MD (229), MP1(232). White Devil, The. MCLE(5626), MD(920), MP3(1131).

Wedekind, Frank. Awakening of Spring, The. MCLE(297), MD(49), MP3(79). Earth-Spirit. TCP(425). Pandora's Box. TCP(428).

Wedemeyer, General Albert C. Wedemeyer Reports! SCL (5002), 1959a(271).

Wedgwood, C. V. Coffin for King Charles, A. SCL(785), 1965a(45). King's War: 1641-1647, The. BM(291), SCL(2448), 1960a(124).

Weidman, Jerome. Enemy Camp, The. SCL(1361), 1959a (71).

Weill, Kurt, Ira Gershwin and Moss Hart. Lady in the Dark. DGAP(334).

Weingartner, Charles and Neil Postman. Teaching as a Subversive Activity. 1970a(303).

Weintraub, Stanley. Beardsley. SCL(333), 1968a(22).

Weiss, Peter. Marat. TCP(432). Persecution and Assassination of Jean-Paul Marat, The. SCLs(222).

Wells, H. G. History of Mr. Polly, The. MCLE(2054), MEF(310), MP2(454). Invisible Man, The. MCLE (2275), MEF(349), MP1(428). Kipps. MCLE(2478), MEF(414), MP2(540). Mr. Britling Sees It Through. MCLE(3086), MEF(516), MP1(600). Time Machine, The. MCLE(5202), MEF(844), MP1(986), SGBN(201). Tono-Bungay. MCLE(5256), MEF(867), MP1(1006), SGBN(206). War of the Worlds, The. MCLE(5566), MEF(933), MP1(1090), PO(178), PON(437).

Welty, Eudora. Bride of the Innisfallen, The. SCL(516), 1955a(35). Delta Wedding. MAF(142), MCLE(1113), MP2(245). Golden Apples, The. MCLE(1781), MP4 (382). Losing Battles. 1971a(175). Ponder Heart, The. MCLE(4179), MP4(1014), SCL(3650), 1954a(213). Short Stories of Eudora Welty, The. MCLE(4787), MP4(1133).

Werfel, Franz. Forty Days of Musa Dagh, The. MCLE (1669), MEU(312), MP1(291). Goat Song. MCLE (1773), MD(302), MP2(370). Song of Bernadette, The. MCLE(4899), MEU(700), MP1(903).

Werth, Alexander. Russia at War, 1941-1945. SCL(4030), 1965a(260).

Wescott, Glenway. Apple of the Eye, The. MAF(31), MCLE(214), MP1(40). Grandmothers, The. MAF(222), MCLE(1821).

Wesker, Arnold. Chips with Everything. MCLE(723), MP4 (132).

Wesley, John. Journal of John Wesley, The. CHL(581). Plain Account of Christian Perfection, A. CHL(608).

West, Anthony. Heritage. SCL(2014), 1955a(118).

West, Jessamyn. Cress Delehanty. SCL(944), 1954a(43).

West, Morris L. Daughter of Silence. SCL(1027), 1962a(93). Devil's Advocate, The. SCL(1153), 1960a(57). Shoes of the Fisherman, The. SCL(4261), 1964a(238).

West, Nathanael. Complete Works of Nathanael West, The. BM(103), SCL(881), 1958a(55). Miss Lonelyhearts. MAF(407), MCLE(3080), MP3(664).

West, Paul. I'm Expecting to Live Quite Soon. 1971a(122).

West, Rebecca. Birds Fall Down, The. SCL(408), 1967a (31). Black Lamb and Grey Falcon. MCLE(428), MN(42), MP1(75). Fountain Overflows, The. SCL (1632), 1957a(73). Train of Powder, A. SCL(4732), 1955a(272).

Westcott, Edward Noyes. David Harum. MAF(127), MCLE (1027), MP1(192).

Westcott, Glenway. Images of Truth. SCL(2165), 1963a(89). Pilgrim Hawk, The. MCLE(3662), MP4(691), SCL (3581), 1968a(240).

Whale, J. S. Christian Doctrine. CHL(1051).

Wharton, Edith. Age of Innocence, The. MAF(4), MCLE (53), MP1(14), PO2(194). Custom of the Country, The. MAF(118), MCLE(967), MP3(243). Ethan Frome. MAF(172), MCLE(1471), MP1(256), PO(263), SGAN(102). Fruit of the Tree, The. MAF(189), MCLE(1703), MP3(406). House of Mirth, The. MAF (273), MCLE(2127), MP1(380). Old Maid, The. MAF(454), MCLE(3364), MP1(679).

Wheeler, A. C. and Edward M. Alfriend. Great Diamond Robbery, The. DGAP(131).

Wheelock, John Hall. By Daylight and in Dream. 1971a(29). Gardner and Other Poems, The. SCL(1710), 1962a (135).

White, E. B. Points of My Compass, The. SCL(3647),

1963a(194). Second Tree from the Corner, The. SCL(4126), 1954a(246).
White, Patrick. Burnt Ones, The. SCL(565), 1965a(22). Riders in the Chariot. MCLE(4452), MP4(1069), SCL(3930), 1962a(246). Tree of Man, The. MCLE (5301), MP4(1232), SCL(4756), 1955a(278). Voss. SCL(4926), 1958a(258).
White, T. H. Once and Future King, The. BM(410), MCLE (3412), MP4(653), SCL(3401), 1959a(183).
White, Theodore H. Making of the President, 1960, The. BM(356), SCL(2838), 1962a(195). Making of the President, 1964, The. SCL(2842), 1966a(164). Making of the President, 1968, The. 1970a(193).
White, William Smith. Taft Story, The. SCLs(307).
Whitefield, George. Journals of George Whitefield. CHL (577).
Whitehead, Alfred North. Process and Reality. WP(921). Religion in the Making. CHL(925).
Whitehead, Don. FBI Story, The. SCL(1498), 1957a(67).
Whitehead, James. Domains. SCL(1210), 1969a(96).
Whitman, Walt. Democratic Vistas. MCLE(1119), MP4(213), MPA5(99). Leaves of Grass. MCLE(2576), MP(160), MP3(554), MPA5(106). Specimen Days. MCLE(4953), MP4(1173), MPA5(114).
Whittier, John Greenleaf. Poetry of Whittier, The. MCLE (4146), MP4(995), MPA5(119). Snow-Bound. MCLE (4873), MP(342), MP1(899), MPA5(125).
Whyte, William H., Jr. Organization Man, The. SCL(3459), 1958a(185).
Whyte-Melville, George J. Digby Grand. MCLE(1176), MEF(157), MP2(253). Market Harborough. MCLE (2931), MEF(475), MP2(632).
Wieman, Henry Nelson. Source of Human Good, The. CHL (1084).
Wilbur, Richard. Advice to a Prophet. SCL(53), 1962a(12). Poetry of Wilbur, The. MCLE(4149), MP4(997). Things of This World. SCL(4595), 1957a(266). Walking to Sleep. 1970a(331).
Wilde, Oscar. De profundis. MCLE(1030), MP4(190). Importance of Being Earnest, The. MCLE(2217), MD (372), MP2(476), POP(141). Lady Windermere's Fan. MCLE(2505), MD(434), MP1(488), POP(144). Letters of Oscar Wilde, The. BM(316), SCL(2600), 1963a (126). Picture of Dorian Gray, The. MCLE(3656), MEF(671), MP1(746), PO(181), SGBN(193). Poetry of Wilde, The. MCLE(4152), MP4(1000).
Wilder, Thornton. Bridge of San Luis Rey, The. MAF(69),

MCLE(503), MP1(86), PO2(247), PON(38), SGAN(177). Cabala, The. MAF(78), MCLE(557), MP1(94). Eighth Day, The. SCL(1291), 1968a(89). Heaven's My Destination. MAF(258), MCLE(1967), MP1(357). Ides of March, The. MAF(290), MCLE(2190), MP1 (413). Our Town. DGAP(313), MCLE(3461), MD(597), MP1(704), SGAP(130), TCP(436). Skin of Our Teeth, The. MCLE(4851), MD(786), MP3(995), SGAP(135), TCP(439).

Wilkinson, Sylvia. Cale. 1971a(32). Killing Frost, A. SCLs(148). Moss on the North Side. SCL(3099), 1967a(225).

William of Ockham. De corpore Christi. CHL(267). William of Ockham: Selections. WP(337).

Williams, C. K. Lies. 1970a(184).

Williams, Charles. All Hallows Eve. MCLE(95), MP4(23). Descent into Hell. MCLE(1125), MP4(218).

Williams, Daniel Day. God's Grace and Man's Hope. CHL (1108).

Williams, Emlyn. George. SCL(1715), 1963a(65).

Williams, Joan. Morning and the Evening, The. SCL(3077), 1962a(209).

Williams, John A. Man Who Cried I Am, The. SCLs(179). Sissie. SCLs(279). Sons of Darkness, Sons of Light. 1970a(281).

Williams, Jonathan. Ear in Bartram's Tree, An. 1970a (105).

Williams, Kenneth P. Lincoln Finds a General. BM(335), SCL(2681), 1960a(140).

Williams, Roger. Bloody Tenent of Persecution, The. CHL (454).

Williams, T. Harry. Huey Long. 1970a(169). P. G. T. Beauregard. BM(428), SCL(3553), 1955a(199).

Williams, Tennessee. Camino Real. TCP(443). Cat on a Hot Tin Roof. BM(63), MCLE(650), MP4(115), SCL (644), TCP(447), 1955a(47). Glass Menagerie, The. DGAP(358), MCLE(1764), MD(300), MP3(418), SGAP (208), TCP(449). Knightly Quest, The. SCL(2454), 1967a(179). Night of the Iguana, The. SCL(3239), 1963a(154). Orpheus Descending with Battle of Angels. SCL(3466), 1959a(193). Streetcar Named Desire, A. MCLE(5023), MP4(1189), SGAP(214), TCP(453). Sweet Bird of Youth. BM(526), SCL(4494), 1960a(263).

Williams, Thomas. High New House, A. SCL(2035), 1964a (130).

Williams, Vinnie. Walk Egypt. SCL(4936), 1961a(281).

Williams, William Carlos. Desert Music and Other Poems,

The. SCL(1131), 1954a(52). Farmers' Daughters, The. SCL(1474), 1962a(119). Imaginations. 1971a (124). In the American Grain. MCLE(2224), MP4 (442). Paterson. MCLE(3521), MP(212), MP3(720). Paterson Five. SCL(3520), 1959a(201). Pictures from Brueghel. BM(432), SCL(3573), 1963a(179). Poetry of Williams, The. MCLE(4155), MP4(1002).

Williamson, Henry. Salar the Salmon. MCLE(4595), MP4 (1088). Tarka the Otter. MCLE(5104), MP4(1203).

Wilson, Angus. Anglo-Saxon Attitudes. SCL(184), 1957a(7). Death Dance. 1970a(98). Middle Age of Mrs. Eliot, The. SCL(3023), 1960a(171). No Laughing Matter. SCL(3283), 1968a(224). Old Men at the Zoo, The. SCL(3373), 1962a(222).

Wilson, Colin. Mind Parasites, The. SCL(3039), 1968a(205).

Wilson, Edmund. Axel's Castle. MCLE(307), MP4(60). Memoirs of Hecate County. SCL(2987), 1960a(162). Patriotic Gore. BM(422), SCL(3523), 1963a(174). Prelude, A. SCL(3672), 1968a(251). Scrolls from the Dead Sea, The. SCL(4096), 1955a(220).

Wilson, Erle. Coorinna. SCL(923), 1954a(40).

Wilson, Harriette. Game of Hearts, The. SCL(1693), 1955a (101).

Wilson, Sloan. Man in the Gray Flannel Suit, The. SCL (2854), 1955a(150).

Wingren, Gustaf. Living Word, The. CHL(1112).

Winston, Richard. Thomas Becket. SCL(4619), 1968a(328).

Winton, Calhoun. Captain Steele. SCL(624), 1965a(32).

Wisdom, John. Philosophy and Psycho-Analysis. WP(1153).

Wison, Colin. Outsider, The. SCL(3487), 1957a(206).

Wister, Owen. Virginian, The. MAF(697), MCLE(5503), MP1(1072).

Wither, George. Poetry of Wither, The. MCLE(4158), MP4(1004).

Wittgenstein, Ludwig. Philosophical Investigations. WP(1160). Tractatus logico-philosophicus. WP(829).

Woiwode, L. What I'm Going to Do, I Think. 1970a(340).

Wolfe, Thomas. Letters of Thomas Wolfe, The. BM(322), MCLE(2629), MP4(538), SCL(2612), 1957a(152). Look Homeward, Angel. MAF(353), MCLE(2738), MP1(517), PO2(267), SGAN(189). Of Time and the River. MAF (451), MCLE(3346), MP1(674). Short Novels of Thomas Wolfe, The. SCLs(271). Web and the Rock, The. MAF(703), MCLE(5597), MP1(1101). You Can't Go Home Again. MAF(732), MCLE(5766), MP1(1142).

Wolfe, Tom. Electric Kool-Aid Acid Test, The. SCL(1301), 1969a(102). Kandy-Kolored Tangerine-Flake Stream-

line Baby, The. SCL(2397), 1966a(135). Pump House Gang, The. SCL(3747), 1969a(271).
Wolfert, Ira. Act of Love, An. SCL(25), 1954a(4).
Wolpert, Stanley. Nine Hours to Rama. SCL(3267), 1963a (157).
Womack, John, Jr. Zapata and the Mexican Revolution. 1970a(360).
Wood, Mrs. Henry. East Lynne. POP(155).
Woodbridge, Frederick James E. Nature and Mind. WP (1021).
Woodham-Smith, Cecil. Great Hunger, The. SCL(1862), 1964a(115). Reason Why, The. SCL(3840), 1954a(225).
Woodworth, Samuel. Forest Rose, The. DGAP(41).
Woolf, Leonard. Beginning Again. SCL(359), 1965a(8). Journey Not the Arrival Matters, The. 1971a(156).
Woolf, Virginia. Between the Acts. MCLE(395), MEF(51), MP3(102). Contemporary Writers. SCL(913), 1967a (53). Granite and Rainbow. MP1(322), SCL(1846), 1959a(101). Literary Essays of Virginia Woolf, The. MCLE(2694), MP4(553). Mrs. Dalloway. MCLE(3108), MEF(533), MP1(607), PO2(118), SGBN(300). Orlando. MCLE(3430), MEF(615), MP1(698). To the Lighthouse. MCLE(5228), MEF(850), MP1(993). Waves, The. MCLE(5583), MEF(940), MP2(1122). Writer's Diary, A. BM(617), SCL(5171), 1954a(301). Years, The. MCLE(5760), MEF(979), MP3(1156).
Woolman, John. Journal of John Woolman, The. CHL(612).
Wordsworth, Dorothy. Journals of Dorothy Wordsworth. MCLE(2389), MP4(481).
Wordsworth, William. Poetry of Wordsworth, The. MCLE (4161), MP4(1007). Prelude, The. MCLE(4233), MP(303), MP3(849).
Wouk, Herman. Marjorie Morningstar. SCL(2907), 1955a (153).
Wright, Constance. Daughter to Napoleon. SCL(1034), 1962a(96).
Wright, Richard. Native Son. MAF(436), MCLE(3236), MP1 (643).
Wright, Richard and Paul Green. Native Son. DGAP(344).
Wyatt, Sir Thomas and Henry Howard, Earl of Surrey. Poetry of Wyatt and Surrey, The. MCLE(4165), MP4 (1010).
Wycherley, William. Country Wife, The. MCLE(907), MD (177), MP2(187). Gentleman Dancing Master, The. MCLE(1732), MD(292), MP3(411). Love in a Wood. MCLE(2767), MD(456), MP3(595). Plain Dealer, The. MCLE(3697), MD(640), MP2(838).